50 YEARS OF
SOLAR SYSTEM EXPLORATION

50 YEARS OF SOLAR SYSTEM EXPLORATION

HISTORICAL PERSPECTIVES

Edited by
LINDA BILLINGS

National Aeronautics and Space Administration
Office of Communications
NASA History Division
Washington, DC 20546

NASA SP-2021-4705

Library of Congress Cataloging-in-Publication Data

Names: Solar System Exploration @ 50 (2012: Washington, D.C.), author. | Billings, Linda, editor. | United States. NASA History Division, issuing body.
Title: 50 years of solar system exploration: historical perspectives / Linda Billings, editor.
Description: Washington, DC: National Aeronautics and Space Administration, Office of Communications, NASA History Division, [2021] "NASA SP 2021-4705." Includes bibliographical references and index.
Summary: "To commemorate the 50th anniversary of the first successful planetary mission, Mariner 2 sent to Venus in 1962, the NASA History Program Office, the Division of Space History at the National Air and Space Museum, NASA's Science Mission Directorate, and the Jet Propulsion Laboratory organized a symposium. "Solar System Exploration @ 50" was held in Washington, D.C., on 25–26 October 2012. The purpose of this symposium was to consider, over the more than 50-year history of the Space Age, what we have learned about the other bodies of the solar system and the processes by which we have learned it. Symposium organizers asked authors to address broad topics relating to the history of solar system exploration such as various flight projects, the development of space science disciplines, the relationship between robotic exploration and human spaceflight, the development of instruments and methodologies for scientific exploration, as well as the development of theories about planetary science, solar system origins and implications for other worlds. The papers in this volume provide a richly textured picture of important developments—and some colorful characters—in a half century of solar system exploration. A comprehensive history of the first 50 years of solar system exploration would fill many volumes. What readers will find in this volume is a collection of interesting stories about money, politics, human resources, commitment, competition and cooperation, and the "faster, better, cheaper" era of solar system exploration"—Provided by publisher.
Identifiers: LCCN 2020003167 (print) | LCCN 2020003168 (ebook) | ISBN 9781626830530 (hardcover) | ISBN 9781626830547 (epub)
Subjects: LCSH: United States. National Aeronautics and Space Administration—History—Congresses.|Planets—Exploration—History—Congresses.|Spaceflight—History—Congresses. | Astronautics—History—Congresses. | Space sciences—History—Congresses. | Outer space—Exploration—History—Congresses.
Classification: LCC TL788.5 .S625 2020 (print) | LCC TL788.5 (ebook) | DDC 919.904—dc23
LC record available at *https://lccn.loc.gov/2020003167*
LC ebook record available at *https://lccn.loc.gov/2020003168*

This publication is available as a free download at *http://www.nasa.gov/ebooks*.

ISBN 978-1-62683-053-0

CONTENTS

Foreword
Linda Billings — vii

Introduction: NASA's Solar System Exploration Paradigm:
The First 50 Years and a Look at the Next 50
James L. Green and Kristen J. Erickson — 1

PART I. Overview — 15

Chapter 1: Exploring the Solar System:
Who Has Done It, How, and Why?
Peter J. Westwick — 17

PART II. Politics and Policy in the Conduct of Solar System Exploration — 33

Chapter 2: Funding Planetary Science:
History and Political Economy
Jason W. Callahan — 35

Chapter 3: The Politics of Pure Space Science, the Essential Tension:
Human Spaceflight's Impact on Scientific Exploration
Roger Handberg — 89

PART III. The Lure of the Red Planet — 107

Chapter 4: Designing Mars Sample Return,
from Viking to the Mars Science Laboratory
Erik M. Conway — 111

Chapter 5: NASA, Big Science, and Mars Exploration:
Critical Decisions from Goldin to Bolden
W. Henry Lambright — 141

PART IV. Public Perceptions, Priorities, and Solar System Exploration — 157

Chapter 6: Survivor! (?) The Story of *S. mitis* on the Moon
Linda Billings — 159

Chapter 7: "Killer Asteroids": Popular Depictions
and Public Policy Influence
Laura M. Delgado López — 185

Chapter 8: The Outer Solar System:
Exploring Through the Public Eye
Giny Cheong — 207

Part V. **Exploring the Outer Solar System** — 223

Chapter 9: Europe's Rendezvous with Titan:
The European Space Agency's Contribution to the
Cassini-Huygens Mission to the Saturnian System
Arturo Russo — 225

Part VI. **Institutional Arrangements in Solar System Exploration** — 239

Chapter 10: Ranger: Circumstances, Events, Legacy
James D. Burke and Harris M. Schurmeier — 241

Chapter 11: Mariner 2 and the CSIRO Parkes Radio Telescope:
50 Years of International Collaboration
John Sarkissian — 251

Chapter 12: International Cooperation in Solar System Exploration:
A Transnational Approach to the History of the
International Solar Polar Mission and Ulysses
Petar Markovski — 285

Epilogue
Linda Billings — 303

Appendix: Program for "Solar System Exploration@50,"
25–26 October 2012 — 307

Acknowledgments — 311

About the Authors — 313

Acronyms — 319

The NASA History Series — 323

Index — 337

FOREWORD

Linda Billings

TO COMMEMORATE the 50th anniversary of the first successful planetary mission—the Mariner 2 flyby to Venus in 1962—the NASA History Program Office, the Division of Space History at the National Air and Space Museum, NASA's Science Mission Directorate, and the Jet Propulsion Laboratory organized a symposium. "Solar System Exploration @ 50" was held in Washington, DC, on 25–26 October 2012.[1]

The purpose of this symposium was to consider, over the more-than-50-year history of the Space Age, what we have learned about the other bodies of the solar system and the processes by which we have learned it. In a call for papers, symposium organizers asked authors to address broad topics relating to the history of solar system exploration, such as the following:

- The various flight projects and their broader implications for the exploration of other solar system bodies.
- The development of space science disciplines and institution building.
- The big questions of planetary science and what has been learned in the 50 years of solar system exploration.
- The relationships of organizations (international, civil/military, etc.) with one another.
- The relationship between robotic exploration and human spaceflight.
- The management of the space science community and the setting of priorities for missions, instruments, and knowledge generation.
- The manner in which scientific knowledge has been acquired, refined, analyzed, and disseminated over time.
- The development of theories about planetary science, solar system origins, and implications for other worlds.
- The development of instruments and methodologies for scientific exploration.

---

1. NASA webcast the entire symposium to reach a broader audience. The webcast is archived here: *http://www.nasa.gov/topics/history/features/SSEat50.html* (accessed 8 January 2020).

The organizing committee received close to 50 proposals for papers. Due to time constraints, the organizing committee could select fewer than half for presentation. Even fewer are included here, as some presenters published their papers elsewhere or otherwise chose not to contribute.[2] One paper included in this volume was not presented at the conference. The agenda for the conference, abstracts of papers, and slide presentations can be found online.[3]

The papers that do appear in this volume nonetheless provide a richly textured picture of important developments—and some colorful characters—in a half century of solar system exploration. A comprehensive history of the first 50 years of solar system exploration would fill many volumes. What readers will find in this volume is a collection of interesting stories about money, politics, human resources, commitment, competition and cooperation, and the "faster, better, cheaper" era of solar system exploration.

Linda Billings
Editor

---

2. The following papers presented at the symposium were published in R. D. Launius, ed., *Exploring the Solar System: The History and Science of Planetary Exploration* (New York: Palgrave Macmillan, 2013): "The Survival Crisis of the Planetary Program," by John Logsdon; "Faster, Better, Cheaper: A Sociotechnical Perspective on the Meanings of Success and Failure in NASA's Solar System Exploration Program," by Amy Paige Kaminski; and "Parachuting onto Another World: The European Space Agency's Huygens Mission to Titan," by Arturo Russo. Russo's paper is reprinted in this volume with permission from Palgrave Macmillan. Wesley Huntress and Mikhail Marov's keynote presentation, "First on the Moon, Venus, and Mars: The Soviet Planetary Exploration Enterprise," drew on their book, *Soviet Robots in the Solar System: Mission Technologies and Discoveries*, (New York: Springer, 2011). Michael Neufeld's paper, "Transforming Solar System Exploration: the Applied Physics Laboratory and the Origins of the Discovery Program," was published in *Space Policy* 30, no. 1 (February 2014). Scott Hubbard's presentation, "Exploring Mars: Following the Water," drew on his book, *Exploring Mars: Chronicles from a Decade of Discovery*, (Tucson: University of Arizona Press, 2011).

3. *http://www.nasa.gov/topics/history/features/SSEat50.html* (accessed 8 January 2020).

INTRODUCTION

NASA's Solar System Exploration Paradigm: The First 50 Years and a Look at the Next 50

James L. Green and Kristen J. Erickson

AFTER MANY FAILURES to get to the Moon and to the planets beyond, Mariner 2 successfully flew by Venus in December 1962. This historic mission began a spectacular era of solar system exploration for NASA and many other space agencies. With the tremendously successful flyby of the Pluto system by the New Horizons spacecraft in July 2015, humankind completed its initial survey of our solar system, and the United States became the only nation to reach every planet from Mercury to the dwarf planet Pluto with a space probe.

Solar system exploration has always been and continues to be a grand human adventure that seeks to discover the nature and origin of our celestial neighbors and to explore whether life exists or could have existed beyond Earth. Before Mariner 2, everything we knew about our solar system came from ground-based telescope observations and from analysis of meteorites. This limited perspective could not begin to reveal the diversity and the true nature of our solar system. In this brief introduction, we address how NASA and other space agencies have approached a comprehensive series of missions for the last half century of solar system exploration.

THE SOLAR SYSTEM EXPLORATION PARADIGM

It is our spacecraft missions that provide the opportunity to get up close and personal with many bodies in the solar system. Mariner 2 was just the first robotic space probe to conduct a successful planetary encounter, the first step

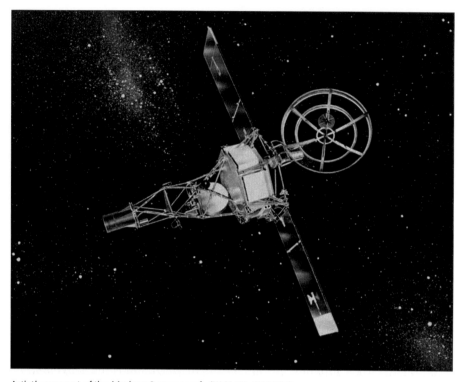

Artist's concept of the Mariner 2 spacecraft. (NASA/JPL: PIA04594)

in a long journey. The scientific instruments on board were two radiometers (microwave and infrared), a micrometeorite sensor, a solar-plasma sensor, a charged-particle sensor, and a magnetometer. These instruments measured the temperature distribution on the surface of Venus, made basic measurements of Venus's atmosphere, discovered the solar wind, and determined that Venus, unlike Earth, has no intrinsic magnetic field.[1] This powerful set of observations fueled our fascination with our cosmic neighborhood and our desire to learn more.

Since Mariner 2, in exploring any particular object, solar system exploration has followed a general paradigm of "flyby, orbit, land, rove, and return samples." A complete campaign may not be performed for each object in the solar system, since not all of our scientific questions can be studied at all objects, and there are difficult technological challenges and financial hurdles to overcome for some types of missions and certain destinations. Moreover, a healthy program of solar system exploration requires a balance between

---

1. Scientific and Technical Information Division, *Mariner-Venus 1962 Final Project Report* (Washington, DC: NASA-SP-59, 1965).

detailed investigations of a particular target and broader reconnaissance of a variety of similar targets. This approach is summarized in Figure 1 for the inner solar system and Figure 2 for the outer solar system, showing progress made in exploration of the major types of solar system bodies. Figures 1 and 2 also show NASA (black, roman text) and international (blue, italic text) space missions, with new mission concepts that have been put forward by the science community as our next steps (red, bold text).

By following the above paradigm in our exploration of the solar system, we have forged a path of significant progress in our knowledge and understanding and a recipe for future exploration as well. For the past 50 years, our primary goals have focused on advancing scientific knowledge of the origin and evolution of the solar system, the potential for life elsewhere, and the hazards and resources present as humans explore space. The quest to understand our origins is universal. How did we get here? Are we alone? What does our future hold? Modern science, especially space science, provides extraordinary opportunities to pursue these questions.

For the last several decades, NASA has sought guidance from the National Research Council (NRC) of the National Academy of Sciences on priorities in solar system exploration. The last two NRC "decadal surveys" of solar system exploration—*New Frontiers in the Solar System: An Integrated Exploration Strategy* (2003) and *Visions and Voyages for Planetary Science in the Decade 2013–2022* (2011)—show the wide diversity in potential targets. The next scientific leap in understanding these targets requires landers, rovers, atmospheric probes, or sample-return missions. The NRC's latest mission recommendations in its last planetary decadal survey are shown in Figure 1 and Figure 2 in bold text. The next planetary science and astrobiology decadal survey 2023–2032, got under way in 2020 and will further refine priorities.

To track spacecraft beyond low-Earth orbit (LEO), NASA developed the Deep Space Network (DSN), which has constantly been upgraded to continue to provide outstanding data tracking, telemetry, and navigation services. Today, all space agencies support large radio-frequency dishes that are coordinated through international agreements between the agencies to meet planetary mission needs. This has worked remarkably well and has naturally forged a set of tracking and navigation standards to the benefit of all.

FLYBY MISSIONS

Flyby missions are designed to obtain the most basic information on their target bodies. Early flyby missions also enabled space agencies to learn to fly between planets. This early trek into the solar system was accomplished with flybys to each planet in our local neighborhood as shown in Figure 1.

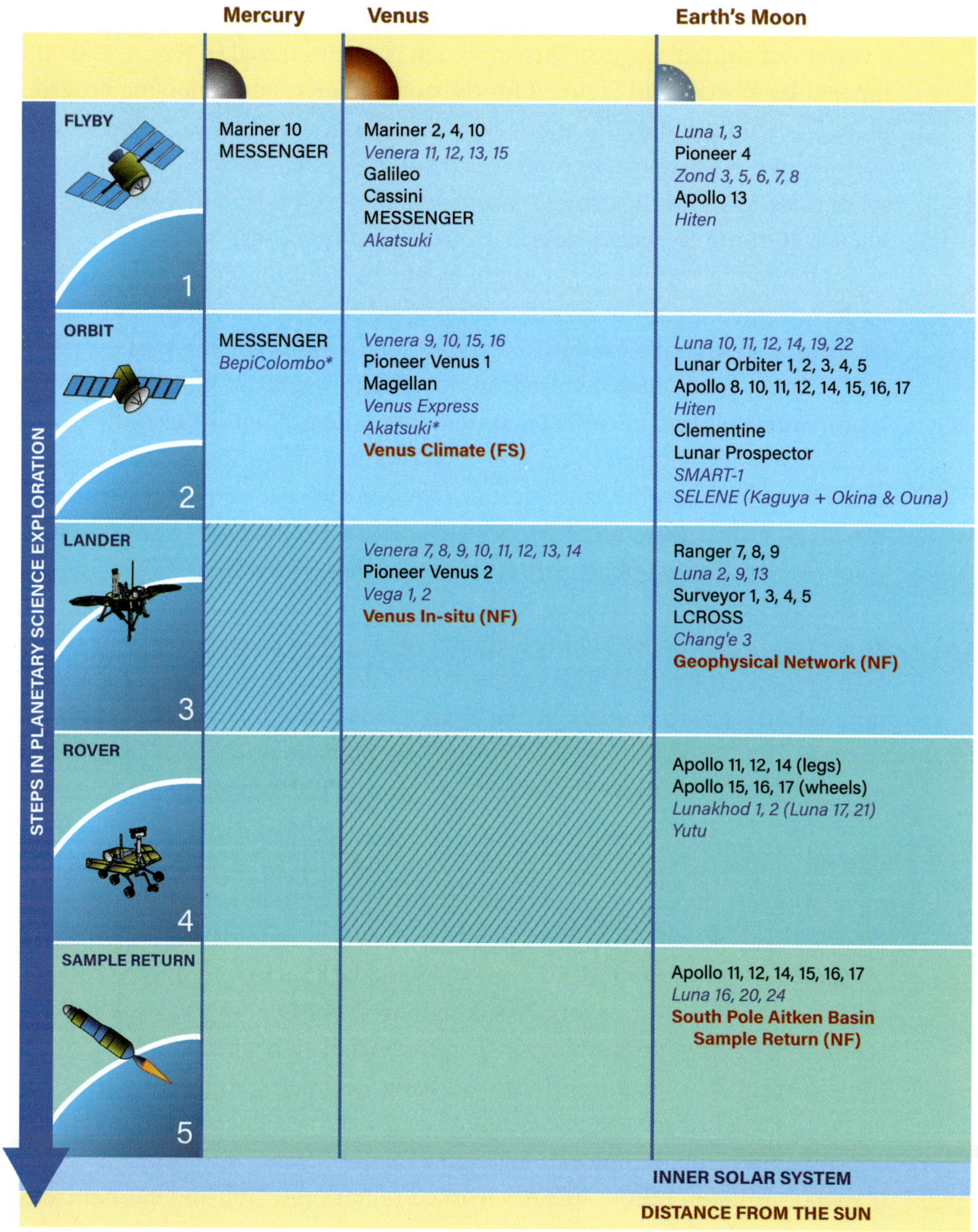

		Mercury	Venus	Earth's Moon
FLYBY	1	Mariner 10 MESSENGER	Mariner 2, 4, 10 *Venera 11, 12, 13, 15* Galileo Cassini MESSENGER *Akatsuki*	*Luna 1, 3* Pioneer 4 *Zond 3, 5, 6, 7, 8* Apollo 13 *Hiten*
ORBIT	2	MESSENGER *BepiColombo**	*Venera 9, 10, 15, 16* Pioneer Venus 1 Magellan *Venus Express* *Akatsuki** **Venus Climate (FS)**	*Luna 10, 11, 12, 14, 19, 22* Lunar Orbiter 1, 2, 3, 4, 5 Apollo 8, 10, 11, 12, 14, 15, 16, 17 *Hiten* Clementine Lunar Prospector *SMART-1* *SELENE (Kaguya + Okina & Ouna)*
LANDER	3		*Venera 7, 8, 9, 10, 11, 12, 13, 14* Pioneer Venus 2 *Vega 1, 2* **Venus In-situ (NF)**	Ranger 7, 8, 9 *Luna 2, 9, 13* Surveyor 1, 3, 4, 5 LCROSS *Chang'e 3* **Geophysical Network (NF)**
ROVER	4			Apollo 11, 12, 14 (legs) Apollo 15, 16, 17 (wheels) *Lunakhod 1, 2 (Luna 17, 21)* *Yutu*
SAMPLE RETURN	5			Apollo 11, 12, 14, 15, 16, 17 *Luna 16, 20, 24* **South Pole Aitken Basin Sample Return (NF)**

STEPS IN PLANETARY SCIENCE EXPLORATION

INNER SOLAR SYSTEM
DISTANCE FROM THE SUN

FIGURE 1. Summary of missions by inner solar system planetary body and steps in planetary exploration: flyby to orbit to lander to rover to returning samples

INTRODUCTION • NASA'S SOLAR SYSTEM EXPLORATION PARADIGM 5

Mars

	Mars	Phobos	Deimos
	Mariner 4, 6, 7 *Mars 4* *Rosetta*	Mariner 9 Viking Orbiter 1, 2 *Phobos 2* Mars Global Surveyor *Mars Express* Mars Reconnaissance Orbiter	Mariner 9 Viking Orbiter 1, 2 Mars Global Surveyor *Mars Express* Mars Reconnaissance Orbiter
Chang'e 1 *Chandrayaan-1* Lunar Reconnaissance Orbiter *Chang'e 2* GRAIL LADEE *Chang'e 3* *Chang'e 5**	Mariner 9 Mars Reconnaissance Orbiter *Mars 2, 5* Viking Orbiter 1, 2 MAVEN *Phobos 2* *Mars Orbiter Mission* Mars Global Surveyor *ExoMars Trace Gas Orbiter* Mars Odyssey *Mars Express*		
	Viking 1, 2 Mars Pathfinder Phoenix InSight *ExoMars Lander**		
	Sojourner MER Spirit MER Opportunity MSL Curiosity Perseverance/Ingenuity *ExoMars Rover**		
	Sample Return (FS)		

COSTS AND RISKS →

LEGEND
FS = Flagship Mission
NF = New Frontiers Class Mission
* To be accomplished

▨ Max Return on Investment Opportunities
Led by Non-U.S.
Mission Concepts

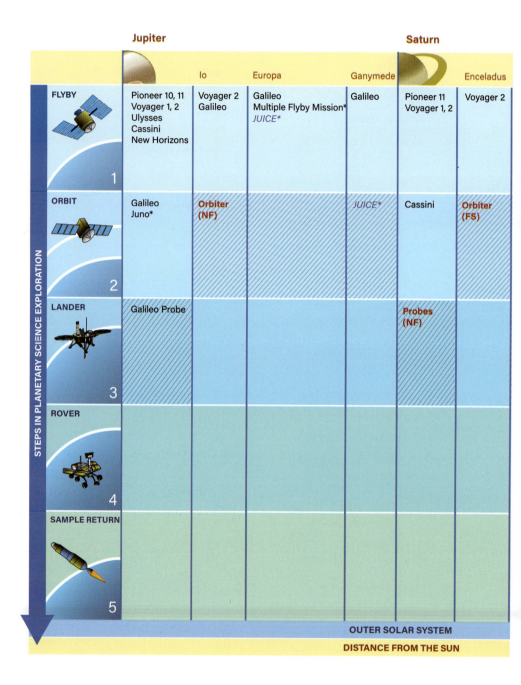

FIGURE 2. Summary of missions by outer solar system planetary body and steps in planetary exploration: flyby to orbit to lander to rover to returning samples

INTRODUCTION • NASA'S SOLAR SYSTEM EXPLORATION PARADIGM 7

	Uranus	Neptune		Dwarf Planets	Asteroids	Comets	
Titan			Triton				
Voyager 2 Cassini	Voyager 2	Voyager 2	Voyager 2	New Horizons	NEAR Shoemaker *Rosetta* Galileo Cassini Deep Space 1 Stardust	ISEE-3/ICE *Vega 1, 2* *Sakigake* *Suisei* *Giotto* Deep Space 1 Stardust – NeXT Deep Impact (EPOXI)	
	Orbiter (FS)			Dawn	NEAR Shoemaker *Hayabusa* Dawn	*Rosetta*	COSTS AND RISKS
Huygens					NEAR Shoemaker	Deep Impact *Philae*	
				Hayabusa *Hayabusa 2** OSIRIS-REx*	Stardust **Surface Sample Return (NF)**	

SMALL BODIES

LEGEND
FS = Flagship Mission
NF = New Frontiers Class Mission
* To be accomplished

 Max Return on Investment Opportunities
Led by Non-U.S.
Mission Concepts

U.S. Mariner and Soviet Venera missions surveyed and inventoried the inner planets Mercury, Venus, and Mars. In this section, we will discuss a few of these examples. The early flyby missions were all about leading the way in how to venture out into the solar system.

The first two Venera spacecraft were designed as flyby missions, but after they failed, the Soviet space program began targeting Veneras directly into the planet Venus, using the planet's extensive atmosphere to slow them down during entry. The Venera 5 and 6 atmospheric probes lasted long enough to provide significant data. Venera 7, designed to survive all the way to the surface, landed and transmitted for about 20 minutes before its battery died.

Space agencies also paid particular attention to Earth's Moon, with Soviet Luna and Zond spacecraft and one early U.S. Pioneer mission. Luna 1 was the first spacecraft to reach the vicinity of Earth's Moon. Although intended to be an impactor, it missed due to an incorrectly timed upper-stage burn during its launch, and it became the first spacecraft to end up orbiting the Sun. Following the first two Zond mission failures, the Soviet Zond 3 mission, after imaging the far side of the Moon, continued well beyond Earth orbit in order to test telemetry and spacecraft systems in deep space.

The principle of gravitational assist was exploited early to provide a method of increasing or reducing the speed of a spacecraft without the use of propellant. The Mariner 10 spacecraft was the first to use gravitational assist to reach another planet by swinging by Venus on 5 February 1974. This maneuver placed it on a trajectory to fly by Mercury a total of three times, twice in 1974 and once in 1975. The MErcury Surface, Space ENvironment, GEochemistry, and Ranging (MESSENGER) mission used the same approach, executing two Venus and three Mercury flybys before entering into orbit around Mercury in March 2011.

As shown in Figure 3, the outer solar system had flybys with two Pioneer and two Voyager spacecraft. The Voyager flyby missions completely changed the way we view the outer solar system. The primary mission of Voyagers 1 and 2 was the exploration of the Jupiter and Saturn systems. After making a string of discoveries there, such as active volcanoes on Jupiter's moon Io and the intricacies of Saturn's rings, the Voyagers' mission was extended. Voyager 2 went on to explore Uranus and Neptune and is still the only spacecraft to have visited these outer ice giant planets.

Voyagers 1 and 2 are currently into the fourth decade of their journey since their 1977 launches. In August 2012, data transmitted by Voyager 1 indicated that it had made a historic entry into interstellar space—the region between the stars, filled with the stellar winds of nearby stars. Scientists hope

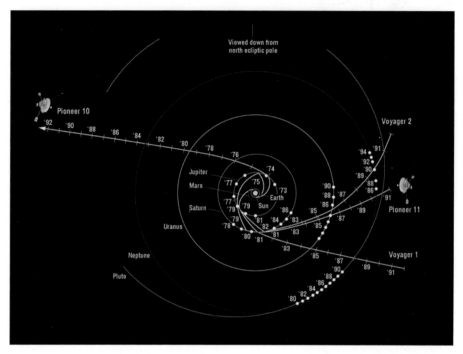

FIGURE 3. Pioneer and Voyager trajectories throughout the solar system. (NASA: 72413 Main ACD97-0036-3)

to learn more about this region when Voyager 2 passes out of the heliosphere and begins measuring interstellar winds.

As part of NASA's New Frontiers program, the New Horizons mission made the first reconnaissance of the dwarf planet Pluto (at 39 AU from Earth) and is now venturing deeper into the distant, mysterious Kuiper Belt, a relic of early solar system formation. New Horizons was launched on 19 January 2006 from Cape Canaveral, Florida, directly into an Earth-and-solar-escape trajectory with an Earth-relative speed of about 16.26 kilometers per second. After a brief encounter with asteroid 132524 APL, New Horizons proceeded to Jupiter, making its closest approach on 28 February 2007. The Jupiter flyby provided a gravity assist that increased New Horizons' speed by 4 kilometers per second. The encounter was also used as a general test of New Horizons' scientific capabilities, as the spacecraft returned data about the planet's atmosphere, moons, and magnetosphere. Most of the spacecraft's post-Jupiter voyage was spent in hibernation mode to preserve on-board systems, except for brief annual checkups. On 15 January 2015, the New Horizons spacecraft successfully came out of hibernation and began its approach phase to the Pluto system, which resulted in the first flyby of the dwarf planet on 14

High-resolution image captured by NASA's New Horizons spacecraft of Pluto's Sputnik Planum basin. (NASA/Johns Hopkins University Applied Physics Laboratory/Southwest Research Institute: PIA20007)

July 2015. With the completion of the New Horizons flyby of the Pluto system, NASA was the first and only space agency to have completed the initial exploration of the solar system.

MISSIONS THAT ORBIT

Beyond flybys, the next most sophisticated type of mission aimed to get a spacecraft into orbit around a solar system object. Data from flyby missions were essential to prioritizing which objects to orbit. High-resolution data from an orbiter mission are essential to planning for a future lander or rover mission.

After flyby missions, scientists wanted to learn much more about the basic properties of our planetary neighbors, such as structure, size, density, and atmospheric and surface composition. NASA's Magellan and the European Space Agency's (ESA)'s Venus Express spacecraft have orbited Venus. The world's space agencies have sent armadas of spacecraft to orbit the Moon and Mars. We have had groundbreaking discoveries with various orbiting missions. To survey the outer planets following the Galileo orbiter to the Jupiter system, Juno, launched in August 2011, arrived at Jupiter in early July 2016, while the Cassini spacecraft orbited Saturn until September 2017.

As our nearest neighbor, the Moon is a natural laboratory for investigating fundamental questions about the origin and evolution of Earth and the solar system. The Lunar Reconnaissance Orbiter (LRO), a robotic mission that has mapped the Moon's surface at high resolution (~1 square meter), is still operating as of this writing. LRO observations have enabled numerous groundbreaking discoveries, creating a new picture of the Moon as a dynamic and complex body.

Planetary scientists have made significant and steady progress in understanding what Mars is like today and what it was like in its distant past. The exploration of Mars is currently being accomplished by an international array of missions from NASA, the European Space Agency and its partner countries, and the Indian Space Research Organization (ISRO). Orbiter missions operating at Mars as of this writing include Mars Odyssey, Mars Express, the Mars Reconnaissance Orbiter, the Mars Atmosphere and Volatile EvolutioN Mission (MAVEN), and the Mars Orbiter Mission.

LANDER AND ROVER MISSIONS

Lander and rover missions enable scientists to acquire "ground truth," measurements so necessary to fully interpret data from orbital missions. The successful landings of the 1-metric-ton[2] Curiosity rover on Mars and the Rosetta mission's Philae probe on comet 67P/Churyumov–Gerasimenko clearly show the ability of our space agencies to explore our solar system at a new level of intensity. Steps like these will allow humans to go beyond this planet and out into the solar system once again.

As of 6 August 2020, Curiosity had been on the surface for eight Earth years. From Curiosity data, we now know that Mars was more Earthlike in its distant past, with rivers, lakes, streams, a thick atmosphere, clouds and rain, and, perhaps, an extensive ocean. Although today Mars is rather arid, scientists now believe vast amounts of water are trapped under the surface of Mars and under the carbon dioxide snow of its polar caps. Water is the key that will enable human activity and long-term presence on Mars.

SAMPLE RETURN

Sample return provides scientists with essential data to understand the geological history of a body. Up to the present, space agencies have collected samples from several solar system bodies, as well as samples of the solar wind. The Apollo program in the late 1960s and early 1970s brought back over 850 pounds of Moon rocks, soils, and regolith. These materials are still being analyzed and yielding significant scientific results. It is also important

---

2. Mars Science Laboratory Landing press kit, National Aeronautics and Space Administration, July 2012, p. 6, *http://www.jpl.nasa.gov/news/press_kits/MSLLanding.pdf* (accessed 8 January 2020).

A self-portrait of NASA's Curiosity rover taken at the rover's location in Gale Crater on Sol 2082 (15 June 2018). (NASA/JPL-Caltech/MSSS; PIA 22486)

to note that many of the meteorites that have fallen on Earth can now be identified with specific solar system bodies such as the Moon, Mars, and Vesta. The comet 81P/Wild (Wild 2) and the asteroid 25143 Itokawa were visited by robotic spacecraft from NASA and the Japan Aerospace Exploration Agency (JAXA), respectively. Both missions returned samples to Earth.

The Mars 2020 rover mission was based on the design of the highly successful Mars Science Laboratory rover, Curiosity. This new rover, named Perseverance, landed on Mars on 18 February 2021 in Jezero Crater. Perseverance carries more sophisticated hardware and new instruments to conduct geological assessments of the rover's landing site, determine the potential habitability of the environment, and directly search for signs of ancient Martian life by contact instruments and by coring and storing rock samples for later return to Earth.

Hitching a ride on Perseverance was another kind of powered craft, the Mars Helicopter Ingenuity. After arriving on Mars and traveling on the belly of Perseverance to a suitable helipad location, Ingenuity demonstrated the first powered flight on another world on 19 April 2021, climbing approximately 10 feet (3 meters) above the ground before hovering and returning to the ground safely.

THE NEXT 50 YEARS

Our robotic solar system explorers have gathered data to help us understand how the planets formed; what triggered different evolutionary paths among the planets; what processes are active; and how Earth formed, evolved, and became habitable. To search for evidence of life beyond Earth, we have used these data to map zones of habitability, study the chemistry of unfamiliar worlds, and reveal the processes that lead to conditions necessary for life.

This overview is not a comprehensive report on past missions. It touches on only a few examples in each of the categories that have defined our approach to solar system exploration for the last 50 years. We are now entering a new era of space exploration as we start to execute more complex missions that will land, rove, and return samples from top-priority targets in the solar system. In Figures 1 and 2, the crosshatched regions indicate the next big steps in the exploration of their target bodies, producing the maximum return based on knowledge acquired from the previous missions. In comparing Figures 1 and 2, it is clear that the inner solar system has been more thoroughly explored. This is understandable since outer solar system missions typically use radioisotope power systems and take many years to arrive at their target bodies.

New technologies will enable space agencies to develop and execute an astounding range of more complicated and challenging missions. We are at the leading edge of a journey of exploration that will yield a profound new understanding of the solar system as our home. NASA is building a Space Launch System (SLS) for human exploration, but its use is also being considered for some deep space robotic missions. The SLS will be more powerful than the Saturn V. If it is used for planetary missions to the outer solar system, direct trajectories rather than inner-solar-system gravity-assist maneuvers would be possible, cutting transit time, typically, by one-third. This launch approach alone would open the outer solar system to a significantly increased rate of missions and discoveries.

Robotic exploration not only yields knowledge of the solar system; it also will enable the expansion of humanity beyond low-Earth orbit. By studying and characterizing planetary environments beyond Earth and identifying possible resources, planetary scientists will enable safe and effective human missions into space. Scientific precursor missions to the Moon enabled the Apollo landings and have made significant progress toward enabling human missions to Mars within the next 50 years. A single-planet species may not long survive. It is our destiny to move off this planet and into the solar system. We are developing the capability to do it.

Acknowledgments

The authors would like to thank Stephen Edberg and Doris Daou for help with graphics and mission information.

PART I
Overview

IN HIS INTRODUCTION TO THIS VOLUME, NASA Chief Scientist Jim Green has described NASA's long-standing paradigm for solar system exploration—flyby, orbit, land and rove, and return samples—and reviewed, from a scientific perspective, the multinational array of robotic missions that have been launched to probe the solar system. In this chapter, historian Peter Westwick provides a wide-reaching and thought-provoking overview of the first 50 years of solar system exploration from a different perspective. He raises important questions along the way, some of which other contributors to this volume address, and some of which remain open, for other historians to answer.

Westwick asks, for example, who are the people who have made solar system exploration possible? The history of human spaceflight tells the stories of the astronauts, cosmonauts, and leading engineers (e.g., Wernher von Braun, Sergei Korolev) who made it possible—not so much for robotic solar system exploration. "After 50 years, we still need a social history of space exploration," he observes.

"Who are the explorers," he asks, "the people, institutions, and nations" that have engaged in exploration? And what exactly *is* "exploration?" he asks. "What does 'exploring' involve?" These questions are especially relevant today, as the line between space exploration and space exploitation is beginning to blur, with proposals for asteroid mining and planetary colonization. Advocacy for human exploration has tended to be driven by profit, he notes. "The profit motive, however, as far as I have seen," he writes, "was largely absent from planetary exploration, which is interesting for a major American enterprise."

Westwick entertains a question that other space historians like to think about: why explore space? Scientists, engineers, and others engaged in exploring space tend to answer the "why" question with stories about "spin-off" benefits, jobs on the ground, national prestige, and educational value. All of these benefits can be supplied by other sorts of scientific and technological enterprises, however. So, the question remains open: why?

Westwick's thoughtful perspective on the first half century of solar system exploration provides an excellent entry to the rest of this volume.

CHAPTER 1

Exploring the Solar System: Who Has Done It, How, and Why?

Peter J. Westwick

SOME 50 YEARS AGO, NASA's Mariner 2 spacecraft skimmed 20,000 miles over Venus. This first excursion to another planet landed Jet Propulsion Laboratory (JPL) Director William Pickering on the cover of *Time* magazine and as grand marshal of the Rose Parade. In August 2012, many were captivated by Curiosity's landing on Mars. That's the Curiosity spacecraft, not the human spirit of inquiry, although that was certainly present, too. JPL engineers spiced things up by devising a landing sequence with a preposterous, Rube Goldberg flavor. They knew better than anyone what was riding on the landing: a $2 billion rover, for starters, but also, perhaps, the national appetite for solar system exploration itself. Curiosity's success may have ensured that the United States, at least, will continue to explore the solar system, so that the history considered in this volume will continue.

Mariner and Curiosity bookend the first 50 years of solar system exploration. In between, robotic explorers have met triumphant success and epic failure; they have seen ring spokes and blueberries and have dealt with Great Galactic Ghouls and faces on Mars. These 50 years have taught us remarkable new things about the solar system. They have also taught us a great deal about ourselves. We now can look outward to our solar system and contemplate all we have learned about it. We also can drop our gaze back to Earth and consider what deep-space exploration tells us about our own human history over the last 50 years.

WHO HAS DONE IT?

The first question is, who are the explorers—not the robots, but the people, institutions, and nations who built them? Let's start with the people. After 50 years, we still need a social history of space exploration.[1] Who are these people, and what do they do all day? How have they changed over 50 years, and how has the work changed? What are their backgrounds? How do they balance work and personal life? What do they do when they are not working, and how does that affect their work?

We know a bit about the types of people involved—for starters, mostly men. Engineering and systems management was an overwhelmingly male preserve for the first half of this period. Women in the space program have been studied in relation to the astronaut corps, but much remains to be done for solar system exploration.[2] The number of women present in JPL's mission control for Curiosity was a marked contrast to all the men running Mariner, and how that happened is an interesting story. Still, though, the engineers on Curiosity are mostly male.

They are also mostly white. NASA has not had a sterling record of minority representation,[3] especially at higher levels, although that has changed recently. One might also think about socioeconomic classes. When we think of the people involved in solar system exploration, we mostly think about white-collar engineers and managers and neglect the many other people involved in the enterprise: machinists, security guards, secretaries—some

---

1. Glen Asner, "Space History from the Bottom Up: Using Social History to Interpret the Societal Impact of Spaceflight," in S. J. Dick and R. D. Launius, eds., *Societal Impact of Spaceflight* (Washington, DC: NASA SP-2007-4801, 2007), pp. 387-406; Sylvia Doughty Fries, *NASA Engineers in the Age of Apollo* (Washington, DC: NASA SP-4104, 1992); Yasushi Sato, "Local Engineering and Systems Engineering: Cultural Conflict at NASA's Marshall Space Flight Center, 1960–1966," *Technology and Culture* 46 (July 2005): 561–583.
2. Margaret Weitekamp, *Right Stuff, Wrong Sex: America's First Women in Space Program* (Baltimore: Johns Hopkins University Press, 2004); Bettyann Kevles, *Almost Heaven: The Story of Women in Space* (New York: Basic Books, 2003; Kim McQuaid, "'Racism, Sexism, and Space Ventures:' Civil Rights at NASA in the Nixon Era and Beyond," in *Societal Impact of Spaceflight*, pp. 421–449; Donna Shirley, *Managing Martians* (New York: Broadway Books, 1998); M. G. Lord, "Cold Warrior's Daughter," in Peter J. Westwick, ed., *Blue Sky Metropolis: The Aerospace Century in Southern California* (Berkeley: University of California Press, 2012), pp. 45–53.
3. NASA's Marshall Space Flight Center and the University of Alabama-Huntsville History Department organized a symposium, "NASA in the 'Long' Civil Rights Movement," 16–17 March 2017, at the U.S. Space and Rocket Center in Huntsville, AL. The symposium aimed to address "the civil rights experiences across NASA that not only explore the experience of African Americans, but also of women, immigrants, and other politically/legally marginalized groups."

Glenn Research Center Propulsion Systems Laboratory Control Room. (NASA: C-1998-00279)

of whom share the excitement of space exploration, others of whom do not. One JPL janitor said the most exciting thing about the Viking landing was the large rat that ran across the room and jumped into a trash can.

Next, what institutions explore the planets? Looking just at the United States, we have universities, government labs, and industrial corporations, for starters. Each type of institution has different goals and cultures, and sometimes those goals and cultures include things besides solar system exploration. How do university scientists interact with industry engineers? How does academic culture intersect the profit motive of contractors and the government's demand for accountability? Consider JPL, to take an example entirely at random. JPL started as an Army rocket laboratory, and even after embracing planetary spacecraft as its main mission, JPL continued to work on Earth sciences, astronomy, and, at times, substantial military programs—up to one-fourth of its total program in the 1980s. All these other programs, especially the military ones, affected how JPL built planetary spacecraft, from Ranger to "faster, better cheaper." And the relationship between civil and military space is by no means confined to JPL.

There is also much talk now about private industry and space exploration, the so-called alternative-space movement, also known as alt-space, New

Space, or Space 2.0. Most public attention here has focused on the human spaceflight program, with SpaceX ferrying supplies to the International Space Station (ISS), and on potential space tourism. But some private groups have also tried to get into the planetary game, from AMSAT (Radio Amateur Satellite Corporation) in the 1980s to Astrobotic Technology and other teams competing for the Google Lunar XPRIZE.

The variety of American space institutions leads us to consider which other countries have done solar system exploration and why. For much of the last 50 years, it was mostly the United States and the Soviet Union/Russia, joined more recently by various European nations, Japan, China, and India. We'll return to some of these countries in a moment. Let us first note that international comparisons of, say, the types of people building spacecraft—their gender, ethnicity, socioeconomic class—might be illuminating. Consider the bureaucratic politics of the Soviet Union, with the Ministry of General Machine Building (MOM), the Space Research Institute of the Russian Academy of Sciences (IKI), and the various design bureaus, and how these dynamics shaped the Soviet space program. Differences include relations between civilian and military space programs. China, for example, has less distinction between civilian and military space institutions—in part because it followed American suggestions in the late 1970s to embrace the U.S. model and integrate the two realms.[4]

Nations collaborated as well as competed in space, and space exploration has provided fertile ground for diplomatic or international history.[5] Looking abroad also raises interesting questions about colonialism—that is, colonialism here on Earth, not space colonization. One might consider the Soviets launching spacecraft out of what is now Kazakhstan, or the French launching rockets out of French Guiana.[6] Consider also the far-flung tracking stations of the Deep Space Network, which confronted apartheid at its South Africa site. How did such interactions affect the work?

---

4. E. A. Feigenbaum, *China's Techno-Warriors: National Security and Strategic Competition from the Nuclear to the Information Age* (Stanford, CA: Stanford University Press, 2003): 128–134.

5. E.g., Walter A. McDougall, *…the Heavens and the Earth: A Political History of the Space Age* (New York: Basic Books, 1985); John Krige, *Fifty Years of European Cooperation in Space* (Paris: Beauchesne, 2014); J. Krige, A. Long Callahan, and A. Maharaj, *NASA in the World. 50 Years of International Collaboration in Space* (New York: Palgrave Macmillan, 2013); Asif Siddiqi, "Competing Technologies, National(ist) Narratives, and Universal Claims: Towards a Global History of Space Exploration," *Technology and Culture* 51 (April 2010): 425–443.

6. Peter Redfield, *Space in the Tropics: From Convicts to Rockets in French Guiana* (Berkeley, CA: University of California Press, 2000).

Mars Pathfinder rover team with Sojourner model, 1994.. (NASA: P-45061)

HOW IS IT DONE?

Solar system exploration, despite the title of this volume, is of course not 50 years old. Astronomers and natural philosophers have been studying the planets for millennia, and planetary science is still done today by telescope from Earth. But when we talk about "exploration," we're talking about going to the planets, not studying them from a distance. And that explains our focus on the last 50 years. What's special about this period is the technology of rockets, which put humans and machines into outer space.

There has been a long-running debate over machines versus humans in the U.S. space program. Thus far, only robotic travelers have reached other planetary bodies, except for the Moon. How do we define "exploration?" What does "exploring" involve? Herodotus, the ancient Greek historian known as the Father of History, provided tales of what he saw or heard on his travels, including such marvelous creatures as giant, camel-eating ants and flying snakes. As Herodotus knew, it is not enough just to go somewhere new; we want to hear about what's there. You went to a new place? What did you see?

So what is the record we expect to get back from other planets? It can't be a traveler's tale. What is it, then? Numbers? That is, do we just go there and count things? Take pictures? Collect physical samples? The answers to these questions help determine the technologies deployed, such as cameras versus counters, as well as who is looking at the return—for instance, geologists versus physicists. These choices affect spacecraft design, such as the showdown between spin stabilization and three-axis stabilization, pitting fields-and-particles against imaging, atmospheric physics versus geology, and NASA's Ames Research Center versus JPL.

Several chapters in this volume will touch on the evolution of spacecraft technology: from orbiters to landers to rovers, from retrorocket landings to airbags to sky cranes, from flagship missions to faster-better-cheaper. Let us not forget the fun factor, for the engineers building these things. Take the Mars rovers. Here is a marvelous technical challenge: take this car, deliver it 35 million miles to another planet, land it softly on the ground there, and drive it around. Engineers can provide all the technical arguments they want for sky cranes and airbags, but, deep down, perhaps they just thought these were cool ideas and wanted to try to pull them off.

One prime development of the last 50 years has been computers. These include computers on spacecraft themselves, which drove feedback loops of capability and complexity and also highlighted differences between U.S. and Soviet spacecraft. U.S. designers could change software midflight, which allowed Mariner 9, for instance, to wait out a dust storm on Mars while a hard-wired Soviet spacecraft plunged fatally into the maelstrom. Later spacecraft pushed this flexibility toward the ideal of autonomy, though they have not taken the additional biomorphic step of replication, urged by physicist Freeman Dyson in the 1980s. So we are still, alas, awaiting the promised profusion of "astro-chickens."[7]

But computer miniaturization did raise hopes about a proliferation of tiny spacecraft. Proposals for microspacecraft dated to the late 1970s. (Jim Burke, a contributor to this volume, was a proponent.) The motivation was partly nostalgic, an attempt to return to the scale of the early Explorers. Subsequent advances in technology have spurred more recent talk about nanospacecraft, whatever that might mean, with fantastic plans using not only microcircuits but also micromachined rocket nozzles and reaction wheels. These plans have not gotten off the ground, literally. If anything, size is going in the other direction, to judge from the Mars rovers.

Miniaturization is an interesting path not taken. Why, after 30 years, are we still launching planetary spacecraft the size of SUVs? The issue is only

---

7. Freeman Dyson, *Disturbing the Universe* (New York: Harper & Row, 1979), pp. 194–204.

Goldstone Deep Space Communications Complex in the Mojave Desert, California. (NASA: JPL-28311)

partly technological (the problem of aperture being one constraint); it is also programmatic—that is to say, political and cultural. Part of the appeal of microspacecraft is the democratization of technology, eliminating the need for massive launch vehicles or massive budgets. And yet solar system exploration remains, so far, a monopoly of nation-states. In other words, how-we-do-it continues to reflect who-does-it.

Computers were not just on spacecraft. They also had a role sitting on desktops here on Earth, including not just computers used at the front end of missions, in spacecraft design, but also on the back end, for data distribution and analysis. As computers drove data rates from 10 kilobits per second on Mariner, to 100 kilobits on Voyager, to 100 kilobytes on Galileo, and ever upward, data management became as much a part of exploration as building spacecraft. Some planetary scientists these days probably have little to do with spacecraft; they just sit at their computers and sift through mountains of downloaded data, often in concert with a whole distributed network of similarly desk-bound investigators. Are all these people also "explorers"?

While we're talking about technology, and the front end and back end of missions, let us recognize what we might call the middle. The vital link between the spacecraft and the downloaded data is the Deep Space Network. The DSN is easy to forget because it is here on Earth, in distant places, with the U.S. node out in the remote Mojave Desert. DSN engineers are not on TV when a spacecraft arrives at a planet, but they are crucial to getting it there and hearing from it. They have saved the bacon of spacecraft designers on several occasions, and they have defined the state of the art in telecommunications and coding theory. They, too, are explorers.

Finally, "How do we do it?" suggests another basic question. The definition of "exploration" often has connotations of novelty. At what point does that term no longer apply to the planets? We no longer talk much about explorers on Earth—those intrepid souls who ventured across deserts and oceans, or to mountain peaks and the poles. This does not mean there is nothing left on Earth to explore—far from it—but that we now think of this more as science than exploration. This is a loss. The urge to be first to a place has inspired some of humankind's most remarkable achievements. Is space exploration similarly losing its romantic appeal? Consider the names of deep-space missions. We have gone from Mariner, Ranger, Viking, and Voyager to Mars Polar Lander, Mars Climate Orbiter, and Mars Science Laboratory. Romance gives way to practicality in many long-term relationships.

This development has programmatic implications. Do we revisit one planet, such as Mars, to extend our database, or do we seek new places—comets or asteroids, or outer-planet satellites—for broader knowledge? And if space exploration has lost its romantic appeal, how does it inspire the amazing dedication of the people who build these spacecraft? Will they put in 100-hour weeks to launch yet another science lab to Mars? And how about the American public? Will they lose interest when the novelty and romance of deep space travel dwindle? Will familiarity breed contempt? And that leads us to our next question: why do it?

WHY DO IT?

Over the past 50-plus years, NASA has probably spent over $50 billion exploring the planets. There is also the investment of human resources: many thousands of highly trained and dedicated people, with very valuable skills, at NASA Centers, universities, and contractors across the country. What did we get for this investment? Why do it?[8] Public information officer Jurrie van der Woude at JPL responded to this question cryptically: if you have to ask, I couldn't tell you.[9] But the U.S. taxpayer, at least, demands a better answer.

---

8. See Steven J. Dick's series of essays Why We Explore at *http://history.nasa.gov/Why_We_/Why_We_01pt1.html* (accessed 28 July 2020). See also Stephen J. Pyne, *Voyager: Seeking Newer Worlds in the Third Great Age of Discovery* (New York: Viking, 2010).
9. David Swift, *Voyager Tales: Personal Views of the Grand Tour* (Reston, VA: American Institute of Aeronautics and Astronautics [AIAA], 1997), p. 395.

In 1970, a nun in Zambia named Sister Mary Jucunda wrote to NASA scientist Ernst Stuhlinger, asking how he could propose spending billions of dollars to explore Mars when children were starving on Earth. Stuhlinger laid out several justifications, which have become litany:[10]

- The federal budget is broken up by agency and is not a zero-sum exercise, so the money couldn't just shift to fight hunger or poverty.
- Understanding other planets helps us understand climate and geology here on Earth and hence improve agriculture, fisheries, and so on.
- Space exploration highlights our common humanity and encourages international cooperation; thus, it helps overcome suffering from national strife.
- If nations do compete, better for them to do so in outer space than through wars here on Earth.
- Space exploration inspires young people to pursue science and engineering, and their future discoveries will help humanity.
- And, finally, the spinoff argument: it stimulates new technologies that find applications on Earth.

Plenty of ink and bytes have been spilled on this debate, and the Curiosity landing revived this issue among the chattering classes. You can look at it two ways. On the one hand, all those billions would pay for an awful lot of school textbooks or food for the poor. On the other, Curiosity cost less than what the Pentagon is spending every week in Afghanistan. (Or insert your favorite comparison here: the current planetary program costs the equivalent of one Starbucks coffee for every American each year, or Americans spend more on dog toys every year, and so on.)

But the fact is that a billion dollars is a lot of money. Leave aside the many other social priorities: what about scientific priorities? Genomics, particle physics, astronomy, and materials science could do a lot with a billion dollars. Or just think how many historians of science a billion dollars could support.

Polls consistently suggest that only a quarter of the American public is interested in space (and even fewer are knowledgeable about it).[11] That is,

---

10. Roger Launius, "Why Explore Space? A 1970 Letter to a Nun in Africa," 8 February 2012, *Roger Launius's Blog*, available at *https://launiusr.wordpress.com/2012/02/08/why-explore-space-a-1970-letter-to-a-nun-in-africa/* (accessed 8 January 2020).
11. Charles Pellerin, "NASA Strategic Planning," 13 April 1993 (JPL 259, 23/252). See also Roger D. Launius, "Public Opinion Polls and Perceptions of U.S. Human Spaceflight," *Space Policy* 19, no. 3 (August 2003); William Sims Bainbridge, "The Impact of Space Exploration on Public Opinions, Attitudes, and Beliefs," in *Societal Impact of Spaceflight*, pp. 1–74; Linda

three-fourths of Americans aren't interested in space. But then recall the media hordes who descended upon JPL for Viking and Voyager, or track the web traffic for Pathfinder, the Mars Exploration Rovers, and Curiosity. And let us not forget Carl Sagan, whose *Cosmos* book and TV series touched not quite billions and billions, but many millions of people in the 1980s, followed by Neil de Grasse Tyson's *Cosmos* reboot in 2014. But then why did none of the major TV networks break into their programming to show the Curiosity landing live?[12]

NASA expends a lot of effort trying to understand this paradox. How to bridge the apathy gap and sustain interest in exploration? It is not just a matter of outreach. NASA has always been very attentive to publicity, from the Mercury 7 and Apollo through Curiosity, and from *Life* magazine to TV and on to today's web-based social media and apps. JPL's first deep-space mission proposals ranked public relations ahead of science or engineering goals. But NASA managers perceived decades ago that space missions apparently do not change how Americans vote, and thus how Congress votes.[13]

Space exploration resonates with deep American values, not least the frontier metaphor, and Americans take great pride in it. In October 2012, a million people lined the streets of Los Angeles—a million people, in LA, that bastion of civic apathy!—to watch a Space Shuttle crawl by at 2 miles per hour. Endeavour was only heading crosstown, to a museum, not into outer space, yet its transit was still a major public happening. The chief of the Los Angeles Police Department (LAPD) said he had never seen a crowd so positive and proud.[14] But when those same people stepped into the polling booth two weeks later, they probably did not pull the lever based on a candidate's space policy.

The next two chapters in this volume will ponder the politics of space, including shifting ideologies of spaceflight. As the highest expression of

---

Billings, "50 Years of NASA and the Public: What NASA? What Publics?," in Steven J. Dick, ed., *NASA's First 50 Years: Historical Perspectives*, NASA SP-2010-4704 (Washington, DC: NASA, 2010), pp. 151–181.

12. While the major TV networks may not have covered the landing live, Ustream reported that its "live stream of NASA's Curiosity rover landing garnered more interest than primetime Sunday television." According to a company spokesperson, 3.2 million people in total had checked the stream at some point during the landing, with a peak of 500,000 people watching at the same time. Adi Robertson, "Ustream Mars Curiosity broadcast numbers beat primetime CNN, company says. The Verge, 8 August 2012, *https://www.theverge.com/2012/8/8/3228405/ustream-mars-landing-numbers*

13. E.g., Hans Mark's comments at National Academy of Sciences colloquium, 26–27 October 1981, collection JPL 150, box 5/folder 49, JPL archives.

14. Los Angeles Police Department press release, "Mission 26 – The Big Endeavor NR12430rl," 15 October 2012, *http://nkca.ucla.edwww.lapdonline.org/southwest_news/news_view/52150* (accessed 7 September 2021).

socially directed technical progress, the early space program received its main support from politicians on the left. But by the late 1960s, as liberals shifted federal attention toward social problems, conservatives were abandoning fiscal austerity and embracing the vision of space as new frontier, a way to rekindle the old pioneer spirit. Thus conservative media commentator George Will, no friend of federal activity, viewed Voyager as "a smashingly successful government program."[15] Liberal commentators, for their part, came to view the frontier image as an emblem of imperial conquest, military adventure, environmental damage, and corporate profiteering.[16] Hence public opinion polls in the early 1980s showed that conservatives were more likely than liberals to support the space program.[17]

Some people extended the frontier image to space as a new realm for commerce. Capitalist ideology certainly animates the alt-space movement.[18] The profit motive, however, appears largely absent from solar system exploration, which is interesting for a major American enterprise. There was excited talk about space mining and space solar power in the 1970s, though the groups pushing such projects—the L5 Society and their brethren—were not themselves building spacecraft. Today, there is the Google Lunar XPRIZE, but as a ploy to spur private investment, the prize is an implicit admission that no marketplace exists in space. So, while many institutions have made money building planetary spacecraft (and others have lost it), the justification for those missions was not commercial. We have not launched these spacecraft to make money.

So why do we do it? Here we have to look at the broader context, at what else has happened over the last 50 years. For more than half the period, that context was the Cold War. One reason the U.S. government supported solar system exploration for many years was to beat the Soviets, in this case in the battle for hearts and minds, in international status and prestige. This reason

---

15. Quoted in David Morrison, *Voyages to Saturn*, NASA SP-451 (Washington, DC: NASA, 1982), p. 93.
16. Roger D. Launius and Howard E. McCurdy, "Epilogue: Beyond NASA Exceptionalism," in Launius and McCurdy, eds., *Spaceflight and the Myth of Presidential Leadership* (Champaign, IL: University of Illinois Press, 1997), pp. 221–250, on pp. 234–240. See also Andrew Butrica, *Single Stage to Orbit: Politics, Space Technology, and the Quest for Reusable Rocketry* (Baltimore: Johns Hopkins University Press, 2003).
17. NBC News poll results, in Laurily Epstein to Louis Friedman, 30 November 81 (JPL 150, 11/146).
18. See W. Patrick McCray, *The Visioneers: How a Group of Elite Scientists Pursued Space Colonies, Nanotechnologies, and a Limitless Future* (Princeton, NJ: Princeton University Press, 2012) and W. Patrick McCray, "From L5 to X Prize: California's Alternative Space Movement," in Westwick, ed., *Blue Sky Metropolis*, pp. 171–193.

often rose and fell with the temperature of the Cold War: one heard it often in the 1960s, less so amid détente in the 1970s, but then more again in the 1980s, when Soviet Mars proposals led to jokes about it becoming the Red Planet, in more ways than one.

Then the Cold War ended. Justifications for space exploration have changed over time. In the 1990s, as the superpower standoff gave way to global competition in the high-tech economy, justifications shifted from maintaining international strategic standing to fueling the engines of economic growth. Solar system exploration, in this argument, supported the high-tech aerospace industry, incubated new technologies, and, perhaps most important, inspired young Americans to careers in science and engineering.

Perhaps to compensate for the mundane justification of economic competitiveness, the end of the Cold War also encouraged more transcendent motives, in particular the possibility of finding life elsewhere in the cosmos. The search for extraterrestrial life in a way turned solar system exploration into a biology program, which meshed with wider scientific and economic interests in biotechnology. Recall, however, all those American flags waving around JPL mission control during the 2012 Curiosity landing and the 2004 Mars Exploration Rover landings. Space exploration as a vehicle for national pride and patriotism was not just a Cold War phenomenon.

As to the motivation for other spacefaring countries: for the countries of Europe, it was perhaps less patriotism and more a way to foster European integration, while balancing American scientific and technological hegemony. In Europe, too, economic competitiveness was a motive—that is, space missions were seen as a stimulus, or perhaps a subsidy, for high-tech industry—and even stronger and earlier than in the United States. The same was true for Japan. National pride remains a powerful factor, especially for nations experiencing that other key development of the 20th century, postcolonialism. For a developing country like India, a space program symbolizes status as a modern international power, much as nuclear weapons do. (And let us not forget that civil space programs remain a barely veiled signal of military space capability.) But in countries like India and China, where hundreds of millions of people struggle with desperate poverty despite pell-mell modernization, the basic question—is it worth it?—is more acute. How can these countries justify spending a billion dollars on space?

In short, motivations for space exploration have reflected the broadest historical developments of this time: the Cold War, postcolonialism, global economic development, and high-tech industry.

These developments explain why we've done it. The follow-on question is: what have we got for it? Some people, like Stuhlinger, like to cite the spinoffs from space exploration. There are certainly examples like computer animation, solar-power technology, and telecommunications coding algorithms. A fun example is the Super Soaker squirt gun, invented by a JPL engineer.[19] But arguing that CGI movies and Super Soakers justify solar system exploration is a thin reed. Justifying a program with spinoffs seems a tacit admission that the primary returns are insufficient.

And that primary justification, science, may suffice. Consider what we have learned about our solar system. The Ranger and Surveyor spacecraft returned evidence that the Moon had not always been cold and hard, though they could not resolve competing theories about lunar origin.[20] Mariner flights confirmed Venus to be a "hellhole," with 900°F surface temperatures and pressures 90 times greater than on Earth.[21] Mariner images of Mercury's craters, meanwhile, supported the "Great Bombardment" theory for the early history of the solar system, which reinforced catastrophist theories of Earth's geological and biological history.[22] Voyager and its successors Galileo and Cassini turned the outer planets and their moons from blurry smears on astronomers' plates to complex, diverse, individual bodies, from the sulfurous calderas of Io to the icy ocean of Europa, each undergoing dynamic processes—external bombardment to the point of cracking or splitting entirely, or flexing gravitationally, outgassing, and erupting, seemingly almost living and breathing.

Planetary missions, in short, revealed the solar system to be full of marvels: methane lakes, miles-high geysers, volcanoes, supersonic winds, canyons thousands of miles long and several miles deep, mountains that dwarf Everest, and off-kilter magnetic fields. They thus helped to correct the geocentric perspective of planetary scientists—evident, for example, in the surprise at volcanic and tectonic activity in cold outer regions of the solar system.

---

19. David Kindy, "The accidental invention of the Super Soaker," Smithsonian Magazine, 21 June 2019, *https://www.smithsonianmag.com/innovation/accidental-invention-super-soaker-180972428/* (accessed 7 September 2021).
20. Clayton R. Koppes, *JPL and the American Space Program* (New Haven, CT: Yale University Press, 1982), pp. 182–183; see also Ronald E. Doel, *Solar System Astronomy in America: Communities, Patronage, and Interdisciplinary Science, 1920–1960* (Cambridge, New York: Cambridge University Press, 1996), pp. 134–150; Stephen G. Brush, *A History of Modern Planetary Physics*, vol. 3, *Fruitful Encounters: The Origin of the Solar System and of the Moon from Chamberlin to Apollo* (Cambridge, New York: Cambridge University Press, 1996), pp. 218–233.
21. John Noble Wilford in the *New York Times* (25 August 1981), quoted in Koppes, p. 250.
22. Brush, *Fruitful Encounters*, pp. 131–138; Ronald E. Doel, "The Earth Sciences and Geophysics," in *Science in the Twentieth Century*, ed. John Krige and Dominique Pestre (Amsterdam: Routledge, 1997), pp. 391–416, on 396, 406.

Artist's concept of New Horizons reaching Pluto. (NASA/Johns Hopkins University Applied Physics Laboratory/Southwest Research Institute: PIA19703)

More fundamental still is the possibility of extraterrestrial life, thanks to evidence of water on Mars, Europa, and Enceladus, and liquid hydrocarbons on Titan.

All these findings suggest that we shift our frame of reference. It is not what we as individual taxpayers get out of solar system exploration, but rather what we as a species gain from it. Some see solar system exploration as a "third age" of human exploration, a fundamental turning point in human history comparable to the oceanic voyages of Columbus and Cook.[23] We could look rather to science. Physicist Niels Bohr said that science is "the gradual removal of prejudices." If so, then solar system exploration might rank with the Copernican and Darwinian revolutions in removing the prejudices of geocentrism and anthropocentrism.

---

23. E.g., Pyne, *Voyager: Seeking Newer Worlds in the Third Great Age of Discovery* Again, reference is to the book in toto, not to a specific passage; Mark Washburn, *Distant Encounters: The Exploration of Jupiter and Saturn* (New York: Harcourt, 1983), p. 140.

WHO CARES?

So far, we have considered three questions: who did it, how did they do it, and why? Let us add a fourth: why write about the first 50 years of solar system exploration? This chapter began with the observation that 50 years of solar system exploration has taught us a lot about our solar system, but equally about ourselves here on Earth. What does solar system exploration tell us about the last 50 years of history?

For example: how does the history of solar system exploration change our view of the Cold War, postcolonialism, the information revolution, or globalization and economic development? If the United States is, indeed, in strategic decline, or at least facing increasing competition, how are these developments shaping solar system exploration? Note that in 2011, amid confusion over U.S. space goals, China announced an aggressive 5-year plan for soft lunar landers and sample returns.[24] What about the future of the nation-state itself? Will the rise of transnational, multinational, nonstate, or substate actors introduce new approaches to solar system exploration? For one thing, it suggests that historians find alternatives to the state-centered narratives we usually use for the Space Age.[25, 26] Can we consider how post-Fordism and postmodernism affected the planetary enterprise? What about climate change? In the 1970s, Malthusian concerns about overpopulation, resource scarcity, and pollution sparked calls for space colonization. Will global climate change similarly encourage solar system exploration?

Historians of solar system exploration should be pretty good at big pictures, since our frame of reference is the entire solar system. But we should remember to step back occasionally and think about the big historical picture—how our work connects to broader developments. Space history can be an insular field, despite the examples of books like Walter McDougall's *…the Heavens and the Earth*, which showed how space history can shed light on fundamental historical changes. Our work should not just speak to other space historians but rather should reach out to general historians, as well as the general public.

---

24. "China welcomes world's scientists to collaborate in lunar exploration," China National Space Administration, 15 January 2019, *http://www.cnsa.gov.cn/english/n6465652/n6465653/c6805232/content.html* (accessed 7 September 2021). China's Chang'e-3 spacecraft landed on the Moon in 2013, and its Chang'e-4 spacecraft achieved the world's first *soft landing* on the *far side of the Moon* on 3 January 2019.
25. Martin Collins, "Production and Culture Together: Or, Space History and the Problem of Periodization in the Postwar Era," in *Societal Impact of Spaceflight*, pp. 615–630.
26. Siddiqi, "Competing Technologies," pp. 425–443.

That includes the need for critical voices. Many space historians study this topic because we ourselves started out as space buffs, but we should include the viewpoints of the unbelievers. Solar system exploration is a human enterprise, and it thus reflects not just the great achievements of humankind but also human foibles and failings. Let us appreciate the achievements of space exploration, but let us also consider the costs.

Let us also recognize that our topic runs up to the present, where the ice gets thin for historians. Times change, and so do historians' judgments. Sir Walter Raleigh warned, "Whosoever, in writing a modern history, should follow truth too near the heels, it may haply strike out his teeth." Or, as Zhou Enlai supposedly said to Henry Kissinger, when asked about the meaning of the French Revolution: "It's too soon to tell." But let us begin.

PART II
Politics and Policy in the Conduct of Solar System Exploration

THE NEXT TWO CHAPTERS explore how politics and policy shaped the first 50 years of solar system exploration—how bureaucrats, scientists, politicians, and others collaborated and competed to set science, mission, and funding priorities.

Aerospace analyst Jason Callahan describes the political economy of solar system exploration, explaining how varied and competing interest groups ("stakeholders," in today's parlance) have come together to advocate and set priorities for solar system exploration. He discusses the role of external advisory groups, such as the NASA Advisory Council (NAC) and the National Research Council's Space Studies Board. And he shows how funding for solar system exploration is, nonetheless, subject to other influences.

Using a very informative set of charts and tables, Callahan lays out the history of federal funding for solar system exploration in the context of overall NASA spending and the federal budget picture. He shows how funding for solar system exploration—like funding for any other federal enterprise—is a reflection of national priorities at any given time. His chapter is "must" reading for any and all who are engaged in advocating for solar system exploration.

Political scientist Roger Handberg addresses the politics of funding for solar system exploration from a different angle, exploring how demands for the funding of bigger-ticket human spaceflight programs have affected solar system exploration and space science writ large. From the beginning, as he points out, space science and human spaceflight have been intertwined, and the "robotic versus human" debate about the course of space exploration has been persistent.

Handberg raises the question of whether, in the post–Space Shuttle era, space science can, or will, be a partner in NASA's grand plans for human exploration. And he wonders whether space science today is best located in NASA or perhaps in some other federal agency.

CHAPTER 2

Funding Planetary Science: History and Political Economy

Jason W. Callahan

PLANETARY SCIENCE IN THE UNITED STATES is a public activity, in that the federal government provides nearly all the funding for it and the vast majority of its resources are managed by a federal administration. Over the past 50 years, scientific communities, the executive branch, and the legislative branch have negotiated to varying degrees of success the direction, scale, and composition of this effort.

In this time, the scientists, engineers, technicians, managers, accountants, students, and others involved in all of the activities of planetary science have coalesced into a coherent scientific community. Furthermore, they have adapted to the shifting federal bureaucratic landscape with three important effects:

1. Despite many factions, the community now acts with a great deal of unity.
2. The community strategizes in terms of programs rather than projects.
3. The community, using the first two points, has developed a systematic method for bounding the options for planetary science activities from which politicians and policymakers choose.

Although the planetary science community has made great strides in communicating its goals, funding for planetary science has not followed a stable trajectory over the last 5 decades. Because NASA spending constitutes a minor fraction of the federal budget, which itself is a relatively small part of the U.S. economy, factors determining the allocation of resources to solar system exploration are not always within the control of Agency leadership or the science community. Understanding NASA's place in the U.S. economic environment helps explain some of the perennial turmoil that typically surrounds the annual budget process. It also sheds light on the influence of national priorities, an important factor to consider as the planetary science community tries to convey the necessity of a continuing solar system exploration program. This chapter considers planetary science in the context of the federal budget, other federal research and development activities, and other space science activities at NASA.

This chapter also analyzes the history of the U.S. space program, which is marked by major decisions of presidents, members of Congress, and NASA Administrators. The role of the space science community is integral to understanding the importance of NASA's scientific program and the value of federal investment in science and technology generally. Members of the planetary science community have played a vital role in shaping the U.S. space program by defining options available to national leadership. They have also played a critical part in forming methods by which scientific communities communicate among themselves, with other communities, and with stakeholders.

BUDGETING FOR EXPLORATION

The first thing to recognize when looking at the U.S. economy is that, at least in the last three decades, there is little correlation between the Gross Domestic Product (GDP) and spending. In times of recession, federal spending goes up. In times of expansion, federal spending goes up.[1]

The financial indicators shown in figure 1 demonstrate one other somewhat disturbing trend over the last five decades. Beginning in the late 1970s (labeled "A"), government expenditures outpaced receipts consistently, and the federal debt grew at a rate matching, and often outpacing, the rate of increase in GDP. The result of this expanding debt is an increasing cost to the federal government each year to pay just the interest on the debt, without bringing down the principal. Interest on U.S. federal debt in 2010 cost $414 billion, roughly 23 times the NASA budget that year. This is not to suggest that the United States would necessarily spend more on exploring the solar system if it carried less debt, but it demonstrates that an increasing debt load

---

1. See the Appendix for this chapter on page 79 for an explanation of the sources of data for the charts in this chapter and the methods by which the author prepared the charts.

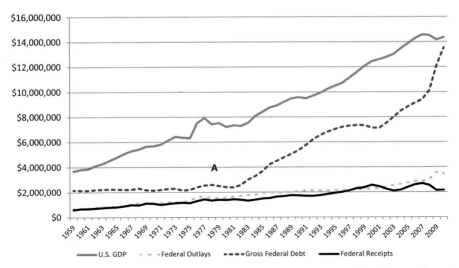

FIGURE 1. GDP, federal outlays, federal debt, and federal receipts, 1959–2010 (in millions, adjusted to 2010 dollars).

can place a significant burden on limited resources. As figure 1 clearly demonstrates, NASA has not encountered a budgetary environment quite like this before.

One fundamental function of government is the allocation of resources, and one of the clearest indications of national priorities is the level to which they are funded. Nearly every resource that is not money still costs money. Therefore, examining the fluctuation of funding levels in a government budget can shed light on the relative standing of national priorities. Situating planetary science within the federal budget is necessary for understanding the role that solar system exploration plays in the federal environment.

The federal budget is broken into two categories: mandatory spending and discretionary spending, as shown in figure 2. Mandatory spending involves Social Security, Medicare, Medicaid, and other programs that do not require an annual appropriations bill from Congress. Discretionary spending includes everything that requires appropriations legislation, including the Departments of Defense (DOD), Education, Energy, Commerce, and Justice, as well as NASA. The largest expenditure in the discretionary budget by far is defense, and so it is common to see budget numbers broken into defense and nondefense discretionary categories.

Figure 3 shows NASA's budget line in the context of nondefense discretionary spending. NASA averaged between 2 and 2½ percent of the discretionary budget—and roughly 6½ percent of the nondefense discretionary budget—from the early 1960s to the end of the Apollo program. But since the

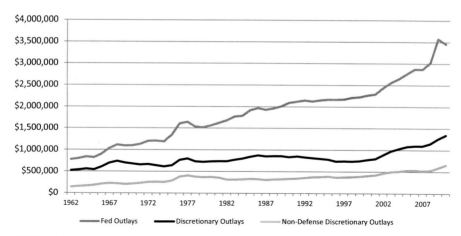

FIGURE 2. Federal budget outlays, 1962–2010 (in millions, adjusted to 2010 dollars).

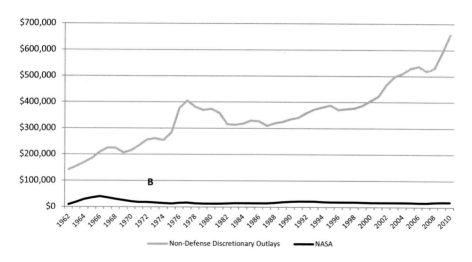

FIGURE 3. Nondefense discretionary and NASA budgets, 1962–2010 (in millions, adjusted to 2010 dollars).

end of Apollo (labeled "B"), it has averaged less than 5 percent of nondefense discretionary spending.

Figure 4 provides a comparison of the nondefense discretionary line to the budget for the Department of Defense. The budget lines for NASA, the Department of Energy (DOE), the National Institutes of Health (NIH), and the National Science Foundation (NSF) are at the bottom of the graph. Along with the Department of Defense, these organizations receive the highest budgets in the federal government for science and technology research.

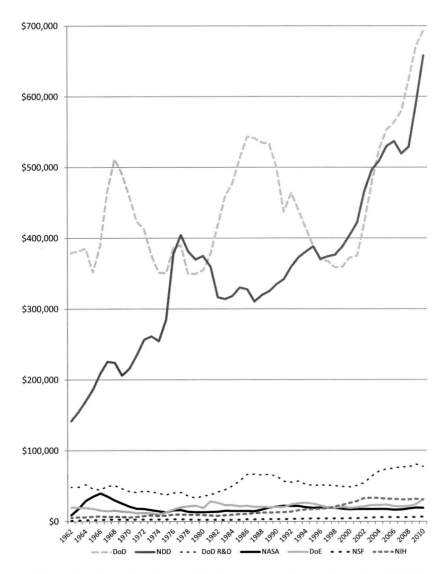

FIGURE 4. Nondefense discretionary, DOD, NASA, National Science Foundation (NSF), National Institutes of Health (NIH), and Department of Energy (DOE) outlays, 1962–2010 ($M, adjusted to 2010 dollars)

Figure 5 displays the organizations with the largest research budgets in the nondefense discretionary line. The term "nondefense" means only that these budget lines are outside of the Department of Defense, not that they are completely removed from any military application. There is, in fact, a fair amount of discourse between researchers in the civilian and military worlds, but that is outside the scope of this research.

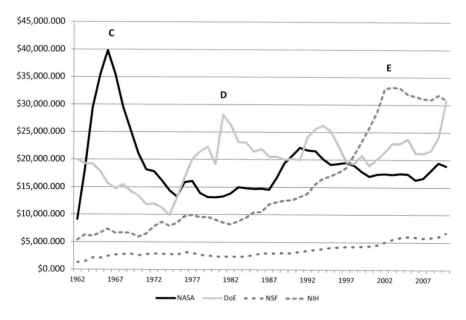

FIGURE 6. NASA, NSF, NIH, and Department of Energy outlays, 1962–2010. (in millions, adjusted to 2010 dollars)

Figure 5 provides a representation of shifting research priorities for the nation over the last five decades. In the 1960s, the focus on the Moon landing is represented by a spike in NASA's budget (see "C"). In the 1970s, the focus moved toward energy (see "D"), seen in the Department of Energy budget line. Beginning in the 1980s and lasting for the next 20 years, the shift toward health and medicine in the NIH budget line is evident (see "E").

Following the spike in each of these budget lines, funding seems to reach equilibrium, give or take a few billion dollars. What this demonstrates is that, barring a renewed interest in space as a national priority on the scale of the space race of 1957–69, NASA is unlikely to see a significant increase in its budget. A far more likely scenario is that projects and programs within NASA will continue to compete for resources at or near current levels—again, give or take a few billion dollars.

As an interesting comparison, figure 6 shows the Department of Defense research and development (R&D) budget line with those of the nondefense R&D agencies. Again, there are upward shifts during periods in which defense R&D increased as a national priority, particularly in the 1980s and following the 11 September 2001 attacks. It is also interesting to note that the defense increase in the 1980s correlates with a decrease in Department of Energy spending (see "F"), which had been on the rise through the 1970s.

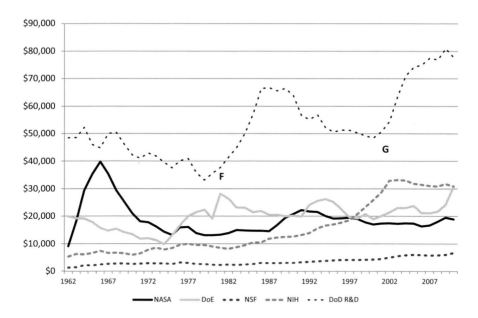

FIGURE 6. DOD research and development (R&D), NASA, NSF, NIH, and Department of Energy outlays, 1962–2010 (in millions, adjusted to 2010 dollars).

And the defense spending increase beginning in 2001 coincides with a downturn in spending on the National Institutes of Health (see "G"), a clear R&D priority through the previous 20 years. Federal R&D spending is by no means a zero-sum game, but figure 6 does illustrate the dynamic nature of national priorities and, by extension, the risks and rewards of aligning an organization's goals and activities with U.S. national priorities.

So, where do NASA and the field of planetary science fit into this picture?

NASA has averaged 1.2 percent of the federal budget, though this average is skewed by the massive investment in the human spaceflight program during the 1960s. In recent decades, the average is below 1 percent. As seen in figure 7, space science as a whole averaged less than 20 percent of NASA's budget over the last 50 years, while the planetary science portion of that budget averaged about 6.5 percent. Factoring out the anomaly of NASA's space race activities in the 1960s, these averages are all a bit lower.

Delving into the NASA space science budget, divided by the themes of planetary science, astrophysics, heliophysics, and Earth science, allows a comparison of trends in space science funding over five decades, but the methodology is inherently inexact. NASA has not always used this arrangement to allot science funds. In fact, it is quite new, historically speaking. NASA's budgets have been constructed in at least a dozen different arrangements over the years, making it extremely difficult to parse them into

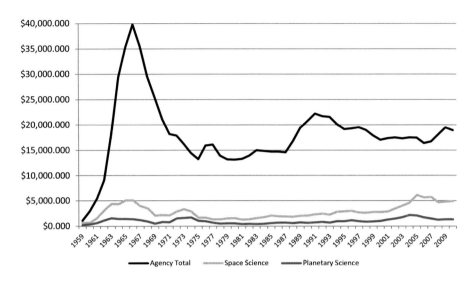

FIGURE 7. NASA budget, 1959–2010 (in millions, adjusted to 2010 dollars).

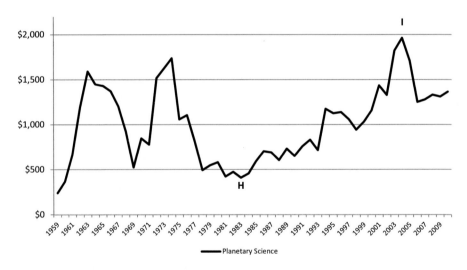

FIGURE 8. Planetary science outlays, 1959–2010 (in millions, adjusted to 2010 dollars).

consistent budget lines. (See the Appendix for this chapter on page 79 for further information regarding these divisions.)

Planetary science was the dominant portion of NASA's space science budget in the mid-1970s. Prior to that period, many space science efforts were attached to the human spaceflight program, and, following it, the planetary community met with increasing competition from astrophysics, Earth science, and heliophysics. When looking at the history of funding for solar

FIGURE 9. Planetary science and astrophysics outlays (in millions, adjusted to 2010 dollars).

system exploration, as shown in figure 8, the budget line happens to divide into decades, with peaks in three of them and a trough between the last two. The lowest part of the planetary science line shows why the 1980s are often referred to as the "lost decade" of planetary science (see "H"). Between 2003 and 2006 (see "I"), planetary science enjoyed its highest level of funding ever.[2]

The astrophysics budget, shown in figure 9, has clearly taken a very different historical path, initially overshadowed by planetary and lunar efforts, space physics missions, and other NASA priorities (which in turn were driven by the Cold War space race to a large degree). The astrophysics budget began a long, upward path in the mid-1970s, as NASA embarked on the early design of the four Great Observatories.[3]

Figure 9 shows that, following the Viking program in the 1970s (see "J"), planetary science received consistently less funding than astrophysics for the next 20 years, though the two funding lines were not entirely dissimilar.

In the early days at NASA, heliophysics was closely associated with space physics, and knowledge gained from experiments conducted in these fields

---

2. This was due in part to an accounting change temporarily placing the funds for the Deep Space Network (averaging nearly $300 million a year in 2010 dollars) in the planetary science budget line.
3. Nancy Grace Roman, "Exploring the Universe: Space-Based Astronomy and Astrophysics," in John M. Logsdon, ed., *Exploring the Unknown: Selected Documents in the History of the U.S. Civil Space Program*, vol. 5, *Exploring the Cosmos* (Washington, DC: NASA SP-2001-4407, 2001), pp. 501–543.

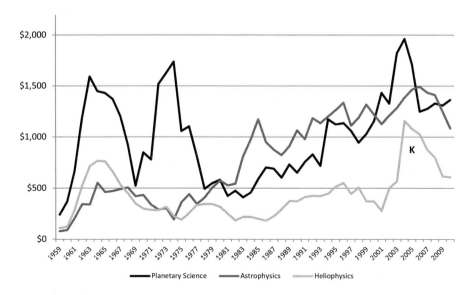

FIGURE 10. Planetary science, astrophysics, and heliophysics outlays (in millions, adjusted to 2010 dollars).

also provided a better understanding of launch environments and communications, among other technical fields required for space exploration.

Funding for heliophysics since the 1960s, as seen in figure 10, has remained below that of the other space science themes, though the heliophysics budget did see a significant increase in the early 2000s (see "K"), in line with other increases in space science funding.

Figure 11 shows that Earth science had a somewhat slow start at NASA but became a more pronounced priority for stakeholders in the early 1990s (see "L"). In the early 2000s, NASA attempted to bring the funding levels of all four themes into closer alignment with one another (see "M"), though all NASA science budgets experienced a downward trend even before the worldwide economic downturn in 2008. The downturn in budgets coincides with U.S. involvement in two wars, along with other domestic issues faced by the nation.

Since WWII, Congress has generally accepted scientific priorities in federally funded civil science endeavors recommended by the appropriate scientific communities, provided that those communities could demonstrate a consensus on priorities. The allocation of resources to support scientific priorities, however, often depends on how those scientific priorities align with a broader national agenda, predicated in terms of national security, geopolitics, or domestic policy. A brief discussion of events in each decade of NASA's planetary science efforts can help demonstrate how interactions between

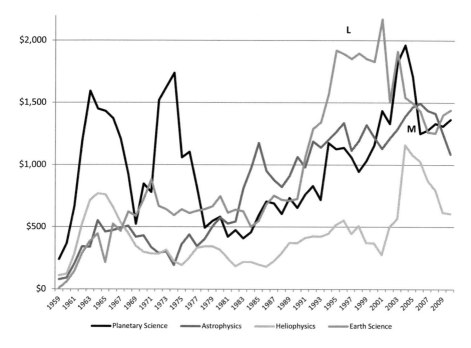

FIGURE 11. Planetary science, astrophysics, heliophysics, and Earth science outlays (in millions adjusted to 2010 dollars).

NASA, the rest of the planetary science community, and government stakeholders have worked to establish the federal allocation of resources for solar system exploration and how those interactions have evolved.

THE POST-WORLD WAR II PERIOD THROUGH THE 1950S

If the U.S. civil space program was formed as a Cold War counter to Soviet space efforts, why did NASA engage in planetary science so early in its space program, and why does the effort continue?

The answer to these questions dates back to the post–WWII period and involves communities of researchers in fields as disparate as radio and radar research, cosmic-ray research, ionospheric physics, and meteorology. Scientists in these communities began to coalesce around the idea that data required to answer some of their most pressing questions could be obtained only by placing scientific instruments outside Earth's atmosphere. Early work in this area involved mounting instruments atop captured German V-2 rockets. These experiments were developed by researchers at Johns Hopkins University's Applied Physics Laboratory (APL), the California Institute of Technology's Jet Propulsion Laboratory (JPL), and the Naval Research

Laboratory (NRL), among others.[4] To coordinate their research, these scientists formed the Upper Atmosphere Rocket Research Panel (UARRP), an unofficial, nonmilitary panel that met to discuss and plan rocket research.[5]

THE INTERNATIONAL GEOPHYSICAL YEAR

A group of scientific leaders in several of these space-related fields met in 1950 to discuss the best path forward for their research. Their host was James Van Allen, a physicist at APL and a member of the UARRP who would go on to have a substantial impact on the field of planetary science. The group included Sydney Chapman, a British geophysicist; Lloyd Berkner, head of Brookhaven National Laboratory; Fred Singer at APL; J. Wallace Joyce, a geophysicist with the Navy and adviser to the Department of State; and Ernest H. Vestine from the Department of Terrestrial Magnetism at the Carnegie Institution. The outcome of this meeting was the group's proposal to the International Council of Scientific Unions (ICSU) for an International Geophysical Year (IGY), modeled on the International Polar Years that were held in 1882–83 and 1932–33. The IGY would take place from July 1957 to December 1958.[6]

The purpose of the IGY was to bring together researchers from various fields and nationalities to address fundamental scientific questions about Earth's geomagnetic field, oceans, atmosphere, and more. Some of the research was not space-related, and some involved sounding-rocket or satellite instruments. Many of the scientific questions addressed during the IGY required vast resources to address, resources that were beyond the reach of individual scientists, academic departments, or even most military labs. By consolidating efforts into a unified enterprise—brought together by the nongovernmental ICSU—scientists in fields as varied as astronomy, geodesy, chemistry, physics, biology, math, radio, and geography were able to obtain financial and logistical support from their governments. This support included military resources not normally associated with science, such as large naval vessels and helicopters for the transport of heavy equipment and personnel to remote locations across Earth, ballistic missile expertise for launching several sounding rockets, and two lines of U.S. scientific satellites along with their tracking and support networks.

---

4. Homer E. Newell, *Beyond the Atmosphere: Early Years of Space Science* (Washington, DC: NASA SP-4211, 1980), *https://history.nasa.gov/SP-4211/ch4-4.htm*, chapter 4, p. 2.
5. Ibid., chapter 4, p. 4.
6. Constance McLaughlin Green and Milton Lomask, Vanguard: A History (Washington, DC: NASA SP-4202, 1970, *https://history.nasa.gov/SP-4202/chapter1.html*), chapter 1.

In terms of governance and national security, the first U.S. satellite program, Vanguard, initiated as a U.S. contribution to the IGY, also was intended to establish satellite overflight as a benign and useful activity.[7] It is extremely unlikely that President Dwight D. Eisenhower's administration would have funded Vanguard had it not constituted a critical step toward establishing U.S. satellite overflight as a peaceful activity, thus providing a justification for later reconnaissance satellites.

While U.S. achievements in Earth and space science during the IGY were in many regards overshadowed by the Soviet launch of Sputnik and the ensuing space race, the IGY was an important formative experience for the nascent space science community.

FORMING NASA

By the end of 1957, the Soviet Union had placed the first artificial satellite, called Sputnik, into orbit. The space race was on, and the United States was trying to determine how best to compete. Lawmakers began consulting with anyone who might have insight into how to best the Soviets in space, including many of the scientists who represented the United States during the IGY. Several prominent researchers called to testify before Congress were members of the Rocket and Satellite Research Panel (RSRP), a successor to the UARRP. Among them were Homer Newell from NRL; William Pickering from JPL; and James Van Allen, by then at the University of Iowa. All had participated in the IGY. The RSRP produced a proposal (which ultimately received support from the American Rocket Society) for "A National Mission to Explore Outer Space" and delivered it to Congress.[8]

"In the interest of human progress and our national welfare," this document began, "it is proposed that a national project be established with the mission of carrying out the scientific exploration and eventual habitation of outer space." It is clear from this initial statement that science was at the forefront of the proposal, at least on equal footing with a human spaceflight program. "It is essential that the National Space Establishment be scientific in nature and in concept and be under civilian leadership and direction."

---

7. Walter A. McDougall …*the Heavens and the Earth: A Political History of the Space Age* (New York: Basic Books, 1985), p. 123.
8. Rocket and Satellite Research Panel, "A Proposal to Explore Outer Space—A Proposal by the Rocket and Satellite Research Panel," in *Hearings Before the Preparedness Investigating Subcommittee of the Committee on Armed Services*, U.S. Senate, 85th Cong., 1st and 2nd sess., part 2, pp. 2135–2136 (Washington, DC: U.S. Government Printing Office, 1958).

This establishment "…should be funded on a long-term basis, not dependent upon direct military appropriations nor upon any of the military services."[9]

Eilene Galloway, National Defense Analyst and later Senior Specialist in International Relations (National Defense) with the Legislative Reference Service of the Library of Congress, assisted Senator Lyndon Johnson[10] during his subcommittee's review of the RSRP's proposal. She recalled:

> While our first reaction was that we faced a military problem of technology inferiority, the testimony from scientists and engineers convinced us that outer space had been opened as a new environment and that it could be used worldwide for peaceful uses of benefit to all humankind, for communications, navigation, meteorology and other purposes. Use of space was not confined to military activities. It was remarkable that this possibility became evident so soon after Sputnik and its significance cannot be understated.[11]

When Congress passed the National Aeronautics and Space Act of 1958, which formed NASA, the first objective listed for the new administration (under Section 102(c)(1)) was, "expansion of human knowledge of phenomena in the atmosphere and space."[12]

---

9. Ibid. Members of the RSRP clearly thought through their recommendations thoroughly, going so far as to pronounce a funding level they felt would be appropriate, stating, "The magnitude of the venture will require a strong dedication of purpose on the part of our people. The country must provide the necessary resources and money to accomplish the mission. That means, among other things, an expenditure of some $10 billion over the next decade." In fact, NASA would spend nearly $35 billion in its first decade, in actual dollars. Adjusted to 2010 dollars, that total is close to $232 billion.
10. Eilene Galloway, "Sputnik and the Creation of NASA: A Personal Perspective," in *National Aeronautics and Space Administration: 50 Years of Exploration and Discovery*, web publication available at *http://www.nasa.gov/50th/50th_magazine/index.html* (accessed 13 January 2020). Johnson was chairman of the Preparedness Investigating Subcommittee of the Senate Committee on Armed Services at the time.
11. Ibid.
12. National Aeronautics and Space Act of 1958, Public Law 85-568, 72 Stat. 426, signed by President Eisenhower on 29 July 1958. Record Group 255, National Archives and Records Administration, Washington, DC.

THE 1960S

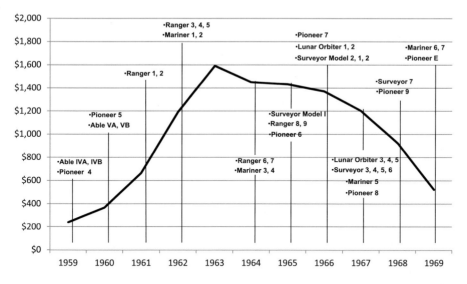

FIGURE 12. Planetary science actual expenditures, 1959–69 (in millions, adjusted to 2010 dollars) by launch dates.[13]

Defining Roles in Space Science

Following NASA's formation, a conflict arose over who would assume responsibility for determining the Agency's strategic direction in science. The National Academy of Sciences had formed a Space Science Board (SSB), drawing on members of IGY technical panels on rocketry and Earth satellites, and the new board adopted many of the advisory functions of the Rocket and Satellite Research Panel. In 1959, SSB Executive Director Hugh Odishaw and Chairman Lloyd Berkner fought for a more active role in NASA's programmatic direction. Their efforts were rebuffed by Homer Newell, NASA's assistant director for space science, and Hugh Dryden, Deputy Administrator of the Agency. The National Academy of Sciences

---

13. Able IVA, Able IVB, Able VA, and Able VB were also known as Pioneer P-1, Pioneer P-3, Pioneer P-30, and Pioneer P-31, respectively. Pioneers 6, 7, 8, and 9 measured the solar wind flow, magnetic fields, and electron density in space, and they observed the energy spectra, fluxes, and direction of solar and galactic cosmic rays. Pioneer E was a similar mission but was lost in a launch failure. Arguably, these were space physics missions, not planetary science missions. In the FY 1968 and FY 1969 budgets, NASA moved the Pioneer program from the Lunar and Planetary Exploration line to the Astronomy and Space Science line. In all other years, the Pioneer program fell under the Lunar and Planetary Exploration line, so the missions are counted as planetary missions here.

was a nonprofit organization,[14] and the SSB operated under a contract with NASA. Dryden and Newell wrote into the contract in 1959 that the National Academy of Sciences would provide studies helping to set the Agency's scientific priorities, leaving NASA to determine its own programmatic strategy.[15] This arrangement would remain fundamentally unchanged for more than three decades, though the SSB would gradually increase its influence.

In 1961, Soviet cosmonaut Yuri Gagarin became the first person to orbit Earth. This event, coming soon after a presidential election won largely on allegations of a U.S. "missile gap" and its implications for U.S. global standing, heightened national concern about U.S. technological inferiority. After speaking with advisers, newly inaugurated President John F. Kennedy decided that sending an astronaut to the Moon before the Soviets could accomplish the feat represented the best opportunity for the United States to demonstrate superiority over the Soviets in space.[16] This decision, based on geopolitical and national security considerations specific to the Cold War, had significant ramifications for NASA's direction and its planetary science aspirations.

President Kennedy selected James Webb as his NASA Administrator, and Webb moved quickly to reorganize the Agency. He established an Office of Tracking and Data Acquisition, Office of Manned Space Flight, and Office of Space Science at NASA Headquarters. Webb's move raised the visibility and stature of science at NASA considerably by placing science on an equal level with human spaceflight hierarchically, though science still trailed the human spaceflight program in prioritization. Webb promoted Homer Newell to Director of the Office of Space Science, and Newell created three scientific divisions: Geophysics and Astronomy, Lunar and Planetary, and

---

14. The National Academy of Sciences operates under a congressional charter, first signed by President Abraham Lincoln in 1863. The National Research Council, an organization tasked with conducting the vast majority of studies and reports for the National Academy of Sciences (and later all of the National Academies), was established in 1916. The National Academy of Engineering was established in 1964, followed by the National Academy of Medicine in 1970. All four organizations are now collectively known as the National Academies. The Space Science Board was renamed the Space Studies Board in 1989.
15. Naugle, *First Among Equals: The Selection of NASA Space Science Experiments* (Washington, DC: NASA, NASA SP-4215, 1991, *https://history.nasa.gov/SP-4215/ch3-2.html#3.2.4*. The position of assistant director for space science was the highest space science position at NASA under Administrator T. Keith Glennan and reported to the director of spaceflight. Administrator James Webb reorganized NASA in 1961 to include the Office of Space Science, headed by an Associate Administrator.
16. John Logsdon, *The Decision to Go to the Moon* (Cambridge, MA: MIT Press, 1970), pp. 391–392.

Life Sciences.[17] Newell established a Space Science Steering Committee with six subcommittees, which, in coordination with NASA Field Centers and Headquarters, would determine the programmatic direction for NASA's science efforts.[18] All members of the Space Science Steering Committee were NASA employees, an arrangement that greatly isolated programmatic decisions from broader space science community input.

REWORKING THE SYSTEM

The Apollo lunar landing mission became an overriding national priority, and nearly every aspect of NASA reoriented to one degree or another to support the race to the Moon. NASA's early solar system and solar system exploration efforts focused heavily on lunar exploration, with the exception of the Mariner and Pioneer programs. NASA began planning in 1960 for a class of robotic space explorers to replace the Mariner family. This new class of spacecraft, called Voyagers, would consist of considerably larger and more powerful platforms, allowing for more capable science payloads. Rather than flybys like most Mariner missions, Voyager spacecraft would be orbiters, providing researchers with greatly extended opportunities for data collection. The Voyager architecture could also incorporate a landing craft, allowing scientists to place instruments on the Martian surface. NASA designers anticipated the heavy-lift capabilities of the new Saturn launch vehicles to propel the massive Voyagers into orbit and beyond.[19] However, retooling NASA for the Apollo program prioritized lunar and human spaceflight missions over solar system exploration. Saturn vehicles were in short supply, and delays in building the Atlas-Agena launch vehicle pushed launch dates for the Mariner program further into the future.

Without critical Martian data from Mariner and no heavy-lift rocket, Voyager's designers found themselves without a mission. Congress cut

---

17. Naugle, *First Among Equals*, https://history.nasa.gov/SP-4215/ch7-1.html#7.1.3. The Office of Space Science became the Office of Space Science and Applications in 1981, was renamed the Office of Space Science in 1992 (briefly known as the Office of Planetary Science and Astrophysics) and became the Science Mission Directorate in 2005.
18. Ibid. The steering committee consisted of only four members: the assistant director and the chief scientist for lunar and planetary programs, and the assistant director and the chief scientist for the satellite and sounding rocket program. The six subcommittees were Aeronomy, Astronomy and Solar Physics, Ionospheric Physics, Energetic Particles, Lunar Sciences, and Planetary and Interplanetary Sciences.
19. Edward C. and Linda N. Ezell, *On Mars: Exploration of the Red Planet, 1958–1978* (Washington, DC: NASA SP-421, 1984), pp. 83–84, 86.; Clayton R. Koppes, *JPL and the American Space Program: A History of the Jet Propulsion Laboratory* (New Haven and London: Yale University Press, 1982), pp. 188–190.

funding for Voyager, though according to congressional staffers, the cuts were "primarily the result of other higher priority programs, not simply disapproval of Voyager."[20] This was the first time Congress eliminated a NASA program through funding cuts. NASA reallocated the remaining funds from Voyager to the rising costs of the lunar effort. While much of the design work done for Voyager would be used for the Viking mission to Mars, and the name Voyager would be attached to an entirely new project in short order, the original Voyager program's elimination presented the planetary science community with a stark new reality.

The cancellation heightened the intensity of the scientific community's criticism of NASA's programmatic strategy and the insularity of the Space Science Steering Committee. Scientists external to NASA felt Agency leadership was not providing them a proper forum to advise on NASA science programs. Responding to these criticisms, NASA Administrator Webb established the Lunar and Planetary Missions Board in 1967 and the Astronomy Missions Planning Board in 1968.[21] The purpose of the boards was to strengthen NASA's ties with the academic science community and provide input to Agency planning efforts. The Lunar and Planetary Missions Board formed the programmatic strategy for planetary science through the 1970s, including the Viking program, the Pioneer-Venus missions, and the outer-planets program that would eventually be named Voyager. In 1971, NASA expanded its advisory structure, placing the two boards within a NASA Space Program Advisory Council.

Also in 1968, the SSB published *Planetary Exploration, 1968–1975*,[22] its first evaluation of NASA's planetary program. The report did not carry the same significance with stakeholders as contemporary decadal surveys do, but it served as another outlet of communication for the planetary science community beyond the Lunar and Planetary Missions Board and its panels.

Funding for Apollo peaked in 1967, two years before the success of the Apollo 11 lunar landing. After that, the Apollo program put another five landers on the surface of the Moon, completed the Skylab project, and flew the U.S. portion of the Apollo-Soyuz Test Project, but funding for NASA continued to decline throughout these missions, with little political support for the space agency's plans to expand human activities in space. For many in the space science community, the shift in fortune for the human spaceflight

---

20. Ezell and Ezell, *On Mars*, p. 128.
21. Newell, *Beyond the Atmosphere*, https://history.nasa.gov/SP-4211/ch12-3.htm.
22. Space Science Board, National Research Council, *Planetary Exploration 1968–1975* (Washington, DC: The National Academies Press, 1968).

effort seemed a natural progression. The astronauts had completed their mission, and now it was time to engage in a more robust robotic effort to explore the solar system.

THE 1970S

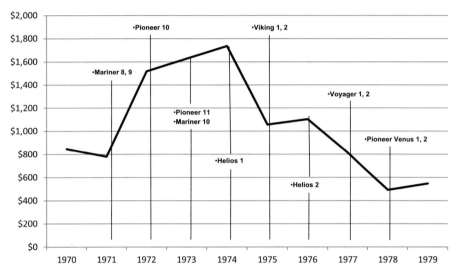

FIGURE 13. Planetary science actual expenditures, 1970–79 (in millions, adjusted to 2010 dollars) by launch dates.[23]

The Scientific Community and the "Grand Tour"
In 1965, a graduate student at JPL discovered that a rare planetary conjunction was imminent, set to occur in the late 1970s. Jupiter, Saturn, Neptune, and Uranus would all be on the same side of the Sun, potentially allowing a spacecraft to follow a gravity-assisted trajectory passing all four planets. The outer planets would not be in a similar alignment for another 176 years, so

---

23. The Helios project was an international cooperative project between the governments of the United States and West Germany. The scientific objectives were to investigate the properties and processes in interplanetary space in the region near the Sun, to within about 0.3 AU. The United States supplied the spacecraft, three instruments, the launch vehicle, and tracking and data support for the first phase of the mission. Again, Helios was arguably a space physics mission and was even budgeted in the Astronomy and Space Physics line in the FY 1968 and FY 1969 NASA budgets. All other years of the Pioneer program were budgeted in the Lunar and Planetary Exploration budget. Therefore, the Helios missions are included here.

NASA had 10 years to plan a mission or forego the opportunity for nearly two centuries.[24]

The initial mission plan became known as the "Grand Tour" and involved flying two spacecraft past Jupiter, Saturn, and Pluto in 1977 and another two craft by Jupiter, Saturn, and Neptune in 1979. As planning for the mission progressed into 1970, the projected cost began to creep toward $1 billion over the span of less than a decade (or roughly $5.6 billion in 2010 dollars), causing consternation throughout the planetary science community, the White House, and Congress.[25] NASA's overall budget was falling precipitously from the heights of the Moon race as the Apollo program lost public and congressional support and the Nixon administration tried to contend with the spiraling costs of the war in Vietnam. There was almost no political interest in another large space mission, and the President imposed a new method of doing business on the space agency. NASA would have to fund any new program starts from its existing budget rather than requesting additional funds.[26]

Of equal importance to the budget challenges, the scientific community did not agree on what outer-planets missions should take precedence. One faction favored the Grand Tour, but another felt that an orbital mission to Jupiter brought greater scientific value for less cost and would not jeopardize smaller missions to destinations such as Venus. The Grand Tour also faced opposition from proponents of a large space telescope who felt that the outer-planets mission would compete for resources. NASA requested that the SSB review its outer planets program in four separate reports between 1968 and 1971. The first two reports[27] supported the Grand Tour concept, but the third report stated, "While the study group realizes the uniqueness of the natural opportunity and the importance of the planetary observations that could be accomplished, it does not place the [Outer Planetary System] Grand Tour in the base or intermediate budget level categories because of the impact of its cost on the possibilities for accommodating other highly desirable scientific missions at these funding levels. The collective value of

---

24. Peter J. Westwick, *Into the Black: JPL and the American Space Program, 1976–2004* (New Haven and London: Yale University Press, 2007), p. 19.
25. Henry C. Dethloff and Ronald A. Schorn, *Voyager's Grand Tour: To the Outer Planets and Beyond* (Old Saybrook, CT: Konecky & Konecky, 2009), pp. 61–62.
26. David Rubashkin, "Who Killed the Grand Tour? A Case Study in the Politics of Funding Expensive Space Science," *Journal of the British Interplanetary Society* 50 (1997): 177–184.
27. Space Science Board, *Planetary Exploration 1968–1975*; Space Science Board, National Research Council, *The Outer Solar System: A Program for Exploration* (Washington, DC: The National Academies Press, 1969).

these smaller missions is considered to have higher scientific priority than the Grand Tour."[28] Congress was unwilling to back a program that didn't have the support of its own scientific community, and the Nixon administration, never a staunch supporter of the space program, favored the Space Shuttle program over a large scientific mission.[29]

In 1971, NASA approved the Mariner-Mars 1973 mission to follow the Mariner-Mars 1969 and Mariner-Mars 1971 missions. Mariner-Mars 1973, which eventually evolved into the Viking program, beat out the Grand Tour for funding based primarily on a lower estimated cost. NASA management canceled funding for the Grand Tour effort due to several factors, including prioritization of the Shuttle Program and a large space telescope, but soon endorsed another plan offered by the Agency's Office of Space Science and Applications—a Jupiter/Saturn mission based on existing Mariner spacecraft. The SSB supported this new mission plan in a 1971 report,[30] and the project also received support from the White House Office of Management and Budget (OMB).

Recognizing that the upcoming planetary alignment presented a unique opportunity, OMB offered to restore funding to the scaled-back effort, which would not affect overall funding for NASA. The Agency replanned the mission to include just two spacecraft. The proposed cost of the new program, now called Voyager, was roughly one-third the amount of the estimated cost of the Grand Tour. This change of plans allowed NASA to accomplish both a deep-space mission to the outer planets and the 1975 Viking mission to Mars in the same decade. NASA launched the two Voyager spacecraft in 1977. The first flew past Jupiter and Saturn, and the second visited Jupiter, Saturn, Neptune, and Uranus. Both spacecraft survived well beyond their expected lifetimes. NASA has extended their operations several times, and, at this writing, the Voyagers are still probing the edges of the solar system.

Growing Pressures on the Planetary Science Community

In 1972, President Richard Nixon endorsed the Space Shuttle as a low-Earth orbit transportation system for NASA, the Department of Defense, and industry partners, recognizing that the Shuttle's promise of lower-cost

---

28. Space Science Board, National Research Council, *Priorities for Space Research 1971–1980* (Washington, DC: The National Academies Press, 1971), p. 14.
29. Michael Meltzer, *Mission to Jupiter: A History of the Galileo Project* (Washington, DC: NASA SP-2007-4231, 2007), p. 27. See also Rubashkin, "Who Killed the Grand Tour?"
30. Space Science Board, National Research Council, *Outer Planets Exploration 1972–1985* (Washington, DC: The National Academies Press, 1971), p. 2.

launches served economic and national security interests, as well as providing NASA with a new human spaceflight objective following the end of the Apollo program. In 1974, anticipating the arrival of the Shuttle as NASA's single option for transport to space, Administrator James Fletcher reorganized the Agency. He centralized control over all launch vehicle activities in the Office of Manned Space Flight, meaning that the Office of Space Science no longer controlled the selection and scheduling of launch vehicles for science missions but would instead have to compete with other users for a place on the Shuttle launch manifest. This arrangement would have a tremendous impact on the planetary launch schedule for decades.

Another issue with wide-ranging implications for planetary science involved the size of projects. In the late 1960s, many in the science community had become concerned by the rising cost and complexity of planetary missions. Large flagship missions launched less frequently than smaller, less expensive projects, resulting in fewer opportunities for scientists to fly experiments. The impact of fewer missions fell disproportionately on graduate students and early-career professionals, with an increasingly negative impact on the field over time. Larger missions also allowed for less flexibility in budgeting when resources inevitably became scarce.[31]

Attempting to address these concerns, the SSB published a report in 1968 proposing a class of spin-stabilized satellites for orbiting Mars and Venus at each launch opportunity.[32] Realistically, only low-cost missions could launch so frequently. NASA responded with a Planetary Explorer program, intended as an ongoing series of small, inexpensive missions, and selected the Pioneer Venus Orbiter and Multiprobe as its first project. The project competed with the Viking and Voyager programs for funding, and rising development costs for the Space Shuttle placed increasing pressures on NASA's budget. With no other new missions starting, the scope and cost of the Pioneer-Venus mission grew as scientists clamored to join the project or be left waiting indefinitely for the next Venus mission. By the time Pioneer-Venus launched in 1978, the project bore little resemblance to the small, inexpensive mission it was intended to be. This dynamic began to characterize planetary missions of the 1970s and 1980s.

---

31. Stephanie A. Roy, "The Origin of the Smaller, Faster, Cheaper Approach in NASA's Solar System Exploration Program," *Space Policy* 14 (1998): 153–171.
32. Space Science Board, *Planetary Science: 1968–1975*, p. 5.

THE 1980S

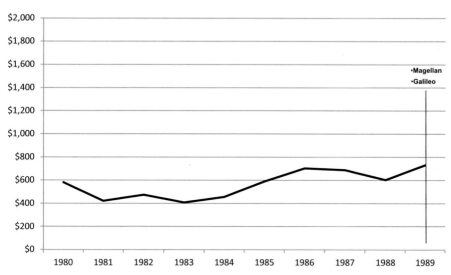

FIGURE 14. Planetary science actual expenditures, 1980–1989 (in millions, adjusted to 2010 dollars) by launch dates.

Conflicting Science and National Priorities
Between 1974 and 1977, the planetary science budget dropped by nearly 60 percent, as NASA and the space community were unable to convince lawmakers or President Gerald Ford's administration that solar system exploration was a national priority requiring the funding levels of the early decade. Having launched Viking and the Voyagers, the planetary science community expected some reduction in the budget. But by 1977, as NASA began to plan for its next planetary mission, the budget situation proved daunting. The Agency's new mission, initially called the Jupiter Orbiter Probe, would have to compete for a shrinking portion of a NASA budget eroded by cost overruns in the Shuttle Program. Strong support for another program slated to begin in 1978, a space telescope called Hubble, backed by the space science community, Congress, and the White House, further complicated the challenging budget environment.

Recognizing the difficulty of proposing two major science programs in the same year, NASA management worked to ensure that Hubble supporters and Jupiter Orbiter supporters would not denigrate each other's projects publicly in an effort to gain congressional support, warning the two camps that divisiveness could erode lawmakers' support for both projects. Congress approved funding for Hubble and the Jupiter Orbiter, demonstrating the efficacy of NASA's strategy, but success came at a high cost. Toward sustaining a unified planetary science community, NASA made the Jupiter Orbiter a program promising all things to all people. The Agency encouraged all subdisciplines in planetary science to participate in the program, and it mutated into an incredibly complex and inevitably expensive undertaking.[33] Nevertheless, NASA's success in obtaining funding to start both programs demonstrated the strength of a unified space science community.

Ronald Reagan won the 1980 U.S. presidential election on a platform dedicated to reducing government spending, particularly nondefense discretionary spending, and in its first year, the new administration began looking for ways to curb or cut expenditures. The Jupiter Orbiter program, by then named Galileo, underwent a new round of scrutiny. Jay Keyworth, the President's science advisor, and David Stockman, the head of OMB, thought that NASA's planetary science program was no longer likely to produce scientific results valuable enough to justify the expense. They believed NASA should focus on Shuttle-based science programs like the Hubble Space Telescope. The fact that the President's science advisor, who was also the head of the White House Office of Science and Technology Policy, did not see value in the planetary science program indicated a distinct breakdown in communications among NASA, the planetary science community, and one of their most influential stakeholders.[34]

NASA rallied quickly, declaring the Galileo spacecraft nearly complete and asserting that canceling the mission at this stage would actually cost more than completing it. Managers at JPL also tried another strategy, attaching Galileo to national security goals by highlighting the spacecraft's autonomous operations capabilities. The technology allowing Galileo to operate at distances precluding direct communication with Earth, according to this line of reasoning, could also be used to operate military and reconnaissance satellites in the event that a nuclear weapon destroyed their ground control stations. A small contingent of influential members of the House of Representatives agreed and sent letters to OMB in support. Though the effectiveness of this strategy is not clear, JPL Director Bruce Murray stated publicly that he believed this action saved Galileo from cancellation.[35]

---

33. Meltzer, *Mission to Jupiter*, pp. 27, 35–36.
34. John M. Logsdon, "The Survival Crisis of the U.S. Solar System Exploration Program in the 1980s," in *Exploring the Solar System: The History and Science of Planetary Exploration*, ed. Roger D. Launius (New York: Palgrave Macmillan, 2013), pp. 57–58.
35. Meltzer, *Mission to Jupiter*, pp. 35–36.

A New Advisory Arrangement

Despite the rescue of the Galileo mission, NASA's planetary science program faced fundamental challenges in regaining any semblance of the momentum it had experienced in previous decades. In an effort to regroup, NASA leadership looked to the broader space science community. Since the Agency's founding, NASA leaders had engaged outside experts through a series of advisory boards, following the tradition of the National Advisory Committee for Aeronautics, the original federal infrastructure transferred to NASA at its formation in 1958. In 1977, recognizing the seriousness of budget reductions to the space program, NASA leadership under Administrator Robert Frosch combined the Agency's Space Program Advisory Council (originally established from the Lunar and Planetary Sciences Planning Board and the Astronomy Planning Board in 1971), Aerospace Safety Advisory Panel, and Research and Technology Advisory Council into a NASA Advisory Council (NAC). The NAC became an independent entity tasked with advising the NASA Administrator on science program concerns. The Administrator retained control of the NAC by appointing its members. NAC subcommittees were populated with outside experts in an effort to keep NASA grounded with the broader science community.[36] The NAC was not intended to compete with the SSB. Rather, NAC members supported the SSB strategic recommendations by supplying the Agency with programmatic recommendations.

In the early 1970s, the SSB established a standing committee dedicated to issues in planetary science. This Committee on Planetary and Lunar Exploration (COMPLEX) led the effort to produce recommendations for a coordinated line of planetary science strategies in a series of reports: *Report on Space Science—1975*,[37] *Strategy for Exploration of the Inner Planets: 1977–1987*,[38] and *Strategy for the Exploration of Primitive Solar-System Bodies—Asteroids, Comets, and Meteoroids: 1980–1990*.[39]

---

36. The NAC advises the NASA Administrator, while the Science Committee advises the head of NASA's science organization (Director of the Office of Space Science when the NAC was established, Associate Administrator of the Science Mission Directorate today). See https://www.nasa.gov/offices/nac/home/index.html (accessed 13 January 2020).
37. Space Science Board, National Research Council, *Report on Space Science—1975* (Washington, DC: The National Academies Press, 1976).
38. Committee on Planetary and Lunar Exploration, Space Science Board, National Research Council, *Strategy for Exploration of the Inner Planets: 1977–1987* (Washington, DC: The National Academies Press, 1978).
39. Committee on Planetary and Lunar Exploration, Space Science Board, National Research Council, *Strategy for the Exploration of Primitive Solar-System Bodies—Asteroids, Comets, and Meteoroids: 1980–1990* (Washington, DC: The National Academies Press, 1980).

It is important to note that while the COMPLEX reports evaluated NASA's planetary program, they did so from a scientific rather than programmatic standpoint. That is, they evaluated the Agency's prioritization of science goals and did not advocate for specific missions. As a result, the studies had influence within NASA and the planetary science community and rarely affected the actions of policy makers in Congress or the White House.

In 1980, responding to declining space science budgets, the NAC formed a Solar System Exploration Committee (SSEC) to provide programmatic recommendations in support of scientific recommendations from COMPLEX. Initially chaired by John Naugle, retired NASA Chief Scientist, former Director of NASA's Office of Space Science, and head of NASA's planetary program from 1967 to 1974, the SSEC attempted to provide an overarching strategy for the planetary science program so that mission selections would be based on their ability to support the strategy rather than on scientific merit alone. The committee believed such an arrangement would result in new missions building on the success of preceding missions, providing a more thorough justification for an ongoing solar system exploration effort at NASA. Naugle pressed this course of action based on his success in the late 1960s working with the Lunar and Planetary Missions Board in NASA's Office of Space Science and Applications.[40]

NASA's Mars Observer spacecraft rides a Titan 3/Orbital Stage booster toward its mission to Mars. Liftoff occurred at 1:05 p.m. (EDT), 25 September 1992. (NASA: S92-46925)

---

40. Logsdon, "The Survival Crisis of the U.S. Solar System Exploration Program in the 1980s," pp. 63–64.

Attempting to Create a Balanced Program

The SSEC 1983 report[41] called for a new low-cost mission program established as a line item in NASA's budget. This action would ensure continuity and sustainability in solar system exploration by establishing a three-tier approach to mission development, with small, medium, and flagship missions delineated by cost. The new low-cost program, titled Planetary Observer, did not involve reducing the size of missions but rather sought to reduce costs through the use of heritage systems, hardware proven on previous missions, and standardized spacecraft. In concept, attaching scientific instruments to a standard platform reduced development costs and might even result in economies of scale if NASA used enough of the standardized craft. The program did not require a reduction in size of spacecraft because NASA planned to launch all planetary missions on the Shuttle with a specially configured Centaur upper stage designed to provide far more lift capability than most science missions required. The Shuttle Centaur, following many delays in development, never flew.[42]

NASA selected its first Planetary Observer mission in 1984. The Mars Geoscience/Climatology Orbiter, later renamed Mars Observer, did not adhere to the concept of using heritage technologies. All but one of its instruments required significant development, which greatly increased the mission's costs. The project did, however, make use of a heritage spacecraft design, adapting one used for an earlier Earth science mission.

The loss of the orbiter Challenger in 1986 delayed launch dates for NASA's entire queue of science missions while the Shuttle fleet was grounded. As the nation debated the future of the Shuttle Program, Mars Observer's 1990 launch date was pushed to 1992. Instead of waiting for the Shuttle to return to flight, NASA opted to fly Mars Observer atop a Titan III expendable launch vehicle with a Transfer Orbit Stage. The spacecraft completed its 11-month journey to Mars, but three days prior to orbit insertion, NASA lost contact with the spacecraft. The Mars Observer Mission Failure Investigation Board found that the most likely cause of failure was a pressurized fuel leak. The reason for the leak was never identified, but the board suggested that it might have been the result of a fuel tank designed for operation in Earth's

---

41. Solar System Exploration Committee, NASA Advisory Council, *Planetary Exploration Through the Year 2000: A Core Program*, pp. 17–18.
42. Virginia D. Dawson and Mark D. Bowles, *Taming Liquid Hydrogen: The Centaur Upper Stage Rocket, 1958–2002* (Washington, DC: NASA SP-2004-4230, 2004), p. 189.

atmosphere, not for a long flight in frozen interplanetary space.[43] NASA planned another Planetary Observer mission, the Lunar Geoscience Orbiter, but following Mars Observer's two-year launch delay, NASA reallocated the project's funds to a Mars sample-return mission study.[44] Subsequently, no new Planetary Observer missions materialized.

Naugle's push for broader strategies in planning space science missions served to unite the scientific community in support of NASA's programs, but it did not result in reducing mission costs or increasing funding for space science at NASA. Lower spending levels for space science aligned with President Reagan's goal to reduce nondefense discretionary spending. While it is not clear that any planetary science strategy would have met with support from the Reagan administration's science team, SSEC reports of the 1980s presented entirely science-focused programmatic strategies at a time when policy makers were focusing on science efforts supporting national security.

A Change in Launch Policy

In 1986, with no planetary missions launched in eight years and—following the loss of Challenger—none likely to launch for several more years, the NAC's Space and Earth Science Advisory Committee (SESAC) released a report, "The Crisis in Space and Earth Science," which called for a reevaluation of how NASA selected, built, and flew space science missions.[45] Many of the committee's findings aligned with SSEC reports, but SESAC also called on NASA to reintroduce expendable launch vehicles into its space transportation fleet. President Reagan had declared in August that NASA would no longer launch commercial satellites. His United States Space Launch Strategy, issued in December, stated that the Shuttle fleet would "maintain the Nation's capability to support critical programs requiring manned presence and other unique [Space Transportation System] capabilities."[46] Thus,

---

43. Mars Observer Mission Failure Investigation Board, "The Mars Observer Mission Failure Investigation Board Report," submitted to the NASA Administrator 31 December 1993, available at *http://spacese.spacegrant.org/Failure%20Reports/Mars_Observer_12_93_MIB.pdf* (accessed 30 July 2020).
44. Roy, "Origin of the Smaller, Faster, Cheaper Approach," p. 155.
45. Space and Earth Science Advisory Committee, NASA Advisory Council, "The Crisis in Space and Earth Science: A Time for a New Commitment" (Washington, DC: NASA, November 1986) pp. 38–51.
46. President Ronald Reagan, "Statement by the President," 15 August 1986, Office of the Press Secretary, Washington, DC; The White House, Fact Sheet, NSDD-254, "United States Space Launch Strategy," 27 December 1986, NASA Historical Reference Collection, NASA History Division, NASA Headquarters, Washington, DC (hereafter "NASA HRC").

payloads would fly aboard the Shuttle only if they required astronaut support or some other Shuttle capability not available on another launch vehicle. The administration established this requirement for the sake of astronaut safety and also to support the development of a U.S. commercial launch industry. As a result of this policy, NASA would have to add expendable launch vehicles to its fleet for robotic space missions, just as the SESAC report had recommended. The policy change represented a confluence of national and space science priorities and had a wide-ranging impact on NASA's entire portfolio of science flight projects.

Strategic Changes in Advisory Structure
Following the SSEC and SESAC reports, both of which called for NASA to implement an overarching science strategy, NASA's Office of Space Science and Applications (OSSA) introduced a strategic planning process in 1987. Under OSSA Director Lennard Fisk, the office released its first annual strategic plan in 1988.[47] The scientific community embraced the process because it provided transparency for NASA's mission plans, and NASA contractors supported the strategic plan because it enabled them to more effectively establish their own long-term strategies. The plan also provided the scientific community with a more unified voice on programmatic matters, as it laid out the order in which NASA would approve projects. It was clear, then, that completion of one project's development would allow for the start of the next project in line.

In 1989, under Chairman Louis Lanzerotti, the Space Science Board changed its name to the Space Studies Board to reflect an expansion of SSB activities. Prior to the 1990s, the SSB's reports tended to focus on relatively narrow fields within each of the disciplines in space science. The one exception was astronomy, for which the board had long issued reports relating to the discipline in its entirety. For example, the SSB issued its first decadal report, on ground-based astronomy priorities, in 1964.[48] The SSB expanded the scope of its next report, addressing *Astronomy and Astrophysics for*

---

47. Lennard Fisk, interview by Rebecca Wright for the NASA Headquarters Oral History Project, Ann Arbor, MI, 8 September 2010, found at the Johnson Space Center (JSC) History Office Oral History Project website, *https://historycollection.jsc.nasa.gov/JSCHistoryPortal/history/oral_histories/NASA_HQ/Administrators/FiskLA/FiskLA_9-8-10.htm* (accessed 30 July 2020).
48. National Academy of Sciences, *Ground-Based Astronomy: A Ten-Year Program* (Washington, DC: The National Academies Press, 1964).

the 1970s,[49] and has issued decadal reports on astronomy and astrophysics roughly every 10 years since that time. The astronomy and astrophysics community has used these reports effectively to communicate priorities to NASA and lawmakers. As a result, NASA's astronomy and astrophysics budget has experienced far less fluctuation over the years than other space science disciplines.

By contrast, through the 1970s and 1980s, the SSB's Committee on Planetary Exploration (COMPLEX) issued a series of reports on scientific priorities for the study of the inner planets, the outer planets, primitive solar system bodies, extrasolar planet detection, and the origins and evolution of life. Following the model of the astronomy community, COMPLEX would focus on setting scientific priorities for all of planetary science, rather than addressing subfields separately.

An Executive Call for a New Direction

Following the Challenger tragedy in 1986, the White House increased NASA's budget to replace the lost Shuttle. The increase was meant to be temporary, but the incoming George H. W. Bush administration decided to use the adjusted budget as a baseline to support a new direction for NASA. The budget increase did not benefit planetary science, as the direction the White House wanted to pursue centered on human spaceflight. White House motivations for pointing NASA in a new direction, though, would have a tremendous impact on planetary science. The Bush administration wanted NASA to operate in a more innovative manner, taking advantage of new technologies and management concepts to reduce the cost of spaceflight. To this end, President Bush proposed the Space Exploration Initiative (SEI), a multidecade program intended to take astronauts back to the Moon and eventually to Mars. At the request of the White House, NASA managers provided plans to achieve this new strategic direction,[50] but the President's National Space Council found NASA's plans too expensive, castigating Administrator Richard Truly for not adhering to the goal of using innovative strategies to cut costs.[51] Conflict between NASA and the White House quickly brought an end to the SEI, but not the White House's strategic goal of cost-conscious

---

49. National Academy of Sciences, *Astronomy and Astrophysics for the 1970s* (Washington, DC: The National Academies Press, 1972).
50. NASA, "Report of the 90-Day Study on Human Exploration of the Moon and Mars," internal NASA study prepared for NASA Administrator Richard Truly, November 1989, available at *http://history.nasa.gov/90_day_study.pdf* (accessed 30 July 2020).
51. Thor Hogan, *Mars Wars: The Rise and Fall of the Space Exploration Initiative* (Washington, DC: NASA SP-2007-4410, 2007), pp. 92–93.

innovation, which would have significant ramifications for the planetary science community in the coming decade.

THE 1990S

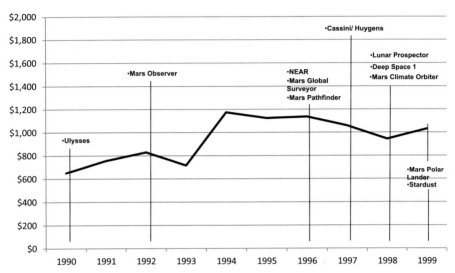

FIGURE 15. Planetary science actual expenditures, 1990–99 ($M, adjusted to 2010 dollars) by launch dates.

The Bush administration's National Space Council, led by Vice President Dan Quayle, concluded that Administrator Truly was not the man to initiate changes at NASA. His replacement, in what would be the last year of the Bush administration, was a rising star from the defense side of the U.S. space program named Daniel Goldin. Goldin caught the attention of Quayle and the National Space Council through his work with the Strategic Defense Initiative Organization on short-schedule, low-cost space technology demonstration projects. Goldin was a proponent of horizontal management structures and projects executed under short time constraints, believing that longer schedules allowed design changes, which in turn caused budgets to grow.

In 1992, President George H. W. Bush chose Goldin as the new NASA Administrator and tasked him with the mission of changing NASA's space exploration culture from the top down. Goldin came to NASA intent on shaping it into an organization less averse to risk and willing to abandon what he saw as outdated methods and thinking. In NASA's Planetary Exploration Division, Goldin accepted plans to implement a Discovery program, which would solicit proposals for small, cost-capped missions led by a Principal Investigator, rather than having mission science parameters determined by

NASA. With the Discovery program, Goldin oversaw the formation of what the planetary science community had been trying to establish for over two decades: a sustainable small-mission program.[52]

Faster, Better, Cheaper

The methods Goldin wanted to implement for managing missions, adapted from a series of small projects he had overseen at TRW Space and Technology Group for the Strategic Defense Initiative Organization, were characterized as "faster, better, cheaper" (FBC) in a speech by Vice President Dan Quayle.[53] FBC methods involved small, streamlined teams in which members had expertise in several fields, so that no aspect of the project was isolated from the rest of the team. Projects run under FBC reduced layers of management and oversight and launched within three years of project selection. Goldin promised to cancel any Discovery program mission that went over budget.[54]

In 1994, following on the astronomical community's success with reports conveying scientific priorities for a decade, the SSB's COMPLEX released *An Integrated Strategy for the Planetary Sciences: 1995–2010*,[55] which evaluated NASA's entire planetary science effort, established the most important scientific goals of the field, and recommended a path forward for research. The report was relatively well received by the community, including NASA, and also caught the attention of lawmakers. Though NASA's overall budget decreased, the budget for planetary science at NASA was increasing in the mid-1990s due to several factors. The Space Shuttle Program had recovered from the Challenger tragedy and a string of technical mishaps and seemed to be on track; the Hubble Space Telescope was launched in 1990 and its faulty mirror corrected in 1993; and the 1996 announcement by NASA's astrobiology program regarding claims of fossil evidence of Martian life in the ALH84001 meteorite[56] rekindled national interest in Mars exploration. The

---

52. Michael J. Neufeld, "Transforming Solar System Exploration: The Origins of the Discovery Program, 1989–1993," *Space Policy* 30, no. 1 (2013): 5–12.
53. Roy, "Origin of the Smaller, Faster, Cheaper Approach." p. 163.
54. Howard E. McCurdy, *Faster, Better, Cheaper: Low-Cost Innovation in the U.S. Space Program* (Baltimore, MD: Johns Hopkins University Press, 2001) p. 25.
55. Committee on Planetary and Lunar Exploration, Space Studies Board, National Research Council, *An Integrated Strategy for the Planetary Sciences: 1995–2010* (Washington, DC: The National Academies Press, 1994). The publication is widely known as the Burns Report, named after Joseph A. Burns, the chair of COMPLEX at the time.
56. D. S. McKay, E. K. Gibson, Jr., K. L. Thomas-Keprta, H. Vali, et al., "Search for Past Life on Mars: Possible Relic Biogenic Activity in Martian Meteorite ALH84001," *Science* 273.5277 (16 August 1996): 924.

impact of *An Integrated Strategy for Planetary Sciences* is difficult to gauge, given all of the other factors affecting planetary science at the time of its release, but the report served as a relatively unbiased set of goals by which lawmakers could judge the effectiveness of U.S. investment in the field.

In the report, COMPLEX stated that the scientific study of Mars should focus on global circulation and climate history, with a study of the polar region key to the latter objective. In 1995, NASA instituted a Mars Surveyor program composed of two spacecraft, Mars Climate Orbiter (MCO) and Mars Polar Lander (MPL), which lifted off in the 1998 Mars launch window. NASA developed both missions under the FBC rubric. The Mars Climate Orbiter made it to Mars, but just as it was entering orbit, NASA lost all communication with the spacecraft. Just six weeks later, the Mars Polar Lander arrived at the planet. The lander had no way to communicate with Earth during its automated descent phase, but NASA expected to hear from the spacecraft shortly after it landed. No communication came.

The public treated the loss of two Mars missions within a six-week span as a topic of ridicule, while lawmakers viewed the events as an indication of structural weaknesses within the space agency. NASA convened the Mars Climate Orbiter Mishap Investigation Board and the Mars Polar Lander Special Review Board to determine what went wrong. In its initial report, the Mars Climate Orbiter Board determined that data entered into the software by JPL in metric units was interpreted by a contractor as English Standard units, meaning that the spacecraft had interpreted data measured in newton-seconds as though it were measured in pound-force seconds. This error resulted in the spacecraft adjusting its trajectory incorrectly before orbital insertion, pushing it far deeper into the atmosphere than intended. The spacecraft either burned up due to friction or bounced off the atmosphere into space.[57] The Mars Polar Lander Board found that the spacecraft had probably entered the Martian atmosphere as planned, but when its landing legs deployed, they likely bounced slightly and triggered a pressure sensor that told the spacecraft it had reached the surface. Informed by the sensor that it had landed, the spacecraft likely shut off its thrusters while it was still some 40 meters in the air, fell to the surface, and shattered on impact.[58]

---

57. Mars Climate Orbiter Mishap Investigation Board, "Mars Climate Orbiter Mishap Investigation Board Phase I Report," delivered to the NASA Administrator 10 November 1999, available at *http://sunnyday.mit.edu/accidents/MCO_report.pdf* (accessed 30 July 2020).

58. JPL Special Review Board, "Report on the Loss of the Mars Polar Lander and Deep Space 2 Missions," delivered to the NASA Administrator on 22 March 2000, available at *http://spaceflight.nasa.gov/spacenews/releases/2000/mpl/mpl_report_1.pdf* (accessed 30 July 2020).

A second report issued by the Mars Climate Orbiter Board[59] addressed management issues that led to the technical miscommunication between JPL and its contractor. The board found that the FBC strategy did not adequately assess risk in space projects. The emphasis on meeting cost and schedule placed pressures on project management to cut corners in planning, developing, and testing, and lack of oversight meant that mistakes slipped through. Some observers outside NASA characterized the problems with FBC as inevitable and believed that in the cutting-edge technology programs pursued by NASA, managers and engineers had to "pick two" of the FBC pillars, but not all three. That is, a spacecraft that was built faster and cheaper would incur larger risks. It would not be better.

When he first proposed the FBC initiative, Administrator Goldin acknowledged that risks would increase. He even said he expected a failure rate of 10 percent in FBC projects.[60] With costs and schedules reduced so significantly, he believed, the program would still return greater value per dollar than projects run under standard systems engineering methods. Goldin's assertion was never proved or disproved, as NASA discontinued the FBC strategy after the loss of the two Mars projects. To that point, FBC missions were running at a failure rate closer to 15 or 20 percent, but the small number of missions did not allow for a measure of any statistical significance.[61] Some of the tenets of FBC, such as employing multidisciplinary expertise and reducing the layers of project management, remain strategies in smaller NASA missions. Strict adherence to cost and schedule deadlines at the potential expense of unreasonably high risks, however, is no longer a NASA strategy for small planetary missions.

In the end, Goldin applied FBC philosophies to the Discovery program, a small-missions program the planetary science community had advocated for many years. The community did not push back against the new methods Goldin introduced, but when an independent report found fault with FBC, the community also did not rush to the defense of Goldin's initiatives. Ultimately, the Discovery program remained a viable platform for a sustained small-mission strategy, and FBC was abandoned. The community-sponsored effort remained, while the executive-backed effort did not.

---

59. Mars Climate Orbiter Mishap Investigation Board, "Report on Project Management in NASA," delivered to the NASA Administrator on 13 March 2000, available at *http://science.ksc.nasa.gov/mars/msp98/misc/MCO_MIB_Report.pdf* (accessed 13 January 2020).
60. McCurdy, *Faster, Better, Cheaper*, p. 129.
61. Ibid., p. 131.

The Influence of the International Planetary Science Community

In the late 1980s and early 1990s, tensions formed between White House policies, NASA's administration, and the interests of space scientists wishing to collaborate with international partners. In the late 1970s, NASA had proposed a joint venture with the European Space Agency (ESA) called the International Solar Polar Mission (ISPM). ESA, formed in 1975 to represent 10 founding Western European nations in space-related activities, became the primary operating organization for the European space science community. The member countries of ESA have always funded the organization at far lower levels than NASA's budget, but ESA has steadily increased its capabilities while cultivating a program of world-class science and technological development. Both the U.S. and European space science communities recognize the potential benefits of international collaboration from a financial and intellectual standpoint and so have often pursued cooperative endeavors.

The proposed ISPM mission consisted of two spacecraft in polar orbits around the Sun, nearly perpendicular to the ecliptic plane. NASA and ESA were to build one orbiter apiece and launch both by Space Shuttle in 1983, then use a gravity-assist maneuver to place the spacecraft into their correct orbits.

In 1982, due to budget restrictions imposed by the Reagan administration and rising costs of Shuttle development, NASA canceled its ISPM spacecraft. The two space organizations reworked their agreement so that ESA would provide a single spacecraft for a new solar mission, NASA would provide a launch vehicle, and both organizations would contribute instruments. This arrangement would allow scientists on both sides of the Atlantic access to any data returned by the spacecraft. Although the new mission, named Ulysses, eventually flew, ESA took umbrage at NASA's unilateral decision to cancel the initial agreement without consultation and adjusted its strategy for future partnerships with NASA.[62] This incident would play a significant role in a later joint venture between the two space agencies, the Cassini-Huygens mission to Saturn.

In a 1983 report, *Planetary Exploration Through the Year 2000*, the NASA Advisory Council's Solar System Exploration Committee supported a joint mission with ESA to send an orbiter to Saturn along with a probe to land on one of Saturn's moons, Titan.[63] The mission remained in the concept

---

62. John Krige, "NASA as an Instrument of U.S. Foreign Policy," in *Societal Impact of Spaceflight*, ed. Steven J. Dick and Roger D. Launius (Washington, DC: NASA SP-2007-4801, 2007), p. 217.
63. Solar System Exploration Committee, *Planetary Exploration*, p. 9.

stage through most of the 1980s, but by 1988 ESA had selected it as the next mission in its planetary program. NASA soon followed suit, and the two organizations named the mission Cassini-Huygens (for the orbiter and the probe, respectively). Both organizations designated the large undertaking as a flagship mission, which represented a more evenly divided partnership than previous joint efforts. ESA's member nations were keen to demonstrate that Europe had reached a point of technological maturity in space science that compared favorably with that of the United States, placing the two space organizations on equal scientific footing.

Administrator Goldin found the size and scope of the mission at odds with the reforms he was attempting to enact and rescinded U.S. involvement in the project. Leadership at ESA, recalling the outcome of ISPM, found it unacceptable that the United States would once again back out of a large international endeavor, effectively canceling the mission unilaterally. ESA representatives vigorously communicated their position to NASA management, the U.S. State Department, and Vice President Al Gore, indicating that such action by the United States would call into question its reliability as a partner in any large scientific or technological endeavors in the future. The Europeans had some leverage in this tactic, given that the White House was courting ESA involvement in the International Space Station (ISS) effort.[64] In its transition from Space Station Freedom to the ISS, the space station program had become a U.S. national priority for distinctly post–Cold War geopolitical and national security reasons (primarily due to the collapse of the Soviet Union in 1991 and the possibility of Russian involvement in the space station). ESA considered Cassini-Huygens a priority of its various member nations for reasons of international prestige but also for the large project's ability to increase the capabilities of member nations' aerospace industrial base. In this case, a confluence of national priorities played out on an international scale. In the end, Administrator Goldin acquiesced, and Cassini-Huygens continued toward its successful launch in 1997.

---

64. Krige, "NASA as an Instrument," p. 216.

THE 2000S

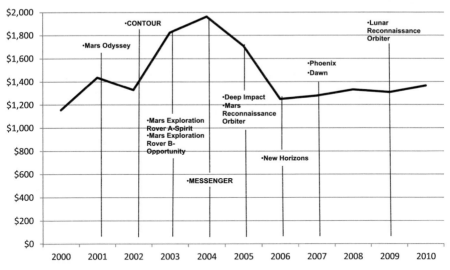

FIGURE 16. Planetary science actual expenditures, 2000–10 ($M, adjusted to 2010 dollars) by launch dates.

Decadal Surveys

In 2001, Ed Weiler, NASA's Associate Administrator for Space Science, requested that the SSB undertake a new study of priorities for solar system exploration in the next decade, modeled on the decadal surveys conducted by the SSB for astronomy and astrophysics. The resulting document, published in 2003 and titled *New Frontiers in the Solar System: An Integrated Exploration Strategy*,[65] became the first decadal survey for planetary science. The term "decadal survey" refers to a specific kind of report conducted by the SSB, and while the board has produced other sorts of reports on scientific priorities for various fields over the period of a decade, those reports have been conducted differently than decadal surveys have been. The differences may relate to the level of community involvement, including smaller or fewer committees, less public outreach, or less rigorous external review. Procedures for a decadal survey are very precise.

Later that decade, NASA also requested that the SSB conduct decadal surveys for Earth science, biological and physical sciences (often referred to as microgravity research), and heliophysics. Thus, the decadal survey became

---

65. Solar System Exploration Survey, National Research Council, *New Frontiers in the Solar System: An Integrated Exploration Strategy* (Washington, DC: The National Academies Press, 2003).

the uniform measure of scientific priorities for NASA's entire space science portfolio, informing the NAC's Space Science Advisory Committee and its various subcommittees as they created roadmaps for NASA's divisions. The roadmaps evaluated scientific objectives and missions in finer technical and economic detail, which in turn informed Division Directors as they formed each portion of NASA's strategic plan.[66]

The SSB's 2003 decadal survey for planetary science provided recommendations from the science community for a Mars lander project, a program of medium-sized planetary missions called New Frontiers, and a mission to Pluto. It also prioritized the most important questions in planetary science. It contained one other notable feature: a more detailed list of mission recommendations. Previous reports assessed science priorities, and some discussed the types of missions required to advance knowledge on those priorities, but they rarely discussed specific missions without a request from NASA. The 2003 survey represented a significant shift, demonstrating the SSB's willingness to delve into the programmatic direction of NASA, an area previously reserved for the NASA Advisory Council.

A New Golden Age

The first decade of the new millennium proved to be a renaissance for Mars exploration due to an increase in the number and diversity of missions to the Red Planet. In 2000, responding to a "Mars Program Independent Assessment Team Report,"[67] NASA Administrator Goldin appointed Scott Hubbard to the new position of Mars program director. The Mars program became a subdivision of the Planetary Science Division in NASA's Office of Space Science. Hubbard's plan was to establish a long-term strategy for Mars exploration, in which each mission would contribute to the goals of the overall program rather than flying discrete, unrelated science missions.[68] The Mars Odyssey orbiter, initially planned as part of the canceled 2001

---

66. Ibid. See the preface for more details on the Office of Space Science. The Government Performance and Results Act (GPRA) of 1993 required NASA's strategic plan to be renewed every three years (updated by the GPRA Modernization Act of 2010).
67. Mars Program Independent Assessment Team (MPIAT), "Mars Program Independent Assessment Team Report," delivered to the NASA Administrator on 14 March 2000, available at http://www.nasa.gov/news/reports/MP_Previous_Reports.html (accessed 31 July 2020). The MPIAT examined the systemic causes for the failure of the Mars Climate Orbiter and the Mars Polar Lander. In conjunction with technical reports by the accident investigation boards for MCO and MPL, the MPIAT report represents the end of the "faster, better, cheaper" initiative at NASA.
68. Scott Hubbard, *Exploring Mars: Chronicles from a Decade of Discovery* (Tucson, AZ: The University of Arizona Press, 2011) pp. 18–19.

Mars Surveyor program, launched in 2001. In addition to acquiring science data, and in concert with the Mars Global Surveyor already in orbit, Mars Odyssey would serve as a communications link for future rover missions. In 2003, NASA launched the highly successful solar-powered Mars Exploration Rovers, named Spirit and Opportunity, with the goal of providing ground data to support orbital observations indicating evidence of past liquid water on the surface of Mars. NASA selected the Mars Reconnaissance Orbiter (MRO), which competed with the MER rovers for the 2003 Mars launch window, as the next Mars mission. MRO launched in 2006 and provided the most detailed mapping of the Martian surface to date. Based on the success of NASA's Explorer and Discovery small-mission programs, Hubbard and his team initiated the competitively selected Mars Scout small-mission program. The first Mars Scout was the Phoenix lander, a project originally slated as a Mars Surveyor mission. Phoenix launched in 2007 to examine the polar ice caps of Mars. By the end of the decade, NASA had started work on the first flagship mission to Mars since Viking, the Mars Science Laboratory.

With an increased budget in the 2000s, NASA's overall planetary program benefited from a high rate of missions. The Discovery program's MESSENGER spacecraft, launched in 2004, became the first U.S. mission to Mercury since Mariner 10 in 1973. MESSENGER flew past the small planet three times in complicated deceleration maneuvers before becoming the first spacecraft to orbit Mercury. In 2001, NASA established the New Frontiers program for medium-class missions, based on the success of the Discovery program, and intended to launch a new spacecraft every three years. In 2006, the first New Frontiers mission, New Horizons, lifted off toward Pluto as the first spacecraft dedicated to the study of the dwarf planet.[69] The second New Frontiers selection candidate, a solar-powered mission to Jupiter called Juno, launched in 2011 on a six-year mission. In 2009, NASA launched the Lunar Reconnaissance Orbiter (LRO) and the Lunar CRater Observation and Sensing Satellite (LCROSS) aboard the same Atlas Centaur launch vehicle. The two satellites were part of a Lunar Precursor Robotic program, intended to support NASA's Constellation human spaceflight program. President Barack Obama canceled the Constellation program in 2010, but LRO and LCROSS completed their missions. LCROSS examined a dust plume created by the mission's depleted Centaur upper stage when it impacted the lunar surface, while LRO provided three-dimensional mapping data of the entire lunar surface.

---

69. In 2006, the International Astronomical Union (IAU) formally defined the term "planet," and Pluto fell outside the definition. The IAU designated Pluto as a dwarf planet.

NASA continued to expand its studies of asteroids and comets in the 2000s. The COmet Nucleus TOUR (CONTOUR) mission, intended to fly past at least two comet nuclei, launched in 2002. It failed following the ignition of its third-stage rocket motor. The exact cause of the failure was unknown, though the mishap investigation board found that the most likely cause was overheating of the spacecraft by the solid rocket motor exhaust plume.[70] NASA launched another Discovery mission to study comets, Deep Impact, in 2005 with far greater success. The Deep Impact spacecraft fired an impactor into the nucleus of a comet and photographed the resulting plume, revealing new information about the contents of comets. The spacecraft continued on an extended mission, named EPOXI, studying two other comets. The Dawn spacecraft, another Discovery mission, lifted off in 2007 to study the two largest objects in the asteroid belt. It reached the first, the protoplanet Vesta, in 2011, and arrived at the dwarf planet Ceres in 2015.

Congress and the White House provided NASA's planetary science program with an unprecedented level of resources in the mid-2000s, but that level began to decline in the face of two wars and an economic decline on a scale unknown in the United States since before World War II. Once more, national priorities have shifted, and the planetary science community continues to face the challenge of demonstrating to lawmakers that solar system exploration is worthy of a significant national investment, despite competition for resources from other sectors of government.

CONCLUSION

The planetary science community coalesced from a number of groups with disparate goals and interests. This community has adapted to changing politics, policies, and priorities, both inside and outside the community, and now speaks with a significantly unified voice. Members of this community have formed organizational structures that formalize the community's goals and strategy, establish consensus within the community, and ensure that the community's voice is heard by the federal organizations charged with executing the nation's solar system exploration activities. These organizations—the SSB, various NASA advisory groups, and their predecessors—have adapted over the last 50 years and now present the community's strategies in terms of programmatic goals rather than individual projects, allowing for

---

70. Comet Nucleus Tour Mishap Investigation Board, "Comet Nucleus Tour Mishap Investigation Board Report," delivered to the NASA Administrator on 31 May 2003, available at *https://www.nasa.gov/home/hqnews/2003/oct/HQ_03324_contour.html* (accessed 31 December 2013).

longer-term planning and broader participation by the community. With a unified voice and a long-term programmatic strategy, the planetary science community is able to affect the course of U.S. solar system exploration by providing policy-makers with a range of options from which to choose.

Today, planetary scientists exercise more influence over policy-making at the federal level, speaking to the strengths of a structured community with institutionalized methods of consensus building. Beyond the scope of this essay (but worth considering) are the drawbacks to the institutionalization of community consensus-building efforts, such as the fact that consensus must by definition stifle the voices of minority opinions. Which viewpoints and objectives have been marginalized and for what reasons? In seeking too broad a consensus, might the community become risk-averse? To what degree might large programs and projects draw broader constituencies, ensuring a bias toward "big science?"

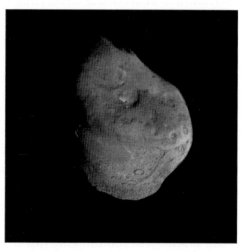

Composite image of Tempel 1 comet taken by Deep Impact spacecraft. (NASA/JPL/UMD: PIA02142)

And while the planetary community has proven increasingly effective at realizing broadly shared goals in previous decades, the path to the current structure of organizations representing the community was not inevitable. Prior to NASA's formation, policy-makers considered continued militarization of U.S. space efforts. After establishment of the civil space agency, the space science community outside of NASA and the civil servants who ran the Agency's space science program clashed over who would determine strategic and programmatic direction. In later decades, Congress and the White House occasionally suggested moving space science efforts to another agency, such as the National Science Foundation, or even abandoning space-based planetary research altogether.

The evolution of the planetary science community—its gradual development from a simple form to something more complex—is represented in the story of the groups and organizations within the community. Prior to NASA's formation in 1958, a nascent space science community consisted of a small group of researchers whose interests lay in a relatively common direction.

There were no official bodies duly appointed to represent the interests of its membership. The closest thing to a recognized organization was the Upper Atmosphere Rocket Research Panel (UARRP), formed by a group of scientists to better coordinate their research and limited resources. As these researchers learned more about this previously unexplored realm, space research increased in complexity, and the coordinating group became more ambitious, culminating in the planning and execution of the International Geophysical Year.

As the U.S. government became more interested in space, Congress and the White House sought out a community of knowledgeable experts whose experience and opinions could guide U.S. policy on early space efforts. Evidence suggests that Congress and President Dwight Eisenhower's Science Advisory Committee held the recommendations of the UARRP in high regard.[71] Many of the panel's recommendations found their way into the text of the National Aeronautics and Space Act of 1958, centralizing space exploration in an institution responsible for exploring the atmosphere and space immediately surrounding Earth, as well as the solar system beyond—and, when appropriate, coordinating that research with international partners.

With the formation of NASA, the National Research Council (the body within the National Academy of Sciences—and later the National Academies—primarily responsible for conducting studies) established the Space Science Board. NASA, along with the National Science Foundation and the Department of Defense, agreed to pay the National Research Council for specific studies from the SSB on the direction and effectiveness of the nation's scientific activities in space. Initially, the authority of the SSB in planning NASA activities was not clear, and the board pushed to have a determining input in mission selection, while NASA preferred to keep that function internal.

Thus, in the early decades of the relationship between the two organizations, the SSB rarely delved into NASA's programmatic territory. By the late 1960s, the relationship had changed, as NASA began to request SSB studies evaluating overarching research strategy while also engaging the planetary science community on programmatic issues through the Lunar and Planetary Missions Planning Board. Since 1977, NASA has maintained a link to the broader space science community by inviting non-NASA scientists to participate in NASA Advisory Council (NAC) functions, but the SSB also

---

71. Newell, *Beyond the Atmosphere*. See *https://history.nasa.gov/SP-4211/ch9-4.htm*.

has served to communicate the community's interests to NASA and other government stakeholders.

When planetary science began to compete with the fields of astrophysics, Earth science, heliophysics, and microgravity research for limited resources, the threat arose that these space science communities might pit themselves against one another, with the potential to disrupt the presentation of a unified voice when communicating the interests of space science writ large. By the early 2000s, witnessing the success of the SSB's decadal survey process for astronomy and astrophysics, NASA requested that the SSB undertake a decadal survey for planetary science. The survey provided recommendations from the science community on programs within NASA and prioritized the most important questions in planetary science. Prioritization allowed NASA flexibility in the event of budget cuts, cost overruns, or unexpected circumstances, and directed the Agency toward a strategy that the planetary science community supported. The survey also explained NASA's rationale for its programmatic choices to Congress and demonstrated that those choices were supported by the science community. The planetary survey represented a shift in programmatic decision-making for NASA, as it included more detailed programmatic recommendations than most previous SSB works.

That trend continues with the most recent decadal survey, *Vision and Voyages for Planetary Science in the Decades 2013–2022*,[72] which outlines scientific and general programmatic recommendations and includes guidelines on how priorities should shift in differing budget scenarios. Congress has often instructed NASA to fund studies on various topics and now regularly includes language in legislation directing NASA to execute the recommendations of SSB decadal surveys. In recent years, excerpts from decadal surveys have appeared in congressional authorization legislation, indicating the high regard in which members of Congress now hold these reports.

The slow shift in focus from the NAC to the SSB in making programmatic recommendations represents an interesting dynamic. The NAC is an organization independent from the NASA program offices, but it is internal to NASA. The NASA Administrator has the authority to implement NAC recommendations, or not, and the council does not publish many formal studies. The SSB, by contrast, is external to NASA and conducts studies for the Agency on a contractual basis. Nearly all SSB reports are available to the public, and the board regularly briefs Congress on findings. As a result,

---

72. Committee on the Planetary Science Decadal Survey, Space Studies Board, National Research Council, *Vision and Voyages for Planetary Science in the Decades 2013–2022* (Washington, DC: The National Academies Press, 2012).

programmatic recommendations from the NAC tend to remain within NASA, which is part of the executive branch of government, while those from the SSB are generally available to the legislative branch, as well as being circulated in the broader scientific community. As the SSB takes on more responsibility for strategic and programmatic direction in U.S. space science and the NAC's role in science shifts to advising NASA on how well it is adhering to the decadal surveys, the power to determine the direction of U.S. space science shifts in a subtle manner from the executive to the legislative branch.

This shift may bode well for the planetary science community. As history has demonstrated, practitioners in all of the various fields that make up this community have always had a hand in shaping the direction of U.S. exploration of the solar system, though often that power has been subtle or indirect. Choices made by presidents, lawmakers, and administrators often seem to be the critical factors in determining the course of solar system exploration, but the choices those individuals make are bounded by the options presented to them by special committees, congressional testimony, advisory boards, and the like. And again, as history demonstrates, the planetary science community has adapted over decades, organizing to become a very effective voice in decision-making.

The SSB decadal surveys for planetary science represent the consensus of the community on scientific and, increasingly, programmatic priorities. Congress seems to recognize there is a unified constituency for space science, and it is treating that community's requests as increasingly legitimate by tying NASA's funding to legislation making aspects of decadal study recommendations into law.

APPENDIX: BUDGET TABLES

Attempting to disaggregate the NASA budget into the current themes within the Science Mission Directorate (planetary science, astrophysics, heliophysics, and Earth science) is difficult for at least three reasons:

First, the current arrangement of the themes has existed only since 2005, which makes comparing historical budgets from year to year difficult. For example, prior to the FY 2006 White House budget request for NASA, Earth science and heliophysics lines were combined in an Earth-Sun Connection theme. For several decades before that, Earth science was not budgeted in the space science budget line, but in a space applications line. Heliophysics did not exist as a separate theme for most of NASA's history and was housed instead in the space physics portion of the Astronomy and Space Physics budget line.

A second, thornier problem lies in assigning many missions to any specific theme. Particularly in the early days of NASA, many spacecraft (or sounding rockets, or balloons) carried instruments that could reasonably be characterized as collecting data for two or more space science themes. As an example, early ionospheric studies might support Earth science and heliophysics. And what if the ionosphere in question is on another planet?

The manner in which NASA prepares budgets for its programs, particularly smaller programs, presents a third challenge. In more than 50 years of sounding rockets and balloon programs, NASA broke their budget lines out by theme only once (in the FY 1971 budget), and never by project or flight. In some years, the Explorer program budget line was divided by project for large and medium missions but not the Small Explorer (SMEX) class of projects. In other years, Explorers were placed under a separate budget line and were not broken out at all.

These examples are intended to demonstrate some of the challenges faced in producing the tables below. Many assumptions and judgment calls lie behind the seemingly specific numbers in these charts. Documentation exists for all of the choices made by the author, but that documentation is not presented here due to the fact that the resulting spreadsheets would require two or three times the pages needed for the rest of the chapter. As a result of imperfect data provided in the source material, the author cautions against using the numbers below as definitive. That said, the trending indicated from year to year can be viewed as accurate because the numbers, while potentially inaccurate, are inaccurate by sums of millions of dollars at most. When comparing budget lines measured in billions, this inaccuracy has a negligible effect on comparative aspects of the data.

All NASA budget numbers come from the President's Annual Budget Request for NASA. The numbers represent fiscal years, not calendar years.

Numbers for any given year come from the NASA budget two fiscal years following the year in question (e.g., the 1980 budget numbers come from the FY 1982 NASA budget). This was done in order to record actual rather than requested budget numbers. The President's budget is only a request to Congress, which must then authorize and appropriate the actual budget, rarely exactly as requested. While budget actuals reported in the President's budget request two years later are not necessarily the final numbers (due to multiyear contractual obligations and other mitigating factors), they are as accurate as a researcher is likely to find over the span of NASA's history.

In FY 1974, the federal government voted to alter the financial year to align with a new budgeting structure.[73] In order to continue funding the government during this shift, Congress introduced a Transitional Quarter between the end of FY 1976 and the beginning of FY 1977. In Tables A1, A2, A3, and A4, the funds for the Transitional Quarter are divided evenly between 1976 and 1977. Conversion factors for Tables A1, A2, A3, and A4 came from the Oregon State University Political Science Department.[74]

TABLE A1. *NASA Historical Budget Numbers for Planetary Science, Astrophysics, Heliophysics, and Earth Science, 1959–2010*

Year	Planetary Science Budget Actual		Astrophysics Budget Actual		Heliophysics Budget Actual		Earth Science Budget Actual	
	$Million	$Million, adjusted to 2010 dollars	$Million	$Million, adjusted to 2010 dollars	$Million	$Million, adjusted to 2010 dollars	$Million	$Million, adjusted to 2010 dollars
1959	31.883	239.719	10.299	77.436	14.511	109.105	0.988	7.425
1960	49.996	367.617	12.247	90.051	16.602	122.074	7.930	58.309
1961	91.019	664.372	27.822	203.080	38.906	283.985	19.610	143.139
1962	164.631	1,192.978	47.121	341.457	72.650	526.449	39.696	287.652
1963	222.802	1,591.443	47.492	339.229	100.198	715.700	54.051	386.079
1964	205.762	1,449.028	78.414	552.211	109.038	767.873	63.177	444.908
1965	206.027	1,430.743	66.470	461.597	109.559	760.826	30.991	215.215

(continued on next page)

---

73. For further details, see Bill Henniff, Jr., Megan Suzanne Lynch, and Jessica Tollestrup, "Introduction to the Federal Budget Process: CRS Report for Congress" (Washington, DC: Congressional Research Service, 3 December 2012), available at *http://www.fas.org/sgp/crs/misc/98-721.pdf* (accessed 3 August 2020).

74. The conversion tables can be found at *https://liberalarts.oregonstate.edu/spp/polisci/faculty-staff/robert-sahr/inflation-conversion-factors-years-1774-estimated-2024-dollars-recent-years/individual-year-conversion-factor-table-0*.

CHAPTER 2 · FUNDING PLANETARY SCIENCE: HISTORY AND POLITICAL ECONOMY

Year	Planetary Science Budget Actual		Astrophysics Budget Actual		Heliophysics Budget Actual		Earth Science Budget Actual	
	$Million	$Million, adjusted to 2010 dollars	$Million	$Million, adjusted to 2010 dollars	$Million	$Million, adjusted to 2010 dollars	$Million	$Million, adjusted to 2010 dollars
1966	204.300	1,371.141	70.473	472.973	98.232	659.275	78.053	523.846
1967	184.150	1,203.595	75.245	491.797	81.858	535.020	71.300	466.013
1968	147.500	921.875	81.171	507.319	71.910	449.438	99.500	621.875
1969	87.923	523.351	70.400	419.048	58.500	348.214	98.665	587.292
1970	150.900	847.753	76.570	430.169	53.082	298.213	128.304	720.809
1971	144.900	779.032	62.750	337.366	53.207	286.059	163.960	881.505
1972	291.500	1,518.229	55.554	289.344	54.546	284.094	127.729	665.255
1973	331.969	1,627.299	61.584	301.882	64.617	316.750	130.594	640.167
1974	392.482	1,736.646	43.317	191.668	50.683	224.261	133.875	592.367
1975	261.200	1,057.490	89.136	360.874	47.179	191.008	158.148	640.275
1976	287.982	1,103.379	114.628	439.188	66.422	254.490	159.330	610.460
1977	225.632	811.626	95.602	343.892	92.448	332.547	174.858	628.986
1978	147.200	492.308	121.076	404.936	103.124	344.896	191.600	640.803
1979	182.400	547.748	168.044	504.637	114.856	344.913	221.100	663.964
1980	219.900	581.746	217.468	575.312	119.332	315.693	281.510	744.735
1981	175.600	421.103	219.802	527.103	103.898	249.156	255.450	612.590
1982	210.000	474.041	240.774	543.508	81.689	184.400	282.423	637.524
1983	186.400	407.877	370.294	810.271	100.006	218.832	285.800	625.383
1984	217.400	456.723	463.607	973.964	103.994	218.475	238.400	500.840
1985	290.900	590.061	579.426	1,175.306	97.774	198.325	270.300	548.276
1986	353.600	702.982	478.280	950.855	91.020	180.954	342.500	680.915
1987	359.200	689.443	456.550	876.296	117.550	225.624	390.700	749.904
1988	327.700	603.499	446.950	823.112	158.000	290.976	389.200	716.759
1989	416.600	732.162	518.650	911.511	212.050	372.671	403.400	708.963
1990	390.848	652.501	637.386	1,064.083	222.049	370.699	434.199	724.873
1991	473.700	757.920	612.271	979.634	257.829	412.526	662.300	1,059.680
1992	534.221	830.826	763.306	1,187.101	273.371	425.149	828.002	1,287.717
1993	475.598	717.342	754.614	1,138.181	280.248	422.697	888.054	1,339.448
1994	798.400	1,174.118	818.100	1,203.088	303.500	446.324	1,065.000	1,566.176
1995	786.287	1,124.874	884.685	1,265.644	361.372	516.984	1,341.800	1,919.599
1996	818.621	1,136.974	962.756	1,337.161	398.426	553.369	1,360.800	1,890.000
1997	779.489	1,059.088	819.681	1,113.697	328.231	445.966	1,361.600	1,850.000

(continued on next page)

Year	Planetary Science Budget Actual		Astrophysics Budget Actual		Heliophysics Budget Actual		Earth Science Budget Actual	
	$Million	$Million, adjusted to 2010 dollars	$Million	$Million, adjusted to 2010 dollars	$Million	$Million, adjusted to 2010 dollars	$Million	$Million, adjusted to 2010 dollars
1998	706.151	944.052	891.531	1,191.886	379.703	507.624	1,417.300	1,894.786
1999	787.751	1,031.088	1,008.647	1,320.219	284.590	372.500	1,413.800	1,850.524
2000	912.839	1,155.492	963.668	1,219.833	292.015	369.639	1,443.400	1,827.089
2001	1,165.290	1,435.086	917.498	1,129.924	224.913	276.986	1,762.200	2,170.197
2002	1,095.800	1,328.242	1,000.200	1,212.364	412.900	500.485	1,241.400	1,504.727
2003	1,539.500	1,824.052	1,087.300	1,288.270	479.700	568.365	1,613.000	1,911.137
2004	1,699.455	1,962.419	1,203.013	1,389.161	1,003.320	1,158.568	1,335.280	1,541.894
2005	1,531.245	1,708.979	1,312.661	1,465.023	965.760	1,077.857	1,340.440	1,496.027
2006	1,156.021	1,249.752	1,381.992	1,494.045	949.897	1,026.916	1,325.600	1,433.081
2007	1,215.600	1,278.233	1,365.000	1,435.331	830.800	873.607	1,198.500	1,260.252
2008	1,312.600	1,329.889	1,395.600	1,413.982	787.600	797.974	1,237.400	1,253.698
2009	1,288.100	1,309.045	1,229.900	1,249.898	607.800	617.683	1,377.300	1,399.695
2010	1,364.400	1,364.400	1,086.000	1,086.000	608.000	608.000	1,439.300	1,439.300

TABLE A2. *Federal Budget Data, 1959–2010*

The federal budget data came from the White House Office of Management and Budget historical tables.[75]

Year	U.S. GDP		Total Federal Outlays		Gross Federal Debt		Federal Gov't. Receipts	
	Real, $Million	$Million, adjusted to 2010 dollars	Real, $Million	$Million, adjusted to 2010 dollars	Real, $Million	$Million, adjusted to 2010 dollars	Real, $Million	$Million, adjusted to 2010 dollars
1959	490,200	3,685,714	92,098	692,466	287,465	2,161,391	79,249	595,857
1960	518,900	3,815,441	92,191	677,875	290,525	2,136,213	92,492	680,088
1961	529,900	3,867,883	97,723	713,307	292,648	2,136,117	94,388	688,964
1962	567,800	4,114,493	106,821	774,065	302,928	2,195,130	99,676	722,290
1963	599,200	4,280,000	111,316	795,114	310,324	2,216,600	106,560	761,143
1964	641,500	4,517,606	118,528	834,704	316,059	2,225,768	112,613	793,049
1965	687,500	4,774,306	118,228	821,028	322,318	2,238,319	116,817	811,229
1966	755,800	5,072,483	134,532	902,899	328,498	2,204,685	130,835	878,087

(continued on next page)

---

75. The OMB historical tables can be found at *https://www.whitehouse.gov/omb/historical-tables/*.

	U.S. GDP		Total Federal Outlays		Gross Federal Debt		Federal Gov't. Receipts	
Year	Real, $Million	$Million, adjusted to 2010 dollars	Real, $Million	$Million, adjusted to 2010 dollars	Real, $Million	$Million, adjusted to 2010 dollars	Real, $Million	$Million, adjusted to 2010 dollars
1967	810,000	5,294,118	157,464	1,029,176	340,445	2,225,131	148,822	972,693
1968	868,400	5,427,500	178,134	1,113,338	368,685	2,304,281	152,973	956,081
1969	948,100	5,643,452	183,640	1,093,095	365,769	2,177,196	186,882	1,112,393
1970	1,012,700	5,689,326	195,649	1,099,152	380,921	2,140,006	192,807	1,083,185
1971	1,080,000	5,806,452	210,172	1,129,957	408,176	2,194,495	187,139	1,006,124
1972	1,176,500	6,127,604	230,681	1,201,464	435,936	2,270,500	207,309	1,079,734
1973	1,310,600	6,424,510	245,707	1,204,446	466,291	2,285,740	230,799	1,131,368
1974	1,438,500	6,365,044	269,359	1,191,854	483,893	2,141,119	263,224	1,164,708
1975	1,560,200	6,316,599	332,332	1,345,474	541,925	2,194,028	279,090	1,129,919
1976	1,967,800	7,539,464	419,780	1,608,351	628,970	2,409,847	338,676	1,297,609
1977	2,203,200	7,925,180	457,206	1,644,624	706,398	2,541,000	396,175	1,425,090
1978	2,217,500	7,416,388	458,746	1,534,268	776,602	2,597,331	399,561	1,336,324
1979	2,501,400	7,511,712	504,028	1,513,598	829,467	2,490,892	463,302	1,391,297
1980	2,724,200	7,206,878	590,941	1,563,336	909,041	2,404,870	517,112	1,368,021
1981	3,057,000	7,330,935	678,241	1,626,477	994,828	2,385,679	599,272	1,437,103
1982	3,223,700	7,276,975	745,743	1,683,393	1,137,315	2,567,302	617,766	1,394,506
1983	3,440,700	7,528,884	808,364	1,768,849	1,371,660	3,001,444	600,562	1,314,140
1984	3,844,400	8,076,471	851,805	1,789,506	1,564,586	3,286,945	666,438	1,400,080
1985	4,146,300	8,410,345	946,344	1,919,562	1,817,423	3,686,456	734,037	1,488,919
1986	4,403,900	8,755,268	990,382	1,968,950	2,120,501	4,215,708	769,155	1,529,135
1987	4,651,400	8,927,831	1,004,017	1,927,096	2,345,956	4,502,795	854,288	1,639,708
1988	5,008,500	9,223,757	1,064,416	1,960,250	2,601,104	4,790,247	909,238	1,674,471
1989	5,399,500	9,489,455	1,143,744	2,010,095	2,867,800	5,040,070	991,105	1,741,837
1990	5,734,500	9,573,456	1,252,993	2,091,808	3,206,290	5,352,738	1,031,958	1,722,801
1991	5,930,500	9,488,800	1,324,226	2,118,762	3,598,178	5,757,085	1,054,988	1,687,981
1992	6,242,000	9,707,621	1,381,529	2,148,568	4,001,787	6,223,619	1,091,208	1,697,058
1993	6,587,300	9,935,596	1,409,386	2,125,771	4,351,044	6,562,661	1,154,335	1,741,078
1994	6,976,600	10,259,706	1,461,753	2,149,637	4,643,307	6,828,393	1,258,566	1,850,832
1995	7,341,100	10,502,289	1,515,742	2,168,443	4,920,586	7,039,465	1,351,790	1,933,891
1996	7,718,300	10,719,861	1,560,484	2,167,339	5,181,465	7,196,479	1,453,053	2,018,129
1997	8,211,700	11,157,201	1,601,116	2,175,429	5,369,206	7,295,117	1,579,232	2,145,696
1998	8,663,000	11,581,551	1,652,458	2,209,168	5,478,189	7,323,782	1,721,728	2,301,775

(continued on next page)

Year	U.S. GDP		Total Federal Outlays		Gross Federal Debt		Federal Gov't. Receipts	
	Real, $Million	$Million, adjusted to 2010 dollars	Real, $Million	$Million, adjusted to 2010 dollars	Real, $Million	$Million, adjusted to 2010 dollars	Real, $Million	$Million, adjusted to 2010 dollars
1999	9,208,400	12,052,880	1,701,842	2,227,542	5,605,523	7,337,072	1,827,452	2,391,953
2000	9,821,000	12,431,646	1,788,950	2,264,494	5,628,700	7,124,937	2,025,191	2,563,533
2001	10,225,300	12,592,734	1,862,846	2,294,145	5,769,881	7,105,765	1,991,082	2,452,071
2002	10,543,900	12,780,485	2,010,894	2,437,447	6,198,401	7,513,213	1,853,136	2,246,225
2003	10,980,200	13,009,716	2,159,899	2,559,122	6,760,014	8,009,495	1,782,314	2,111,746
2004	11,676,000	13,482,679	2,292,841	2,647,622	7,354,657	8,492,676	1,880,114	2,171,032
2005	12,428,600	13,871,205	2,471,957	2,758,881	7,905,300	8,822,879	2,153,611	2,403,584
2006	13,206,500	14,277,297	2,655,050	2,870,324	8,451,350	9,136,595	2,406,869	2,602,021
2007	13,861,400	14,575,605	2,728,686	2,869,281	8,950,744	9,411,928	2,567,985	2,700,300
2008	14,334,400	14,523,202	2,982,544	3,021,828	9,986,082	10,117,611	2,523,991	2,557,235
2009	13,937,500	14,164,126	3,517,677	3,574,875	11,875,851	12,068,954	2,104,989	2,139,216
2010	14,359,700	14,359,700	3,456,213	3,456,213	13,528,807	13,528,807	2,162,724	2,162,724

TABLE A3. *NSF, NIH, and DOE Budget Data, 1959–2010*
The budget data for the National Science Foundation and the Department of Energy came from the White House Office of Management and Budget historical tables.[76] The budget data for the National Institutes for Health are appropriations data, not budget actuals. This means that the data are not the same as the other budget data to which they are being compared. Since the author was only examining trends in data over time, and since no budget actual data were readily available for NIH, the author felt that the use of appropriations data was acceptable in this case. The differences between appropriations and budget actuals are generally small, though not insignificant. Speaking in a broad sense, appropriations numbers tend to be slightly higher than budget actual numbers. The difference, at the small agency or institute level, is usually in hundreds of thousands or low millions of dollars. The author is confident that, while the budget line displayed in figures IV, V, and VI for the NIH budget may be incrementally higher than the budget actuals, the trending is accurate over the five-decade span. The budget data for NIH came from the NIH 2012 Almanac.[77]

---

76. The OMB historical tables can be found at *https://www.whitehouse.gov/omb/historical-tables/*.
77. The NIH 2012 Almanac was accessed at *http://nih.gov/about/almanac/appropriations/part2.htm* (accessed 5 August 2020).

Year	NSF Outlays $Million	NSF Outlays $Million, adjusted to 2010 dollars	NIH Appropriations $Million	NIH Appropriations $Million, adjusted to 2010 dollars	DOE Outlays $Million	DOE Outlays $Million, adjusted to 2010 dollars
1959			291.817	2,194.113		
1960			399.380	2,936.618		
1961			551.023	4,022.066		
1962	183.000	1,326.087	740.206	5,363.812	2,755.000	19,963.768
1963	206.000	1,471.429	880.241	6,287.436	2,700.000	19,285.714
1964	310.000	2,183.099	867.369	6,108.232	2,726.000	19,197.183
1965	309.000	2,145.833	959.159	6,660.826	2,579.000	17,909.722
1966	368.000	2,469.799	1,100.519	7,386.034	2,343.000	15,724.832
1967	415.000	2,712.418	1,014.254	6,629.111	2,253.000	14,725.490
1968	449.000	2,806.250	1,076.461	6,727.881	2,474.000	15,462.500
1969	490.000	2,916.667	1,109.757	6,605.696	2,393.000	14,244.048
1970	464.000	2,606.742	1,061.007	5,960.713	2,393.000	13,443.820
1971	522.000	2,806.452	1,212.847	6,520.683	2,200.000	11,827.957
1972	567.000	2,953.125	1,506.156	7,844.563	2,299.000	11,973.958
1973	585.000	2,867.647	1,762.565	8,640.025	2,304.000	11,294.118
1974	647.000	2,862.832	1,790.425	7,922.235	2,233.000	9,880.531
1975	662.000	2,680.162	2,092.897	8,473.267	3,230.000	13,076.923
1976	836.500	3,204.981	2,521.680	9,661.607	4,365.000	16,724.138
1977	856.500	3,080.935	2,763.092	9,939.178	5,573.000	20,046.763
1978	803.000	2,685.619	2,842.936	9,508.147	6,412.000	21,444.816
1979	870.000	2,612.613	3,189.976	9,579.508	7,441.000	22,345.345
1980	912.000	2,412.698	3,428.935	9,071.257	7,260.000	19,206.349
1981	976.000	2,340.528	3,569.406	8,559.727	11,756.000	28,191.847
1982	1,099.000	2,480.813	3,641.875	8,220.937	11,656.000	26,311.512
1983	1,055.000	2,308.534	4,023.969	8,805.184	10,590.000	23,172.867
1984	1,193.000	2,506.303	4,493.588	9,440.311	10,990.000	23,088.235
1985	1,309.000	2,655.172	5,149.459	10,445.150	10,586.000	21,472.617
1986	1,536.000	3,053.678	5,262.211	10,461.652	11,025.000	21,918.489
1987	1,547.000	2,969.290	6,182.910	11,867.390	10,692.000	20,522.073
1988	1,644.000	3,027.624	6,666.693	12,277.519	11,165.000	20,561.694
1989	1,736.000	3,050.967	7,144.765	12,556.705	11,386.000	20,010.545
1990	1,821.000	3,040.067	7,576.352	12,648.334	12,083.000	20,171.953
1991	2,064.000	3,302.400	8,274.739	13,239.582	12,472.000	19,955.200

(continued on next page)

Year	NSF Outlays $Million	NSF Outlays $Million, adjusted to 2010 dollars	NIH Appropriations $Million	NIH Appropriations $Million, adjusted to 2010 dollars	DOE Outlays $Million	DOE Outlays $Million, adjusted to 2010 dollars
1992	2,230.000	3,468.118	8,921.687	13,875.096	15,515.000	24,129.082
1993	2,429.000	3,663.650	10,335.996	15,589.738	16,933.000	25,539.970
1994	2,605.000	3,830.882	11,299.522	16,616.944	17,830.000	26,220.588
1995	2,814.000	4,025.751	11,927.562	17,063.751	17,608.000	25,190.272
1996	2,988.000	4,150.000	12,740.843	17,695.615	16,195.000	22,493.056
1997	3,093.000	4,202.446	13,674.843	18,579.950	14,458.000	19,644.022
1998	3,143.000	4,201.872	15,629.156	20,894.594	14,414.000	19,270.053
1999	3,246.000	4,248.691	17,840.587	23,351.554	15,879.000	20,784.031
2000	3,448.000	4,364.557	20,458.556	25,896.906	14,971.000	18,950.633
2001	3,662.000	4,509.852	23,321.382	28,720.914	16,319.000	20,097.291
2002	4,155.000	5,036.364	27,166.715	32,929.352	17,669.000	21,416.970
2003	4,690.000	5,556.872	28,036.627	33,218.752	19,379.000	22,960.900
2004	5,092.000	5,879.908	28,594.357	33,018.888	19,892.000	22,969.977
2005	5,403.000	6,030.134	28,560.417	31,875.465	21,271.000	23,739.955
2006	5,510.000	5,956.757	29,178.504	31,544.329	19,649.000	21,242.162
2007	5,488.000	5,770.768	29,607.070	31,132.566	20,116.000	21,152.471
2008	5,785.000	5,861.196	30,545.098	30,947.414	21,400.000	21,681.864
2009	5,958.000	6,054.878	31,238.000	31,745.935	23,683.000	24,068.089
2010	6,719.000	6,719.000	30,916.345	30,916.345	30,778.000	30,778.000

TABLE A4. *DOD Budget Data, 1959–2010*

Budget data for the Department of Defense and DOD Research and Development spending came from the White House Office of Management and Budget historical tables.[78]

Year	DOD Budget Outlays $Million	DOD Budget Outlays $Million, adjusted to 2010 dollars	DOD R&D Outlays $Million[2]	DOD R&D Outlays $Million, adjusted to 2010 dollars
1959			4,950.000	37,218.045
1960			5,517.000	40,566.176
1961			6,466.000	47,197.080
1962	52,345.000	379,311.594	6,689.000	48,471.014

(continued on next page)

---

78. The OMB historical tables can be found at *https://www.whitehouse.gov/omb/historical-tables/*.

Year	DOD Budget Outlays		DOD R&D Outlays	
	$Million	$Million, adjusted to 2010 dollars	$Million[2]	$Million, adjusted to 2010 dollars
1963	53,400.000	381,428.571	6,792.000	48,514.286
1964	54,757.000	385,612.676	7,419.000	52,246.479
1965	50,620.000	351,527.778	6,623.000	45,993.056
1966	58,111.000	390,006.711	6,675.000	44,798.658
1967	71,417.000	466,777.778	7,649.000	49,993.464
1968	81,926.000	512,037.500	8,071.000	50,443.750
1969	82,497.000	491,053.571	7,762.000	46,202.381
1970	81,692.000	458,943.820	7,519.000	42,241.573
1971	78,872.000	424,043.011	7,639.000	41,069.892
1972	79,174.000	412,364.583	8,238.000	42,906.250
1973	76,681.000	375,887.255	8,529.000	41,808.824
1974	79,347.000	351,092.920	8,960.000	39,646.018
1975	86,509.000	350,238.866	9,284.000	37,587.045
1976	100,753.500	386,028.736	10,497.000	40,218.391
1977	108,375.500	389,839.928	11,366.000	40,884.892
1978	104,495.000	349,481.605	10,726.000	35,872.910
1979	116,342.000	349,375.375	11,045.000	33,168.168
1980	133,995.000	354,484.127	13,469.000	35,632.275
1981	157,513.000	377,729.017	15,739.000	37,743.405
1982	185,309.000	418,304.740	18,363.000	41,451.467
1983	209,903.000	459,306.346	20,566.000	45,002.188
1984	227,411.000	477,754.202	23,850.000	50,105.042
1985	252,743.000	512,663.286	28,165.000	57,129.817
1986	273,373.000	543,485.089	33,396.000	66,393.638
1987	281,996.000	541,259.117	34,732.000	66,664.107
1988	290,360.000	534,732.965	35,605.000	65,570.902
1989	303,555.000	533,488.576	37,819.000	66,465.729
1990	299,321.000	499,701.169	38,247.000	63,851.419
1991	273,285.000	437,256.000	35,330.000	56,528.000
1992	298,346.000	463,990.669	35,504.000	55,216.174
1993	291,084.000	439,040.724	37,666.000	56,811.463
1994	281,640.000	414,176.471	35,474.000	52,167.647
1995	272,063.000	389,217.454	35,356.000	50,580.830

(continued on next page)

Year	DOD Budget Outlays		DOD R&D Outlays	
	$Million	$Million, adjusted to 2010 dollars	$Million[2]	$Million, adjusted to 2010 dollars
1996	265,748.000	369,094.444	36,936.000	51,300.000
1997	270,502.000	367,529.891	37,702.000	51,225.543
1998	268,194.000	358,548.128	37,558.000	50,211.230
1999	274,769.000	359,645.288	37,571.000	49,176.702
2000	294,363.000	372,611.392	38,279.000	48,454.430
2001	304,732.000	375,285.714	41,157.000	50,685.961
2002	348,456.000	422,370.909	44,903.000	54,427.879
2003	404,744.000	479,554.502	53,778.000	63,718.009
2004	455,833.000	526,366.051	61,510.000	71,027.714
2005	495,308.000	552,799.107	66,467.000	74,181.920
2006	521,827.000	564,137.297	69,323.000	74,943.784
2007	551,271.000	579,675.079	73,716.000	77,514.196
2008	616,073.000	624,187.437	75,783.000	76,781.155
2009	661,049.000	671,797.764	79,708.000	81,004.065
2010	693,586.000	693,586.000	77,591.000	77,591.000

CHAPTER 3

The Politics of Pure Space Science, the Essential Tension: Human Spaceflight's Impact on Scientific Exploration

Roger Handberg

FROM THE U.S. SPACE PROGRAM'S INCEPTION in October 1958, human spaceflight has been deeply intertwined with the space science programs at NASA. Space science writ large existed prior to NASA, but the Agency's creation, offering the possibility of access to space, helped focus public and congressional attention more intently on what was considered an exotic field known to most only through Chesley Bonestell's and others' artistic fantasies of planets and the vehicles that humans would use to fly and live in space. The illustrations depicted a human adventure reaching out to the planets and beyond, one that appealed to early generations of space enthusiasts.

Bonestell's glamorous and imaginative scenarios were rarely accurate except to exhibit the loneliness and beauty of other worlds, and they grabbed public attention. Remember that this period was just past the age of Percival Lowell's "canals on Mars" claims, at least as far as the public was aware. Bonestell did not lay out any agenda for space exploration. That was his collaborator Wernher von Braun's task, with his vision of humans pushing out into outer space.[1] Von Braun's vision, often unacknowledged, still dominates discussions of future U.S. human spaceflight endeavors. These two types, the

---

1. The most famous pictures appeared in Willy Ley's *The Conquest of Space* (New York: Viking, 1949). For some of the images, go to "Chesley Bonestell" on the *Cosmic Café and Outer Space Art Gallery* website, *http://www.outer-space-art-gallery.com/chesley-bonestell.html* (accessed 6 August 2020).

artist and the dreamer, made outer space a real destination possibility for humans, not just a figment of science fiction. So, from before the beginnings of the U.S. space program, human spaceflight and space science have existed as uneasy partners and collaborators, continuing with the establishment of NASA and its emphasis on human spaceflight along with space science.[2]

SETTING THE STAGE

The title for this chapter is drawn from a book published in the 1960s, *The Politics of Pure Science*, in which author Daniel Greenberg described a disconnect between the high-minded goals of science and the way in which decisions about how to conduct and fund that science were made.[3] My purpose here is not to expose, but rather to determine how to judge the impact of two complementary but often competing perspectives on future directions for the U.S. space program, embodied in the concepts of robotic missions and missions including a human presence.

The linkage between space science and human spaceflight comes (from the perspective of space science) in the form of a Faustian bargain. Human exploration dominates popular media coverage of the space program, while space scientists feel that their efforts have actually moved space exploration further ahead. The science program, from this view, is one steady, usually systematic progress marred by occasional accidents or glitches. Yet others may view space science differently. Take, for example, the 2012 landing of Curiosity on Mars. A burst of media coverage occurred, but much of it focused on people, not on the science of the mission. Rather, after Curiosity returned its first images, coverage shifted focus to a scientist's Mohawk haircut and a dance video put out by fans spoofing JPL personnel.[4] Using

---

2. The National Aeronautics and Space Act, Pub. L. No. 111–314 124 Stat. 3328 (18 December 2010). Section 20112 (a) (2) directs NASA to "arrange for participation by the scientific community in planning scientific measurements and observations to be made through use of aeronautical and space vehicles, and conduct or arrange for the conduct of such measurements and observations;…."

3. Daniel S. Greenberg, *The Politics of Pure Science* (New York: New American Library, 1967). Greenberg published two later books on the politics of science: *Science, Money and Politics: Political Triumph and Ethical Erosion* (Chicago: University of Chicago Press, 2001) and *Science for Sale: The Perils, Rewards, and Delusions of Campus Capitalism* (Chicago: University of Chicago Press, 2007).

4. Patrick Kingsley, "Mars Curiosity Rover: Upstaged by NASA Mohawk Guy," *Guardian* (6 August 2012), http://www.guardian.co.uk/fashion/shortcuts/2012/aug/06/mars-rover-curiosity-nasa-mohawk-guy (accessed 8 October 2012); Denise Chow, "We're NASA and We Know It," *Space.com* (16 August 2012), http://www.space.com/17140-mars-rover-music-video-spoof-lmfao.html (accessed 8 October 2012).

social media to generate public attention and interest is not a problem, but it reflects the reality that to keep public attention on space science, one must go all out. The Hubble Space Telescope, the star of NASA science with its imagery, has experienced a decline in public attention even as its science has become more spectacular. How many images can you use as a screen saver? The same phenomenon has impacted Curiosity as it settled into the work of scientific exploration and public attention shifts to the newest Mars rover, Perseverance.[5]

The essential tension that exists between the space science community and the human spaceflight community arises over how funds are allocated and which specific strands of space science should be a priority.[6] Parts of space science are explicitly in support of the human exploration program. Other major areas are distant. Politically, all must ultimately justify their existence and their budgets based on some value to the larger program within which they exist. The requirement that NASA programs be justified is a critical one because they are publicly funded; their audiences are not always their scientific peers or even their peers within the Agency itself. For example, NASA's Search for Extraterrestrial Intelligence (SETI) program and its High Resolution Microwave Survey (HRMS) project, which began operations in 1992, were abruptly canceled by Congress in 1993 after sustaining some public ridicule by several members.[7] There is some evidence that SETI research is not dead at NASA, but it is extremely low-profile, embedded in

---

5. One can see this effect comparing the following headlines: Emi Kolawole, "Mars Rover Curiosity Takes First Sample of Soil on the Mars (photo)," *Washington Post* (8 October 2012), http://www.washingtonpost.com/blogs/innovations/post/mars-rover-curiosity-takes-first-sample-of-soil-on-the-red-planet-photo/2012/10/08/d08da152-1163-11e2-ba83-a7a396e6b2a7_blog.html (accessed 9 October 2012). and, Elizabeth Howell, "NASA's Perseverance Mars rover landing: Why do we keep going back to the Red Planet?" Space.com (18 February 2021), https://www.space.com/why-return-to-mars-perseverance-rover-landing (accessed 19 April 2021). For a positive spin on the cost of Curiosity, but also, more generally, planetary missions, see Casey Dreier, "Curiosity Comes Cheap—Why the Latest Mars Rover (and All Planetary Exploration) Is a Steal," *The Planetary Society* (9 August 2012), http://www.planetary.org/blogs/casey-dreier/20120809-curiosity-comes-cheap.html (accessed 9 October 2012).

6. The essential tension is the subject of Thomas Kuhn's first forays into his pursuit of the question of when scientific revolutions occur. See his *The Structure of Scientific Revolutions* (Chicago: University of Chicago Press, 1962). It is the conflict or tension between the established view of what physical reality is and the pressure exerted by newer evidence and theories.

7. Stephen J. Garber, "Searching for Good Science: the Cancellation of NASA's SETI Program," *Journal of the British Interplanetary Society* 52 (1999): 3–12.

Artist's concept of Kepler-186f, the first Earth-size planet in the habitable zone. (NASA Ames/SETI Institute/JPL-Caltech: PIA17999)

other programs including the Kepler mission to search for extrasolar planets, focusing especially on Earth-size planets in or near the habitable zone.[8]

What occurs within the space science community is a multi-track process in which the various broadly defined disciplinary communities within it work out a framework for establishing funding priorities while the human spaceflight community works on keeping a viable flight program alive. All of this activity occurs against a background of the primacy of human exploration on NASA's agenda. Conflicts occur at several levels: within the sub-disciplines of space science; among the major themes within space science, including planetary science, Earth science, heliophysics, and astrophysics; and between the scientific community and the human space exploration community.

Priorities arise within the space science community through decadal-survey recommendations, developed under the auspices of the National Research Council for NASA—a politicized process. What further complicates the process is that decadal surveys can, depending on the area they cover, address space-based and ground-based research projects. The astronomy and astrophysics decadal survey directly confronts this division—one currently exacerbated by cost overruns and schedule delays for NASA's James Webb Space Telescope (JWST). Fortunately for the JWST, the story of

---

8. *https://www.nasa.gov/mission_pages/kepler/overview/index.html* (accessed 8 August 2021).

its predecessor, the Hubble Space Telescope, with its problems but eventual triumph, provides support for pressing forward regardless of current problems because the science will be so productive. The politics here are driven by conflicting community interests and aggressive space science entrepreneurs who lobby for specific programs. Within NASA, those priorities are worked out in the context of specific missions (supposedly chosen based on their excellence and scientific value) to be funded at what rate. For example, the $2 billion Alpha Magnetic Spectrometer-02 (AMS-02), presently on the International Space Station, was an audacious experiment that absorbed resources and was behind schedule. What protected it in the end was its high cost. It was too costly to cancel. In addition, its extensive international team created political support beyond the usual suspects in the United States.[9]

Efforts to expand the funding "pie" for the space science community have occurred by pursuing several pathways. One has been to expand the amount of funding appropriated for such activities. Since the Apollo program, NASA has chronically defined itself as underfunded. For years, advocates for NASA have cited 1 percent of the federal budget as a necessary goal in order to sustain a robust space program. This is an overly optimistic perspective, based on what is now clearly a historical anomaly—the early years of the Apollo program (1964–67), when NASA's budget accounted for around 4 percent of the federal budget.[10]

The spaceflight community works to ensure that funding and commitments are supported in Congress and the executive branch to continue specific flight vehicles such as the Space Shuttle and various attempts at a successor. Given that NASA budgets are finite, sharp controversies occur over the rate and size of spaceflight funding. In times of need, the space science community is, in effect, taxed to support the more important—according to Agency leadership—human spaceflight endeavors. The latter can draw in Congress as members act to protect constituent interests in protecting jobs and companies. NASA leadership has sought presidential engagement to initiate and fund human spaceflight projects, but this approach has proven repeatedly to be a weak reed to rely on given other presidential priorities. NASA efforts have fallen on deaf ears in Congress and the White House.

---

9. *https://ams.nasa.gov/index.html*. The cost of this project is estimated at $2 billion. Tia Ghose, "Dark Matter Possibly Found by $2 Billion Space Experiment, *Space News*, 3 April 2013, *https://www.space.com/20490-dark-matter-discovery-space-experiment.html* (accessed 7 September 2021).

10. Perry D. Clark, "Viewpoint: One Percent for NASA, a Big Benefit for Humankind," *MLive.com*, 22 July 2011, updated 21 January 2019, *https://www.mlive.com/opinion/muskegon/2011/07/viewpoint_one_percent_for_nasa.html* (accessed 25 November 2020).

The second approach has been to slice the budget pie into thinner pieces, providing the illusion of a bigger program. NASA's "faster, better, cheaper" mantra of the 1990s was the most public version of this approach.[11] It was not a response aimed at expanding space science's share of the budget, but rather an effort to expand human spaceflight's share. By sending space science off to a cheaper realm, this approach enabled the human spaceflight side of the house to continue on a path of business as usual after NASA's 1993 crisis (see below).

CONFLICTING PRESSURES—NOT REINFORCING

Human spaceflight at NASA has been considered the public face of the U.S. space program since its inception, manifested in displays of astronauts for publicity purposes. The Mercury 7 were the prototype astronaut-heroes and remained so even as spaceflight became, in principle, more routine and safer. Two Shuttle losses during flight, one during liftoff and the other during reentry, returned an aura of extreme danger to the astronaut's public persona. The takeaway from these two tragedies was that human spaceflight is inherently dangerous and that NASA was committed to its continuation. Return to flight was not just a technical task but an absolute priority within the Agency. This human spaceflight focus has led to a series of abortive efforts at Shuttle replacement. A controversial analysis of these efforts suggests that $20 billion over 20 years was "wasted" or misspent.[12] From the perspective of the space science community, this commitment contrasts with the much smaller commitment to space science over a similar time period in which greater success was achieved. Post-Shuttle human space flight programs have floundered, thus far, due to cost factors and technical issues not solvable within expected budgets.

NASA leadership's vision is bounded by its relations with Congress, especially at the committee and subcommittee level (see figure 1), and the executive branch, especially the Office of Management and Budget (OMB). Public attention provides a constant backdrop to Agency leadership actions

---

11. Lt. Col. Dan Ward, "Faster, Better, Cheaper Revisited: Program Management Lessons from NASA," *Defense AT&L* (March–April 2010), https://apps.dtic.mil/dtic/tr/fulltext/u2/1016355.pdf (accessed 23 September 2012).
12. Marcia Smith, "Did NASA Really Waste $20 Billion in Cancelled Human Space Flight Programs?" *Space Policy Online*, 22 September 2012, http://www.spacepolicyonline.com/news/did-nasa-really-waste-20-billion-in-cancelled-human-space-flight-programs (accessed 9 October 2012). There is some dispute over whether the total cited is accurate, but the political point is made, given that the chart cited here is from a congressional website, *http://culberson.house.gov/reps-culberson-wolf-posey-and-olson-introduce-the-space-leadership-act/*.

and reactions. The operative assumption is that publicly visible failures will generate a decline in public support for the program. What is feared, or more disruptive, is members of Congress and their constituents. NASA Centers and JPL are significant local economic engines, so changes affecting them, especially declines in funding, generate intense congressional interest and backlash. These interests play out in the struggle over space science funding, where members from California and Maryland aggressively resist reprogramming funds from space science to support human spaceflight.

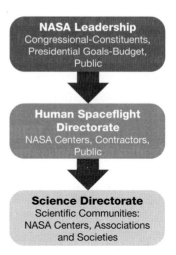

FIGURE 1. Major players.

A PATTERN OF BEHAVIOR

Conflict over resource allocation to space science and human spaceflight was muted in NASA's early days because of the newness of the field.[13] Scientists flocked to space science in pursuit of new opportunities. Within the space science field, this influx created some controversy as established space scientists (a small, intimate group) confronted demands from newcomers for access to funding and flight opportunities.[14] In addition, the newcomers challenged supposed cozy situations where established space scientists judged each other's work, creating an appearance of a closed shop. Meanwhile, NASA decided that it would run the space science enterprise through a Headquarters division or directorate. External players such as the National Research Council (NRC) and its Space Science (later Space Studies) Board (SSB), the National Science Foundation (NSF), and various disciplinary associations would operate in an advisory capacity. Internally, NASA reorganized the space science program several times in pursuit of maximum efficiency and responsiveness to upper-level management and to the science and engineering communities that actually implemented the program.

One early decision was to have a scientist and an engineer fill the two top slots at NASA. This decision reflected the reality that space science involves

---

13. For a more intimate and detailed analysis of the early years, see Homer E. Newell, *Beyond the Atmosphere: Early Years of Space Science* (Washington, DC: NASA SP-4211, 1980).
14. John E. Naugle and John M. Logsdon, "Space Science: Origins, Evolution, and Organization," in *Exploring the Unknown: Selected Documents in the History of the U.S. Civil Space Program*, ed. John M. Logsdon, vol. 5, *Exploring the Cosmos* (Washington, DC: NASA SP-4407, 2001), pp. 8–15.

both science and technology. A failure to understand science and technology requirements for a mission could result in disaster. Also, early on, it became clear that as space science disciplines evolved away from their terrestrial roots, space science projects were becoming a bit of a gamble. If a mission failed, it was unlikely to be repeated quickly, meaning that scientists working on it over years or decades might have only one shot at conducting the experiments they saw as essential for advancing knowledge. In the earliest days, some of NASA's planetary missions often launched in pairs—such as Vikings 1 and 2 and Voyagers 1 and 2—doubling the chance of a data return. Reorientation or diversion of space science program funding could turn a subdiscipline into a virtual intellectual desert for a generation, as ambitious newcomers either chose not to enter the field or moved off into other areas.

Concurrent with the startup of the space science arm of the Agency, the Apollo program announced by President John F. Kennedy in May 1961 was already under way. With NASA virtually on a war footing, it meant that budgets were ample, at least for a time. The impact of Apollo on the space science program was real. JPL, for example, was tasked with landing (actually crash-landing) on the lunar surface to assess the composition of the Moon rather than pursuing its preferred mission of studying Mars or Venus. JPL's lunar odyssey involved a series of missions that failed for an assortment of reasons (see chapter 14). JPL's lunar craft carried television cameras rather than scientific equipment. The focus of these missions was on identifying landing locations for Apollo missions.[15] Even more telling was the fact that the Apollo landings on the lunar surface did not produce the flow of scientific data that some expected. Astronaut Harrison Schmitt, a trained geologist, was the only scientist to fly on an Apollo mission (17, the last). The last two planned Apollo missions, with significant science components, were canceled. For space science, Apollo was a diversion, although some science was accomplished once Apollo requirements had been met. The later Ranger missions photographed areas of interest to science. What was clear during and after Apollo was the relative priorities of science and human spaceflight as reflected in their relative shares of the NASA budget.

The end of the Apollo program left human spaceflight in danger. NASA's Apollo Applications program, established in 1968 to develop science-based human spaceflight missions using hardware developed for the Apollo program, depended on the Saturn 5, which was determined to be too expensive for use in future missions. The Skylab missions in the early 1970s, along

---

15. Amy Paige Snyder, "NASA and Planetary Exploration," in Logsdon, *Exploring the Unknown*, vol. 5, pp. 272–277.

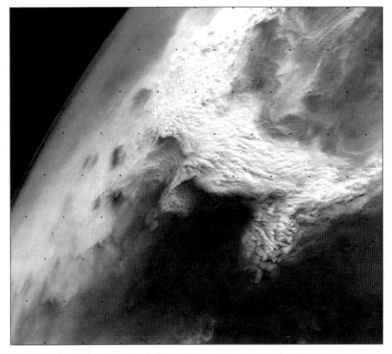

FIGURE 2. Viking Orbiter 2 image of a large dust storm over the Thaumasia region on Mars. (NASA/JPL: PIA02985)

with the Apollo-Soyuz Test Project, were the dying embers of Apollo.[16] NASA's prime directive became getting a follow-on human spaceflight program approved. In 1969, President Richard Nixon rejected human spaceflight recommendations from his Space Task Group on cost grounds. After much skirmishing, in January 1971 President Nixon approved the Space Shuttle Program, only one component of the Task Group's recommendations. The Space Shuttle was conceived as transportation to and from a low-Earth-orbit space station. Nixon rejected the space station proposal.[17]

The 1970s turned out to be a "golden age" for space science at NASA as planetary missions reached out to Mars, Venus, and the outer planets. Major successes of this period include the Viking mission to Mars. Viking's search

---

16. "Skylab: 1973–1974," *https://historycollection.jsc.nasa.gov/JSCHistoryPortal/history/skylab.htm* (accessed 25 November 2020); "Apollo-Soyuz Test Project," *https://www.nasa.gov/mission_pages/apollo-soyuz/index.html* (accessed 25 November 2020).

17. Space Task Group, "The Post-Apollo Space Program: Directions for the Future, September 1969." A truncated portion can be seen at *http://www.hq.nasa.gov/office/pao/History/taskgrp.html* (accessed 23 September 2012).

for life was unsuccessful, but the mission yielded tremendous amounts of data, including observations of Martian seasons. Another success was the Voyager program, which sent two spacecraft on a "grand tour" of the outer planets. They are still heading into interstellar space.[18] Other missions flew to Venus, Saturn, and Jupiter. All of these mission successes suggested that the future for space science was bright.

Unfortunately, Space Shuttle development was absorbing more resources than expected because the Shuttle Main Engine and the heat shield tiles for the Shuttle were proving difficult to develop. These cost overruns were devastating because it was clear, given the economics of the day—hyperinflation and economic slowdown—that additional funding was not to be had. NASA leadership pursued several angles in order to overcome the funding shortfall. After some lobbying, President Jimmy Carter was persuaded to establish as national policy that all U.S. government payloads would fly on the Space Shuttle.[19] This decision was seen as securing the Shuttle's future by keeping the flight volume up, allowing greater efficiency. Fixed costs would be amortized over more flights. In addition, the Shuttle would also carry domestic commercial payloads. The only challenger to the Shuttle's monopoly was the European Ariane expendable launch vehicles. Arianes had limited payload capacity. At the same time, modern communication satellites were growing in size, requiring larger boosters to get to orbit. The impact of Carter's decision was that all space science payloads would have to be compatible with human missions to and in orbit. This decision magnified the cost of science missions, a cost seen as unnecessary by the space science community. Meanwhile, the U.S. Air Force bitterly resisted any attempt to totally end its expendable launch vehicle (ELV) program. The Air Force wanted to maintain control over its access to space, and there was the fear of a single-point failure if the Shuttle fleet was grounded for any reason.

With the 1980 presidential election, Ronald Reagan came to office with a mandate to reduce nondefense federal spending. His budget director, David Stockman, proposed a significant cut in the NASA budget, $604 million, effectively reducing it by about 10 percent, meaning all new starts were killed off except for the Galileo mission to Jupiter.[20] The following year

---

18. "Viking Mission to Mars," *http://nssdc.gsfc.nasa.gov/planetary/viking.html* (accessed 23 September 2012); "Voyager: The Interstellar Mission," *http://voyager.jpl.nasa.gov/* (accessed 23 September 2012).
19. Presidential Directives 37 and 42: *https://www.jimmycarterlibrary.gov/research/presidential_directives* (accessed 8 August 2021).
20. Galileo Legacy Site, *http://solarsystem.nasa.gov/galileo/* (accessed 23 September 2012).

saw catastrophe.[21] NASA Administrator James Beggs announced that the Agency "would be willing to eliminate its solar system exploration program altogether as long as the Space Shuttle and other space projects retained adequate funding."[22] The Hubble Space Telescope survived cuts, along with Galileo, after much debate and politics. The newly established Planetary Society arose in defense of space science since it was clear that NASA leadership's agenda was to advance human spaceflight before all else.

Space science thus entered an awkward era in which missions and vehicles grew larger and larger—becoming, in the words of one critic, "Christmas trees," loaded with multiple and possibly incompatible instruments. The explanation was simple: because space science missions now had to be human-rated, their costs grew.

Sadly, the Shuttle program encountered a major crisis when the orbiter Challenger exploded during liftoff on 28 January 1986. NASA leadership subsequently maintained a singular focus on "return to flight." This crisis in human spaceflight had implications for space science in several ways. Unlike the 1970s, the 1980s were a lost decade for science missions. Only Magellan—a Venus radar mission—and Galileo were launched during that decade, both by the Shuttle in 1989. The Hubble Space Telescope had to wait until 1990 for its launch on the Shuttle.

The real budgetary crisis for space science came after another human spaceflight initiative, the space station, got under way. Since Nixon's 1972 decision approving the Shuttle development, NASA had aggressively pursued the space station as the next logical step. The Space Shuttle was intended to be a construction and heavy-lifting vehicle, not a test bed for science experiments. Orbiters could be refitted for long-duration missions but were incapable of leaving low-Earth orbit for exploration. Supplying the space station was the Space Shuttle's mission, but there was no space station to supply. In 1984, over objections from his staff, President Ronald Reagan proposed in his State of the Union address to start a space station program. The initial proposal was for an $8 billion project to be operational in 1992. Neither happened. As the space station ran through a series of budget projections and redesigns that went in opposite directions, the budget went up and the number of missions for it went down.[23]

---

21. Roger Handberg, *Reinventing NASA: Human Spaceflight, Bureaucracy, and Politics* (Westport, CT: Praeger, 2003), pp. 60–61.
22. Snyder, "NASA and Planetary Exploration," pp. 290–291.
23. Handberg, *Reinventing NASA*, chapter 4.

By 1993, a crisis arose over burgeoning cost overruns for the space station and Shuttle programs. Funding issues grew so serious that some analyses predicted that human spaceflight could consume NASA's entire budget. In 1991, this concern had led to an unprecedented public attack on the space station by 14 science associations such as the American Physical Society. Their objections arose in response to budget caps negotiated between President George H. W. Bush and Democrats in Congress.[24] This deal gave President Bush enormous difficulties inside the Republican Party since it combined tax increases with the budget caps. It especially infuriated conservative Republicans, since Bush had famously told them, "Read my lips, no new taxes," at the 1988 Republican National Convention.[25]

The cost of NASA's human spaceflight program precipitated a political crisis in 1993 when, in a continuing debate over appropriations, the Superconducting Super Collider and space station projects were subjected to up-or-down votes. The space station survived by one vote in the House of Representatives, while the Collider was shut down. Why one survived and the other did not is a subject of some debate. The strongest explanation was that NASA had distributed contracts for the space station nationwide, ensuring a broad constituency, while the Collider was essentially a Texas-Louisiana program.[26]

The result of these conflicts was that the space station and Space Shuttle programs were reorganized in an attempt to reduce costs. Space Station Alpha, renamed Space Station Freedom in the last years of the Reagan administration, was yet again redesigned and was recast as a component of U.S. foreign policy. The Clinton administration–era redesign, eventually renamed the International Space Station (ISS),[27] was smaller and included the Russian Federation as a partner for several reasons. Russian space technology was first-class and cheap, and it provided jobs for Russian engineers and scientists who might otherwise be tempted to leave Russia, taking their knowledge of militarily significant space technology with them. NASA handed off the Space Shuttle Program to a Boeing–Lockheed Martin joint venture called the United Space Alliance, which would manage Shuttle

---

24. Eliot Marshall, "Tilting at the Space Station," *Science* (19 July 1991): 256–258.
25. *http://www.ontheissues.org/celeb/George_Bush_Sr__Tax_Reform.htm* (accessed 30 September 2012).
26. Roger Handberg, "Congress, Constituency, and Jobs: The Superconducting Super Collider, the Space Station and National Science Policy," *Technology in Society* 23 (2001): 177–194.
27. Roger Handberg, "The Fluidity of Presidential Policy Choice: The Space Station, the Russian Card, and U.S. Foreign Policy," *Technology in Society* 20 (1998): 421–439.

refurbishment and flight preparation. The objective of these changes was to improve NASA's control over human spaceflight spending and thus facilitate other Agency activities, including space science and aeronautics, the latter being particularly important to international competitiveness.

When the Mars Observer spacecraft, launched on a Titan III ELV, was lost in 1993, NASA's Mars program hit a dead end. There was no money available to fly another mission of similar profile, given that the Mars Observer was a billion-dollar program. Mars Observer had been freed from the earlier requirement of human rating, but the mission reflected the dominance that requirement had over space science at the time.

For space science missions, NASA Administrator Daniel Goldin pushed for a new approach called "faster, better, cheaper." The goal of this approach was to reverse the trend of science missions growing larger and more expensive, the abortive Mars Observer mission being one much-cited example.[28] "Faster, better, cheaper" science mission programs initiated at NASA included the Discovery program in 1992, the New Millennium program in 1995, an expanded Mars exploration program with a mission planned every two years, and the Origins program. According to NASA:

> Through Goldin's aggressive management reforms, annual budgets have been reduced, producing a $40 billion reduction from prior budget plans. He implemented a more balanced aeronautics and space program by reducing human space flight funding from 48 percent of NASA's total budget to 38 percent and increasing funding for science and aerospace technology from 31 to 43 percent....
>
> Goldin also cut the time required to develop Earth- and space-science spacecraft by 40 percent and reduced the cost by two-thirds, while increasing the average number of missions launched per year about four times. During the same time, Space Shuttle costs were reduced by about a third, while all safety indicators and mission capabilities have achieved significant improvements.[29]

The point of the "faster, better, cheaper" exercise was cost control. The reality was more brutal. ISS cost overruns were growing, despite the fact that expenditures were supposed to be capped based on the Bush-Congress tax-and-cap deal. Through the 1990s, a resurgence in space science occurred

---

28. The discussion here draws heavily from Handberg, *Reinventing NASA*, chapter 6, and Snyder, "NASA and Planetary Exploration," pp. 294–298.
29. "Daniel Saul Goldin," NASA History Office, *http://history.nasa.gov/dan_goldin.html* (accessed 30 September 2012).

thanks to the Discovery program and the revitalized Mars exploration effort. The Hubble Space Telescope was repaired, opening new vistas for astronomers and astrophysicists probing questions related to the origins of the universe and the potential for life on other planets.[30]

Astronomy was not immune to budget pressures at NASA. Activity had picked up during the 1960s through the Apollo Applications Program's Apollo Astronomy Mount (AAM). Astronauts were to operate the telescope. The applications program was canceled just as Apollo reached its crescendo. The AAM flew on Skylab missions, but for astronomers that event was passé. Their view was that humans only complicated operations and could not match a robotically operated telescope that could conduct long-duration observations.

NASA's space-based Great Observatories were designed to be deployed by the Space Shuttle, a supposedly cheaper alternative to expendable launch vehicles. Instead, Shuttle launches added to the high costs of these missions. The Great Observatories covered much of the electromagnetic spectrum: the Compton Gamma Ray Observatory, the Chandra X-ray Observatory, the optical Hubble Space Telescope, and the infrared Spitzer Space Telescope. Only Spitzer flew to orbit on a Delta rocket.[31]

Earth science was a continuing priority but was swamped at times by the gold-rush attitude about the Apollo program. However, photos taken of the lunar surface provided support for the idea of creating images of land masses on Earth.[32] Space-based observation of Earth has major military, economic, and social potential, which created an artificial schism in how Earth observation was approached. The military, with its early warning and reconnaissance missions, pursued acquiring the most precise images possible, down to the centimeter in accuracy. Ironically, since the mid-1990s some of the military's earliest observations, acquired by the National Reconnaissance Office, have been declassified for use in long-term environmental monitoring studies. NASA's Earth Resources Technology Satellite (ERTS), launched in 1972 and later renamed Landsat 1, was restricted from acquiring such precise images, as were weather satellites at that time, for national security reasons. These resolution restrictions continued until the end of the Cold War, when

---

30. Nancy Grace Roman, "Exploring the Universe: Space-Based Astronomy and Astrophysics," in Logsdon, *Exploring the Unknown*, vol. 5, pp. 501–545.
31. Ibid. pp. 532–541.
32. John H. McElroy and Ray A. Williamson, "The Evolution of Earth Science Research from Space: NASA's Earth Observing System," in *Exploring the Unknown*, ed. John M. Logsdon, vol. 6, *Space and Earth* Sciences, pp. 441–473.

they were gradually lifted in response to commercial pressure for higher-resolution imagery. NASA Earth science missions became controversial as they were gradually pulled into the debate over environmental change, especially questions of climate change. The George H. W. Bush administration sought to build a large-scale program in 1991 called Mission to Planet Earth, involving flying multiple missions to assess various facets of Earth's environment. Pursuing this initiative—"dedicated to understanding the total Earth system and the effects of natural and human-induced changes on the global environment"[33]—meant pushing off any need to take a position that might adversely affect the President's position within the Republican Party while providing political cover at that year's United Nations Conference on Environment and Development (UNCED) in Rio de Janeiro.[34]

By 2001, NASA had returned to its former situation of budget overruns in the human spaceflight program, and the bow wave had become too large to be ignored. The George W. Bush administration reacted by cutting ISS funding again, this time by eliminating a crew return vehicle; canceling the joint NASA-DOD X-33 and X-34 next-generation launch vehicle programs; and further reducing ISS capabilities. NASA's ISS partners rejected the latter decision since the reduction would mean that their research modules would never be flown to the ISS and employed for research. Matters came to a head on 1 February 2003, when the orbiter Columbia broke up during reentry, killing seven crewmembers. The Space Shuttle Program entered its final stages as the Columbia Accident Investigation Board stated that the Shuttle was an experimental vehicle whose continued flight was problematic. The Agency was able to restart Shuttle flight in July 2007, but it was now on a pathway to Shuttle Program shutdown.

In January 2004, President George W. Bush announced the Vision for Space Exploration (VSE), a long-term program aimed at returning humans to the Moon and ultimately sending people to Mars. A lunar base would become a test bed for long-duration stays in outer space. NASA stood up a Constellation program to develop the Ares 1 expendable launch vehicle and the Orion crew vehicle. Subsequently, a heavy cargo lifter, the Ares 5, would be built to move large quantities of equipment and supplies to Earth orbit for departure to the Moon and other locations. Another program, Prometheus, was established to develop nuclear propulsion for missions to the outer

---

33. Mission to Planet Earth, *http://www.hq.nasa.gov/office/nsp/mtpe.htm* (accessed 24 September 2012).
34. United Nations Conference on Environment and Development, Rio de Janeiro, 3–14 June 1992, *https://www.un.org/en/conferences/environment/rio1992* (accessed 25 November 2020).

planets. The Space Shuttle Program was to shut down in fall 2010 once ISS construction was complete. NASA would abandon the ISS in 2016. The plan was to shift funding required for the Shuttle Program and the ISS Program to the new Ares rockets and the Orion capsule. With insufficient political support for an Apollo-scale effort, funding for new programs would have to come from existing programs. One effect of these decisions was to focus NASA science funding on areas directly supporting the human spaceflight effort. This situation was similar to the one that occurred in the 1960s when support of the Apollo program was the priority to which space science had to adapt. Early betting was on a "new series of orbiters and landers" for the Moon, and for Mars an "additional 2009 mission, 2011 lander, and sample return."[35] NASA's European and Japanese ISS partners got their Columbus and Kibo modules lifted to the ISS while a continuing controversy over launching the AMS-02 particle-physics detector experiment to the ISS was finally resolved in 2011.

By the time of the arrival of President Barack Obama's administration in January 2009, the Constellation program was behind schedule and over budget. Given growing national economic difficulties, NASA was under pressure to get costs in line. The Obama administration established an expert committee (known as the Augustine Committee, after its chairman Norman Augustine) to review NASA's human spaceflight program. Its report in October 2009 described the Constellation program as untenable due to costs and schedule delays and insufficient political support to fix the program's problems.[36] Meanwhile, the ISS approached completion, with NASA clearly losing control over the Station due to the termination of Space Shuttle flights and consequent dependence on Russia for access to the ISS. One sign of this changed situation was the extension of the ISS lifespan from 2016 to 2020, possibly 2028. Other partners in the ISS felt that the money they had invested in the project would be wasted if it were to be terminated in 2016.

The Augustine Committee's recommendation was for the United States to finish out its tenure on the ISS and restart the quest for a Shuttle replacement for use in exploration beyond LEO, possibly to an asteroid or some other locations. Returning to the Moon was not a priority, although it could be one option. The Ares 1 flew one partial test and was shut down, while work on the Orion spacecraft was to be recycled into what became known

---

35. Andrew Lawler, "Scientists Fear Collateral Damage from NASA's Revised Vision," *Science* 303 (26 March 2004): 1952–1953.
36. Review of the U.S. Human Spaceflight Plans Committee, *Seeking a U.S. Spaceflight Program Worthy of a Great Nation* (Washington, DC: NASA, October 2009).

as the Space Launch System (SLS). The SLS was to become the U.S. ticket to explore beyond LEO. It might service the ISS, but that was not the SLS mission. Quite the contrary, it was to go outward. What made the debate in 2009–11 more raucous is that the issue of constituent jobs became an even stronger priority in Congress given the economic recession. Also, there was a split in the congressional space coalition. Members with space launch constituencies were the most vocal, demanding that the administration move quickly to replace the Space Shuttle. Others, such as Senators Barbara Boxer (D-CA) and Barbara Mikulski (D-MD) were aggressive in protecting their constituents at JPL and Goddard Space Flight Center. It was clear that NASA was going to shed a significant portion of its contractor workforce with no immediate prospects of return. After the Apollo shutdown, most contractors at Kennedy Space Center (KSC), for example, had disappeared for a time, but there was a clear expectation that the Shuttle Program would return workers to the local economy, whereas NASA's Marshall Space Flight Center and Johnson Space Center were more sheltered because their role was preparing for the Shuttle. Congressional antagonism toward the Obama administration inflamed NASA budget negotiations. In December 2010, agreement was reached that the SLS would proceed while the commercial sector would be challenged, with government support, to handle crew and payload launches to the ISS and LEO. Commercial crew and cargo service is now underway.

For space science missions of any type, the federal deficit plus political antagonisms make planning and implementation difficult. Continuing constraints on NASA's budget raise the prospect of severe disruption of research across all space science disciplines.

WHAT DOES IT MEAN?

Space science is clearly an important part of NASA's mission, but it cannot be the Agency's top priority given the hold that human spaceflight has on NASA leadership and the public. Space science is a public good, while human exploration is said to be more than that—an expression of the human spirit, according to some views. Congress—especially members who have a NASA facility located in their district or state—remains focused on constituent jobs as priority number one, with little concern about the content of those jobs. The public is impressed by space activities, but not so much that these activities rank ahead of other social priorities. Space science has attempted to rally the troops with regards to fending off funding cuts in support of the human spaceflight program. Their tools include the National Academy of Sciences' decadal surveys.[37] These outside interventions are often important in guiding future program development, but when budgets go down, these reports are not definitive.

From the perspective of the human spaceflight program, space science remains a passenger that helps justify missions, but it is not terribly important otherwise. For example, life sciences projects have been passengers on the ISS from the beginning, though with budget cuts they are among the first to go. Those science projects clearly have only one purpose from the perspective of Agency leadership: to justify having a crewmember present to run an experiment that in many cases could be turned on from Earth as happens in other situations.

It may be time to reconsider where space science should be located in government. With NASA now out of the business of running a space taxi service, the Agency might do well to focus on the deep exploration program that it has longed for, at least rhetorically. The Space Shuttle Program was a distraction because it focused the Agency on maintaining a delivery schedule. NASA human spaceflight officials are already suggesting that the SLS might carry some space science missions beyond LEO. Space science needs some leverage in decision-making, which it presently does not possess.

The argument after the Challenger disaster was that Agency leadership had been obsessed with avoiding what they perceived as embarrassing launch delays. With SLS development as a priority at NASA, space science could become a partner in exploration beyond LEO. But such a step might require spinning off space science from NASA to NSF or the National Academy of Sciences. Both agencies had made runs at becoming the nation's space science agency in the early days of the space program but lost out to congressional "pork" politics. NASA facilities were established in the districts or states of congressional leaders such as then–Senate Majority Leader Lyndon Johnson. The Apollo program was a second Tennessee Valley Authority for southern states that did not benefit the first time around. The other reason they lost was the hold the von Braun model of space exploration held over the discussions of how to organize the space program, with the military seen as leading expeditions to explore new worlds.

---

37. One example is the Committee on a Decadal Strategy for Solar and Space Physics (Heliophysics) *Solar and Space Physics: A Science for a Technological Society* (Washington, DC: National Research Council, National Academy of Sciences, 2012).

PART III
The Lure of the Red Planet

THE FIRST 50 YEARS of Mars exploration at NASA were marked by great successes—such as the twin Viking orbiter/lander missions, the Mars Exploration Rovers Spirit and Opportunity, and the Mars Science Laboratory (a.k.a. Curiosity)—and costly failures—such as the loss of the Mars Observer, Mars Climate Orbiter, and Mars Polar Lander missions in the 1990s. This period was also marked by tension between robotic and human exploration plans for Mars, between Moon and Mars exploration plans, between Big Science and the "faster, better, cheaper" approach. Funding for Mars exploration has waxed and waned over the years, as have NASA's international partnerships for missions to the Red Planet.

The next two chapters in this volume address two critical aspects of NASA's plans for Mars exploration: the importance of sample return and the interplay between science and politics.

Historian Erik Conway documents NASA's decades of planning for a mission to collect samples of Mars and bring them back to Earth. Mars sample return has been a top priority in the space science community for 40 years. Conway explains how and why the science community identified Mars sample return as a top goal and considers why it has been as yet unachievable. That said, NASA's Mars 2020 mission, launched in summer 2020, is designed to cache samples that are intended to be retrieved by a future sample-return mission. NASA's fiscal year 2020 budget request included $109 million for a Mars sample-return mission, proposed to be launched as early as 2026.

Artist's concept of the proposed Mars Sample Return mission. (NASA/JPL: PIA05488)

Mission architectures for Mars sample return are, and always have been, as Conway notes, "complex, technologically challenging, and expensive." In his chapter, he documents the evolution of Mars sample-return mission architectures from the 1970s to 2012. Getting to Mars has always been the easy part; containing Mars samples in a pristine state, getting them off the surface of Mars, and returning them to Earth has always been the hard part. Given the cost and complexity of such a mission, Conway points out that planning for Mars sample return is now necessarily an international endeavor. The latest mission architecture has been offered by the joint NASA–European Space Agency (ESA) International Mars Analysis of Returned Samples Working Group, which published a draft architecture and science management plan for the return of samples from Mars in 2018.[1]

Political scientist Henry Lambright explores what he calls "the disconnect between the long-term perspective of scientists and the short-term perspective of politicians." In his chapter, he documents the role of the NASA Administrator in setting goals and objectives for Mars exploration, starting with Dan Goldin (1992–2001) and ending with Charlie Bolden (2009–17), showing how Administrators must negotiate between the sometimes oppositional cultures of science and politics.

---

1. T. Haltigin, C. Lange, R. Mugnuolo, and C. Smith, "A Draft Mission Architecture and Science Management Plan for the Return of Samples from Mars: Phase 2 Report of the International Mars Architecture for the Return of Samples (iMARS) Working Group," *Astrobiology* 18, suppl. 1 (1 April 2018): S-1–S-131, *https://doi.org/10.1089/ast.2018.29027. mars*, 2018.

Goldin's successor Sean O'Keefe was a public administrator (a "bean-counter" by some accounts) who had served in the White House Office of Management and Budget and the Department of the Navy and was a protégé of Vice President Dick Cheney. Subsequent Administrator Mike Griffin "was the consummate rocket engineer," Lambright writes, and a strong advocate for human exploration.

Goldin, who is NASA's longest-serving Administrator to date, is best known for his advocacy of a "faster, better, cheaper" approach to space exploration, which affected NASA's plans for the robotic exploration of Mars. During his tenure, he had to deal with the loss of three missions to Mars and the frenzy that broke out in 1996 after NASA researchers claimed they had found fossil evidence of microbial life in a Martian meteorite. He reconfigured NASA's Mars exploration program to "follow the water" and established an astrobiology research program, reasserting the Agency's interest in the search for evidence of extraterrestrial life in the solar system. (NASA's Astrobiology program is now focused on contributing instruments and experiments to missions that will explore potentially habitable environments in the solar system.)

O'Keefe was in charge of responding to President George W. Bush's Vision for Space Exploration, a proposal to send humans back to the Moon and then on to Mars. Lambright writes that O'Keefe "made Mars science a priority at the expense of other science programs." Griffin, who had headed NASA's Space Exploration Initiative Office in the late 1980s, took over implementation of the Moon-Mars program, emphasizing plans for human missions and also making a hard decision to delay the launch of the Mars Science Laboratory for two years.

Charlie Bolden, President Barack Obama's appointee to head NASA, was an ex-astronaut, a retired Marine major general, and the Agency's first African American Administrator. Bolden had to oversee the Obama administration's stand-down of Bush's Moon-Mars program, reconfigure NASA's plans for human and robotic exploration of Mars, and develop Obama's Asteroid Initiative, which featured a plan to bring an asteroid into the vicinity of the Moon's orbit and send astronauts to explore it. The Trump administration canceled plans for a human mission to an asteroid. However, NASA's Near-Earth Observations program, which had been made a key element of the Asteroid Initiative and consequently received a larger budget, remains in operation, with its larger budget intact.

NASA's Mars Science Laboratory mission, launched in 2011, landed the Curiosity rover on the Red Planet on 5 August 2012. At the time of this writing, Curiosity had been exploring the surface of Mars for seven years. The mission's experiments are focused on answering this question: Did Mars ever have the right environmental conditions to support microbial life?

On 18 November 2013, NASA launched its Mars Atmosphere and Volatile EvolutioN (MAVEN) mission, which entered Mars orbit on 22 September 2014. MAVEN, which was still conducting science operations at the time of this writing, was designed explore the Red Planet's upper atmosphere, ionosphere, and interactions with the Sun and solar wind.

On 14 March 2016, the European Space Agency launched its ExoMars Trace Gas Orbiter to Mars, arriving on 16 October 2016. On 5 May 2018, NASA launched its Interior Exploration using Seismic Investigations, Geodesy, and Heat Transport (InSight) mission to Mars. InSight, developed by the Jet Propulsion Laboratory, is the first robotic planetary explorer designed to study in depth the "inner space" of Mars: its crust, mantle, and core. NASA's Mars 2020 mission and ESA's ExoMars 2020 rover mission to Mars will continue our exploration of the Red Planet.

Also at the time of this writing, in addition to these recent missions, three workhorse missions were still conducting science operations at Mars: NASA's Mars Odyssey orbiter, in operation since 2001 (now NASA's longest-lasting spacecraft at Mars); ESA's Mars Express orbiter, which arrived at the Red Planet in December 2003; and NASA's Mars Reconnaissance Orbiter, in operation since 2006.

At the time of this writing, NASA was responding to the Trump administration's directive to return people to the Moon by 2024 and to send people to Mars by 2033. Politics likely will sort out NASA's Mars priorities: scientific exploration, sample return, and human missions. Both of the chapters in this section shine a light on the vagaries of politics—both outside and inside NASA.

CHAPTER 4

Designing Mars Sample Return, from Viking to the Mars Science Laboratory[1]

Erik M. Conway

EVEN BEFORE NASA'S twin Viking landers made their way to the surface of Mars, planetary scientists wanted to acquire samples and send them back to Earth. In the first post-Viking "decadal survey" of priorities for exploring the inner planets, conducted by the National Academy of Sciences' Committee on Planetary and Lunar Exploration (COMPLEX), Mars sample return was advertised as the proper means of investigating "questions the answer to which are less dependent on the locale of the investigation, but more on the sophistication of the techniques that can be brought to bear."[2] Chaired by California Institute of Technology meteorite specialist Gerry Wasserberg, this 1978 COMPLEX study framed the ambitions of planetary scientists into the present day. The National Academy's 2011 decadal survey of priorities in planetary science, chaired by Cornell University astronomer Steven Squyres, made a Mars sample-return mission (called "MAX-C," for Mars Astrobiology Explorer-Cacher) its number-one priority for 2013–22.[3]

---

1. Portions of this chapter have appeared in Erik M. Conway, *Exploration and Engineering: The Jet Propulsion Laboratory and the Quest for Mars* (Baltimore: Johns Hopkins University Press, 2015).
2. National Research Council, *Scientific Exploration of the Inner Planets: 1977–1987* (Washington DC: National Academies Press, 1978), p. 36, *https://doi.org/10.17226/12379*.
3. National Research Council, *Vision and Voyages for Planetary Science in the Decade 2013–2022* (Washington, DC: National Academies Press, 2011), p. 4, *https://doi.org/10.17226/13117*.

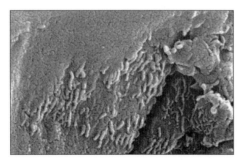

Electron microscope image showing microscopic tube-like structures within ALH84001, a fragment of a Martian meteorite found in Antarctica. (NASA/JSC: S96-12299)

Between those two studies, more than three decades apart, there have been a multiplicity of design studies for Mars sample-return missions. All of these studies have evolved architectures that are complex, technologically challenging, and expensive. And none has yet come to fruition. The closest NASA has come to sample-return is the Mars Science Laboratory/Curiosity mission, initially conceived of as a sample-return rover. As flown, it was intended to demonstrate heavy payload capacity and precision landing for a Mars sample-return campaign planned for the late 2010s and early 2020s.

DREAMING OF SAMPLES FROM MARS

This desire for Mars sample return has remained stable, and perhaps even grown stronger, despite the scientific community's inability to actually get, and keep, the mission "sold" to NASA and, perhaps more importantly, to the White House Office of Management and Budget. The push for Mars sample return persists despite the equally strong belief in the scientific community that Earth already holds samples of Mars, in the form of meteorites collected in Antarctica. One in particular, Allen Hills meteorite ALH-8401, has even been asserted by some NASA scientists to contain evidence of life on Mars—hotly disputed evidence, to be sure, but those disputes have not called into question the meteorite's origin.[4] It is widely accepted to have come to Earth from Mars, spalled off the Red Planet by some titanic collision, probably millions of years ago.

During the decades that planetary scientists have dreamed of sample return, NASA has undergone great changes. Its share of the federal budget has shrunk dramatically, from 4.5 percent in its peak year, 1964, to 0.45 percent in 2011.[5] It built, operated, and then retired its Space Transportation System, popularly called the Shuttle. It also built and continues to operate

---

4. Kathy Sawyer tells this story well in *The Rock from Mars: A Detective Story on Two Planets* (New York: Random House, 2006).
5. NASA Office of Inspector General, Office of Audits, "NASA's Challenges to Meeting Cost, Schedule and Performance Goals," report no. IG-12-021, 27 September 2012, p. 8.

the International Space Station, with a coalition of foreign partners, relying on Russian launch vehicles for transportation after repeated failures to develop its own Shuttle replacement. The Agency has seen human expeditions to Mars and to the Moon proposed and then canceled due to lack of political interest. Where once NASA could draw on the Cold War rhetoric of competition with the Soviet Union as justification for an expansive program of exploration, that rhetoric had become ineffective by the 1980s, if not earlier, and the Agency now struggles to justify funding for its human spaceflight ambitions.

Space enthusiasts like to paint NASA as "exceptional," having a grand mission to fulfill that should exempt it from the normal political give-and-take in Washington, but it has never been like that.[6] It has to compete with other elements of government for congressional votes and dollars, without the large geographic or social constituencies possessed by most other federal agencies.[7] And for the last few decades, NASA has failed to play the political game sufficiently well to fund human spaceflight and robotic science without substantial impacts (see figure 1). One impact is obvious. The Agency now must rely on foreign partners to sustain the International Space Station, due to five separate failures to obtain sufficient funds to complete a new human-rated U.S. launch vehicle.[8] Another is less so. In its efforts to protect, let alone expand, its human program, NASA has repeatedly curtailed the ambitions of its scientific program. One victim, though not the only one, has been Mars sample return. Plans for sample return were canceled in 1991, 2000, and 2011.

Each sample-return study has provided the technical basis for those that followed it, and some of the flown (but not specifically sample-return–oriented) Mars missions have contributed technical knowledge that has in turn altered engineers' assessment of sample-return architectures. The result has been a gradual, intermittent improvement in the technical capacity to perform a Mars sample-return mission. But that improving technological base has not led to improved chances of funding. While NASA is

---

6. Roger D. Launius and Howard McCurdy, "Epilogue: Beyond NASA Exceptionalism," in *Spaceflight and the Myth of Presidential Leadership*, ed. Roger D. Launius and Howard McCurdy (Chicago: University of Illinois Press, 1997), pp. 221–244.
7. Richard S. Conley and Wendy Whitman Cobb, "Presidential Vision or Congressional Derision? Explaining Budgeting Outcomes for NASA, 1958–2008," *Congress & the Presidency* 39 (2012): 51–73.
8. These were President Ronald Reagan's National Aerospace Plane; President George H. W. Bush's National Launch System; President Bill Clinton's X-43 "VentureStar" public-private partnership with Lockheed; another Clinton initiative, the Orbital Space Plane; and President George W. Bush's Ares.

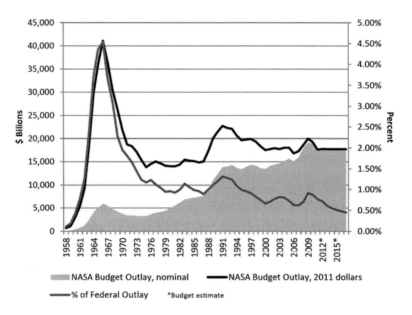

FIGURE 1. Historical NASA budget as a percentage of the federal budget. From NASA Office of the Inspector General, "NASA's Challenges to Meeting Cost, Schedule, and Performance Goals," 27 September 2012.

closer to having the technical capacity to carry out this longstanding scientific goal than it has ever been, it is less able to carry it out than it was just a handful of years ago.

EARLY VISIONS OF MARS SAMPLE RETURN, 1978 TO 1993

In a 1974 study, the Space Science Board (SSB) had argued for Mars sample return as a long-term goal, a stance rejected by COMPLEX in 1978. The point of dispute was whether sample return should be seen as an end in itself or merely one technique to be used in a more comprehensive program of exploration. COMPLEX argued that both in situ research—science performed from orbit or on the surface of Mars—and returned samples were necessary: "A minimal base of information is necessary to guide the choice of a sample to define and address substantial and important scientific questions in a definitive way and to ensure the acquisition of a sufficient variety of materials, and with adequate documentation."[9] In situ science was necessary to provide this base of information, and to some degree in situ science needed to precede sample return.

---

9. "Report of the Committee on Lunar and Planetary Exploration (COMPLEX), Space Science Board, Assembly of Mathematical and Physical Sciences," National Research Council, 1978.

This COMPLEX study presented two possible future surface mission scenarios, one for in situ exploration and one for sample return. The in situ mission scenario required "substantial mobility" in order to explore areas of 10–100 kilometers. This mobile robot was to have the ability to pick up and test samples of rock and soil during its traverse and to provide chemical analyses and "high-quality macroscopic and microscopic imaging" of its collections. In short, COMPLEX sought a robotic geologist for its in situ mission. The sample-return mission, in some respects, was more modest. The sample-return lander the committee envisioned might need mobility within "a selected area of a few meters" but could also be stationary as long as it could choose samples within the small area around it (that is, as long as it would have a Viking-like sampling arm.) The stationary lander also needed to have "basic imaging and chemical analytical capabilities"[10] so that scientists could choose the best samples.

One interesting aspect of this COMPLEX study is that, relative to the surface exploration scenarios, orbital science was deemphasized. The study did not ignore the utility of orbiting platforms. Indeed, some of its priorities, such as atmospheric science, were explicitly discussed as better performed from orbit. But the panel chose not to include any specific orbital science scenarios, perhaps due to the tremendous success, and popularity, of the Viking landings the year before. From a public image perspective, merely sending another orbiter to Mars might have seemed retrogressive, despite the reality that much new science could still be accomplished from orbit.

COMPLEX, then, chose for the Martian future the most expensive and technologically ambitious paths forward. The technology to build and operate a long-range, semi-autonomous rover on Mars did not exist in 1978. But engineers of that era did try. JPL had acquired an engineering model of the Apollo-era Lunar Rover from NASA Marshall Space Flight Center and equipped it with the cameras and other sensors needed to operate autonomously. And in 1978, the JPL team had even gotten it to work, after a fashion. The rover had moved itself a few centimeters in a test that October, taking an entire day to do it. But it had to be hooked up to the largest, fastest mainframe owned by JPL's parent, the California Institute of Technology—a Digital Equipment Corporation KL10—to do anything at all. The size of a large room, the KL-10 could not possibly be sent to Mars. So while the demonstration had been successful in a narrow technical sense, it was widely

---

10. All quotations are from COMPLEX, p. 51.

perceived as a failure. This effort demonstrated the impracticality of a Mars rover with 1970s computing.[11]

From a financial perspective, a follow-on Mars rover mission—or, for that matter, any kind of Mars surface mission—was equally unlikely. NASA's principal focus during the 1970s was construction of the Space Transportation System, the famous Shuttle. The Shuttle Program overran its budget repeatedly, and an agreement worked out in 1973 between the Nixon administration and Congress deferred any new starts for planetary missions for five years in order to help fund it. (The Agency's aeronautics budget was also cut for the same reason.) The next planetary mission approved, the Galileo mission to Jupiter, was supported in the 1978 budget. But the 1980 election brought in a presidential administration that was hostile to civilian science and initially sought to eliminate solar system exploration entirely. It was 1984 before new planetary missions were approved.

By this time, it had become clear to program managers at NASA Headquarters, including then-head of planetary science Geoffrey Briggs, that a lower-cost approach to solar system exploration was necessary. In recognition of this fiscal reality, NASA commissioned a new decadal survey from the Space Science Board that was split into two chunks, a "core program" of missions that did not require technological innovation to carry out, and an "augmented" program that included technologically advanced missions like sample return. Published in 1987, the "augmented" program of exploration baselined what had been the more technologically ambitious of the two versions of sample return given in the 1978 study, the long-range rover.

NASA established a Mars Rover Sample Return Science Working Group after the Augmented Program was published. JPL scientist Donald Rea headed the effort, with engineering deputies from JPL and from Johnson Space Center. In April 1988, Rea told the working group that their target was a launch in 1998. "This is thought to be essential if the U.S. program is not to be surpassed by the Soviet missions to Mars in the mid and late 1990s," according to the meeting's notes.[12] The rover definition portion of the study was assigned to JPL engineer Donna Shirley, who recruited robotics specialists from JPL. Her study, like the 1978-era studies, brought into focus again the slowness of technologically feasible Mars rovers. Their notional rover designs were based on 17-day missions, and they concluded that in that time, a rover might only be able to travel a few dozen kilometers.

---

11. Brian Wilcox, interview by author, 6 June 2006.
12. Mars Rover Sample Return Science Working Group, "Minutes of the Sixth Meeting of the Mars Rover Sample Return Science Working Group," 8–9 April 1988, p. 1.

These results were unsatisfying to the collected scientists. They did not like the fact that the rover would be stationary for long periods of time while waiting for instructions from Earth or that it would travel at best only dozens of kilometers. The preceding, late-1970s effort to plan a rover/sample-return mission had assumed, quite unrealistically, that the rover would collect samples across hundreds of kilometers, allowing a detailed examination of Martian geology.[13]

Shirley made an effort to get the scientists to think more clearly about what they really needed a rover to achieve. They had been thinking along the lines of what her engineering team called a "Godzilla" rover—a huge, robust, but dumb robotic vehicle carrying a large payload. The Godzilla rover was looking to be too heavy for a Shuttle launch and would need to go on a Titan IV/Centaur, the most powerful (and expensive) expendable rocket. Some estimates made it marginal even for the Titan. In short, she needed them to start thinking about a more reasonable rover.[14]

The chastened science working group responded with reduced ambitions. At the science working group's next meeting in January 1988, chairman Michael Carr of the U.S. Geological Survey had members work out goals for three different mission variants. Rover capability was the distinguishing feature of the three. In the simplest version, the rover had to travel no more than 100 meters from the lander, would carry few instruments, and would have its data processing and analysis needs handled by the lander, not on board. It would collect samples identified by the lander's instruments and would perform no analysis of its own. This rover would be, in short, merely a "sample gathering device."[15]

This minimal mission would be the least expensive and might be possible with a single Titan/Centaur launch. It placed the rover and sample-return vehicle in a single package, a particularly attractive option as it meant the rover would not have to find its way to an ascent vehicle that landed nearby. Because landing accuracies on Mars had uncertainties of tens of kilometers, even a very accurate pair of landings could leave the two vehicles too far apart for the rover's capabilities. This element of mission risk could only be

---

13. Mars Rover Sample Return Science Working Group, "Notes and Handouts from the Mars Rover Sample Return Science Working Group Meeting," 6–7 August 1987, pp. 34–56. Shirley puts this story slightly differently in her memoir; see Donna Shirley, *Managing Martians* (New York: Broadway Books, 1998), pp. 122–123.
14. Mars Rover Sample Return Science Working Group, "Notes and Handouts from the Fourth Mars Rover Sample Return Science Working Group," 23–24 November 1987, pp. 4, 106–110.
15. Mars Rover Sample Return Science Working Group, "Notes and Handouts from the Fifth Mars Rover Sample Return Science Working Group," 11–12 January 1988, p. 2.

reduced by a significant research and development program to enable greater landing accuracy, which would raise mission costs substantially.

The working group's other two mission concepts were two-launch efforts, reflecting the limitations of available launch vehicles. In one version, the rover would be capable of traveling 10–20 kilometers. Because it would be collecting samples far from the ascent vehicle, it would have to carry its own analytic instruments to characterize samples prior to collection so that Earthbound scientists could evaluate their potential value. The rover would also have to be a driller to provide a core sample of several meters' depth. In the other version, the rover would be capable of traversing 100 kilometers over two Mars years. It would be a true "robot geologist," with a wide variety of analytic capabilities of its own and "science alarms" that would stop the rover if it traversed scientifically interesting locations.[16]

This longest-range "regional" rover mission drew the least discussion at the January meeting. It was clearly beyond the state of the engineering art, and it was slowly becoming clear to the scientists that while competition with the Soviet Union for Martian glory might be heating up, NASA appeared to have neither the funds for nor the interest in a mission of that scale. Technologically, it would not be feasible for a "Big Mission" in 1998. The JPL robotics program seemed to be making progress toward limited autonomy, so a "local rover" appeared to be within reach.

By the beginning of 1989, the sample-return teams had defined the "local" rover mission variant as its baseline mission, with a few modifications. An imaging orbiter would fly first, in 1996, carrying the big camera necessary to enable landing site selection and safety imaging. A rover, communications orbiter, and ascent/Earth return vehicle would all go in 1998.[17] As things stood in early 1989, though, funding needs for even this limited version of sample return seemed far out of reach.

But the political situation in Washington was about to change.

SAMPLE RETURN AND THE SPACE EXPLORATION INITIATIVE

On 20 July 1989, President George H. W. Bush said in a speech:

> In 1961 it took a crisis—the Space Race—to speed things up. Today we don't have a crisis; we have an opportunity. To seize this opportunity, I'm not proposing a 10-year plan like Apollo; I'm proposing a long-range, continuing commitment.

---

16. Ibid., pp. 3–4.
17. Mars Rover Sample Return Science Working Group, "Notes and Handouts of the Eleventh Meeting of the Mars Rover Sample Return Science Working Group," 23–24 February 1989, pp. 51–55.

First, for the coming decade, for the 1990s: Space Station Freedom, our critical next step in all our space endeavors. And next, for the new century: Back to the Moon; back to the future. And this time, back to stay. And then a journey into tomorrow, a journey to another planet: a manned mission to Mars.[18]

NASA responded to Bush's announcement with a "90-Day Study" of how to meet these goals.[19] This effort pulled in the Mars Rover Sample Return Science Working Group, which suddenly found itself charged with defining all of the robotic missions to Mars that would have to precede a human landing.[20] At JPL, systems engineer and soon-to-be Mars Observer deputy manager Glenn Cunningham was assigned to coordinate the precursor mission studies. His team got started on 1 August. Cunningham's directions were to develop a robotic program that would include launches to Mars every 26 months, provide the scientific and technological information needed to enable human missions, be implemented exclusively by the United States, and not exceed $1.5 billion per year.[21] Johnson Space Center personnel would define human mission needs.

The Mars robotic precursor plan that evolved from this effort called for a second Mars Observer flight in October 1996, in the event that Mars Observer itself failed. Then a "Mars Global Network" mission would be launched in December 1998. The Network mission would be followed by a sample-return mission in 2001, using the "local rover" concept for sample collection. In 2003, large, high-resolution imaging and communications orbiters would fly to Mars. Finally, beginning in 2005, longer-range rover and sample-return missions would be launched in alternating opportunities through 2011.[22] The later rover missions would target chosen human landing sites to provide detailed site surveys to certify their safety.[23]

Vice President Dan Quayle's National Space Council was horrified by the 90-Day Study's price tag. Quayle had NASA Administrator Richard Truly

---

18. "Remarks on the 20th Anniversary of the Apollo 11 Moon Landing," Public Papers of President George H. W. Bush, 20 July 1989, https://bush41library.tamu.edu/archives/public-papers/712 (accessed 15 January 2020).
19. Thor Hogan, *Mars Wars: The Rise and Fall of the Space Exploration Initiative*, (Washington, DC: NASA-SP-2007-4410, 2007), pp. 53–54.
20. Glenn Cunningham, interview with author, July 2006; JPL briefing package, Code EI Mid-Term Review of JPL Support of 90 Day Study [briefing package], 15 September 1989, courtesy of Cunningham.
21. JPL briefing package, p. B-6.
22. JPL briefing package, pp. E-1–E-34.
23. Report of the 90-Day Study, p. 3-11;. Hogan, p. 58.

remove the offending cost estimates from the public version of the study, and he had the Space Council staff start looking for less expensive options. The council also embarked on a public relations strategy aimed at discrediting the report, knowing that the costs would leak out anyway.[24] It was obvious that Congress would not finance a program of this magnitude. Salvaging the Moon-Mars agenda—dubbed the Space Exploration Initiative (SEI)—meant finding a way to make it cheaper—or at least make it appear cheaper.

The 90-Day Study was released in December 1989, as the President's fiscal year 1991 budget was being prepared for submission to Congress. In an early sign of trouble, the White House Office of Management and Budget reduced NASA's SEI-related request substantially, although it still allowed an increase in the Agency's budget. In Congress, however, most agencies were facing cuts, not increases, and NASA was no different. A White House "space summit" convened on 1 May 1990 failed to convince congressional leaders that the new initiative was worth funding. Two more damaging revelations in 1990—that the newly launched Hubble Space Telescope had a flaw in its primary mirror and that two of NASA's four Space Shuttle orbiters had developed dangerous hydrogen leaks—hurt the Agency's technical credibility and political chances.[25]

It did not help the administration's case that the SEI, a quintessential Cold War–era giant space endeavor, happened to be working its way through the political process at the same time that the Soviet Union was collapsing. Soviet leader Mikhail Gorbachev had embarked on a series of political and economic reforms in 1985 that had been intended to strengthen the nation's destitute economy, but they had the opposite effect. Political freedoms Gorbachev introduced undermined the Communist Party and its hold on the USSR as well as the USSR's hold on the states of Eastern Europe. Cheering crowds dismantled one of the Cold War's greatest symbols, the Berlin Wall, in November 1989 before a shocked American television audience. East and West Germany merged during 1990, and the Soviet Union itself dissolved in December 1991. The new Russian Federation, as the Soviet Union's core state was renamed, did not even retain control of the USSR's old launch facilities at Baikonur, which were in the newly independent state of Kazakhstan.

In this atmosphere, the House Appropriations Committee chose to remove all SEI-related funds from NASA's fiscal year 1991 budget while still allowing an increase in NASA's overall budget. It specifically deleted funding for a Lunar Observer mission and new human missions and launch vehicles.

---

24. Hogan, *Mars Wars*, p. 63.
25. Hogan, *Mars Wars*, pp. 65, 75–81.

The Senate agreed. The White House continued to promote the initiative, and although NASA officials continued to act as if it could be revived, it was effectively over.[26]

Geoff Briggs at NASA Headquarters had converted the Mars Rover Sample Return Science Working Group into the Mars Science Working Group in mid-1989. The reconstituted group met in August 1990, where a major topic of discussion was the ramifications of cuts for Mars science. The budget would no longer support a sample-return mission of any description. Yet sample return was still a top desire of scientists. Only a few years would elapse before it reappeared in NASA's plans.

SAMPLE RETURN IN THE FASTER, BETTER, CHEAPER ERA

During the 1990s, NASA embarked on new approaches to developing low-cost robotic space missions. This period of experimentation is referred to as the "faster, better, cheaper" era at the Agency.[27] This era resulted in the first Mars sample-return mission proposal to make it out of the "pre-project" study phase into project status. That sample-return project did not last long, but several Mars missions undertaken in the 2000s were influenced by it, and the Mars Science Laboratory/Curiosity mission is an indirect derivative.

After the loss of the Mars Observer in 1993, NASA created its first Mars exploration program proposing a funded sequence of missions rather than following its old approach—of seeking funding for single missions via "new start" proposals. This program was called Mars Surveyor, and it was intended to achieve at least one launch every Mars opportunity (i.e., every 26 months). Surveyor-funded projects were to be launched in 1996 (Mars Global Surveyor), 1998 (Mars Climate Orbiter and Mars Polar Lander), and 2001 (an orbiter-lander pair was planned, but only the orbiter, Mars Odyssey, was completed). The Surveyor program was supposed to launch a two-part sample-return mission in 2003 and 2005. Given the small budget allocated to the Surveyor program, originally about $200 million a year, NASA structured the sample-return mission as a partnership with the French space agency Centre National d'Études Spatiales, or National Center for Space Studies (CNES).

The sample-return mission architecture developed by NASA and CNES in 1998 involved sending a large lander to Mars in 2003, with a

---

26. Hogan, *Mars Wars*, pp. 110–112, 124–125, and 128–135.
27. For a more complete discussion, see Howard McCurdy, *Faster, Better Cheaper: Low-Cost Innovation in the U.S. Space Program* (Baltimore: Johns Hopkins University Press, 2001).

sample-collecting rover like the one proposed in the 1978 COMPLEX study.[28] The rover, expected to be about 120 kilograms in mass (the Mars Exploration Rovers were 180 kilograms), was to roll down a ramp from the lander to the surface, gather a variety of samples, put them into a multichambered sample container, and return the container to the lander. The lander would also have a solid-fuel rocket intended to fire the sample container into a low Mars orbit (see figure 2). In 2005, a CNES-built orbiter would reach Mars, collect the sample container from orbit, encapsulate it in a return vehicle, and shoot it back to Earth. NASA would also launch a second sample-return lander in 2005, with the French orbiter to return that sample as well. This approach would keep the Surveyor program's funding profile manageable.

The sample-return lander was to be a derivative of the Lockheed Martin–built Mars Polar Lander, which was under development at the time. The budget for the new lander was $130 million, slightly more than the total Climate Orbiter/Polar Lander spacecraft budget of $120 million. Within budget, the new lander had to be "gigantized," scaled up from the Polar Lander's 290 kilograms to slightly more than 1,000 kilograms; sample collection and transfer systems for rover, lander, and orbiter had to be developed; the sample-return rocket and Earth return vehicle had to be developed; and the rover had to be developed.[29] The new rover was to be a derivative of the Athena rover design chosen for the 2001 Mars Surveyor lander, which itself was an enlarged version of the Mars Polar Lander. The new rover also had to meet a more stringent set of planetary protection requirements than those that had been imposed on the Polar Lander, and techniques to meet these requirements had to be developed. Not only did the rover design have to protect Mars from contamination by Earth, it also had to ensure that the sample would neither contaminate Earth nor be contaminated by Earth when sent back. This capability had to be designed into the sample collection and transfer system.

All these new developments were technologically risky, and in aerospace engineering, technical risk and cost risk amount to the same thing. Each new technology that has to be developed imposes a difficult-to-quantify cost risk, so a project involving many new technologies has a very high probability of large cost overruns. Project managers typically mitigate cost risk by holding financial reserves roughly scaled to the number of new technical

---

28. Overview in "James F. Jordan and Sylvia L. Miller, "The Mars Surveyor Program Architecture," presented at the 1999 IEEE Aerospace Conference, held 7 March 1999 in Aspen, CO.

29. Masses from Edward A. Euler, "The Mars Sample Return 'Workhorse' Lander," 1999 American Astronomical Society (AAS) National Conference, 16–18 November 1999.

FIGURE 2. The sample return lander concept derived from the Lockheed Mars Polar Lander design, 1999. (This image was slightly altered from the original by removing dimensions. From Edward A. Euler, "The Mars Sample Return 'Workhorse' Lander, 1999 AAS National Conference, November 16–18, 1999, copy in HMEC, Mars Program and Sample Return Documents, MSR 03:05.)

developments being undertaken. Given the low budget available for this edition of Mars sample return, this approach was not possible.

It did not matter, in the end. The 2003/2005 sample-return project died when its technical forerunner, the Mars Polar Lander, disappeared during its descent to Mars on 3 December 1999. Both the Surveyor 2001 lander and sample-return 2003/2005 lander projects had been built around the assumption that the Polar Lander would succeed (in aerospace jargon, this is called "success oriented"), validating the basic entry, descent, and landing methodology spacecraft builder Lockheed Martin had chosen for these missions. Instead, the Polar Lander's failure convinced NASA and JPL officials that the design had deep flaws. Loss of confidence in the design led NASA to terminate both projects the following year. The demise of the Polar Lander also led NASA to abandon its "faster, better, cheaper" experiment and reestablish more stringent technical requirements and oversight, bringing attendant increases in mission costs.

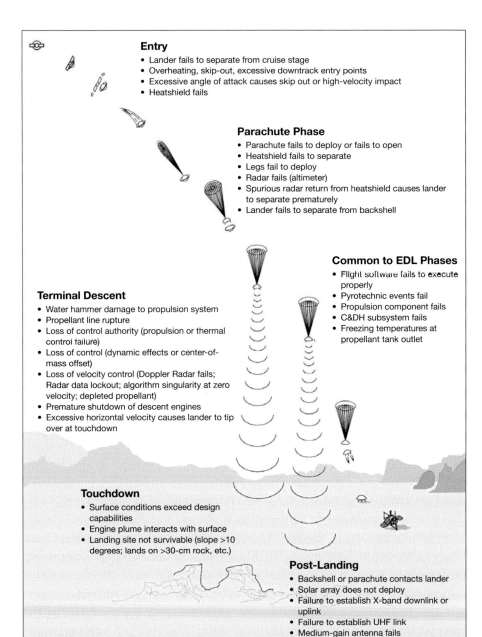

Diagram from JPL report on the failure of the Mars Polar Lander. (JPL Special Review Board, Report on the Loss of the Mars Polar Lander and Deep Space 2 Missions, 22 March 2000, JPL-D 18709, p. 22)

Yet it took time for NASA to cancel the 2003/2005 lander-sample-return project, and in the months between the loss of the Polar Lander and receipt of a formal cancellation order, JPL sample-return engineers (and their superiors) knew that they still had to show up to work. So they put their time into a pair of informal studies that drew on what they had learned about sample return over the previous two years of effort. This short period of time and thought had profound effects on the architecture of sample return and on technologies they conceived of as necessary to accomplish it.

THE "BUBBLE TEAM" AND LARGE-LANDER STUDIES

During the short life of the sample-return project, many of the engineers involved had reached the conclusion that the basic architecture they were using was deeply flawed. Whatever might have gone wrong with Polar Lander, they no longer believed the Lockheed Martin lander could be scaled up so much, so easily. The lander's legs could not be scaled up enough to provide much ground clearance due to constraints imposed by the size of available launch-vehicle aerodynamic shrouds, rendering the lander vulnerable to rocks. Longer legs also would leave the lander vulnerable to a "tip-over" problem. As the rover would start to move across the lander deck, the vehicle would see a center-of-gravity shift that might tip the whole thing over, especially if it had landed on a sloped surface. And there were still more problems. So they set out to find a new architecture that would resolve some of these challenges.

The effort to conceive a better Mars landing method was embedded within a JPL Mars Exploration Office–initiated review of sample return. Set up in February 2000, the review's purpose was actually to protect the sample-return architecture from being reviewed externally—perhaps by Johnson Space Center, which wanted a role in any Mars sample-return effort but had not gained much of a foothold in the sample-return effort as it was being implemented in 2000. So the review was structured to prevent major changes to the architecture, which might then be used as justification for reassessing institutional roles. Separate teams were to review each component of the mission—the Earth return vehicle, the lander, the Mars ascent vehicle. This review became known as the "bubble team study" around JPL.[30]

Brian Muirhead, who had been spacecraft development manager for the Mars Pathfinder mission, led the bubble team looking at lander architecture, along with Tom Rivellini, Bill Layman, and Dara Sabahi. Muirhead did not think the bubble team's charter provided enough flexibility. He did not think

---

30. Dara Sabahi oral history, 28 July 2008; Tomasso Rivellini oral history, 14 November 2008. (JPL Oral History Collection.)

that the Lockheed Martin legged lander made any sense when scaled up to the size necessary to carry out sample return, so he ignored the charter and had his team redesign the lander entirely.[31]

This group devised some newish options for the lander. Back in the 1960s, there had been some investigation of what was called a "pallet lander." The pallet lander concept replaced the legs with a structure that would absorb the lander's impact energy by crushing, exactly like the "crumple zones" on passenger cars. One advantage of the pallet approach was that the lander deck would be closer to the ground than it would be on the legged lander. This feature would make disembarking the large sample-return rover easier and provide less potential for a "tip-over" disaster.[32] The pallet lander also had two clear disadvantages. It had pressurized propellant tanks underneath its top deck, and these tanks could not be allowed to be punctured or crushed, so the "crumple-zone" structure had to be designed to protect them. And because this structure was designed to be destroyed on impact, the test program necessary to verify its performance under a wide variety of Mars-like environmental conditions was going to be expensive.[33] But the team still thought it better than the legged lander.

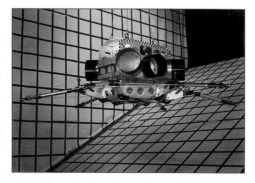

FIGURE 3. A small-scale mechanical drop test model of the "pallet lander" concept, complete with rover mock-up. (JPL/Caltech)

The other option the team considered became known as the 4pi airbag lander. This was derived from the Mars Pathfinder approach of having a rocket-equipped backshell zero out vertical velocity before dropping the lander on the surface. Like Pathfinder, this lander would be protected by a set of airbags on impact. Unlike Pathfinder, the airbags would also provide a self-righting system. (Pathfinder's self-righting was performed by metal lander petals, not by airbags.) And instead of using solid rockets, the backshell would be equipped with a throttleable liquid-fueled rocket. A throttleable rocket would enable more precise control over touchdown velocity, so

---

31. Sabahi oral history, 28 July 2008; Rivellini oral history, 14 November 2008.
32. Tomasso Rivellini, "From Legs to Wheels," Rivellini Mars Science Lab collection, HMEC; Rivellini oral history, 14 November 2008.
33. Sabahi oral history, 28 July 2008; Rivellini oral history, 14 November 2008.

the airbags in this concept would not have to be as robust (and heavy) as Pathfinder's had been.

Muirhead's team also decided to remove the Mars ascent vehicle from the lander and put it on the sample-collection rover—a big change, as it meant a much larger rover. The team's mechanical engineers were sensitive to allowable mechanical tolerances and thought that the task of getting the rover back onto the sample-return lander, in the proper mechanical alignment to deposit the samples into the ascent vehicle's receiving mechanism, was much too hard to do from 150 million miles away. If the rover were to carry the sampling apparatus and ascent vehicle bolted to its own deck, this problem went away. Components could be aligned while still sitting in JPL's clean room.[34]

This redesign attempt never came to anything final, though. Due to changing leadership in JPL's Mars office during March and April, the bubble-team study was redirected into a different set of studies. Barry Goldstein got an assignment to look at establishing a new line of competed Mars missions, while James Graf took charge of a "large-lander study" that absorbed the work and membership of Muirhead's bubble team. With sample return no longer in the cards, the large-lander study's purpose was to figure out how to land a big enough payload to carry out sample return without actually doing sample return. On the recommendation of John Casani, Graf recruited Lockheed Martin's Steve Jolly to the lander team so that the company's point of view was also represented.[35]

This large-lander study team further developed the bubble team's pallet and airbag concepts, while a subgroup argued for a third approach. Jolly, Rob Manning, and Dara Sabahi thought the team was not taking a radical enough approach. Sabahi explained later, "You have a rover with a very capable mobility system. We should just suspend the rover on the backshell and land with the wheels."[36] With no lander or airbags to egress from, egress is not a problem. The rover's wheels would roll off most rocks. Because the rover's center of gravity would be low, it would not be as likely to tip over on a high slope as a taller legged lander carrying a rover. To this troika, the most obvious solution was to get rid of all the impediments to the rover.

They did not win the argument with the larger group, though. There were two issues that they could not resolve within the study period. The first was whether the backshell's propulsion system could control terminal velocity precisely enough to assure a touchdown speed of no more than about

---

34. Rivellini oral history, 14 November 2008.
35. Sabahi oral history, 28 July 2008.
36. Sabahi oral history, 28 July 2008.

2 meters per second, the most a reasonable rover suspension system could handle. This was principally a question of how good Doppler radars really were. Rivellini explained later that the Polar Lander's problematic radar had raised a lot of questions about the performance of radars on Mars that simply could not be addressed without much more research.[37] The second issue was one of controllability. How would the backshell keep control of a rover dangling on a cable 10 or 20 meters below it? If the rover started to swing on the end of its cable, could a reasonable control system stop it before touchdown?

Without answers to those questions, the team shelved the wheel-landing idea and kept the pallet and 4pi airbag lander concepts alive. The Mars program office ultimately funded a technology-development task to build and test proof-of-concept models of both.[38] Meanwhile, above the heads of these engineers, officials at JPL and NASA Headquarters were engaged in an effort to restructure the overall Mars program. Cancellation of the 2001 lander led directly to the question of what to send to Mars in the 2003 launch opportunity—a revamped 2001 lander or something else. By May 2000, JPL had proposed, and NASA had conditionally accepted, what was originally called the Mars Geological Rover and became the Mars Exploration Rover mission, which used a Mars Pathfinder–based entry and landing architecture instead of Lockheed Martin's Viking-like architecture.

Separately from the short-range effort to figure out what to do in 2003, the Mars program leadership had also sponsored an effort to make a "roadmap" for Mars exploration over the next decade. The roadmap was designed to overcome the technological incoherency of the Surveyor program's mission set—the program's inability to select missions that would build capabilities needed for the long-sought sample return due to the program's focus on competed missions. The roadmap swept in a "Mars Surveyor Orbiter," baselined for a 2005 launch. The pallet lander became the basis of a "Mars Smart Lander" project that would launch in 2007, along with a "Telecommunications Orbiter" to be developed jointly with the Italian Space Agency. The Telecom Orbiter was justified by the high data rates that the Smart Lander was supposed to be capable of and by the program's intent to carry out sample return, now penciled in for 2011. The Smart Lander project's technological purpose was to demonstrate new precision landing technology and prove the ability to land payloads large enough to accomplish sample return, around 1,000

---

37. Rivellini oral history, 14 November 2008.
38. Tom Rivellini, Robust Landing ATD Task Overview, January 2001, Rivellini Mars Science Lab collection; Rivellini oral history, 14 November 2008; Sabahi oral history, 28 July 2008.

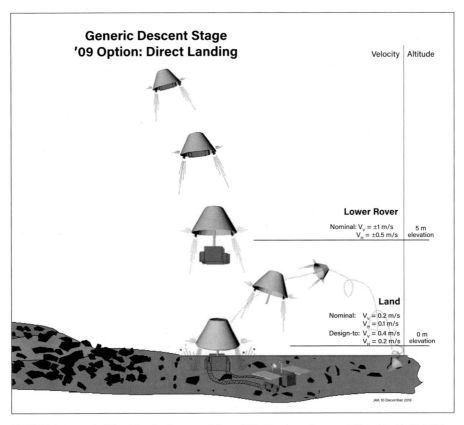

FIGURE 4. An early "direct landing" concept, from EDL Storyboard presentation, March 15, 2000. (Tommasso Rivellini, JPL/Caltech)

kilograms. This new Mars program also envisioned selecting the first Mars Scout mission in 2002 for a 2007 launch.[39]

The Mars Surveyor Orbiter was the first of these roadmap projects to be initiated. Like other orbiter missions in the Mars program, it was to be developed under a systems contract, but not necessarily with Lockheed Martin. NASA leaders wanted the contract recompeted. And since the new orbiter's launch date of August 2005 was now comfortably far in the future, they also planned to solicit instruments via NASA's standard Announcement of Opportunity process. Late in 2000, JPL assigned Jim Graf as project manager, and Graf approached Rich Zurek and asked what he thought scientists' biggest desire for future Mars exploration was likely to be. Zurek told him

---

39. "NASA's First Scout Mission Selected for 2007 Mars Launch," NASA Headquarters, Release 03-256, 4 August 2003, *https://www.nasa.gov/home/hqnews/2003/aug/HQ_03256_mars_scout.html* (accessed 8 August 2021).

higher data rates.⁴⁰ During the 1990s, there had been an enormous improvement in both computing technology and digital imaging technology. By 2000, it was possible to build a camera that would simply overwhelm the ability of, say, Mars Global Surveyor's telecommunication system to send its imagery back to Earth. The amount of data that could be returned from Mars was limited by a number of factors—the power available in Mars orbit, the size of the spacecraft's antenna, the data compression scheme in use, or the availability of time on the Deep Space Network. In drafting the request for proposals, Graf had his project team specify a dramatic increase in data rate for bidders' prospective spacecraft.

From the standpoint of sample-return strategy, the new orbiter's function was to enable safer landings through very-high-resolution imaging. The Mars Orbiter Camera aboard the Mars Global Surveyor spacecraft lacked sufficient resolution to image rocks of sufficient size to endanger a lander, but it would be possible to build such a camera in the early 2000s. It would simply need a big spacecraft to carry it (and a high data rate to get its imagery back to Earth.) The alternative, designing landers to survey their own landing sites during the descent phase and maneuver to avoid rocks, would be possible but difficult. Merely testing a spacecraft that would be able to decide on its own where to land would be challenging, because under JPL's rules, every option available to the spacecraft, and every combination of options, had to be tested. The test program would expand exponentially as the spacecraft's flexibility increased. It would be far simpler, and less expensive, to have humans on Earth look at high-resolution images of landing sites and verify ahead of time sites free of hazards. The orbiter's strategic purpose was primarily engineering support. The mission gained the name Mars Reconnaissance Orbiter (MRO), reflecting this strategic function as an intelligence-gathering asset.

The project could anticipate having much greater resources to draw on. NASA's Mars program budget increased from $248.4 million in fiscal year (FY) 2000 to $428 million in FY 2001. Some of this increase went to the Mars Exploration Rover (MER) mission, but a significant amount was specifically for the Reconnaissance Orbiter. Mars program officials Scott Hubbard and James Garvin had gone to the NASA budget examiner at the Office of Management and Budget in January 2001 to argue for an expanded Reconnaissance Orbiter mission scope.⁴¹ In order for the Mars program to launch a big smart lander later in the decade and sample return in the 2010s,

---

40. James Graf oral history, 12 January 2009, JPL Oral History Collection.
41. Scott Hubbard, *Exploring Mars: Chronicles from a Decade of Discovery* (Tucson: University of Arizona Press, 2011), pp. 135–138.

officials had to figure out where to send those missions by the late 2000s. The Orbiter mission should be able to identify water-bearing minerals and map near-surface ice in pursuit of understanding Martian habitability as well as identify locations most likely to be both safe and interesting. Garvin explained later, "We convinced [NASA budget examiner Steve] Isakowitz that just like a big telescope can find the stars to look at, MRO is the eye in the sky over Mars to refine where we need to go. Instead of 30,000 sites that MGS tells us are pretty cool, let's downsize it to the 100 top places to go on Mars for the next twenty-five years."[42] NASA's MRO budget authority subsequently increased substantially, from $455 million to $633 million.[43]

WHITHER THE MARS SMART LANDER?

During 2003 and 2004, the Mars Smart Lander project saw a major realignment. After the large-lander study of 2000 had closed down, Tom Rivellini had run a technology task designed to further investigate two approaches conceived during the study, the pallet lander and the 4pi airbag lander. His engineers had built scale models and tested them in a variety of simulated Martian terrains to help them understand how each would perform. In part due to problems the Mars Exploration Rover project had with its airbags, the pallet lander had become the baseline design for the Smart Lander. As the mission concept stood in 2001, the Smart Lander's goals were to demonstrate active hazard avoidance during terminal descent, precision landing, and increased mobility, as well as the capacity to land such a large vehicle safely.

In parallel with engineering studies of the lander, a science definition team had been established to develop a scientific rationale for the mission. Chaired by Raymond Arvidson of Washington University in St. Louis, it was chartered in April 2001 and completed its report in October. This team argued that the Smart Lander should achieve "major scientific breakthroughs" while preparing the way for sample return.[44] The Smart Lander, with a notional cost of $750 million, was too expensive an opportunity to waste on engineering demonstrations alone.

Because the technological purpose of the Smart Lander was to demonstrate the ability to safely land a large payload, the lander—about 800

---

42. James Garvin, interview with the author, 17 August 2010.
43. G. Scott Hubbard, James Garvin, and Edward J. Weiler, "Mars Reconnaissance Orbiter Formulation Authorization," 17 January 2001, JPL D-22733; J. Edward Weiler to Director, JPL, "2005 Mars Reconnaissance Orbiter Project Phase A to B Confirmation," 10 May 2002, JPL D-22734.
44. Smart Lander Mission Science Definition Team, "NASA Mars Exploration Program Mars 2007 Smart Lander Mission Science Definition Team Report," 11 October 2001, appendix 1, 25.

kilograms in mass—was to have about 100 kilograms available for payload. For a sample-return mission, that 100 kilograms would be allocated primarily to an ascent vehicle intended to place collected samples in Mars orbit. But for the Smart Lander mission, it was available for scientific instruments. The science definition team took the availability of a large payload mass as an opportunity to propose two very different and equally ambitious missions: a Mobile Geobiology Explorer and a Multidisciplinary Platform. The Geobiology Explorer would feature a large, autonomous rover aimed at looking for the chemical signatures of past life on Mars, while the platform would be a fixed lander designed to drill 5 to 10 meters beneath the surface and analyze the resulting samples. Either would be, in their words, "the capstone mission for this decade."[45]

A variety of factors biased the Smart Lander decision toward the rover. The pallet lander was designed to facilitate rover egress; developing it was unnecessary for a fixed driller, which could use a gigantized Viking-like three-legged lander. Scientists wanted regional-scale surface mobility for sample return anyway, to ensure that they could obtain the most scientifically desirable samples. JPL engineers, having originated Mars surface mobility, wanted to expand their capabilities. During early 2002, JPL performed trade studies on four variants suggested by the science definition team: lander vs. rover and solar vs. radioisotope power.

Expanding possibilities for this mission, unsurprisingly, produced a rapid cost escalation, and later in 2002 a "design to cost" study was convened to bound the options. JPL's Dan McCleese cochaired this study with Jack Farmer of Arizona State University. This Project Science Integration Group (PSIG) used the results of a recent Mars Exploration Program Analysis Group study to argue for a lander mission focused on determining the habitability of ancient Mars. Finalized in June 2003, this mission concept called for a large rover with a somewhat smaller payload than the Geobiology Explorer, but with essentially the same focus. Reflecting a desire for breakthrough science, McCleese's group argued for significantly more money for the mission: "The PSIG and the MSL [Mars Smart Lander] Project doubt that the resources, as presented to PSIG, for MSL will be sufficient to fund the payloads needed to meet the science floors of scientifically supportable missions."[46]

---

45. Ibid., p. 2.
46. Mars Science Laboratory Mission, "Project Science Integration Group Final Report," 6 June 2003, quotation from p. 7; C. W. Whetsel, "The End of the Beginning: Mars Science Laboratory Mission at PDR," MSL_through_confirmation_whetzel.ppt, 6 October 2006.

Artist's concept of Curiosity's skycrane maneuver. (NASA/JPL-Caltech: PIA14839)

At the same time, JPL engineers were souring on the pallet lander concept. It would require an expensive developmental testing program, just as the airbag landers had, because numerical analysis was not sufficient to fully characterize the pallet structure's ability to collapse predictably while still protecting the fuel tanks and assorted propulsion hardware. Rover egress from the pallet at a variety of slopes and rock abundances would also have to be tested. In contrast, the "landing on wheels" approach, which they had started to refer to as "skycrane" after the Sikorsky S-64 Skycrane helicopter, had begun to look more and more promising. It would not require the sort of developmental test program the pallet lander would, and it would simplify some other engineering problems—such as load paths through the structure and packaging and integration of a radioisotope thermoelectric generator (RTG) power source if NASA chose that path. The skycrane was a much more tractable problem analytically, since at the moment of touchdown only the rover would touch the ground. The descent stage stayed hovering above it, then flew off and crashed after the cable connecting them was cut. It did not have to survive the crash or protect a payload. The descent stage and rover could be tested separately, and there was no egress problem. A rough cost-estimating exercise put the skycrane's development cost at about one-third that of the pallet lander.[47] By the time of an October 2003 mission concept

---

47. Anon., "Pallet and Skycrane," March 2003, Rivellini MSL materials; C. W. Whetsel, "The End of the Beginning."

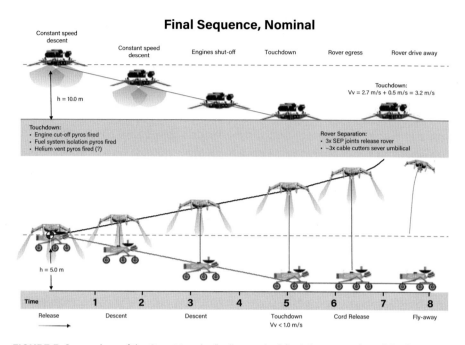

FIGURE 5. Comparison of the Smart Lander "pallet version" final descent to that of the "rover on a rope" version, from the MSL Touchdown System Selection Peer Review, 7 May 2003. (Courtesy: Tommasso Rivellini, JPL/Caltech)

review, JPL engineers had settled on the skycrane approach, and the overdetermined rover decision was made as well. The skycrane would lower a rover, based upon the sample-return rover sketched out in the bubble-team studies of 2000, to the surface of Mars on cables.

The Committee on Planetary and Lunar Exploration of the National Academies had reviewed NASA's Mars strategy during 2002, and it joined the MSL Science Definition Team and Project Science Integration Group in advocating for remaking the Smart Lander into a productive science mission. In particular, they advocated dropping solar power for nuclear power on future landed missions to achieve longer mission lives and increase science return. Accordingly, the Smart Lander's rover gained two RTGs for power.[48] The decision to use RTGs also contributed to a decision to delay the mission's launch to 2009.

Reflecting the changed nature of the mission from technology demonstration to high-yield science, the project was renamed Mars Science

---

48. COMPLEX, "Assessment of Mars Science and Mission Priorities," National Academy Press, 2003, pp. 4, 102–103.

Laboratory.⁴⁹ In later years, NASA and JPL management would regret keeping the same acronym, MSL, for two rather different mission concepts. But in 2003, it seemed clever. The mission budget was expanded to pay for the expanded concept, to $1.6 billion.

THE DEMISE OF SAMPLE RETURN

The Mars program that NASA laid out in 2000 envisioned carrying out a sample-return campaign beginning in 2011, with the launch of a Smart Lander–derived sample-collection and -caching rover. But in 2004, the year after the Smart Lander was rescoped into the Science Laboratory, the winds began to shift against sample return again. While NASA Administrator Dan Goldin had been pushing in the late 1990s for a presidential decision in 2004 to send astronauts to Mars, he had left NASA in 2001. His successor, Sean O'Keefe, got a different presidential decision that year—to return astronauts to the Moon. This was articulated in President George W. Bush's Vision for Space Exploration. The Vision was predicated on an overall increase in the NASA budget of about $3 billion per year, with the rest of the cost of a return to the Moon to be borne by shutting down the Space Shuttle Program in 2010 and diverting its funding line to the new Moon program. An almost immediate revolt against the idea from within the President's own party ensured that it was never fully funded, and heavy-lift launch vehicle development started with much less than its anticipated financing and never did acquire full funding.⁵⁰

This situation caused NASA leaders to begin raiding other budgets to fund the Moon program. At a meeting in May 2005, NASA's Mars program staff found that the Mars program's contribution to the new lunar effort would be about $3 billion over the next five years. NASA's FY 2006 budget runout had projected the Mars budget increasing to nearly $1.3 billion per year by 2010.⁵¹ Under the new budget plan, Mars would receive only $648 million in fiscal year 2010. Jim Garvin, then NASA's Mars program scientist, remembered later, "The senior leaders of the Agency said, 'Mars has to go.' It was ironic they said that in the space of it succeeding so well, but sometimes too much

---

49. C. W. Whetsel, "The End of the Beginning," ; Brian Muirhead, Mars Science Laboratory Mission Concept Review, "Flight System Trade Studies and Reference Design," 28–29 October 2003, Rivellini MSL History files.
50. Review of Human Spaceflight Plans Committee, "Seeking a Human Spaceflight Program Worthy of a Great Nation," *https://www.nasa.gov/offices/hsf/home/index.html*, pp. 58–59; chart I on p. 59.
51. NASA Fiscal Year 2006 Budget Estimates, 107488main_FY06_low (1).pdf,; NASA Fiscal Year 2007 Budget Estimates, 042458main_FY07_budget_full (1).pdf.

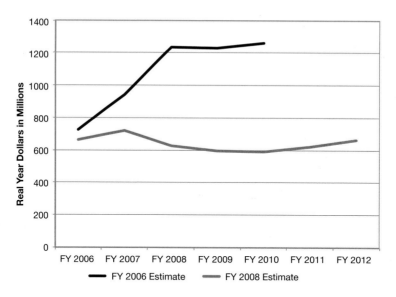

FIGURE 6. Evolution of the Mars Budget, I: The 2006 and 2008 Fiscal Year estimates with 5 year outruns. Data from President's budget submissions.

success breeds that kind of contempt."[52] The Mars program budget was cut again in 2007; the actual FY 2010 budget was $438.2 million.[53]

The $3 billion cut to the Mars program knocked sample return "off the planning horizon," to quote an *Aviation Week & Space Technology* writer.[54] Since the just-approved Mars Science Laboratory and its skycrane-like landing system were intended to demonstrate large payload delivery capability for sample return, this cut removed its programmatic purpose. It remained a valuable scientific mission but became somewhat of an orphan. The technology development program for sample return, known as "Safe on Mars" and including the very important sample collection and handling systems, was a victim of the cut, and until 2009 the Mars program had no meaningful technology development funds. The Telecommunications Orbiter was also cut from the program. Instead, the program would have to depend on the Mars Reconnaissance Orbiter far outliving its design life in order to serve the MSL rover when it got to Mars. When NASA approved the second Scout mission,

---

52. Garvin interview.
53. NASA Fiscal Year 2012 Budget Estimates, P-2, 516674main_FY12Budget_Estimates_Overview.pdf; NASA Fiscal Year 2010 Budget Estimates, 345225main_FY_2010_UPDATED_final_5-11-09_withver.pdf, SCI-86.
54. Jefferson Morris, "NASA's Mars Budget Now Stable But Tight, Official Says," *Aviation Week & Space Technology* (16 January 2007).

MAVEN, it required the mission to carry a relay like MRO's despite being in a very poor orbit for relay services.

Yet scientific advocacy for sample return continued. A committee of the Space Studies Board criticized NASA in 2008 for what it saw as the cessation of any relevant Mars sample-return work and called for restarting technology investment.[55] That year and into 2009, a NASA Mars Architecture Team met to try to construct a new, less expensive variant of sample return that would begin in 2018 with a medium-size rover (smaller than MSL but larger than the MERs) for astrobiology investigations and sample collection. This medium-sized mission became known as MAX-C, short for Mars Astrobiology Explorer-Cacher. Here the idea was to collect samples with the MAX-C rover and, when the sample container was full, leave the cache on the surface. A later mission, to be launched in 2020 or perhaps 2022, would land nearby, send a collection rover to grab the sample container, and launch it back to Earth. To try to reduce NASA's cost, the MAX-C mission was to be integrated with a European effort called ExoMars, which was to send the first European rover to Mars.

Yet 2008 proved a poor year in which to restart sample-return planning. The banking crisis of that year resulted in a focus on budget cutting, and NASA was not spared. The Constellation program also ran far over budget. In 2009, the incoming Obama administration, faced with shrinking tax revenues and growing costs, reopened the question of whether to develop a new launch vehicle. Portions of the aerospace industry had never been happy with the Constellation program's focus on the development of a Shuttle-derived, government-owned and -operated launch vehicle. The United States already had commercial launch vehicles capable of servicing the International Space Station (ISS) with cargo, and they could be improved to carry astronauts as well. The builders of those rockets, understandably, wanted the government's business. They found inroads into the new administration sometime in 2008, and the administration empaneled yet another blue-ribbon review of NASA's exploration policy. That panel concluded that Constellation needed about $59 billion more than its fiscal year 2010 White House budget guidelines, or $159 billion over the next decade. Completion on schedule would need, in

---

55. Committee on Assessing the Solar System Exploration Program, Space Studies Board, Division on Engineering and Physical Sciences, National Research Council, *Grading NASA's Solar System Exploration Program: A Midterm Review*, National Academies Press, Washington, DC, 2008, p. 40.

essence, an increase in the NASA budget of about $6 billion per year.[56] That was not in the cards.

The administration formally terminated the Constellation program in 2010, having already begun shutting it down and transitioning to a new effort, which it called the Commercial Crew Development program. This was an expansion of another Bush administration effort, commercial cargo development, which sought to replace the Shuttle's cargo-carrying capacity to the ISS with commercially procured launch vehicles. The administration's intended budget for this program was about $800 million per year, with much of the rest of Constellation's funding going to technology development, including heavy-lift propulsion technology.[57] Congress, however, insisted on a parallel "heavy-lift" launch vehicle development patterned on Constellation's Ares V rocket—and mandated it without funding it. In fact, the enacted fiscal year 2012 budget cut NASA by about $700 million overall. Funds for heavy-lift development came from reducing funds for the commercial crew program to about half of what the administration had requested.[58]

The fiscal year 2011 and 2012 budget submissions had projected NASA being flat-funded at $18.5 billion overall, with its science directorate also flat-funded at $5.1 billion for the next five years. Much of the cut in 2012 came from funds that had once financed Shuttle operations, so the Agency's bet that it could retain those funds for its commercial crew development and heavy-lifter developments did not pan out. In order to expand funding for the commercial crew effort back to what it had intended in 2011, it again had to raid other accounts. The science directorate's contribution to the commercial crew development was about $162 million.

That $162 million contribution, though, hides the true damage to planetary science, which was cut by $309 million.[59] The "missing" $309 million largely went to fund an enormous cost overrun on the James Webb Space Telescope, which was approved for development in 2004 for a $2.5 billion budget but by 2010 exceeded $8 billion.[60] The $309 million cut to the planetary science budget amounted to a slice of about 20 percent. Mars exploration received the largest cut in absolute dollars, $226.2 million, or 40 percent

---

56. Augustine, p. 84.
57. NASA Fiscal Year 2011 budget request, costs from p. iv.
58. NASA Office of Inspector General, Office of Audits, "NASA's Challenges to Meeting Cost, Schedule and Performance Goals," report no. IG-12-021, 27 September 2012, p. 28.
59. NASA FY 2013 budget request, SC-3.
60. John Casani, chair, "James Webb Space Telescope Independent Comprehensive Review Panel Final Report," 5 November 2010, https://www.nasa.gov/pdf/499224main_JWST-ICRP_Report-FINAL.pdf

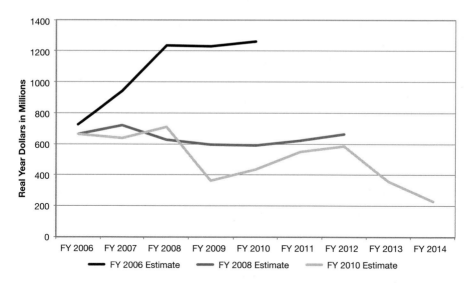

FIGURE 7. Evolution of the Mars Budget, II: The 2006, 2008, and 2010 Fiscal Year estimates with 5-year outruns. Data from President's budget submissions.

of its previous budget. The smaller lunar science program begun in the Bush administration was zeroed out in 2015, and outer-planets science was cut by about a third.[61]

The consequence of the cut to the Mars program was the immediate termination of NASA's participation in two missions that were being jointly developed with the European Space Agency: a Trace Gas Orbiter to study the Martian atmosphere after a launch in 2016, and the ExoMars mission in 2022 that would land Europe's first planetary rover using JPL's skycrane landing technology. The European Space Agency salvaged these missions by partnering with Russian space agency Roscosmos instead.

The NASA budget reached its low point in fiscal year 2013, at $16.9 billion.[62] Although it was projected to sink even lower under the terms of the 2011 Budget Control Act, Congress actually began adding funds a year later and, by fiscal year 2016, had reached $19.3 billion.[63] The remarkable turnaround in NASA's fortunes included the planetary science budget, and while a Mars Sample Return mission had still not been funded as of 2016, a "Mars

---

61. NASA FY 2013 budget estimates, 632697main_NASA_fy13_budget_summary_508.pdf, PS-1.
62. NASA Operating Plan for Public Law 113-6 Appropriations, August 1, 2013, *https://www.nasa.gov/sites/default/files/files/FY_2013NASA_OperatingPlanEnclosure1_13SEP2013.pdf* (accessed 18 August 2020).
63. Jeff Foust, "NASA Receives $19.3 Billion in Final 2016 Spending Bill," *SpaceNews.com* (16 December 2015), *http://spacenews.com/nasa-receives-19-3-billion-in-final-2016-spending-bill/* (accessed 16 January 2015).

2020 Rover" mission based upon the Mars Science Laboratory mission was approved. It was to be equipped to collect and store samples for retrieval by a later mission, reflecting the continued interest in returning bits of Mars to Earth. But the return would not happen prior to the late 2020s.

CONCLUSIONS AND RUMINATIONS

The story told here is one of scientists continuing to promote a consistent goal across decades, engineers trying to deliver that achievement, and both being undermined by the vagaries of budgets and politics. Engineering and science have made progress toward sample return without having succeeded in creating the necessary political conditions to get sample return funded. It may not be in their power to do so. One thread of my story has been NASA's parallel effort to develop a new human-rated launch vehicle in the same time period, which has failed in precisely the same way. Just as NASA's scientists have not been able to create a political alliance strong enough to keep funding for Mars sample return, NASA's human spaceflight advocates (a much larger and politically well-connected group centered in Texas, Alabama, and Florida) have not been able to forge a political alliance substantial enough to get a new launch vehicle completed after several tries over nearly three decades.

If fiscal challenges have prevented the achievement of Mars sample return, they have not particularly constrained engineering. The restoration of more traditional engineering conservatism after the demise of "faster, better, cheaper" had the unexpected effect of fostering innovation in Mars landing technology. The temporary programmatic rejection of the Lockheed Martin legged-lander design for sample return after the Polar Lander's loss, combined with JPL's engineers' efforts to devise a safer way to land large payloads, led them from the pallet lander to the skycrane. Yet in contrast, rover surface mobility has not seen rapid improvement. The Mars Exploration Rovers, designed to travel a kilometer in three months, went much further over a much longer period. The Mars Science Laboratory (MSL) rover is not significantly faster. "Curiosity," as the MSL rover is named, has the capabilities that scientists of the 1970s desired, but still not the level of mobility. It averages tens of meters per day of movement, not kilometers. Thus the "regional rover" of the 1978 COMPLEX study has still not been achieved. In that arena of engineering, innovation has not made much progress against scientists' desires.

CHAPTER 5
NASA, Big Science, and Mars Exploration: Critical Decisions from Goldin to Bolden

W. Henry Lambright

IN AUGUST 1996, Dan Goldin, NASA Administrator, met with Dan McCleese of the Jet Propulsion Laboratory (JPL) and a team of scientists McCleese was leading. There was excitement in the air. A group of NASA and academic scientists had recently announced claims that they had detected evidence of fossilized bacterial life in a Mars meteorite.

"What's the next step?" Goldin demanded to know. "Mars sample return!" McCleese and others replied. "OK," said Goldin. "Can you do it in 2001?" "No," they said. "We don't know where to go. A mission that soon would be a shot in the dark, like Viking. We have to go at it in a systematic way." Goldin pushed more for an early date, but in the end said: "OK, do the right thing in terms of science. But the political process will tell us how fast we can go."[1]

This brief exchange epitomizes much about NASA's Mars Exploration Program. There are recurring themes. These include the search for extraterrestrial life; the issue of how to go, and how fast; the goal of Mars sample return; and the disconnect between the long-term perspective of scientists and the short-term perspective of politicians.

The exchange also highlighted the role of the NASA Administrator as a "boundary spanner" between science and politics, trying to find a way to encompass the requirements of both cultures.

---

1. Dan McCleese, interview by author, 30 March 2011.

The aim of this chapter is to gain greater understanding of the big decisions that have shaped NASA's robotic Mars Exploration Program over the past 20 years by focusing on the role of the NASA Administrator in those decisions. By definition, the NASA Administrator is a political executive. As an executive, he is in charge of a federal agency and is expected to look "down and in." As a political appointee, he is a presidential agent, confirmed by the Senate and accountable to the public. He must look "up and out." As Goldin indicated in comments above, scientists may say where a program should go, but politicians will determine the resources to get there. They may also disagree about the destination. The NASA Administrator tries to influence the decision-making process involving direction and pace of what is a Big Science program. He operates in a political environment, increasingly a global political context. Does the NASA Administrator help or hinder Mars exploration—or is he irrelevant to it?

APPROACH

Any government program features hundreds, even thousands of decisions. But some are clearly more important than others. They may be called strategic. They typically pertain to program initiation, implementation, reorientation, and termination. These are decisions that are chiefly about change or maintenance in a program. Many individuals and groups try to influence those decisions. The NASA Administrator has more opportunity to exert influence than most other claimants because of his position and formal role in a hierarchy. He is the face of the Agency to its political masters.

Influence, however, is mercurial. It rises and falls. Influence depends on an Administrator's personality and skills, as well as the context in which he operates. He has semi-autonomy. There are times in history when opportunities for leadership are present and other times when they are not, owing to constraints. Most Administrators in public and private life have been maintainers. Others have had occasions to be change agents. The biggest decisions about Mars exploration have been about change in an ongoing sequence of choices and events.

The NASA Administrator is responsible for the Agency as a whole and usually is most attentive to NASA's dominant program—human spaceflight. But the Administrator also is attentive to other programs that are either especially expensive or controversial or both. More than perhaps any other robotic space endeavor, Mars exploration generates issues that land on the Administrator's desk. The robotic Mars Exploration Program tends to be a priority not only for NASA's Science Mission Directorate, but also for NASA as a whole. At least, that has been so since 1992, when Dan Goldin became

Administrator. Most NASA Administrators see the ultimate goal of human spaceflight to be Mars. Robotic exploration is a precursor to human exploration. The possibility that Mars has or had life also gives the robotic program a special panache with the public. Programs with a high public visibility and potential for controversy get a NASA Administrator's attention.

What have been the strategic decisions that have driven the Mars Exploration Program since 1992? How have NASA Administrators influenced decision-making? What have been the impacts of the decisions made? Have NASA Administrators made a difference in Mars policy?

The leaders in question during the 20-year period under consideration have been Dan Goldin (1992–2001), Sean O'Keefe (2001–05), Michael Griffin (2005–09), and Charles Bolden (2009–17). To be sure, many others are involved in the process that leads to and from big decisions. But the focus in this paper is on NASA Administrators and their influence. Administrators can affect decisions through both their executive and political roles. As executives, they choose priorities, appoint managers, adjust budgets, and organize the Agency for implementation. As political actors, they must sell their decisions internally and externally though rhetoric and coalition-building. Few human beings are equally blessed in all the talents required for NASA leadership. They must do the best they can in the period during which they serve. Leadership matters, critically so in Big Science. But leadership is hard.

DAN GOLDIN (1992–2001)

Age 51 at the time of his appointment, Goldin was born in New York City and had a B.S. in mechanical engineering from the City College of New York.[2] He worked for five years at NASA's Lewis (now Glenn) Research Center in Ohio before moving to TRW, a large aerospace firm in California. There he rose through the ranks and was Vice President and General Manager for Space when called to Washington. Most of his activities over the years were in classified national security programs. Although not known widely, in the "black" space world he was highly regarded.

Goldin came with a reputation for being intense, even intimidating, in style; visionary; and hard-working. He called himself a change agent, and that was what President George H. W. Bush wanted. He had fired Goldin's predecessor Richard Truly in part because he had not championed enthusiastically Bush's Moon-Mars human exploration initiative. That was not a problem

---

2. The Goldin section is based on a monograph by W. Henry Lambright, *Transforming Government: Dan Goldin and the Remaking of NASA* (Washington, DC: IBM, 2001), as well as ongoing research on the history of the robotic Mars program sponsored by NASA.

for Goldin. He was passionate about Mars, and that was one reason Bush chose him and why he accepted. Bush's Moon-Mars program went nowhere with Congress, as Goldin soon discovered, but he saw robotic exploration as an area where he could make progress toward the Red Planet. He replaced the Science Mission Director he had inherited with Wesley Huntress, and later—when Huntress left—with Ed Weiler. He found them both able and supportive of his Mars goals.

Goldin was retained as NASA Administrator by President Bill Clinton because Goldin's faster, better, cheaper efficiency approach to program management fit well with Clinton's, and especially Vice President Al Gore's, desire to launch a reinventing-government campaign. Goldin ultimately became their poster boy for the White House (and congressional) drive to accomplish more for less. He also endeared himself to the White House through his leadership in the International Space Station Program. He was responsive to the White House, and so the White House was responsive to him.

The occasion for a big decision involving the Red Planet came in 1993 when NASA's Mars Observer, an orbiter, failed as it approached Mars. Rather than lamenting the loss, Goldin used it to initiate a new Mars Surveyor program based on faster, better, cheaper principles. Calling Mars Observer a $1 billion Battlestar Galactica, Goldin said his new program would lower cost and risk. Instead of putting all experiments in one probe, NASA would divide them into smaller spacecraft sent every 26 months, when the Mars-Earth alignment was optimal. Getting a "program line" in the budget approved by the White House and Congress was important to this fast-paced strategy. In selling the concept of a long-term program to the White House Office of Management and Budget and Congress, Goldin and his Science Associate Administrator, Wesley Huntress, argued that they would get more science done in a less costly way.[3] Mars exploration thus became an ongoing effort, with one mission setting the stage for the next. Goldin said that the robotic Mars Surveyor program, as it was called, was a showcase for his faster, better, cheaper product line. This was an initiating decision that rejuvenated the program at a point when it might otherwise have gone onto the back burner.

Goldin's second big decision was one of reorientation. This came in the wake of the 1996 announcement of the discovery of possible fossil evidence of bacteria in the Martian meteorite ALH84001.[4] As noted above, Goldin

---

3. Wesley Huntress, interview by author, 18 September 2008.
4. "Meteorite Yields Evidence of Primitive Life on Early Mars," NASA press release, 7 August 1996, *http://www2.jpl.nasa.gov/snc/nasa1.html* (accessed 16 January 2020); D. S. McKay,

NASA Administrator Dan Goldin with a model of the Pathfinder Rover. (NASA: goldin1_marspath.jpg)

was advised that NASA had to have Mars sample return (MSR) to answer the life-on-Mars question. MSR was already a long-run goal of the Mars Surveyor program. The search for life was to derive from a gradual and comprehensive effort. There was no deadline, and the search for evidence of extraterrestrial life was downplayed in NASA rhetoric. What Goldin did was make MSR the goal of the Mars Exploration Program, with 2005 as a desired MSR launch date. He also made the search for life a stated goal for NASA and revived the field of astrobiology as critical to it. Even as the existing Mars Surveyor program was implemented, the new effort targeting Mars sample return and creating a broader scientific constituency for it commenced.

But Goldin overreached. His third big decision came in the wake of the two Mars mission failures in 1999. Those failures showed the limits of the faster, better, cheaper approach to decision-making. The existing Mars Surveyor program was ended, along with the accelerated Mars sample-return plan. A new effort, called the Mars Exploration Program, began, aimed at "following

---

E. K. Gibson, Jr., K. L. Thomas–Keprta, H. Vali, et al., "Search for Past Life on Mars: Possible Relic Biogenic Activity in Martian Meteorite ALH84001," *Science* 273, no. 5277 (16 August 1996): 924; Kathy Sawyer, *The Rock from Mars: A Detective Story on Two Planets* (New York: Random House, 2006).

the water."⁵ The new program was slower, more expensive, and, as results showed, better. Mars sample return was set beyond the program's 10-year planning horizon with no definite launch date. Goldin, the change agent, changed himself. He decided that two probes, Spirit and Opportunity (the Mars Exploration Rovers), should go to Mars rather than one. He emphasized that Mars exploration was a NASA priority, not just a science priority, and taxed other Agency divisions to pay for the extra costs that Spirit and Opportunity required.

Goldin, more than any NASA Administrator in history, came into office with a personal Mars agenda. Extremely controversial in management style, he nevertheless set the Agency on a strong trajectory toward the Red Planet during a record-setting nine-and-a-half-year tenure.

SEAN O'KEEFE (2001–05)

Age 45 at the time of his appointment, O'Keefe was born in Monterey, California, and received a bachelor's degree from Loyola University in New Orleans.⁶ He then went to the Maxwell School of Citizenship and Public Affairs at Syracuse University, where he obtained a master's degree in public administration. Not a scientist or engineer, he worked in Washington, DC, for the Defense Department and subsequently on the staff of the Senate Appropriations Committee. When Dick Cheney became Secretary of Defense in 1989, he appointed O'Keefe his comptroller and then Secretary of the Navy. O'Keefe was Deputy Director of the Office of Management and Budget under President George W. Bush in 2005 when the President appointed him NASA Administrator.

O'Keefe did not have Mars on his immediate agenda when he came to NASA. His job was to get financial control of the International Space Station (ISS), which was then absorbing a $4.8 billion overrun.⁷ O'Keefe was seen as a competent, generalist manager, with good political skills and excellent White House and congressional contacts. He delegated Mars robotic policy to Weiler, while he concentrated on the ISS. In February 2003, the Space Shuttle Columbia disintegrated upon returning to Earth's atmosphere.

---

5. Mars Exploration Payload Assessment Group, "Scientific Goals, Objectives, Investigations, and Priorities," 2001, *https://mepag.jpl.nasa.gov/reports/JPL_Pub._01-7_(Part_2).pdf* (accessed 10 March 2021).
6. The O'Keefe section is based on a monograph by W. Henry Lambright, *Executive Response to Changing Fortune: Sean O'Keefe as NASA Administrator* (Washington, DC: IBM, 2005), as well as ongoing research on the history of the robotic Mars program sponsored by NASA.
7. "NASA: Lost in Space?" Taxpayers for Common Sense, 17 July 2001, *http://www.taxpayer.net/library/weekly-wastebasket/article/nasa-lost-in-space* (accessed 17 January 2020).

CHAPTER 5 • NASA, BIG SCIENCE, AND MARS EXPLORATION **147**

NASA Administrator Sean O'Keefe and President George W. Bush in the NASA Headquarters Auditorium on 14 January 2004, when Bush announced the Vision for Space Exploration policy. (White House: P37072-21-BushatHQ-fromWhiteHouse2)

O'Keefe's role abruptly became that of a crisis manager. What O'Keefe did in that year was use his close ties with the Bush White House, especially Vice President Dick Cheney, to forge a new policy for human spaceflight through a presidential decision. Announced by Bush in early 2004, this decision was to send astronauts back to the Moon and then on to Mars and beyond.

This decision appeared at first to be a boon to the robotic program, further buoyed in the O'Keefe years by the success on Mars of the Spirit and Opportunity rovers. A new budgetary wedge was planned to integrate the robotic and human program, with the prospect of joint and enlarged funding over time. O'Keefe's management style was to use budget decisions to drive priorities, and he made Mars science a priority at the expense of other science programs. O'Keefe left NASA in 2005, having reorganized the Agency for the new human exploration mission. Building on what he inherited from Goldin, he set the Science Mission Directorate on what appeared to be an even greater Mars-priority direction.

MICHAEL GRIFFIN (2005-09)

Bush appointed Michael Griffin to succeed O'Keefe as NASA Administrator. Griffin was 55 years old.[8] Born in Aberdeen, Maryland, he received a bachelor's degree in physics from Johns Hopkins University, and then a Ph.D. in aerospace engineering from the University of Maryland. He joined the Jet Propulsion Laboratory shortly after graduation from Maryland and subsequently worked for the Johns Hopkins University Applied Physics Laboratory. In 1989, he joined DOD as Deputy for Technology with President Ronald Reagan's Strategic Defense Initiative Organization (commonly known as Star Wars).

A lifelong true believer in human spaceflight, Griffin left DOD in 1989 to run NASA's new Space Exploration Initiative office following George H. W. Bush's Moon-Mars decision. Not long after that program was killed by Congress, he departed NASA to return to the private sector, eventually the Applied Physics Laboratory.

Griffin was the consummate rocket engineer, with additional academic degrees and a coauthored book, *Space Vehicle Design*, among his credits. Unlike Goldin, who intervened in a range of space decisions and most programs seeking almost constant change, Griffin's style was more that of a highly focused technical manager. His attention and interventions largely aimed at human spaceflight. He was not particularly interested in—or skilled at—the outside political side of his job. He had few helpful contacts in the White House and found dealing with OMB thoroughly unpleasant.

As NASA Administrator, Griffin concentrated on implementing President George W. Bush's Moon-Mars program, called Constellation. He focused on technical and managerial decisions related to the launch vehicle and space capsule associated with Constellation. He delegated the robotic Mars program mainly to his Science Associate Administrators. He had four Science Associate Administrators in his four-year tenure: Ed Weiler, Mary Cleave, Alan Stern, and then Weiler again.

Griffin's primary decision affecting the Mars program when he took office was to replace O'Keefe's "priority" with "balance." Money was spread across various fields, a decision that pushed Mars sample return further into the indefinite future. He sought to tell the President what he regarded as the truth about the cost of human spaceflight but was not rewarded for his honesty with sufficient money. One result was that science and Mars program

---

8. The Griffin section is based on a monograph by W. Henry Lambright, *Launching a New Mission: Michael Griffin and NASA's Return to the Moon* (Washington, DC: IBM, 2009), as well as ongoing research on the history of the robotic Mars program sponsored by NASA.

NASA Administrator Mike Griffin speaking during a visit to the NASA Ames Research Center. (NASA: ACD05-0084-31)

budgets were cut to help fill the gap in human exploration expenses. Griffin and the science community found themselves at odds, much to Griffin's regret. Less money meant a slower pace toward Mars sample return.

Griffin's third Science Associate Administrator was Alan Stern. It was Stern who wanted to be the change agent, and the changes he sought brought him into sharp dispute with JPL and the Mars science community. He played hardball with the most expensive mission of the Mars Exploration Program then under way, the Mars Science Laboratory (MSL). Cost overruns were real and serious.

Stern argued to delay the mission two years and also add a cache to make the mission the initial step toward Mars sample return. Griffin refused the request for delay but went along with the cache idea. When Stern cut the budget for Spirit and Opportunity without telling Griffin, the NASA Administrator and Stern parted ways. What Griffin found was that he needed a more politically astute Science Associate Administrator, and he brought back Weiler, who was then Director of Goddard Space Flight Center, to head the Science Mission Directorate.

Weiler killed Stern's cache but helped persuade Griffin that MSL really needed an extra two years to be technically ready. Delaying MSL was the most important decision about Mars that Griffin made. It meant that the cost of MSL went up substantially. But the success of MSL in 2012 showed the wisdom of the decision.

CHARLES BOLDEN (2009-17)

Charles Bolden, President Barack Obama's choice for NASA Administrator, was a 61-year-old retired marine Brigadier General and ex-NASA astronaut.[9] An African American from Columbia, South Carolina, Bolden had scored many firsts in his career, and he was the first African American appointed to lead NASA. His name was urged on Obama by Senator Bill Nelson (D-FL), at that time the senior Democrat on NASA's authorizing subcommittee in the Senate.[10]

Bolden graduated from the U.S. Naval Academy with a degree in electrical science and went on to a distinguished career as a marine naval aviator, flying many combat missions. For 14 years, he was a member of NASA's astronaut corps, serving on four Space Shuttle missions, including two as commander.[11] He worked as Assistant Deputy Administrator to Goldin in 1992.

Bolden was in private business in Houston when he was asked to return to NASA. He did not particularly want to be NASA Administrator. Having served on various NASA advisory committees in recent years, he knew the Agency's problems and disliked Washington politics. But he was "a good soldier" and could not say no to the President. Although Bolden saw human spaceflight to Mars as NASA's destiny, he did not have a special agenda when he assumed NASA's command. In style, Bolden was friendly, approachable, and positive in outlook. He was a delegator who retained the managers he inherited, including Weiler. His access to the White House was limited. His deputy, Lori Garver, was better connected politically than he. His emphasis was human spaceflight, and his biggest problem was the Constellation program, which was well behind schedule and costing too much. It was not until early 2010 that the fate of Constellation became known, a presidential decision on which Bolden had little influence.

---

9. The Bolden section is based on research under way on the robotic Mars program, as well as the author's long-term research on NASA administrative leadership under IBM sponsorship. Charles Bolden, interview by author, 24 July 2012.
10. Andrew Lawler, "Obama Turns to NASA Veterans to Lead Space Agency," *Science* 324 (29 May 2009): 1125.
11. Bolden served as pilot on STS-31, the Shuttle mission that deployed the Hubble Space Telescope.

NASA Administrator Charles Bolden speaking at the launch of the Mars Atmosphere and Volatile EvolutioN, or MAVEN, mission. (NASA/Kim Shiflett: KSC-2013-4020)

Meanwhile, he did become involved with the robotic Mars program through Weiler. The Associate Administrator for Science worked during the transition from Griffin to Bolden to initiate a joint Mars exploration program with the European Space Agency (ESA). NASA's existing Mars Exploration Program was running its course, and there was no multimission program planned beyond MSL and a small orbiter mission called MAVEN to study Mars's atmosphere. The plan Weiler had was to link with ESA's ExoMars mission, with launches planned in 2016 and 2018, and continue in alliance toward Mars sample return in the 2020s.

On 5 November 2009, Bolden signed a "statement of intent" with his ESA counterpart Jean Jacques Dordain for the joint exploration of Mars, starting with participation in the ExoMars program.[12] Planning at the technical level ensued. The prospective joint program, however, soon became hostage to larger political machinations concerning human spaceflight and NASA's overall budget.

---

12. Doug McCuistion, Director, NASA's Mars Exploration Program, "Overview of NASA and the 'New" Mars Exploration Program," 2010, *https://mars.nasa.gov/news/1030/nasa-and-esas-first-joint-mission-to-mars-selects-instruments/* (accessed 10 March 2021).

On 1 February 2010, the Obama administration's rollout of its budget request for NASA called for killing the Constellation program and building a commercial industry to service the ISS. A major investment would be made in technology development. For science, there was a new priority given to Earth science, owing to White House interest in climate change. Nothing was said of destinations, and the Moon-Mars goal of Constellation vanished.

These decisions were greeted with bipartisan opposition in Congress and dismay within NASA. Both Obama and Bolden were put on the defensive. Bolden argued behind the scenes for the necessity of a destination, especially Mars. In April, Obama sought to respond to what was obviously a political disaster for NASA. He called for a goal to reach an asteroid by 2025 and trip to Mars in 2030s. Congress was not assuaged, and it was not until October 2010 that the White House and Congress reached a compromise that restored part of Constellation, along with funds for commercial spaceflight. NASA would build a heavy-lift rocket and space capsule for the asteroid-Mars goal while relying on the emergent commercial sector for trips to the ISS. Given the Agency's overall budget constraints, the compromise was a considerable burden to NASA. In addition, the James Webb Space Telescope (JWST) had suffered a multibillion-dollar overrun that had to be addressed.[13]

For Bolden, these developments meant that he was caught between the White House and Congress over priorities. For the robotic Mars program, disagreement between NASA's political masters created delays in getting needed decisions. The National Research Council (NRC) in March 2011 lent its weight to Mars sample return as the top priority for solar system exploration over the next 10 years.[14] The first step would be a mission to collect samples.

NASA and ESA proposed a joint Mars rover mission with sample collecting capability for the 2018 ExoMars mission. ESA asked for a letter from Bolden in June 2011 that would commit U.S. funds to ExoMars.[15] Bolden favored the joint activity, but he could not deliver the funding commitment. Weiler, throughout the summer of 2011, negotiated with OMB on the joint program. OMB refused to support a "flagship mission"—that is, the

---

13. James Webb Space Telescope (JWST) Independent Comprehensive Review Panel (ICRP), Final Report, 29 October 2010, *https://www.nasa.gov/pdf/499224main_JWST-ICRP_Report-FINAL.pdf* (accessed 17 January 2020).
14. National Research Council, *Visions and Voyages for Planetary Science in the Decade 2013–2022* (Washington, DC: National Academies Press), 2011.
15. Peter de Selding, "NASA Cannot Launch 2016 ExoMars Orbiter," *Space News* (3 October 2011): 4, 13.

sample-collecting mission—and what it implied for long-term spending. Weiler, utterly frustrated, retired 30 September.[16]

In October, Bolden and Dordain met. Dordain was desperate, as his own funding for ExoMars depended on getting a NASA commitment.[17] Bolden told him he could not act because his budget remained uncertain. They agreed to bring in a third party, Russia, to try to ease the cost burden and make the program they wanted more feasible.

The conversation between Bolden and Dordain continued. Bolden at the same time had negotiations with the head of OMB. His Mars discussions took place amidst sometimes bitter sessions between senior lawmakers and the White House over the human spaceflight program and overall NASA spending.

Between Thanksgiving and Christmas 2011, decisions on NASA's upcoming budget came to a head. NASA had a team of scientists and engineers in Paris negotiating technical requirements for a joint Mars program. Bolden was on the phone with Dordain trying to find ways they could pay for at least the 2018 mission. OMB told Bolden that he would have to choose between JWST and a flagship Mars mission. Owing to political support for JWST, the NASA Administrator knew this was no choice. Bolden called his team in Paris back home. Technically, Bolden made the decision to reject NASA participation in the joint program. The reality was that this decision was forced on him by OMB. What OMB did reflected priorities worked out between the President and powerful forces in Congress. When the NASA budget came out in February 2012, planetary science in general, and Mars in particular, took a huge hit.

Bolden had lost a battle but was not about to give up on Mars. He turned to John Grunsfeld, the new Associate Administrator for Science, and told him that he could not get a flagship Mars program sold during the current Obama term. But he wanted to mount a drive to get a decision by Obama or his successor as President for a new multimission program that the country could afford. He told Grunsfeld:

---

16. "NASA Science Chief Retiring From Agency," *Space News*, 27 September 2011, https://spacenews.com/nasa-science-chief-retiring-agency/ (accessed 24 March 2021); Yudhijit Bhattacharjee, "Ed Weiler Says He Quit NASA Over Cuts to Mars Program," 9 February 2012, http://www.sciencemag.org/news/2012/02/ed-weiler-says-he-quit-nasa-over-cuts-mars-program (accessed 17 January 2020).
17. Frank Morring, Jr., "Picking Up the Pieces," *Aviation Week & Space Technology* (10 October 2011): 46–47; Jean-Jacques Dordain, "Space Shots," *Space News* (17 October 2011): 18.

I want to prepare a program plan for the next administration. It has to lead to Mars Sample Return. NAS-NRC has said it would not support a Mars program without that goal. I want to synergize manned [sic] and robotic space. At worst, I want a major launch initiative [to Mars] in two years. Combine as much as you can. Stop stovepiping. Let's have some technology development. Let's do Mars in a way that is faster, better, and fiscally reasonable.[18]

Bolden ordered Grunsfeld to work with NASA's human spaceflight chief and others to develop an integrated program. Grunsfeld turned to Orlando Figueroa, NASA's former Mars program director, now retired, to head a planning team for a "Mars Next Decade" program.[19] NASA asked the Mars community and JPL for their ideas. Meanwhile, Mars supporters on Capitol Hill decried the cuts and fought to have Obama's February budget request changed by Congress.

On 6 August, prospects for Mars exploration took a turn for the better when the $2.5 billion Mars Science Laboratory rover, Curiosity, landed safely on the Red Planet. Everyone, including President Obama, praised the achievement. The President may have sent NASA a message saying he personally would "protect" the Mars investment.[20] Two weeks after the MSL landing, NASA announced that it would launch a new Mars mission in 2016 called InSight. It would be a moderately priced mission to dig beneath the surface to get better understanding of the Mars interior. It symbolized the intent of the Agency to try to continue with Mars missions at each 26-month opportunity. It was not formally part of NASA's Mars Exploration Program. The money came from another small-mission program called Discovery.

Bolden had suffered a tenure in which he had not been able to promote Mars as a priority to the degree he wished. But in what he thought might be the waning months of his time at NASA, he sought to use the success of Curiosity as a catalyst to maintain momentum in Mars exploration in the hopes that he or his successor could get a "new start" decision from the next administration. The reelection of Obama in November 2012 gave reason for optimism. On 4 December, Grunsfeld announced that the White House

---

18. Charles Bolden, interview by author, 24 July 2012.
19. Marcia Smith, "NASA Starts Planning for Smaller Mars Missions in 2018," Spacepolicyonline.com, 27 February 2012, *https://spacepolicyonline.com/news/nasa-starts-planning-for-smaller-mars-mission-in-2018/* (accessed 17 January 2020); W. Henry Lambright, *Why Mars: NASA and the Politics of Space Exploration* (Baltimore: Johns Hopkins, 2014), p. 247.
20. Alan Boyle, "Obama Tells Mars Rover Team: Let Me Know if You See Martians," NBCNEWS.com, 13 August 2012, *http://cosmiclog.nbcnews.com/_news/2012/08/13/13259297-obama-tells-mars-rover-team-let-me-know-if-you-see-martians* (accessed 17 January 2020).

had approved a $1.5 billion Mars rover mission for 2020. In January 2013, President Obama decided to retain Bolden.

CONCLUSION

The past 20 years of the Mars Exploration Program have been extraordinary. Without question, the program has been a success, despite many bumps in the road. The safe landing of the Curiosity rover is a testament to NASA's ability to manage complex Big Science programs. This particular mission, the climax of the current "follow-the-water" strategy, has received justifiable praise. Indeed, the entire Mars Exploration Program is an example of how to advance Big Science in a difficult, often harsh political environment. The use of orbiters, landers, and rovers in a comprehensive, systematic, step-by-step progression has worked. While the past 20 years are, on the whole, a success story, they have also had their problems, and the future of the Mars Exploration Program today is quite uncertain.

This chapter has focused on big decisions and the role of the NASA Administrator in them over the past two decades. Have Administrators helped, hindered, or been irrelevant to the Mars Exploration Program?

The answer is that they have helped far more than they have hindered progress and always have been relevant. One way or another, major Mars decisions get to the Administrator's desk. Goldin deserves much credit for turning the failure of Mars Observer in 1993 into a catalyst to launch the Mars Surveyor program. This decision put NASA on a Mars trajectory that has continued to this day. His decision to reorient the program with Mars sample return as an accelerated goal was premature and an example of the overreach that marked the faster, better, cheaper strategy in general. This overreach helped lead to two failed missions in 1999. However, Goldin learned from his mistakes and reset the Mars program on a more realistic track before he left NASA.

O'Keefe's contribution lay with his decision to make the robotic exploration program an even higher priority through integrating it with the new Moon-Mars human spaceflight program. Goldin resurrected the search for life as a rationale for the robotic program. O'Keefe gave new emphasis to the robotic program as a precursor for human exploration.

Griffin's initial decisions as Administrator put a damper on the Mars program in order to help other space science endeavors. O'Keefe's "priority" emphasis gave way to "balance" in the science program. Griffin's early appointments for Science Associate Administrator did not endear him to many Mars advocates. However, he helped the Mars program near the end of his tour by protecting Spirit and Opportunity, by bringing Weiler back as Science Associate Administrator, and especially by deciding to delay the Mars Science Laboratory. A postponement of a flagship mission is a very big decision, with significant budgetary implications. Griffin did not want to delay but eventually did so. Delay turned out to be the right decision. Failure of MSL in the budgetary environment of present times would have devastated Mars exploration.

Bolden was tightly constrained in his influence as NASA Administrator by the seemingly endless war between the White House and Congress over the human space program. He was also constrained by the toxic politics of partisan conflict that has meant government by continuing resolution and budgetary uncertainty. With NASA's overall budget capped, OMB unrelenting, and his political masters backing other priorities, he was forced to withdraw from the joint Mars program with ESA. However, he used the successful landing of the Curiosity rover to help initiate a major new Mars rover mission that was at a funding level the White House could accept.

All these Administrators have been pro-Mars. Some have had more administrative power than others; some have been more adroit in their use of power than others. Initially or later in their tenure, they all have made it clear that Mars exploration is not only a space science priority, it is a NASA priority. Most have wanted to better integrate human and robotic programs. Leadership at NASA has taken a relay form, with one Administrator handing off the Mars baton to the next. Not all leaders have run at the same pace, or avoided pitfalls, but all have kept NASA moving forward toward the Red Planet. That is one reason Mars exploration has been such a remarkable success in the past 20 years. It is a long-term, Big Science effort in a constraint-filled, short-term political context. Administrators attempt to provide momentum through their decisions, bridging science and politics.

A scholar once described governmental decision making as the "science of muddling through." So it has been with the Mars Exploration Program—decision-making has been "incremental," "disjointed."[21] The job of the NASA Administrator is to engage as intelligently as possible in this messy but essential process of governing in order to keep the Agency pointed in the Mars direction. The Administrators discussed in this chapter have done that.

---

21. Charles Lindblom, "The Science of Muddling Through," *Public Administration Preview* 19, no. 2 (spring 1959): 79–88.

PART IV
Public Perceptions, Priorities, and Solar System Exploration

THE NEXT THREE CHAPTERS depart from analysis of the science, technology, and politics of solar system exploration to consider public perceptions of solar system exploration and the roles that NASA, the media, and members of the scientific community play in influencing public perceptions, or not.

Linda Billings explores the case of a scientific claim that became accepted as a "fact" without undergoing the standard peer-review process. A claim that *Streptococcus mitis*—a common member of the human oral microbiome—went to the Moon on a NASA Surveyor lunar lander and survived for 32 months in the harsh conditions of the lunar surface was disputed when it was made. Yet the claim became widely accepted as a fact without undergoing formal peer review. The claim maintained its status as scientific and historical fact for decades, until visual evidence surfaced that refuted the claim.

Laura Delgado López examines the idea of the "killer asteroid" in popular culture and in public policy discourse. Though the narrative of mass destruction by means of planetary impact goes back much further in time, she shows how the 1980 Alvarez hypothesis, linking a massive impact event with the extinction of the dinosaurs, boosted public interest in the impact narrative. However, she concludes that pop-culture depictions of impact disasters do not appear to have had much influence on public opinion or public policy.

One recent example of a far-fetched pop-culture depiction of an impending asteroid-impact disaster is the CBS television series *Salvation*, which aired for two seasons in 2017 and 2018. This show followed a plotline in which a graduate student and a billionaire inform the Pentagon that an asteroid is six months away from colliding with Earth. The impending impact is kept secret, as are preparations to deflect the impact. This show likely had no impact on policy-makers. In reality, all known impact hazards are immediately made public, as would be plans for deflecting an asteroid off an impact course with Earth and preparations for impact mitigation in case deflection is not an option. This work is coordinated through the International Asteroid Warning Network (IAWN) and the international Space Mission Planning Advisory Group (SMPAG). Policy-makers in the United States and elsewhere are being kept informed.

The single most influential event affecting the public's (and especially policy-makers') perceptions about asteroid impact risks was not a TV show or a sci-fi movie, but the 15 February 2013 bolide impact event over Chelyabinsk, Russia, in which an asteroid of some 66 feet in size exploded in the atmosphere. The event was widely observed, recorded, and studied in its immediate aftermath—providing the first opportunity for scientists to develop an in-depth understanding of this phenomenon. In the United States, NASA established a Planetary Defense Coordination Office (PDCO) in January 2016, and the National Science and Technology Council (NSTC) Interagency Working Group for Detecting and Mitigating the Impact of Earth-Bound Near-Earth Objects (DAMIEN) published a National Near-Earth Object Preparedness Strategy and Action Plan in June 2018.

Giny Cheong looks at how NASA and JPL worked with the mass media to communicate about the science of the Voyager, Galileo, and Cassini missions to the outer planets and how these communications evolved over time. She considers how the mass media framed the science of these missions, focusing on human interest and human emotions. She concludes with some thoughts about the transition from "old" to "new" media, the shift in news and information "gatekeeping" from mass media to individual consumers, and other factors that are changing the cultural landscape in which science communication takes place. The proliferation of online news and information outlets and social media networks over the past several years provides greater opportunities to inform interested members of the public about what is going on in space exploration. As of this writing, almost two dozen individuals were working on NASA's social media team, and NASA's "flagship" social media accounts included Facebook, Twitter, Instagram, Snapchat, YouTube, Tumblr, Pinterest, Google Plus, LinkedIn, Giphy, Flickr, Ustream, Twitch, Slideshare, and Soundcloud.[1]

---

1. *https://www.nasa.gov/socialmedia* (accessed 9 January 2020).

CHAPTER 6

Survivor! (?) The Story of *S. mitis* on the Moon

Linda Billings

THE STORY OF HOW BACTERIA from Earth survived for more than two years on the surface of the Moon is well known in the annals of the U.S. space program and beyond. In places ranging from peer-reviewed journals to official space-agency sources, Wikipedia, and fringe-y websites such as the self-explanatory "UFO Updates List"[1] and "Cosmic Ancestry" (an archive maintained by a "strong-panspermia" advocate),[2] the account of how technicians at the NASA found viable *Streptococcus mitis* (*S. mitis*) bacteria inside equipment retrieved from the Moon and returned to Earth by astronauts has been replicated widely and reported as fact for decades.

Some skeptics have argued over the years, however, that what have been described as bacteria that survived a roundtrip to the Moon and back were actually bacteria that never left Earth. The story involves a set of claims that were disputed when they were first made public and are still in dispute today.

This chapter will show how this story of the remarkable survival of Earth bacteria in the harsh lunar environment for a prolonged period of time is not

---

1. *http://www.ufoupdateslist.com/1998/sep/m01-001.shtml* (accessed 17 January 2020).
2. *http://www.panspermia.org*. The panspermia hypothesis posits that key elements of life as we know it, such as amino acids, were delivered to Earth from space and are likely found elsewhere. According to the "strong panspermia" hypothesis, a power greater than ourselves created life and spread it throughout the universe. Life on Earth began when fully formed microbes were delivered here from space.

fact but folklore. More than 30 years after the story was first told, it is not likely that it can be proven definitively true or false. However, the evidence now points to "false," largely thanks to the unearthing of old visual records of cleanroom procedures. I make the case here that the claim that *S. mitis* traveled from Earth to the Moon, returned to Earth, and came back to life in a lab does not qualify as scientific truth. I explore this story as an interesting case in the social construction of scientific facts, and I consider how a few pictures can belie thousands of words.

A BRIEF INTRODUCTION TO THE STORY OF *S. MITIS* ON THE MOON

In 1969, astronauts on NASA's Apollo 12 mission to the Moon collected parts of the Agency's Surveyor III robotic lunar lander for return to Earth. In 1971, two technicians who had worked on microbial analysis of the parts at NASA's Manned Spacecraft Center (MSC, now Johnson Space Center) claimed they had been able to grow *Streptococcus mitis* from a swab of the parts. They concluded that *S. mitis* had flown to the Moon on Surveyor III, survived on the surface for 27 months, and come back to life upon return to Earth and more amenable environmental conditions. The implication was that terrestrial microbial life could survive on the surface of the Moon.

NASA subsequently published these findings in a 1972 report, *Analysis of Surveyor 3 Material and Photographs Returned by Apollo 12*.[3] In 1974, the prestigious peer-reviewed journal *Annual Review of Microbiology*[4] published a paper on advances in space microbiology. This paper reported the claim of *S. mitis* surviving on the Moon as fact.

Over the next three decades the *Annual Review* paper was cited in 31 peer-reviewed journal papers, and in places ranging from NASA fact sheets to Wikipedia entries and Web sites, the account of how *S. mitis* survived for 31 months on the Moon and came back to life on Earth was widely replicated as "fact."

The full story of *S. mitis* on the Moon follows.

PART 1: SURVEYOR III GOES TO THE MOON; APOLLO 12 FOLLOWS

On 17 April 1967, NASA launched its robotic Surveyor III spacecraft to the Moon. Surveyor III made a soft landing on the Moon on 20 April 1967, with a suite of instruments including a camera on board. Surveyor III's instruments

---

3. Scientific and Technical Information Office, *Analysis of Surveyor 3 Material and Photographs Returned by Apollo 12* (Washington, DC: NASA, 1972) pp. 239–247.
4. The journal ranked third of 112 microbiology journals included in the 2011 Journal Citation Reports, with an impact factor of 14.345 and a cited half-life of greater than 10.

Apollo 12 astronaut Pete Conrad examining Surveyor 3 before removing its television camera and several other pieces to be taken back to Earth. The Intrepid Lunar Module can be seen in the background. (NASA: AS12-48-7134)

transmitted data and imagery for 14 days, then shut down, mission accomplished. For two years and seven months, Surveyor III sat at its lunar landing site untouched by human hands. In a related development, in 1967 NASA's MSC completed construction of its 8,000-square-meter Lunar Receiving Laboratory (LRL) for handling sample materials to be returned to Earth by Apollo astronauts. The lab included biological facilities, a crew isolation area, and gas-analysis and radiation-counting laboratories.[5]

The stated functions of the LRL were to distribute samples to the scientific community; perform time-critical sample measurements; permanently

---

5. Judy Allton, "25 Years of Curating Moon Rocks," *Lunar News* 57 (1994), *http://curator.jsc.nasa.gov/lunar/lnews/lnjul94/hist25.htm* (accessed 17 January 2020).

A U.S. Navy Underwater Demolition Team swimmer assists the Apollo 12 crew during recovery operations in the Pacific Ocean. (NASA: S69-22271)

store under vacuum a portion of each sample; and perform quarantine testing of lunar material samples, spacecraft, and astronauts. On 14 November 1969, NASA launched its Apollo 12 mission to the Moon, its second lunar landing excursion, with a crew of three astronauts—Charles "Pete" Conrad, Alan Bean, and Richard Gordon, Jr. On 19 November, Conrad and Bean landed their Lunar Module Intrepid about 163 meters away from where Surveyor III sat in the lunar Ocean of Storms. On 20 November, the astronauts retrieved several pieces of equipment from the Surveyor spacecraft, including its camera.

According to records[6] of the Apollo 12 mission, Conrad and Bean stashed the camera in a sample pack, zipped it shut, brought it back to the Lunar Module and stowed it on-board, and took it home to Earth. It is not clear whether any crewmember may have touched the camera with bare hands or breathed on it inside the module. The Apollo 12 crew returned to Earth on 24 November, splashing down in the South Pacific near Pago Pago. Photos

---

6. Scientific and Technical Information Office, "Analysis of Surveyor 3 Material and Photographs Returned by Apollo 12," Washington, DC, NASA, 1972, p. 244; "Surveyor Crater and Surveyor III," Apollo 12 Lunar Surface Journal, *https://www.hq.nasa.gov/office/pao/History/alsj/a12/a12.html* (accessed 17 January 2020).

of the retrieval of the Apollo 12 crew at splashdown show that they were not wearing their protective "biological isolation garments." Once the astronauts were moved from their capsule to an aircraft carrier, they donned their protective garments and entered an isolation unit aboard the carrier. The sample pack containing the Surveyor camera parts was retrieved along with other equipment inside the capsule and returned to the MSC. The sample pack was taken to and quarantined at the Lunar Receiving Laboratory, where "it was placed inside of two Teflon bags and sealed for storage at room temperature."[7] Available NASA records do not clearly indicate who may have handled the camera sample pack in the trip from inside the capsule after splashdown to the carrier and then to the LRL.[8]

PART 2: SURVIVAL ON THE MOON?

On 8 January 1970, LRL personnel began examining the Surveyor camera. Microbial analysis came first, as soon as the camera was opened.[9] Working in a cleanroom environment, technicians performed standard microbial assays, using sterile swabs moistened with sterile saline solution to sample parts of the camera, applying the swabs to containers of nutrient material, and waiting to see if any microbes would grow. After four days of incubation, one sample produced "visible microbial growth." The apparently microbe-laden sample had been taken from foam embedded inside the body of the camera. "The isolate was identified, with confirmation from the U.S. Public Health Service Center for Disease Control…as…*Streptococcus mitis*,"[10] reported two of the technicians involved in the analysis.

In January 1971, at the Second Lunar Science Conference in Houston, results of this analysis were reported, in two separate papers, and later published in conference proceedings. In the first paper, F. J. Mitchell, a U.S. Air Force major assigned to the Preventive Medicine Division of NASA's MSC, and R. H. Ellis, a contractor[11] working at MSC, claimed that the *S. mitis* that had been cultured in the LRL had traveled to the Moon on Surveyor III,

---

7. John D. Rummel, Judy Allton, and Don Morrison, "A Microbe on the Moon? Surveyor III and Lessons Learned for Future Sample Return Missions," *http://www.lpi.usra.edu/meetings/sssr2011/presentations/rummel.pdf* (accessed 17 January 2020).
8. According to John D. Rummel, a former NASA planetary protection officer, it is likely that the astronauts handled the sample pack after splashdown. (Personal communication.)
9. F. J. Mitchell and W. L. Ellis, "Surveyor III: Bacterium Isolated from Lunar-Retrieved TV Camera," in *Proceedings of the Second Lunar Sciences Conference*, vol. 3 (Cambridge, MA: MIT Press, 1971), pp. 2721–2733.
10. Ibid., p. 2727.
11. Ellis worked for Brown and Root-Northrop.

survived on the lunar surface for two and a half years, and, once returned to Earth, revived, and reproduced. NASA had not anticipated the return of Surveyor components to Earth, so it had not conducted any microbial analysis of the Surveyor camera's interior before launch. "Decontamination measures taken before the Surveyor launch did not eliminate the possibility that the spacecraft carried organisms to the moon," they asserted.[12] They noted that conditions during prelaunch vacuum testing and later on the lunar surface could have freeze-dried any biological material on the spacecraft and could have played a role in enabling *S. mitis* to survive on the Moon.

Mitchell and Ellis described the conduct of the Surveyor III camera analysis in great detail. A brief summary of their report follows, starting with cleanroom procedures:

> The…camera was placed in a laminar-outflow hood equipped with high-efficiency particulate air filters…in the LRL astronaut debriefing room, which has an air-conditioning system separate from the system used by the rest of the LRL. Every surface of the…hood which would be exposed to the camera was thoroughly washed twice with isopropyl alcohol prior to the camera being placed in the hood…. Only those personnel directly responsible for disassembling and sampling the TV cameras were permitted in the room. They were clothed in…surgical caps, face masks, and sterile gloves.[13]

Samples taken from the Surveyor camera parts were applied to three different types of growth media for aerobic, anaerobic, and mycological analysis. "The protocol established for the aerobic and anaerobic analyses… contained a system of redundancy and cross-checks designed to identify suspected laboratory contamination…. Obvious cases of laboratory contamination could easily be identified and reported as such," they reported.[14] Swabs from only one sampled surface—a 1-cubic-millimeter piece of foam inside the camera—yielded visible microbial growth.

"Every step in the retrieval of the Surveyor III TV camera was analyzed for possible contamination sources, including camera contact by the astronauts; ingassing in the lunar module and command module during the mission or at 'splashdown'; and handling during quarantine, disassembly, and analysis at the LRL," they said. Mitchell and Ellis dismissed the possibility of contamination by astronauts during retrieval from the Moon as "no viable

---

12. F. J. Mitchell and W. L. Ellis, "Surveyor III: Bacterium Isolated from Lunar-Retrieved TV Camera," p. 2721.
13. Ibid., pp. 2723–2724.
14. Ibid., pp. 2725–2726.

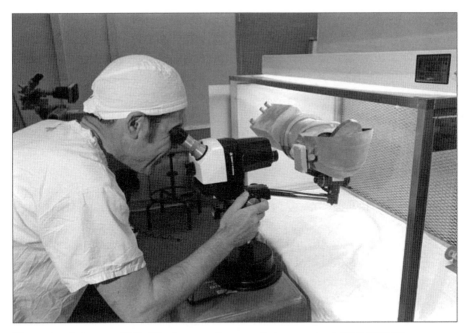

Photo taken in January 1970 of the Surveyor III camera being examined. (NASA: P-10709B)

terrestrial microorganism has ever been detected in the [lunar] samples collected by the astronauts." They also surmised that the camera's shroud "may have provided a formidable barrier to ingassing carrying fine particles, perhaps even the size of a bacterium…. Extreme precautions were taken at all times during the analysis to prevent any handling errors which might have caused contamination."[15]

"The available data indicates," they concluded, "that *Streptococcus mitis* was isolated from the foam sample and suggest that the bacterium was deposited in the Surveyor III TV camera before spacecraft launch."[16]

At the very same meeting, M. D. Knittel, M. S. Favero, and R. H. Green presented a paper in which they reported on the results of microbial sampling of returned Surveyor III electrical cabling.[17] Knittel and Green were both with the Jet Propulsion Laboratory, where Surveyor spacecraft were

---

15. Ibid., pp. 2728–2729.
16. Ibid., p. 2732.
17. M. D. Knittel, M. S. Favero, and R. H. Green, "Microbial Sampling of Returned Surveyor III Electrical Cabling," *Proceedings of the Second Lunar Science Conference*, vol. 3 (Cambridge, MA: MIT Press, 1971), pp. 2715–2719.

developed.[18] Favero was with the Phoenix Field Station of the U.S. Public Health Department. They reported on the results of an experiment they conducted to determine whether terrestrial microbial life, if any had been present on Surveyor III upon launch, could have survived 31 months of exposure to lunar surface conditions. Their findings raised some questions about Mitchell and Ellis's report.

Knittel, Favero, and Green chose to examine a piece of electrical wire bundling running from the Surveyor camera to another part of the spacecraft, because earlier studies had shown that "a high level of microbial contamination [was] associated with wiring bundles."[19] "If, during the actual sampling of the wires," they observed, "a contaminant were accidentally introduced, it would be impossible to separate it from a lunar survivor." Thus "it was necessary," they said, "to perform several simulated assays with a piece of sterile wiring bundle before the lunar sample was assayed. During these simulated assays, all of the procedures that were to be applied in sampling of the Surveyor III cable were used to determine if the sampling could be done without contamination. These procedures increased the confidence that the Surveyor III cable could be examined without contamination."[20]

"Prior to opening the Sealed Environmental Sampling Container containing the Surveyor III cable and other parts," they reported, technicians discovered that it had leaked. "When the [container] was opened, it was found to contain a high concentration of oxygen.... There was concern whether airborne bacterial contamination of the exterior wraps would penetrate to the interior of the wiring bundle." Their work in the lab showed that "if airborne bacteria did pass into the [container] through the leak, the wiring bundle wraps would protect the wires beneath it from contamination."[21]

Their results showed "that no viable microorganisms were recovered from that portion of Surveyor III cable that was sampled.... The prelaunch thermal and vacuum testing of the Surveyor III spacecraft could have accounted for a major reduction in the bacterial contamination," they noted. Knittel, Favero, and Green concluded "that no microorganisms survived on the wiring bundle during its lunar exposure. That is not to say that a microorganism cannot survive exposure to the lunar environment, but only that none

---

18. In their paper (p. 2733), Mitchell and Ellis acknowledged Knittel "for supervising the selection of sampling sites and assisting in the [Surveyor] sampling" and Green for "technical and administrative assistance."
19. Knittel et al., p. 2715.
20. Ibid., p. 2716.
21. Ibid., pp. 2716–2717.

were found on the returned piece."[22] The implication was that if no viable microbes were found on these protected wiring samples, then it would not be likely that any viable microbes would be found on other hardware samples taken from Surveyor III.

NASA subsequently published the findings of both Mitchell and Ellis and Knittel et al., as they were reported at the 1971 Lunar Science Conference in a 1972 report, "Analysis of Surveyor 3 Material and Photographs Returned by Apollo 12."[23]

Did Mitchell and Ellis prove that *S. mitis* could survive on the Moon and come back to life on Earth? Did Knittel, Favero, and Green's findings raise serious doubts about Mitchell and Ellis's claims? Subsequent developments further complicated the story of *S. mitis* on the Moon.

PART 3: HOW A CLAIM BECAME A FACT

In 1974, the prestigious peer-reviewed journal *Annual Review of Microbiology*[24] published a paper by Gerald R. Taylor of NASA Johnson Space Center's Life Sciences Directorate (previously of JSC predecessor MSC's Preventive Medicine Division) that reported on advances in space microbiology.[25] In this paper, Taylor cited the Lunar Science Conference papers by Mitchell and Ellis and by Knittel, Favero, and Green.[26] In his text, however, Taylor noted only the findings of Mitchell and Ellis, as follows:

> Various components of the American Surveyor III spacecraft, which had resided on the moon for 2.5 yr, were returned during the Apollo 12 mission and analyzed for the presence of viable microorganisms.... Except for the presence of *Streptococcus mitis*, which was considered by the investigators to have been deeply embedded within the camera body before it left the Earth, no viable microbes were recovered from any of the tested components.[27]

---

22. Ibid., p. 2719.
23. NASA Scientific and Technical Information Office, "Analysis of Surveyor 3 Material and Photographs Returned by Apollo 12," includes Part A, "Surveyor 3: Bacterium Isolated from Lunar-Retrieved Television Camera," pp. 239–247, http://www.hq.nasa.gov/alsj/a12/AnalysSurvIIIMtrial.pdf (accessed 17 January 2020); M. D. Knittel, M. S. Favero, and R. H. Green, "Microbiological Sampling," pp. 248–252.
24. See footnote 4.
25. Gerald R. Taylor, "Space Microbiology," *Annual Review of Microbiology* 28 (1974): 121–137.
26. Taylor coauthored, with J. Kelton Ferguson and Charles Truby, a paper "Methods Used to Monitor the Microbial Load of Returned Lunar Material," *Applied Microbiology* 20, no. 2 (1970): 271–272, http://www.ncbi.nlm.nih.gov/pmc/articles/PMC376914/?page=1 (accessed 17 January 2020).
27. Taylor, "Space Microbiology," p. 122.

Over the next three decades (1974 to 2006), according to Science Citation Index, Taylor's paper was cited in 31 peer-reviewed journal papers, in publications ranging from *Icarus* and *Infection and Immunity* to *Microbiology and Molecular Biology Reviews*, *Microbiological Research*, *Phytopathology*, and *Trends in Biotechnology*. Meanwhile, in places including NASA fact sheets, Wikipedia entries, and websites ranging from credible to dubious, the account of how *S. mitis* survived for 31 months on the Moon and came back to life on Earth was widely replicated and reported as fact. Thus, the evolution of a scientific claim into a scientific fact occurred.

PART 4: CONTESTING THE CLAIM

After 30 years, though, somebody decided to look into the story. During his second stint as NASA's Planetary Protection Officer (1998–2006), John D. Rummel, a microbial ecologist by training, decided to investigate claims about *S. mitis* surviving on the Moon and coming back to life in the lab, along with competing claims that it could have been the result of lab contamination. He had talked with people having knowledge of the LRL's analysis of the Surveyor III camera who had indicated that cleanroom procedures for the analysis were less than stringent. This chapter will return to Rummel's investigation after a brief discussion of the science of microbes.

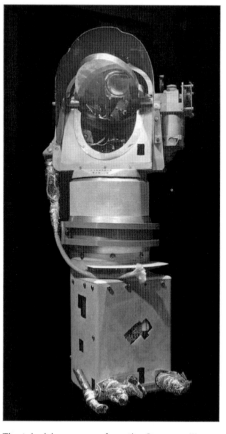

The television camera from the Surveyor III spacecraft on display at the Smithsonian National Air and Space Museum. (Smithsonian National Air and Space Museum: 2006-1139)

A Quick Review: Microbes, Sterilization, and Lunar Quarantine

A quick review of the science of microbes, as it is relevant to this tale, will help to shed light on how the "true story" of *S. mitis* on the Moon has come to be falsified.

As most people know all too well, bacteria are hardy organisms. We live in an era of killer viruses, "super-bugs," and antibiotic-resistant bacteria. The global spread of plant, animal, and human diseases caused by bacteria and other microbes is a growing concern as populations expand and become increasingly mobile. The existence of extremophilic microbial life, an exotic concept just a few decades ago, is now common knowledge. Scientists have found microbial life pretty much everywhere they have looked for it on Earth—in deep-sea hydrothermal vents, kilometers beneath the surface of the planet, at temperatures above the boiling point and below the freezing point of water, in hyper-acidic and hyper-saline conditions, and so on. It is also now well known that some bacteria can form spores—dormant, non-reproductive structures—that enable them to survive harsh environmental conditions, such as temperature extremes and water shortages, and revive and reproduce when conditions improve.[28]

Thanks in part to 50 years of NASA-sponsored exobiology and astrobiology research, it is now common knowledge that bacteria and other forms of microbial life can thrive in virtually every sort of extreme terrestrial environment known to science and that some can survive radical changes in environmental conditions for years, centuries, or longer.[29] This knowledge is spurring the search for evidence of habitable environments and life in our solar system. Solar system exploration has revealed that the subsurface of Mars and the Jovian moons Europa, Ganymede, and Callisto may have liquid water environments that could support life as we know it. Saturn's moon Enceladus appears to have a subsurface liquid water ocean. Saturn's moon Titan is of interest, too, with its dense atmosphere, organic chemistry, and a possible subsurface liquid water ocean. For missions to these targets, planetary protection—the policy and practice of protecting solar system bodies (that is, planets, moons, comets, and asteroids) from contamination by Earth life, and protecting Earth from possible life-forms that may be returned from other solar system bodies[30]—has become a complicated enterprise.

---

28. Take, for example, a microbe discovered in 1956, long before "extremophile" became a household word—*Deinococcus radiodurans*, a bacterium that can survive cold, dehydration, vacuum, acid, and ionizing radiation. The Guinness Book of World Records has named *D. radiodurans* the world's toughest bacterium. See *http://www.genomenewsnetwork.org/articles/07_02/deinococcus.shtml* (accessed 17 January 2020).
29. See, for example, Becky McCall, "Microbes Survive Deep Permafrost," BBC News, 23 February 2005, *http://news.bbc.co.uk/go/pr/fr/-/1/hi/sci/tech/4287579.stm* (accessed 17 January 2020).
30. *https://planetaryprotection.nasa.gov* (accessed 17 January 2020).

Coming back to Earth (and the Moon), what is known about *S. mitis* today? It is not an unusual microbe. According to a "microbe wiki" maintained by Kenyon College, *Streptococcus mitis* are "bacteria that colonize hard surfaces in the oral cavity such as dental hard tissues as well as mucous membranes and are part of the oral flora…. *S. mitis* are not motile, do not form spores, and…live optimally at temperatures between 30 and 35°C…. *S. mitis* is a part of the normal mammal flora."[31] Key points about *S. mitis* to keep in mind as this story progresses are that it is not a spore former and that it likes to live, and is commonly found, in human mouths, at a comfortable 30–35°C.

Did—could—*S. mitis*, indeed, travel from Earth to the Moon, survive more than two years of exposure there to cosmic radiation, extreme high and low temperatures (ranging from around 120°C to around –150°C), and no liquid water at all, only to revive once brought back into familiar terrestrial environs? And why were scientists and engineers even thinking about such a possibility back then?

PART 4 (CONTINUED): CONTESTING THE CLAIM

Even before NASA came to be, the international science community was discussing the possibility of extraterrestrial life and steps that might be taken to prevent forward and back contamination—respectively, the transport of terrestrial microbial life to extraterrestrial environments in the course of solar system exploration and the return to Earth of extraterrestrial microbial life, should it exist, in samples brought back from solar system bodies.[32] In the early days of planning for Apollo missions to the Moon, NASA deemed protecting Earth from possible contamination by extraterrestrial biology a public health issue. Thus, the Agency addressed concerns about possible back contamination by planning for the quarantine of astronauts and material samples returned from the Moon. A key element of the Apollo quarantine program was the construction of a Lunar Receiving Laboratory (LRL)

---

31. *http://microbewiki.kenyon.edu/index.php/Streptococcus_mitis* (accessed 17 January 2020). For the record, *S. mitis* should not be confused with other streptococcus bacteria, such as *Streptococcus pyogenes*, or group A streptococcus, which causes strep throat. See *http://www.mayoclinic.com/health/strep-throat/DS00260/DSECTION=causes* (accessed 17 January 2020).

32. See Michael Meltzer, *When Biospheres Collide: A History of NASA's Planetary Protection Programs* (Washington, DC: NASA SP-2011-4234, 2011) p. 1516; and Steven J. Dick and James E. Strick, *The Living Universe: NASA and the Development of Astrobiology* (New Brunswick, NJ: Rutgers University Press, 2004) pp. 24–29

at NASA's Manned Spacecraft Center (MSC, now Johnson Space Center) to contain and analyze lunar samples.[33]

NASA established an "Unmanned Spacecraft Decontamination Policy" in 1963, "based on acceptance of the scientific opinion that lunar surface conditions would mitigate against reproduction of known terrestrial microorganisms and that, if subsurface penetration of viable organisms were to be caused by spacecraft impact, proliferation would remain highly localized." Nonetheless, spacecraft going to the Moon were subject to decontamination procedures specified in this policy, which was applied to the Surveyor lunar missions.[34] By 1967, NASA had given up on the goal of sterilization for lunar missions and adopted a lunar quarantine policy to prevent contamination of Earth by extraterrestrial life.[35]

With that background established, this story can now fast-forward into the 21st century. I began conducting communication research for the NASA Planetary Protection Program in 2002. In a 10 December 2002 memo responding to a query from me about the story of *S. mitis* as a "lunar survivor," as reported on various websites, Planetary Protection Officer Rummel said:

> The [claim] of *Streptococcus mitis* surviving on the Moon in the Surveyor camera body is almost certainly incorrect. The detection of *S. mitis* in the camera body was the subject of two conference presentations at the 1970 [sic] Lunar Science Conference, but there was no peer-reviewed paper with that result at the time, nor has there ever been. The original papers (gray, very, very, gray) were cited by Jerry Taylor in the 1972 *Annual Reviews of Microbiology*...and got into the peer-reviewed literature that way.[36]

Rummel told me that in 1998, he had gotten in touch with JPL Surveyor Project Scientist Leonard Jaffe about this "survivor" claim and that Jaffe had

---

33. NASA and the U.S. Public Health Service (PHS) agreed to put G. Briggs Phillips, the PHS liaison to the MSC, in charge of lunar quarantine. See Charles R. Phillips, *The Planetary Quarantine Program: Origins and Achievements, 1956–1973* (Washington, DC: NASA SP-1902, 1974) pp. 30–33. In 1963, the PHS detailed Capt. Lawrence B. Hall to NASA to develop a spacecraft sterilization program for the Agency. Hall became NASA's Planetary Quarantine (PQ) Officer. For an extended discussion of quarantine and sterilization during the Apollo era, see Meltzer, *When Biospheres Collide*, pp. 55–59.
34. See Phillips, *The Planetary Quarantine Program*, p. 31.
35. "On August 24, 1967, NASA entered into an Interagency Agreement, 'Protection of the Earth's Biosphere from Lunar Sources of Contamination,' with the Departments of Agriculture; Interior; and Health, Education, and Welfare.... The National Academy of Sciences was also a party to this interagency agreement. NASA subsequently issued a string of implementing documents. See Phillips, *The Planetary Quarantine Program*, p. 31.
36. See footnote 25.

told him "there was a film of the procedure to sample the camera, and that the samplers had broken sterile protocol inadvertently (by placing their sampling tool outside the sterile hood)." Jaffe passed along to Rummel a message he had received from his Surveyor Project colleague Richard Green (the R. H. Green of Knittel, Favero, and Green) about the LRL analysis of the Surveyor III camera. Green had told Jaffe: "Re: the sampling: You were correct, the sampling of the camera was suspect. I took movie film of the entire procedure, and it shows up on it as well. I believe that I still have the film somewhere in storage. If it would be helpful, I could try and find it." Rummel told me his "best guess is that this bug did not, ever, survive even the trip out, let alone the stay on the lunar surface."[37]

In 2004, at an Astrobiology Science Conference held at NASA Ames Research Center in Moffett Field, California, Rummel gave a presentation entitled "Strep, Lies(?), and 16mm Film: Did *S. mitis* Survive on the Moon? Should Humans Be Allowed on Mars?"[38] In his talk, Rummel considered whether "sufficiently stringent procedures" were followed to prevent microbial contamination during collection, delivery, and analysis of the Surveyor III camera. Dissecting Mitchell and Ellis's "*S. mitis*: survivor" claim, he determined that the answer was "no" and asserted that the microbial growth they had reported was the product of lab contamination during analysis. A paper on biological contamination studies of lunar landing sites, published in 2004, coauthored by Rummel, and published in the *International Journal of Astrobiology*, also challenged the claim, as follows:

> One suggestion that bacteria might survive on the Moon came when the crew of Apollo 12 returned to the Earth with selected components from the unmanned Surveyor III probe, including the television camera that had spent over 2 years on the lunar surface. Scientists working at the Lunar Receiving Laboratory (LRL) claimed to have isolated a colony of viable *Streptococcus mitis* bacteria from a sample of foam collected inside the camera housing.... However, all of the other camera components, including an internal section of the electrical cabling, did not contain viable terrestrial bacteria...nor was *S. mitis* found in the test camera that never went to the Moon. Meanwhile, it has been suggested that there is photographic evidence that these bacteria did not survive on the Moon, but instead were isolated due to laboratory contamination of the foam during analysis in the LRL.... Nevertheless, the Surveyor III bacteria controversy illustrates the potential confusion associated with terrestrial biological contamination that can lead to false positive detection

---

37. J. D. Rummel, personal communication with author, 10 December 2002.
38. Rummel provided his PowerPoint presentation to the author.

of life. Future microbiological investigations of the Apollo site materials that have remained on the Moon for over 30 years could help resolve the Surveyor III issue. It also should be emphasized that even if bacteria delivered by lunar spacecraft are inactivated or sterilized on the Moon, due to the harsh surface conditions, organic compounds from dead cells will remain and could leave biomarkers in lunar samples returned to Earth.[39]

PART 5: HOW THE STORY SPREAD

In 2006, I began exploring the story of *S. mitis* on the Moon in earnest, first searching the World Wide Web for accounts. What follows are some highlights, starting with what appear to be official NASA sources.

On 23 May 2006, on a NASA Goddard Space Flight Center web page, I found the following "science question of the week," provided by planetary scientist David Williams of NASA's National Space Science Data Center: "Can anything from Earth live on the Moon?" The answer here was "yes." The Mitchell and Ellis version of the story of *S. mitis* was replicated here: "Scientists concluded that the *S. mitis* was inside the camera originally and had managed to survive on the Moon…for a year and a half [sic]."[40]

At the same time, on a NASA website maintained by Marshall Space Flight Center, I found a much more detailed account of the Mitchell and Ellis version of the story of *S. mitis* on the Moon.[41] Dated 1998 and headlined "Earth Microbes on the Moon: Three Decades After Apollo 12, a Remarkable Colony of Lunar Survivors Revisited," this account reported on "an inadvertent stowaway, *Streptococcus mitis*, the only known survivor of unprotected space travel…. How this remarkable feat [of survival] was accomplished only by *Strep.* bacteria remains speculative." But "the significance of a living organism surviving for nearly 3 years in the harsh lunar environment may only now be placed in perspective, after 3 decades of the biological revolution in understanding life and its favored conditions."

Another NASA record found online, "Apollo 12 Lunar Surface Journal—Surveyor Crater and Surveyor III," includes a transcript of Apollo 12 astronauts Conrad and Bean's conversation while they were on the lunar surface, plus post-flight commentary from them and others, in which they address the

---

39. D. P. Glavin, J. P. Dworkin, M. Lupisella, G. Kminek, and J. D. Rummel, "Biological Contamination Studies of Lunar Landing Sites: Implications for Future Planetary Protection and Life Detection on the Moon and Mars," *International Journal of Astrobiology* 3, no. 3 (2004): 265–271.
40. *http://www.gsfc.nasa.gov/scienceques2002/20030418.htm* (accessed 23 May 2006).
41. This report was found at *https://lsda.jsc.nasa.gov/Document/doc_pubs_citations/PUB001658*.

story of *S. mitis* on the Moon.[42] In postflight comments, Conrad said, "The thing that had the bacteria in it was the television camera. The Styrofoam in between the inner and outer shells. There's a report on that. I always thought the most significant thing that we ever found on the whole g-----n Moon was that little bacteria who came back and lived and nobody ever said s---t about it."

In his postflight comments, "Lunar Surface Journal" contributor Marv Hein, citing the NASA report "Analysis of Surveyor 3 Material and Photographs Returned by Apollo 12," said, "the survival of microbes was anticipated at the time Surveyor III was launched." He noted that the microbes identified by Mitchell and Ellis in their chapter of the report were *S. mitis* cultured from "sample 32 extracted from foam insulation used between 2 aluminum plates of the camera circuit boards and extracted through a hole originally cut for the placement of electronic components. It is estimated that between 2 and 50 cells were isolated from the foam sample. There is significant discussion (in the NASA report) as to how it may have survived." In his postflight comments, journal contributor Ken Glover noted, "There is a distinct possibility that the microbes found in the Surveyor TV camera got there as a result of post-flight contamination. As of 2004, it seems generally accepted that the history of the particular microbes found in the Surveyor III parts will never be resolved."[43]

I also found a classroom "teacher sheet" for grades 9–12, "All About Microbes," developed for a NASA-sponsored project (now defunct) called "NASA Explores," that replicated this "survivor" story.[44] This curriculum supplement included the following "Q&A":

> What unmanned probe unknowingly carried the *Streptococcus mitis* bacteria to the Moon in 1967? How was the bacteria returned to Earth?
>
> *Surveyor 3 carried the bacteria to the Moon, and the crew of Apollo 12 returned it to Earth.*

The source provided to answer this question was the 1998 NASA Marshall story mentioned above.

---

42. http://www.hq.nasa.gov/office/pao/History/alsj/a12/a12.surveyor.html (accessed 17 January 2020).
43. http://www.hq.nasa.gov/office/pao/History/alsj/a12/a12.surveyor.html (accessed 17 January 2020).
44. http://www.nasaexplores.com, no access date, hard copy in author's files.

Beyond the universe of NASA's website, I found further accounts. The following information, for example, came from a reference.com entry on Surveyor III:

> Perhaps Surveyor 3's [sic] most remarkable finding, though, was a complete accident. A common bacteria, *Streptococcus mitis*, was unintentionally present inside the spacecraft's camera at launch. Around 50 to 100 of these bacteria survived dormant in this harsh environment for 3 years, to be detected when Apollo 12 brought the camera back to Earth. The discovery, while paid comparatively little attention at the time, gave some credence to the idea of interplanetary panspermia, but more importantly, led NASA to adopt strict abiotic procedures for space probes to prevent contamination of Mars and other bodies suspected of having conditions suitable for life; most dramatically the Galileo spacecraft was deorbited to avoid impacting Europa.[45]

I also found an interesting "reader forum" hosted by the web news service Space.com in 2004 on the topic "Organisms can survive the vacuum of space." Readers leaned hard toward "yes," and several repeated the story of *S. mitis* surviving on the Moon. "Cosmic Ancestry," a website maintained by an advocate of strong-panspermia theory,[46] retold the story, too, in an entry entitled "Bacteria: The Space Colonists." According to this account, *S. mitis* "had survived for 31 months in the vacuum of the Moon's atmosphere." Noting the strong-panspermia view that, "when the first bacteria colonized the Earth, almost 4 billion years ago, it was by our standards a hostile place," the entry went on to cite accounts of bacteria surviving in spore form for tens of millions of years. Here the story of *S. mitis* surviving a stint on the Moon was used to bolster the case for the seeding of life on Earth from outer space.

An entry on the Lunar and Planetary Institute's website on the Apollo 12 Surveyor III analysis took the middle road, stating:

> A particularly important aspect of the *Surveyor 3* analysis was the search for living material on the spacecraft. *Surveyor* was not sterilized prior to launch, and scientists wanted to know if terrestrial microorganisms had survived for two and a half years in space. One research group found a small amount of the bacteria *Streptococcus mitis* in a piece of foam from inside the TV cameras. They believed that these bacteria had survived in this location since before launch.... Another research group found no evidence of life inside a section of electrical cable. Some people associated with the curation of the

---

45. *http://www.reference.com/browse/wiki/Surveyor_3* (accessed 24 May 2006). This information is no longer available online.
46. See footnote 2.

Surveyor 3 materials have suggested that the one positive detection of life may be the result of accidental contamination of the material after it was returned to Earth.[47]

PART 6: INVESTIGATION OF THE CLAIM YIELDS RESULTS

At Rummel's request,[48] in 2006 I began contacting people at NASA Johnson Space Center who might know something about the Surveyor III camera analysis. Rummel told me that Judith Allton, a curator with JSC's Astromaterials Acquisition and Curation Office, reportedly had a list of film and photographic records of the analysis, so I first contacted her. Allton ultimately found her handwritten list and provided it to us. JSC astromaterials curator Carlton Allen referred us to John F. Lindsay with the Lunar and Planetary Institute's Center for Advanced Space Studies for help with our investigation.[49] Lindsay advised that he was "part of the preliminary examination team on Apollo 12…so have some feel for the way things went—and would enjoy working on the data once again."[50]

I put my research into this matter on hold in late 2006, when Rummel stepped down as Planetary Protection Officer to become NASA's Senior Scientist for Astrobiology. In 2008, Rummel left NASA for East Carolina University, and John Lindsay passed away. Nonetheless, Rummel seemed determined to prove, if possible, that "*S. mitis*: survivor" was actually "*S. mitis*: lab contamination." Ultimately Rummel, Allton, and Don Morrison completed an investigation into the matter, and Rummel reported their results at a workshop in 2011.[51]

As noted above, some microbes survive environmental conditions that are not conducive to reproduction by forming spores. In spore form, microbes are dormant but not dead, and when living conditions improve, the spores can change form and start reproducing again. A spore-forming microbe might be able to survive temperature swings from 120°C to –150°C,

---

47. http://www.lpi.usra.edu/expmoon/Apollo12/A12_experiments_III.html (accessed 17 January 2020).
48. At this time, my work was fully funded by a grant from the NASA Planetary Protection Program. John Rummel served as NASA Planetary Protection Officer from 1997 to 2006.
49. Author e-mail correspondence with Michael Zolensky, Judy Allton, Carlton Allen, John Rummel, and John Lindsay dated 23 May–29 June 2006.
50. Ibid.
51. "The Importance of Solar System Sample Return Missions to the Future of Planetary Science," Lunar and Planetary Institute and NASA Planetary Science Division, The Woodlands, TX, 5–6 March 2011, http://www.lpi.usra.edu/meetings/sssr2011/ (accessed 21 January 2020).

though repeated cycling to 120°C "would have a killing effect," Rummel said at the workshop. However, *S. mitis* is not a spore-forming microbe, and non–spore formers are more sensitive to temperature swings, even under vacuum conditions. According to NASA records, the Surveyor III camera reached a maximum temperature of around 70°C on the Moon. NASA records also showed that *S. mitis* "was…isolated from the [Apollo 12] crew in routine microbial testing." The team's investigation verified that "no viable microbes were isolated from the Surveyor III cables or from any Apollo surface samples returned to Earth" and that "no viable microbes were isolated from 10 of 11 sampling locations (32 of 33 samples) within the camera body." While microbes were isolated from Surveyor III's ground-control camera in small numbers at six locations, "no viable *S. mitis* were ever isolated" from it.[52]

What clinched the trio's investigation, however, was that in 2010, they found the 16-millimeter film records of the 1970 Surveyor III camera analysis at the LRL, "languishing in [an archive in] Maryland." All three researchers viewed and analyzed the films, and "it wasn't pretty," Rummel reported. If the judges on television's *American Idol* were to view the microbiology performances in this case, "those guys would have been out in an early round," he observed. Morrison commented, "The general scene does not lend a lot of confidence in the proposition that contamination did not occur." The films showed lab technicians working in short sleeves with only their mouths and noses covered by masks. At some points they were working with bare hands as well. As Rummel observed, "after all of that, how can you be sure where your microbes came from?"

More specifically, Morrison pinpointed an anomaly in camera foam sampling:

> All of the prior samples were taken with the camera sampling areas on the viewer's left. Before taking the foam sample, a worker inserted his upper body into the [supposedly clean chamber containing the camera] and visually examines the side of the camera that is toward the filter of the [chamber] and away from the viewer. He faces the hidden side of the camera's electronics package and examines it, perhaps exposing it to his respiration. After withdrawing from the [chamber], the camera is rotated so that the side that was toward the filter of the [chamber] and examined by the worker is now the visible face and the camera sampling areas are now on the viewer's right. Immediately after the camera rotation, the foam samples are taken…. The collection of the foam sample concludes the sampling exercise. The foam

---

52. "The Importance of Solar System Sample Return Missions to the Future of Planetary Science."

samples were the last taken. This raises a serious question. Because the worker extended his upper body into the [chamber] and directly faces the area from which the foam sample was taken, it is possible that his exhalations were deposited on the camera, including the foam, causing contamination.[53]

Concurring with Morrison's assessment, Allton noted, "As to general protocol, I will add that the participants were wearing short sleeve scrubs, thus arms were exposed. Also, that the scrub shirt tails were higher than the flow bench level (and would act as a bellows for particulates from inside the shirt). We do not see how the tweezers were handled before the sampling."[54]

FOR THE RECORD: *S. MITIS*—LUNAR SURVIVOR OR POSTFLIGHT INTERLOPER?

On 2 May 2011, aerospace writer Leonard David reported on Rummel et al.'s findings on the news site Space.com.[55] In this article, the story of *S. mitis* on the Moon was reported as "a long-lived bit of Apollo moon landing folklore that now appears to be a dead-end affair." Rummel told David, "The claim that a microbe survived 2.5 years on the moon was flimsy, at best, even by the standards of the time…. The claim never passed peer review, yet has persisted in the press—and on the Internet—ever since."

It appears that the contestation of Mitchell and Ellis's claim has had some effect on the public record. Rummel, Allton, and Morrison's work on the case of *S. mitis* on the Moon is slowly but surely undermining Mitchell and Ellis's original claim. While in 2006, I found numerous websites replicating the story of "*S. mitis*, survivor on the Moon," in 2012 I found only a few sticking with the story. In 2006, I had contacted NASA Goddard's David Williams to advise that the claim he had reported on the Web was contested. A search for the page in 2012 found that it no longer existed. In 2012, at Reference.com's online entry for Surveyor III, at the very same URL that I checked in 2006, a different story about *S. mitis* on the Moon appeared, as follows:

> It is widely claimed that a common bacterium, *Streptococcus mitis*, accidentally contaminated the spacecraft's camera prior to launch and survived dormant in this harsh environment for two and a half years, to be detected when Apollo 12 brought the camera back to Earth in 1969. This claim has been cited as providing credence to the idea of interplanetary panspermia,

---

53. Ibid.
54. Ibid.
55. Leonard David, "Moon Microbe Mystery Finally Solved," Space.com, 2 May 2011, *http://www.space.com/11536-moon-microbe-mystery-solved-apollo-12.html* (accessed 21 January 2020).

but more importantly, led NASA to adopt strict abiotic procedures for space probes to prevent contamination of Mars and other bodies suspected of having conditions suitable for life; most dramatically the Galileo spacecraft was deorbited to avoid impacting Europa. However, NASA officials now no longer support this claim.[56]

At the time of this writing, the Lunar and Planetary Institute's web entry on the analysis of Surveyor III components remained the same in 2012. Not surprisingly, so did "Cosmic Ancestry's."[57] Remarkably, so did the "Science@ NASA" entry (maintained by NASA Headquarters). It had not been revised since it was posted online in 1998. Thus, in 2012, at least one "nasa.gov" web page continued to report, without question or qualification, that *S. mitis* did, indeed, survive for 31 months on the Moon, come back to Earth, and come back to life.

Given the fluid nature of Internet content, it seems that the public record may ultimately reflect that Mitchell and Ellis's claims about *S. mitis* on the Moon are, at best, claims and not proven "facts," and, at worst, discredited assertions. One body of literature that I have not examined at all, and is worth looking at, is textbooks. It will take time to observe whether and how the scientific record may be corrected—perhaps in another annual review.

Meanwhile, the story of *S. mitis* on the Moon remains persistent in the cultural environment. On the 14 September 2012 edition of National Public Radio's *Science Friday* show, host Ira Flatow asked NASA Planetary Protection Officer Catharine Conley (Rummel's successor) about the bioassays of Surveyor III camera parts.[58] Conley said, "It turns out that the way they were taking those samples was about the same level of sterility…as you do in surgery…so they had short-sleeved scrubs, they didn't really have good masks—so the samples that were contaminated were taken at the very end of…this whole sampling process, and just after somebody breathed right that

---

56. Ibid.
57. "Cosmic Ancestry" is maintained by Brig Klyce, a strong-panspermia advocate who advocates the disputed views of Fred Hoyle and Chandra Wickramasinghe on the seeding of Earth with microbial life from space. On his website, Klyce says he "has actively studied evolution, the origin of life, and panspermia since 1980. In 1995, this activity became his primary occupation. Today, he conducts, promotes, and publicizes research pertaining to the strong version of panspermia, which he would like to link with Gaia, calling the synthesis Cosmic Ancestry." Brig attended Princeton University and received a bachelor of architecture degree from the University of Tennessee in 1975. He retired from the textile rental industry in 1995. See http://www.panspermia.org (accessed 21 January 2020).
58. Flatow's question: "Wasn't there a case in one of the Apollo missions where contamination was brought back?" Conley's answer: "This was the return of the Surveyor camera…."

location on the camera, so it probably was contamination after the camera [was] brought back...."[59]

CONCLUSIONS: WHY SHOULD WE CARE ABOUT THE STORY OF *S. MITIS* ON THE MOON?

The study described in this chapter is a special case in the social construction of scientific facts. It shows how a claim became a widely accepted fact without passing the test of peer review; how initial counterclaims that challenged the status of the first claim as a fact seemingly failed to register with expert and non-expert audiences; how a later and perhaps more vigorous counterclaim ultimately led to a solid case against the first claim, with visual evidence playing an important role; and how, consequently, the first claim appears to be losing its status as fact.

Rummel and his colleagues were interested in this case as one that illustrates the importance of stringent compliance with planetary protection policy and procedures.[60] Planetary protection is essential to preserving extraterrestrial environments in their pristine conditions for scientific exploration, and planetary protection requirements for solar system exploration missions aim to prevent any contamination that would obscure chances for finding evidence of life elsewhere. With multiple sites in our solar system being explored as potentially habitable environments and Mars sample return still a top priority for the space science community, planetary protection is an ongoing concern. The prospect of sending humans to extraterrestrial environments that might be habitable for Earth life greatly complicates the task of compliance with planetary protection requirements.

Space-based experiments flown during the Space Shuttle era have shown that some terrestrial bacteria—though not *S. mitis*—can survive exposure to the space environment.[61] And in recent years, microbiology research has

---

59. *https://www.sciencefriday.com/segments/mars-rover-may-be-contaminated-with-earth-microbes/* (accessed 8 August 2021).
60. For information on these policies and procedures, see *http://planetaryprotection.nasa.gov* (accessed 26 August 2020). Rummel continues to work on planetary protection policy through the international Committee on Space Research's Panel on Planetary Protection.
61. See, for example, Rosa de la Torre et al., "Survival of Lichens and Bacteria Exposed to Outer Space Conditions—Results of the Lithopanspermia Experiment," *Icarus* 208 (August 2010): 735–748; Gerda Horneck, David M. Klaus, and Rocco L. Mancinelli, "Space Microbiology," *Microbiology and Molecular Biology Reviews* 74, no. 1 (March 2010): 121–156; Wayne L. Nicholson et al., "Resistance of *Bacillus* Endospores to Extreme Terrestrial and Extraterrestrial Environments," *Microbiology and Molecular Biology Reviews* 64, no. 3 (September 2000): 548–572.

revealed the extent to which humans are teeming with microbial life.[62] The National Institutes of Health's Human Microbiome Project, whose goal is to "characterize the microbial communities found at several different sites on the human body, including nasal passages, oral cavities, skin, gastrointestinal tract, and urogenital tract,"[63] has yielded fascinating results.

According to Todar's *Online Textbook of Bacteriology*, "a human adult houses about 10^{12} bacteria on the skin, 10^{10} in the mouth, and 10^{14} in the gastrointestinal tract. The latter number is far in excess of the number of eukaryotic cells in all the tissues and organs which comprise a human...." By the way, this textbook also notes, "Predominant bacteria in the oral cavity and mucus membranes include streptococci. *S. mitis* is commonly found in the pharynx... and mouth... among other locations." [64]

At the 2011 conference where Rummel et al. presented the results of their investigation, JSC astromaterials curators Carlton Allen, Judy Allton, and colleagues reported on lessons learned from experience with extraterrestrial materials curation, including this one: "Samples will never be cleaner than the tools and containers used to collect, transport, and store them. It is critical to design and monitor spacecraft contamination control during manufacturing and operations."[65] In another presentation at the conference, JSC astromaterials curator Michael Zolensky and NASA scientist Scott Sandford reported some "lessons learned from recent sample return missions"[66]—the Long-Duration Exposure Facility, a test bed for space-based dust collection; Stardust, which collected and returned samples of cometary and interstellar dust; and Hayabusa, which collected and returned samples from the asteroid Itokawa. These three missions were variously plagued with contamination problems before launch, during recovery, and in the processes of analysis and curation. For example, Stardust's aerogel dust capture medium "was

---

62. See, for example, A. Grice et al., "Topographical and Temporal Diversity of the Human Skin Biome," *Science* 5931 (2009): 1190–1192; M. Arumugam et al., "Enterotypes of the Human Gut Microbiome," *Nature* 473 (12 May 2011): 174–180.
63. *http://commonfund.nih.gov/hmp/* (accessed 21 January 2020).
64. *http://www.textbookofbacteriology.net/normalflora_3.html* (accessed 21 January 2020).
65. Carlton Allen, Judith Allton, Gary Lofgren, Kevin Righter, and Michael Zolensky, "Curating NASA's Extraterrestrial Samples—Past, Present, and Future," presented at "The Importance of Solar System Sample Return Missions to the Future of Planetary Science," Lunar and Planetary Institute and NASA Planetary Science Division, The Woodlands, TX, 5–6 March 2011, *http://www.lpi.usra.edu/meetings/sssr2011/presentations/allen.pdf* (accessed 21 January 2020).
66. Mike Zolwnsky and Scott Sandford, "Lessons Learned from Three Recent Sample Return Missions," *http://www.lpi.usra.edu/meetings/sssr2011/presentations/zolensky.pdf* (accessed 21 January 2020).

significantly contaminated during manufacture," according to Zolensky and Sandford, and NASA "bungled… the recovery of LDEF"—the Long-Duration Exposure Facility, a research spacecraft deployed by the Space Shuttle in 1984 and retrieved by the Shuttle in 1990[67]—"degrading the science return from the mission" because it ranked "concerns for human comfort" over LDEF science mission goals.[68]

NASA cleanroom practices have evolved considerably since 1970, from the days of the Surveyor camera analysis, when cleanroom technicians wore short sleeves exposing bare arms, caps that covered the tops of their heads but not all of their hair, and face masks covering only their noses and mouths; to the present-day planetary-protection requirement of "bunny suits" for cleanroom operations that cover and contain the entire body.

Today the scientific consensus is that it is not likely that terrestrial microbes could survive and thrive on the Moon, and this consensus is reflected in NASA's planetary protection policy for the Moon, which designates robotic missions to this target "Category II," that is, forays to a body of "significant interest relative to the process of chemical evolution and the origin of life, but where there is only a remote chance that contamination carried by a spacecraft could compromise future investigations."[69]

In such environments, forward contamination is not a concern. However, there is a concern that in extraterrestrial environments where liquid water might exist, such as on some parts of Mars, it could be possible for terrestrial microbes to thrive and replicate. In these cases, forward contamination is a serious concern, and planetary protection requirements for missions to these environments are strict. In 2005, at NASA's request, a special committee of the U.S. National Research Council (NRC) reviewed planetary protection requirements for missions to Mars, in view of new evidence, collected by recent missions, that Mars had extensive liquid water on its surface billions of years ago—including indications of possible recent liquid water activity on the Martian surface—and accordingly recommended further caution. For missions to regions of Mars where terrestrial microorganisms might survive and grow or where indigenous life might be present—regions that may encompass more of Mars than scientists once thought possible, particularly

---

67. "Long Duration Exposure Facility (LDEF)," *https://curator.jsc.nasa.gov/mic/ldef/* (accessed 21 January 2020).
68. Ibid.
69. *http://planetaryprotection.nasa.gov/categories* (accessed 21 January 2020).

areas deep beneath the Martian surface—the NRC recommended taking special precautions.[70]

With Curiosity, NASA's first astrobiology laboratory on Mars, seeking evidence of past or present habitability on the planet, questions will continue to arise, from the press and the public and the science community, about the possibility of finding life on Mars or in other extraterrestrial environments. With all the terrestrial junk that the U.S. and Soviet/Russian space agencies have deposited on Mars—on purpose and by accident—since the 1970s, some skeptics have raised the question of whether the planet may already be contaminated with Earth life.[71]

For planetary protection, the story of *S. mitis* on the Moon illustrates, among other things, that microbes are everywhere (on Earth), cleanroom procedures for microbial assays cannot be too careful, and meticulous and complete records of such procedures must be made and preserved. For the history and sociology of science, this case shows how a claim that was never subjected to formal peer review and became, and remained, a fact for decades before it was seriously challenged; and how it took visual evidence to finally make the case that multiple sources had made verbally. It also shows how the "paper trails" that researchers like to excavate for information are now intermingled with digital documentation that can be altered at any time, without leaving any visible record of a change. As to evaluating scientific "facts," I offer a journalist's old adage: if your mother says she loves you, check it out.

ACKNOWLEDGMENTS

The author wishes to thank John Rummel, Judy Allton, Don Morrison, David Carrier, and Michael Zolensky for their assistance with this project; NASA Headquarters reference librarians for helping to track down key documents; and NASA's Planetary Protection and Astrobiology programs for supporting this research.

---

70. Committee on Preventing the Forward Contamination of Mars, National Research Council, *Preventing the Forward Contamination of Mars* (Washington, DC: National Academies Press, 2006) [3–5].
71. See, for example, C. P. McKay, "Biologically Reversible Exploration," *Science* 6 (February 2009): 718.

CHAPTER 7
"Killer Asteroids": Popular Depictions and Public Policy Influence

Laura M. Delgado López

IF THE DISASTER of the Carolinas should repeat itself in the vicinity of New York City, all man's handiwork extending over a great oval spreading from Long Island to Ohio, Virginia and Lake Ontario would be completely annihilated. One-half of the people, one-third of the wealth of the United States would be completely rubbed out. The world's greatest metropolis would lie a smoking ruin, land honeycombed by water-filled depressions where the star teeth had bitten deep.[1]

In 1933, reporting on research positing that the Carolina Bays were marked by "meteorite scars" formed by ancient impacts, Edna Muldrow offered this vision of impact effects. The image of American civilization ravaged by the sudden impact of an immense planetary body has been the focal point of dozens of movies, books, and games. Although the most famous are surely the blockbuster films *Armageddon* (1998)[2] and *Deep Impact* (1998),[3] the theme of mass destruction via planetary impact goes back much further in time.

---

1. Edna Muldrow, "The Comet That Struck the Carolinas," *Harper's Monthly Magazine* 168, no. 1003 (1933): 83–89.
2. *Armageddon,* film, directed by Michael Bay (Touchstone Pictures, Jerry Bruckheimer Films, Valhalla Motion Pictures, 1998).
3. *Deep Impact,* film, directed by Mimi Leder (Paramount Pictures, DreamWorks SKG, Zanuck/Brown Productions, Manhattan Project, 1998).

What sustains this common narrative? Is it rooted in real events? What effect, if any, have these stories had on public perceptions of actual asteroid impact hazards? This chapter considers these and other questions while describing the common elements of this narrative of destruction and exploring why it has become so popular.

Although examples prior to the 1990s exist, that decade featured the majority of mass-media storylines showcasing asteroid impact threats. This seemingly exponential growth was likely driven by reactions to a real-world event that was followed the world over, the impact of Comet Shoemaker-Levy with Jupiter in 1994. As examples from the first two decades of the 21st century attest, this narrative is still alive and strong. Two unrelated events on 15 February 2013—the predicted close approach of asteroid 2012 DA14 to Earth and the unpredicted explosion of a meteor over Chelyabinsk, Russia—brought asteroid impact hazards into sharp focus once more and likely gave renewed force to this storyline.

What does the recurrence of this narrative say about public attitudes toward this issue? Popular narratives often reflect deep-rooted societal fears and beliefs.[4] The prevalence of this narrative is suggestive of public concerns about asteroid impacts. Yet what little empirical research exists on the subject, specifically two national polls and a formal survey discussed later in the chapter, contradicts this assumption, showing that people do not see a catastrophic asteroid impact as a real threat. What can explain this sharp contrast between sensational media depictions akin to Chicken Little's famous assertion that "The sky is falling!" and a general public response of "Who cares?"

By referencing the work of Paul Slovic on risk assessment and looking at examples of the impact narrative spanning three decades, I contend that the way that catastrophic impacts are repeatedly represented in fiction (predominantly in film) is, in fact, consistent with the degree of public concern. That is, fictional asteroid impact threats are predominantly a mode of entertainment. I also contend that this enduring fictional narrative does not reflect advances in scientific understanding of asteroid impact hazards. This

---

4. In a previous paper, I argue that a dominant narrative tying space commercialization to a capitalist dystopia reveals deep-rooted fears of the loss of individuality as a result of the disappearance of the state. I suggest that policy-makers need to be aware of conflicting narratives like this that may affect public opinion about real policy issues, such as the commercialization of space. See Laura Delgado, "The Commercialization of Space in Science Fiction Movies: The Key to Sustainability or the Road to a Capitalist Dystopia," presented at the AIAA Space 2010 Conference and Exposition, Anaheim, CA, 30 August–2 September 2010.

Artist's concept of the Comet Shoemaker-Levy 9 impact on Jupiter. (NASA/Don Davis: ARC-1994-AC94-0182)

situation may be a product of the gap between the public and scientific perceptions[5] and understanding of asteroid impact risk.

A LONG, EXPLOSIVE HISTORY

Contrary to what some may believe, the impact threat narrative began much earlier than the Hollywood blockbuster *Armageddon*, with some authors developing the narrative in fiction as far back as the 19th century. (See the chapter's appendix on page 203.)[6]

The 1890s saw the publication of *La Fin du Monde*,[7] a French novel that pondered on the end of the world in the face of a comet striking Earth in the

---

5. This is not to suggest that scientists are not part of the public or audience. The line is drawn rather loosely here to demarcate the sharp contrast between science's understanding of the issue and how it is commonly depicted in fiction.
6. This table, while incomplete, particularly considering narratives that may have developed in other languages, serves to show that the draw of the asteroid impact scenario is not new.
7. Camille Flammarion, *La Fin du Monde* (Paris: Ernest Flammarion, 1894).

25th century. This story reappeared in the 1930s as a film by the same name[8] and was republished as *Omega: The Last Days of the World* in 1999.[9]

In 1933, Edna Muldrow's article, "The Comet That Hit the Carolinas," was published in *Harper's Magazine*. While not fiction, it was rather poetic in evoking the end of the world following a hypothetical massive collision and in articulating the alarming thoughts of some who saw a threat in both asteroids and comets, even the well-known ones:

> We have no assurance that on its next trip Halley's comet[10] may not sideswipe us or that it may not be disintegrated by that time and have become a steady stream of meteors, so that each year we may plunge into its path and be pelted by falling stars of greater or lesser size.[11]

Examples of the asteroid impact narrative in the first few decades of the 20th century appeared as interest in the topic grew following scientific investigations into the Tunguska impact event. Hundreds of fiction and nonfiction accounts have explored what happened in Siberia in 1908—and interest has not died down. As recently as 2010, the National Research Council (NRC) cited the latest research on the Tunguska event in a report on asteroid impact mitigation strategies.[12]

Since Tunguska, other events have renewed interest in the subject of asteroid impacts, producing a flurry of media content. Interest in the subject exploded after 1980, when Luis and Walter Alvarez published their now-famous hypothesis linking the extinction of the dinosaurs with a massive asteroid impact 65 million years ago. Another critical event was the impact of the Shoemaker-Levy 9 comet on Jupiter in 1994. With solar system research confirming the role that impacts have played in transforming not just the

---

8. *La Fin du Monde,* film, directed by Abel Gance (1931).
9. Camille Flammarion, *Omega: The Last Days of the World* (Nebraska: University of Nebraska Press and Bison Books, 1999).
10. Fear over the approach of Halley's comet was part of a general concern over the effects of comets coming into close proximity with the planet. As a nonfiction example, consider Ignatius L. Donnelly's *Ragnarok: The Age of Fire and Gravel*, in which he posited that a comet hit the planet 12 years earlier with globally disastrous effects. In an interesting exception in fiction, H. G. Wells offers a positive storyline in his 1906 novel *In the Days of the Comet*, where a comet changes the composition of the atmosphere and humanity is "exalted" as a result.
11. Muldrow, "The Comet That Struck the Carolinas," *Harper's Magazine* (December 1933): 82.
12. Committee to Review Near-Earth Object Surveys and Hazard Mitigation Strategies, *Defending Planet Earth: Near-Earth Object Surveys and Hazard Mitigation Strategies* (Washington, DC: The National Academies Press, 2010) pp. 13–14.

Four images of Jupiter and the luminous night-side impact of fragment W of Comet Shoemaker-Levy 9 taken by the Galileo spacecraft on 22 July 1994. (NASA/JPL: PIA00139)

face but even the composition of planetary bodies, it became clearer not only that our own planet had been shaped dramatically by continuous impacts, but also that these events were not just a thing of the past.

By the 1990s, this expanding understanding of the impact history of the solar system prompted Congress to task NASA with surveying near-Earth objects (NEOs) and led to a golden era of mass-media treatments of asteroid impact threats, with extinction-level events appearing in over 25 different works of fiction in that decade. Short films, movies, TV programs, and computer games all subjected characters to different versions of the asteroid-impact scenario.

In a survey of 90 "cinematic film, video, and television productions" about asteroids or comets between 1936 and 2004, William Hartwell found that 30 percent addressed impact hazards.[13] Between 1994 and 2004, he noted a marked increase in threat scenarios, with more than half of the productions he surveyed emphasizing impacts. Hartwell claimed the increase was "a direct result" of the Shoemaker-Levy incident.[14]

Interest in the impact-threat narrative has continued into the 21st century. Although not as visible, debate over the non-negligible possibility of asteroid impacts with Earth—and some initial predictions of possible impacts by the asteroids Apophis in 2029 and 2011 AG5 in 2040 (later dismissed)—helped sustain this narrative. In addition, mass-media coverage of predictions of

---

13. William T. Hartwell, "The Sky on the Ground: Celestial Objects and Events in Archeology and Popular Culture," in *Comet/Asteroid Impacts and Human Society, An Interdisciplinary Approach*, ed. Peter T. Bobrowsky and Hans Rickman (Heidelberg, Germany: Springer, 2007), pp. 71–87.
14. Ibid., p. 82.

the end of the world in December 2012, prompted by misinterpretation of a Mayan calendar, led to at least one major motion picture capturing the civilization's end by fiery impact that same year. The close approach of asteroid 2012 DA14, which came within 17,200 miles of Earth, as predicted, on 15 February 2013, and the Chelyabinsk "superbolide" event that coincidentally produced a shower of meteorites over Russia on the same day have already inspired new additions to this list.[15] We can presume that the TV movie *Asteroid v. Earth* (2014)[16] and the 2017 animated short *Asteroids!*[17] are linked to these two high-interest events.

PUBLIC PERCEPTIONS OF THE ASTEROID-IMPACT "THREAT"

Taken at face value, constant references to civilization-ending asteroid collisions with Earth could suggest an underlying fear in a majority of the population. Yet, as mentioned above, when asked about asteroid impact hazards, most people say they do not consider them a believable threat. A 2010 Pew Research Center poll found that a combined 62 percent of respondents said an asteroid hitting Earth by 2050 "will probably not happen" and "will definitely not happen," while a combined 31 percent did entertain the possibility, including 5 percent who said it "will definitely happen." These results are practically identical with those of a 1999 Pew poll that posed the same question.[18]

Howard McCurdy has argued that the idea of an "asteroid impact threat" was first promoted in an attempt to stimulate space exploration after the Apollo era. He has found that the "threat" was not made believable even then: "Warnings about asteroids and comets striking the Earth mobilized a response feeble by comparison to space efforts incited by the Cold War. The Cold War really scared people, and asteroids do not."[19]

---

15. See NASA, "Asteroid 2012 DA14—Earth Flyby Reality Check," 15 February 2013, *http://www.nasa.gov/topics/solarsystem/features/asteroidflyby.html* (accessed 31 April 2013); and Don Yeomans and Paul Chodas, "Additional Details on the Large Fireball Event over Russia on Feb. 15, 2013," NASA, 1 March 2013, *http://neo.jpl.nasa.gov/news/fireball_130301.html* (accessed 31 February 2013).
16. *Asteroid vs. Earth,* TV movie, directed by Christopher Douglas Olen Ray (2014).
17. Boris Kit, "'Asteroids' Getting Rewrite from 'Autobahn' Writer," *Hollywood Reporter* (5 February 2015), *http://www.hollywoodreporter.com/heat-vision/asteroids-getting-rewrite-autobahn-writer-770691* (accessed 14 August 2015).
18. "Life in 2050: Amazing Science, Familiar Threats: Public Sees a Future Full of Promise and Peril," Pew Research Center. *https://www.pewresearch.org/wp-content/uploads/sites/4/legacy-pdf/625.pdf* (accessed 24 March 2021).
19. Howard E. McCurdy, *Space and the American Imagination* (Washington and London: Smithsonian Institution Press, 1997), p. 82.

In 1993, Paul Slovic and K. Peterson conducted a survey of public attitudes and perceptions of asteroid impact hazards, likely the first of its kind. In their sample of 200 college students, impact risk ranked 14th out of 24 on a list of risks to the American public. Even then, this risk was considered to be "distant in time" or "non-immediate."[20]

A COMPELLING NARRATIVE, AN UNBELIEVABLE THREAT

Why does the catastrophic impact narrative keep appearing in pop culture? Why do authors and producers continue to perpetuate it? Three elements make this narrative particularly compelling, especially to moviegoing audiences. Slovic's work on risk assessment, which explores beliefs and perceptions that shape attitudes toward risks, helps to explain how the unique characteristics of this disaster narrative may help sustain it. Slovic and colleagues have developed a matrix that assesses public attitudes toward various risks based on two major factors: "dread risk" and "unknown risk."[21] Together, these factors capture elements that make something seem particularly "risky" to people—an uncontrollable, indiscriminate, catastrophic, or unknown risk. Although asteroid impact risk has not been mapped in their matrix, it is worth noting that "satellite crashes" are pretty high on the high-dread, high-unknown quadrant. But where a satellite crash would have limited effects were it to fall on a populated area, asteroid impact risk is "unique in its combination of very low probability and very great consequence."[22]

The asteroid-impact narrative consistently depicts impacts as catastrophic events. As one scientist has said: "This is also an equal-opportunity hazard, with everyone on the planet at risk from impacts."[23] Paris and New York City make repeated appearances in impact-disaster movies not only because they are so easily identifiable but also because they enable a display of the extent of damage: whether by direct impact, tsunami, or resulting panic, everyone is affected.

Finally, the impact-disaster narrative is all the more compelling because it conveys urgency. Few of the narratives surveyed in this chapter consider the effects of a civilization-ending disaster predicted to occur decades into the future.

---

20. Paul Slovic, "Perception of Risk from Asteroid Impact," in *Comet/Asteroid Impacts and Human Society, An Interdisciplinary Approach*, ed. Peter T. Bobrowsky and Hans Rickman (Heidelberg, Germany: Springer, 2007), pp. 369–382, 379.
21. Paul Slovic, "Perception of Risk," *Science* 236, no. 4799 (1987): 280–285.
22. Slovic, "Perception of Risk from Asteroid Impact," p. 377.
23. David Morrison, "Asteroid and Comet Impacts: the Ultimate Environmental Catastrophe," *Philosophical Transactions of the Royal Society A* 364 (2006): 2041–2054, 2050.

The Near-Earth Object Wide-field Infrared Survey Explorer (NEOWISE), the asteroid-hunting portion of the NASA WISE mission, illustrates an edge-on view of near-Earth asteroids. (NASA/JPL-Caltech: PIA15627)

Instead, feeding into the perception that impacts are unpredictable, these narratives usually depict discovery of an impending impact as a surprise to science and the world. This narrative persists beyond fiction. Despite decades of NEO research that have led to a global system of tracking asteroids and predicting their future orbital paths, the perception that planetary impacts are always unpredictable is rather widespread. Consider that in the case of a tragic shooting in a Colorado movie theater, lawyers for Cinemark USA, in seeking dismissal of lawsuits filed against their client, said, "It would be patently unfair, and legally unsound, to impose on Cinemark…the duty and burden to have foreseen and prevented *the criminal equivalent of a meteor falling from the sky*" [emphasis added].[24]

---

24. Keith Coffman, "Cinemark, USA, Theatre Chain, Seeks Dismissal of Lawsuits in Colorado Mass Shooting," Reuters, 27 February 2012, *http://www.huffingtonpost.com/2012/09/28/ theater-seeks-dismissal-o_n_1921419.html* (accessed 27 September 2012).

Tools of the Trade

A second element that makes the impact-disaster narrative particularly compelling is its visual appeal. Advances in computer simulations and special effects have rendered asteroid impacts incredibly dramatic. Movies and games turn the sequence of an asteroid on its collision course and its eventual impact with Earth into almost a movie in itself. The TV miniseries *Impact* (2009),[25] released a decade after *Deep Impact,* begins not on Earth but just behind the looming menace of an asteroid nearing the planet.

The same tools provide opportunities for even more powerful after-impact visuals: giant tsunamis, explosions, and alterations of Earth's climate are common. From beginning to end, the asteroid-impact narrative affords more opportunities for showcasing advanced special effects than other natural disasters, such as earthquakes or hurricanes.

With impressive computer-generated imagery (CGI) blowing the minds of movie audiences in the 1990s—in the wildly popular *Jurassic Park* (1993)[26] and *Toy Story* (1995),[27] for example—CGI became an expectation by the 2000s. Within a few years of *Armageddon* and *Deep Impact,* an asteroid impact disaster could be depicted vividly for not a whole lot of money.

The visually compelling aspect of an impact is so prevalent that it is noticeable even in nonfiction. Asteroid impacts are afforded extensive, visually compelling sequences even in documentaries where they are just one of several examples of cataclysms, such as in *Last Days on Earth* (2006)[28] and *History Classics: Mega Disasters* (2006).[29] The visual trope of asteroid impact even appears in unlikely places. For example, the TV singing competition *The X Factor* begins with a clip of the program logo flying through space and "crashing" into the planet—much like a meteor would.

The Draw of Space

A third compelling element of the impact narrative is the origin of the threat in space. As McCurdy has explained, after World War II, doomsday scenarios regained popularity. "In earlier times, religious leaders explained how the

---

25. *Impact,* TV miniseries, directed by Mike Rohl (Tandem Communications, ProSieben Television, Impact Films, Province of British Columbia Film Incentive BC, 2009).
26. *Jurassic Park*, film, directed by Steven Spielberg (Universal Pictures, Amblin Entertainment, 1993).
27. *Toy Story,* film, directed by John Lasseter (Pixar Animation Studios, Walt Disney Pictures, 1995).
28. *Last Days on Earth,* documentary, written by George Kachadorian (ABS News 20/20, 2006).
29. *History Classics: Mega Disasters—Episode 5: Asteroid Apocalypse,* documentary series (Creative Differences, 2006).

world might end; in the twentieth century, the public listened to scientists who looked to the sky."[30] Linked with the fear of nuclear bombing, asteroids fell comfortably into a larger space-conscious mindset: "All of the doomsday scenarios, both astronomical and human in origin, fell from the sky."[31] McCurdy has cited several classic science-fiction novels, such as *Rendezvous with Rama* (1972) and *Lucifer's Hammer* (1977), which reflected this idea that both doom and salvation would come from space. McCurdy concluded that the asteroid impact threat was not made believable in real life but suggested that this narrative captured the public's interest as something believable enough in fiction to be entertaining.

Taken together, the three elements discussed above suggest why the asteroid impact scenario has been, and continues to be, a popular motif in movies, books, and games. Nevertheless, despite its prevalence, this popular narrative is far from creating a real-world panic. As the next section describes in more detail, the way the asteroid impact threat is presented only confirms that the "giggle factor" is alive and well.

"Houston, We Have a Problem"
Clichés populate asteroid impact movies, nudging them into the "B" category of science-fiction film. With few exceptions, asteroid impact narratives make for decidedly poor-quality movies, often only made watchable by the special effects used to depict the asteroid on its path of destruction. Narrative gaps, incorrect scientific or technological assumptions, and predictable storylines are common downfalls.

Some prevalent elements of this narrative are as follows:

- **INCORRECT SCIENCE AND TECHNOLOGY**—Most asteroid impact films show a lack of concern for accurately describing the phenomenon, often with surprising results. In the miniseries *Impact*, for example, an asteroid impact on the Moon shifts the balance of mass in the Moon-Earth system so that the gravitational and electromagnetic properties of Earth are thrown completely out of balance. In a scene showing the effects of the Moon reaching the apogee of its new, highly elliptical orbit, people and cars levitate because the gravity of the planet is no longer keeping them on the surface. The same goes for technologies used to address the threat. In *Armageddon* for instance, the Space Shuttle, a low-Earth orbit vehicle, is used to deliver the crew

---

30. McCurdy, *Space and the American Imagination*, p. 70.
31. Ibid., p. 72.

to the surface of an asteroid far beyond low-Earth orbit, where they then use nuclear warheads to destroy it.
- **INFLATED NASA ROLE**—Although real-world discussions of planetary defense are complex, involving issues that include institutional turf and sovereignty concerns, this kind of debate is not considered in the dominant narrative. In most scenarios, NASA is the automatic choice for addressing the threat. The U.S. Department of Defense, which holds the nuclear warheads usually counted on to deflect or destroy the asteroid, tends to play a secondary role.
- **SCIENCE'S LIMITATIONS**—Whereas in the real world, near-Earth asteroid detection and tracking and identification of potentially hazardous asteroids is an ongoing enterprise, in fiction the incoming asteroid usually comes as a last-minute surprise, and science's limitations (particularly in being able to predict the impact) are highlighted. Such is the case of *The Apocalypse* (2007),[32] a movie with a deep-rooted religious argument, where asteroid impacts are the main event of the biblical rapture. Notably, in *Deep Impact,* the asteroid is first identified by a child with a not-so-impressive telescope—not by the powerful ground-based telescopes used by scientists.
- **ASTEROIDS AS THE COVER**—The second most defining element of these movie narratives, besides their high-powered imagery, is that the asteroid impact is rarely the focal point. The impact plays second fiddle to a number of common themes, namely, American values (such as bravery, commitment, and self-sacrifice), the true nature of people (such as selfishness and despair), and family drama (such as mending broken relationships or highlighting personal loss). These insular narratives contrast scenes of global destruction with a focus on one or a few characters.

Since asteroid-impact narratives do not actually revolve around the threat of impact, the takeaway of these storylines appears to be not a deeper understanding of a potential threat, but the successes and failures of individuals in the midst of lively scenes of destruction—believable enough to keep us entertained, but not to keep us up at night.

---

32. *The Apocalypse,* TV movie, directed by Justin Jones (The Asylum, Faith Films, 2007).

ASTEROID IMPACT RISK IN SCIENCE

While the public is entertained by these movies but unconcerned about asteroid impact risks, the scientific community has been preoccupied with the issue for at least three decades. Despite the early work of individuals like Ernst Öpik, which led to the surveying of more than 20,000 meteorites and the development of the first theory of comet formation in the 1930s, and Ralph Baldwin, who first linked lunar craters with impact events in the 1940s, "until the mid-1960s impact cratering…was deemed a curiosity."[33]

The shift in thinking about the risk of asteroid impacts with Earth was the result of a number of developments, notably planetary imaging by NASA's Mariner and Voyager spacecraft in the 1960s and 1970s, which began to show that asteroid impacts with planetary bodies were still occurring. Then, in 1980, Nobel Laureate Luis Alvarez and his son Walter Alvarez identified an asteroid impact with Earth as the event that led to the extinction of the dinosaurs. These developments, along with observations of comet Shoemaker-Levy 9's impact with Jupiter, prompted some scientists to make more urgent appeals to look at the issue.

In 1981, NASA sponsored a "Spacewatch Workshop" in Snowmass, Colorado, whose participants concluded that that risk of an extinction-level event caused by an asteroid or comet impact with Earth "exceeds risk levels that are sometimes deemed unacceptable by modern societies in other contexts."[34] Thus began efforts by the U.S. government to better understand the hazard. The most important development was a 1994 congressional directive to NASA for a comprehensive assessment of potentially hazardous NEOs. The resulting Spaceguard Survey, arguably inspired by Arthur Clarke's science fiction novel *Rendezvous with Rama* and certainly responding to the Shoemaker-Levy 9 impact with Jupiter, began in 1998. Its task was to identify 90 percent of all asteroids larger than 1–2 kilometers in size by the end of 2008. That goal was reached by the end of 2010, so the attention of the program shifted to finding 90 percent of the population larger than 140 meters.[35] In 2005, Congress asked NASA to complete a comprehensive survey of potentially hazardous sub-kilometer-sized asteroids by 2020. This

---

33. Clark R. Chapman and David Morrison, "Risk to Civilization: A Planetary Science Perspective," in *Global Catastrophes in Earth History: An Interdisciplinary Conference on Impacts, Volcanism, and Mass Mortality*, ed. Peter D. Ward (Boulder, CO: Geological Society of America, 1988): pp. 26–27.
34. Ibid.
35. See "Near-Earth Asteroid Discovery Statistics," NASA Near Earth Object Program, http://neo.jpl.nasa.gov/stats/ (accessed 14 August 2015); Lindley Johnson, "Near Earth Object Program," presented at the Single Dish Telescope Workshop, Green Bank, WV, 9–10 June

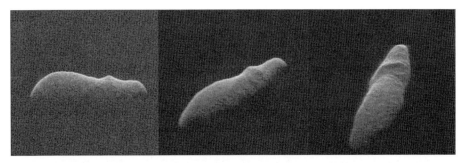

Three radar images of near-Earth asteroid 2003 SD220 obtained on 15–17 December, by NASA's Goldstone Deep Space Communications Complex and the National Science Foundation's Green Bank Telescope in West Virginia. (NASA/JPL-Caltech/GSSR/NSF/GBO: PIA22970)

directive, provided in NASA's authorizing legislation, became known as the George E. Brown, Jr., Near-Earth Object Survey Act.

Because of several government-sponsored studies, workshops, and programs in the United States and abroad related to this subject,[36] scientists' understanding of NEO impact risks has advanced greatly in the past 15 years. NASA's near-Earth observations budget averaged about $4 million a year until 2012, when it rose to $20 million. By 2014, the project's budget was $40 million and the President's budget request for fiscal year 2016 asked for $50 million to continue efforts to identify and track all NEOs that pose an impact threat to Earth.[37] The administration's 2019 budget request for NASA included $150 million for planetary defense.[38]

Not Seeing Eye to Eye: Public and Scientific Perceptions
One key lesson learned from studies of NEOs is that the future orbits of most asteroids can be predicted far in advance—decades or more, an insight that belies the perception that impacts occur at random and with little warning.

2015, *https://science.nrao.edu/science/meetings/2015/planetary-radio-astronomy-future/johnson* (accessed 14 August 2015).

36. For a detailed review of these activities, see Committee to Review Near-Earth Object Surveys and Hazard Mitigation Strategies, *Defending Planet Earth: Near-Earth Object Surveys and Hazard Mitigation Strategies* (Washington, DC: The National Academies Press, 2010).

37. According to NASA 2016 budget documents, the Near-Earth Object Observations (NEOO) project "looks for NEOs that have any potential to collide with Earth and do significant damage to the planet." See "NASA FY 2016 Budget Estimates," *http://www.nasa.gov/sites/default/files/atoms/files/fy2016_budget_book_508_tagged_0.pdf* (accessed 14 August 2015), p. PS-4.

38. *https://doctorlinda.wordpress.com/2018/05/07/whos-doing-what-in-planetary-defense-the-facts/* (accessed 23 January 2020).

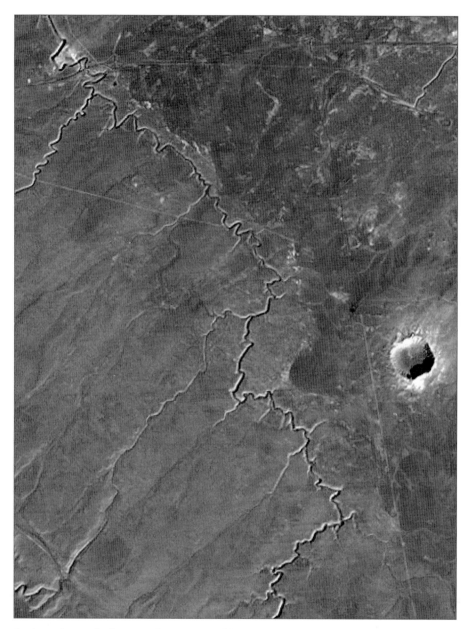

Barringer Crater, also known as "Meteor Crater," is a 1,300-meter (0.8-mile)-diameter, 174-meter (570-foot)-deep hole in the flat-lying desert sandstones 30 kilometers (18.6 miles) west of Winslow, Arizona. (NASA/JPL: PIA03212)

Because the orbits of known asteroids are predictable, scientific concern for asteroid impact risks is not centered on the kind of scenarios depicted in the dominant pop-culture narrative of asteroid impact disaster. This critical element of predictability is completely lost in most of these popular narratives. In like manner, while asteroids and comets that may impact the planet can come in a variety of sizes and cause different kinds of impacts, the vast majority of near-Earth objects are sub-kilometer in size. These sub-kilometer objects rarely make an appearance in fiction. The standard narrative depicts threats from huge asteroids—"the size of Texas," as in *Armageddon*, or 19 kilometers in size, as in *Impact*. The Tunguska impact event of 1908, which scorched or felled trees over an expanse of 2,200 square kilometers (1,367 square miles), is believed to have been caused by an airburst of an approximately 30-meter (98-foot) object.[39] The asteroid that exploded over Chelyabinsk in February 2013 was approximately 20 meters in size.

Walk, Do Not Run, to the Exit
Surveys have already found more than 90 percent of the estimated population of 1-kilometer or larger NEOs. Surveying for sub-kilometer NEOs is under way. Given that the more common sub-kilometer objects could cause considerable destruction upon impact with Earth, the scientific community is calling for increased investment in NEO research and surveying. Even though the National Research Council's Committee to Review Near-Earth Object Surveys and Hazard Mitigation Strategies in its 2010 report mentioned a number of recent wake-up calls "that have highlighted the impact threat to Earth"—such as a meteorite impact in Peru in 2007 and a 2009 impact of another object on Jupiter—its recommendations were not made on the basis of urgency. Instead, the Committee argued that "the time required to mitigate optimally... is in the range of years to decades, but this long period may require acting before it is known with certainty that a NEO will impact Earth."[40] A mismatch between public and scientific perceptions of NEO impact hazards is evident.

Risk research has shown that differences between expert and non-expert risk assessments stem not from differences of opinion over acceptable levels of risk but from different definitions of the concept of risk itself.[41] Further

---

39. Donald K. Yeomans, *Near Earth Objects: Finding Them Before They Find Us* (Princeton, NJ: Princeton University Press, 2013), pp. 5, 118.
40. Committee to Review Near-Earth Object Surveys and Hazard Mitigation Strategies, *Defending Planet Earth: Near-Earth Object Surveys and Hazard Mitigation Strategies*, p. 25.
41. Paul Slovic and Elke U. Weber, "Perception of Risk Posed by Extreme Events," presented at the Risk Management Strategies in an Uncertain World Conference, Palisades, NY, 12–13 April, 2002, pp. 10–11; Mary Douglas and Aaron Wildavsky, *Risk and Culture: An Essay on the Selection of Technical and Environmental Dangers* (Berkeley: University of California Press, 1982); Paul Slovic, *Perception of Risk* (London and Sterling, VA: Earthscan

complicating efforts to explain the risk of NEO impacts with Earth is NEO experts' reliance on probabilistic risk assessments. Quantifying this risk as a 1 in 100,000 chance of an individual dying because of an asteroid impact may not be useful to non-experts.[42] It is clear that while real events can and do engage policy-makers and citizens in the dialogue on NEO impact risks and hazards, that engagement is short-lived. Instead, in the absence of "proof" of an imminent catastrophic impact, interest wanes.

FINAL CONSIDERATION: THE ROLE OF EDUCATION

Calls for improved education on the subject of NEO impact risks and hazards are common in the scientific literature. Two decades ago, Paul Weissman stated that the correct approach "is to carefully prepare the public for the problem by a program of public education."[43] The preface of *Comet/Asteroid Impacts and Human Society* (2007), a book compiling a variety of views from the global science community related to the issue of dealing with comet and asteroid impacts, states, "The International Council for Science (ICSU) recently recognized that the societal implications (social, cultural, political and economic) of a comet/asteroid impact on Earth warrants an immediate consideration by all countries in the world."[44] One of the book's contributors put it even more bluntly: "The challenge for ICSU is the immediate preparation of a worldwide program designed to give people an objective vision about what NEO impacts really mean for humanity."[45]

Publications Ltd., 2000). Slovic's volume includes work by Slovic and other risk experts, including Baruch Fischhoff, Howard Kunreuther, Roger E. and Jeanne X. Kasperson, and Sarah Lichtenstein.

42. Experts participating in an asteroid impact risk communication workshop found that "[q]uantitative and probabilistic scales are of limited value when communicating with non-expert audiences. Qualitative measures of characterizing impact hazards and risks and describing potential impact effects may be more effective communication tools." See "Workshop on Communicating Asteroid Impact Warnings and Mitigation Plans: Workshop Report Prepared for the International Asteroid Warning Network," Secure World Foundation, *http://swfound.org/media/186555/iawn_communication_workshop_report.pdf* (accessed 15 August 2015).

43. Paul R. Weismann, "The Comet and Asteroid Impact Hazard in Perspective," in *Hazards Due to Comets & Asteroids*, ed. Tom Gehrels (Tucson, AZ, and London: University of Arizona Press, 1995), p. 26.

44. Peter Bobrowsky and Hans Rickman, preface to *Comet/Asteroid Impacts and Human Society, An Interdisciplinary Approach*, ed. Peter T. Bobrowsky and Hans Rickman (Heidelberg, Germany: Springer, 2007), pp. V–VII, V.

45. Michel Hermelin, "Communicating Impact Risk to the Public," in *Comet/Asteroid Impacts and Human Society, An Interdisciplinary Approach*, ed. Bobrowsky and Rickman, pp. 495–504.

This reaction originates in a common assumption that credits the public's lack of concern with limited coverage on the issue: people do not care about asteroid impact risks and hazards because they are unfamiliar with them. Weissman, for example, said, "As reporting of random meteorite falls like the 1992 Peekskill, NY[,] event becomes more widespread, public opinion may begin to accept the idea of larger impacts being possible."[46] Today, with fictional depictions and real events involving asteroid impacts well known in popular culture, this sentiment seems to be wishful thinking.

In the end, do popular depictions really serve as "educational targets of opportunities," and do "scientists owe a great debt of gratitude to the Hollywood blockbuster," as one scientist has argued?[47] Or do these depictions perpetuate a view of the asteroid-impact threat that is removed from scientific understanding and, therefore, real risk?

The prevalence of the asteroid-impact narrative as a source of entertainment does not necessarily foster public concern or education. As one prominent risk researcher has observed, given the uniqueness of asteroid impact risks and public perceptions of risks, "it will be hard to generate concern about asteroids unless there is an identifiable, certain, imminent, dreadful threat."[48]

It is difficult to assess the effect of the Chelyabinsk impact event of 2013 on public perception of impact risks, A period of intense interest followed that event, featuring three congressional hearings, the proliferation of videos of the event (one attracted over 4 million views on YouTube) and various social media events involving NASA experts, including a White House Google+ Hangout linked to a close approach of an asteroid in May 2013.

While political support for NEO surveying has increased, as demonstrated with the growth of the NASA NEO observations program budget, the establishment of a NASA Planetary Defense Coordination Office in January 2016, and NASA funding for the Double Asteroid Redirection Test (DART), a mission to be launched in 2021 to demonstrate the kinetic-impact technique for deflecting an asteroid off its orbital path, there is still no strong political will for a space-based NEO survey mission, which would vastly improve detection capability.[49] (Ground-based NEO surveys are limited to nighttime observations when the sky is clear.)

---

46. Weissman, "The Comet and Asteroid Impact Hazard in Perspective," p. 18.
47. Hartwell, *The Sky on the Ground*, p. 83.
48. Slovic, "Perception of Risk from Asteroid Impact," p. 380.
49. It should be noted that there has been progress in the establishment of international coordination mechanisms to facilitate a collective response to a potential NEO threat. While

A poll conducted by the Pew Research Center in 2018 to assess public opinion about priorities in the U.S. civil space program showed that respondents rated monitoring asteroids that could hit Earth as a second-highest priority.[50] Results of an Associated Press–National Opinion Research Center public opinion poll published in May 2019 showed that 85 percent of respondents said it was moderately to very/extremely important for NASA to monitor asteroids and comets that might impact Earth.

The community of stakeholders advocating for greater support of NEO research and planning for planetary defense may find it fruitful to continue to take advantage of real-world events that capture public interest to explain the real science behind the asteroid impact risk predictions and to do it consistently, incorporating lessons learned from the fields of risk communication and risk perception. Such efforts may help to reduce the gap between public and scientific understanding of the issue in the long term—even while the next addition to the cadre of fictional asteroid impact disasters is likely to perpetuate what has already become a standard set of clichés and misrepresentations.

ACKNOWLEDGMENT

This paper is the result of an original idea from Dr. Dwayne Day. I would like to thank him for having inspired and supported the writing of this article.

---

operating independently of the United Nations (UN), the International Asteroid Warning Network (IAWN) and the Space Mission Planning Advisory Group (SMPAG) (established in 2013) were created in response to UN recommendations. IAWN seeks to function as the authoritative source of information on potentially hazardous NEOs, while SMPAG is intended to focus on the development of options should threat mitigation become necessary. For additional background information, see "International Asteroid Warning Network," *http://www.minorplanetcenter.net/IAWN/* (accessed 15 August 2015); and "Space Mission Planning Advisory Group," *http://www.cosmos.esa.int/web/smpag* (accessed 15 August 2015).

50. "Majority of Americans Believe It Is Essential That the U.S. Remain a Global Leader in Space," *http://www.pewinternet.org/2018/06/06/majority-of-americans-believe-it-is-essential-that-the-u-s-remain-a-global-leader-in-space/* (accessed 23 January 2020).

APPENDIX: TIMELINE OF ASTEROID IMPACTS IN WORKS OF FICTION

Year	Name	Country	Notes
1890s			
1890	La Fin du Monde (The End of the World)	France	Novel
1910s			
1910	The Comet	U.S.	Short Film
1930s			
1931	La Fin Du Monde	France	Film
1933	When Worlds Collide	U.S.	Novel
1940s			
1942	The Magnetic Telescope	U.S.	Animated Short Film
1950s			
1951	When Worlds Collide	U.S.	Film
1956	Uchujin Tokyo ni arawaru (Warning from Space)	Japan	Film
1958	La morte viene dallo spazio (The Day the Sky Exploded)	Italy	Film
1959	Starship Troopers	U.S.	Novel
1960s			
1961	Il Pianeta degli uomini spenti (Battle of the Worlds)	Italy	Film
1962	"The Wandering Asteroid"	U.S.	Episode of TV Series *Space Patrol*
1962	Yosei Gorasu (Gorath)	Japan	Film
1968	The Green Slime	U.S./Japan	Film
1968–69	Project SWORD	U.S.	Comic Strip
1970s			
1971	City Beneath the Sea	U.S.	TV Movie
1972	Rendezvous with Rama	U.S.	Novel
1973	Protector	U.S.	Novel
1977	Lucifer's Hammer	U.S.	Novel
1978	The Hermes Fall	U.S.	Novel
1978	A Fire in the Sky	U.S.	TV Movie
1979	Meteor	U.S.	Film
1979	Impact!	U.S.	Novel

(continued on next page)

Year	Name	Country	Notes
1980s			
1980	*Shiva Descending*	U.S.	Novel
1983	*Navstevnici* (*The Visitors*)	Czechoslovakia	TV Series
1984	*Night of the Comet*	U.S.	Film
1985	*Footfall*	U.S.	Novel
1985	*Lucifer's Hammer*	U.S.	Novel (reprint)
1987	*Kikou Senki Doragunaa* (*Metal Armor Dragonar*)	Japan	TV Series
1988	*Kidō Senshi Gundam: Senshitachi no Kiseki* (*Mobile Suit Gundam: Warrior's Locus*)	Japan	Video Game
1990s			
1990	*The Oxygen Barons*	U.S.	Novel
1991	*Double Planet*	U.S.	Novel
1992	*Discours des cometes* (*Comets Speech*)	Canada	Short Film
1993	*The Hammer of God*	U.S.	Novel
1993	*Lucifer's Hammer*	U.S.	Comic Book
1994	*Without Warning*	U.S.	TV Movie
1994	*Outpost*	U.S.	Video Game
1994	"Out of this World"	U.S.	Episode of TV Series *The Magic School Bus: Space Adventures*
1995	*Zombie Holocaust*	U.S.	Video
1995	"Last Days"	U.S.	Episode of TV Series *Sliders*
1995	*The Dig*	U.S.	Computer Game
1995	"Bart's Comet"	U.S.	Episode of TV Series *The Simpsons*
1996	*3 Minutes to Impact*	U.K.	Documentary Film
1996	*The Tomorrow Man*	U.S.	TV Movie
1997	*Starship Troopers*	U.S.	Film
1997	*Doomsday Rock*	U.S.	Film
1997	*Falling Fire*	U.S./Canada	TV Movie
1997	*Asteroid*	U.S.	TV Movie
1997	*Asteroids: Deadly Impact*	U.S.	Documentary Film
1998	*Meteorites!*	U.S.	TV Movie
1998	*Deep Impact*	U.S.	Film
1998	*Armageddon*	U.S.	Film

(continued on next page)

Year	Name	Country	Notes
1998	L'Année de la comète (The Year of the Comet)	France	Film
1998	Nemesis	U.S.	Novel
1999	Cold Fusion	U.K.	Novel
1999	Judgment Day	U.S.	Film
1999	The Last Train	U.S.	TV Series
1999	Omega: The Last Days of the World	U.S.	Novel (reprint)
1999	Rogue Star	U.S.	Novel
2000s			
2000	Tycus	U.S.	Film
2000	Dinosaur	U.S.	Film
2000	Submarine TITANS	U.S.	Video Game
2001	Asteroid	—	Radio Drama
2001	Terraforming Earth	U.S.	Novel
2001	Pearl Harbor II: Pearlmageddon	U.S.	Short Film
2002	"Fail Safe"	U.S.	Episode of TV Series *Stargate SG-1*
2003	Birth of an Age	U.S.	Novel (part of the Christ Clone Trilogy)
2003	Stratos 4	Japan	TV Series
2004	"Impact Winter"	U.S.	Episode of TV Series *The West Wing*
2004	Dr. Lively's Ultimatum	U.S.	Novel
2004	The Meteor	Thailand	Film
2004	PI: Post Impact	Germany/U.S.	Film
2004	"Phantom Planet"	U.S.	TV Series, episode of *Danny Phantom*
2007	Anna's Storm	U.K.	TV Movie
2005	Deadly Skies	U.S./Canada	Film
2005	Meteors: Fire in the Sky	U.S.	Documentary Film
2006	Earthstorm	U.S.	Film
2006	Last Days on Earth	U.S.	Documentary Film
2006	"Asteroid Apocalypse"	U.S.	Episode of TV Series *Mega Disasters*
2007	Days of Darkness	U.S.	Film
2007	Impact Earth (Futureshock: Comet)	U.K.	TV Movie

(continued on next page)

Year	Name	Country	Notes
2007	"Whatever Happened to Sarah Jane?"	U.K.	Episode of TV Series *Sarah Jane Adventures*
2008	*Impact*	Germany/Canada	TV Movie
2008	*Time Messenger*	U.S.	Novel
2008	*Léger tremblement du Paysage* (*A Faint Trembling of the Landscape*)	French	Film
2008	*Skhizein*	French	Short Film
2008	*Advance Wars: Days of Ruin*	U.S.	Video Game
2009	*Meteor*	U.S.	TV Miniseries
2009	*Polar Storm*	U.S./Canada	Film
2009	*The Last Witness: The Protean Explosion*	U.S.	Novel
2010s			
2010	*Meteor Storm*	U.S.	TV Movie
2010	*Meteor Apocalypse*	U.S.	Video
2010	*Shadow in the Sky*	U.S.	Novel of the Last Year Trilogy
2010	*Muumi ja punainen pyrstötähti* (*Moomins and the Comet Chase*)	Finland	Film
2011	*Rage*	U.S.	Video Game
2011	*Exodus*	—	Novel of the Exodus Trilogy
2011	*The Metamorphosis of Timothy Dunn*	U.S.	Novel
2011	*Melancholia*	Denmark/Sweden/France	Film
2011	"Asteroid Heads to Earth"	U.S.	Episode of TV Series *The Onion News Network*
2012	*Seeking a Friend for the End of the World*	U.S.	Film
2012	*The Asteroid*	—	Novel
2012	*Inryu myeongmang bogoseo* (*Doomsday Book*)	South Korea	Film
2012	*Asteroid Crisis*	—	Novel
2012	"Trajectory"	—	Short Story/Podcast
2012	*Newton's Ark*	—	Novel of the Emulation Trilogy
2012	*The Last Policeman*	U.S.	Novel
2014	*Asteroid v. Earth*	U.S.	TV Movie
2017	*Asteroids!*	U.S.	Animated Short

CHAPTER 8

The Outer Solar System: Exploring Through the Public Eye

Giny Cheong

STARTING IN THE LATE 1970S, NASA's Voyager interplanetary mission repeatedly made headlines with new discoveries and spectacular images from the outer edges of the solar system. NASA planned this twin-spacecraft mission to take advantage of an outer-planet alignment of Jupiter, Saturn, Uranus, and Neptune that occurs approximately once every 175 years. Due to cost considerations, NASA initially received funding only for flybys of Jupiter and Saturn. Voyager 2 launched first, on 20 August 1977, arriving at Jupiter in March 1979 and Saturn in November 1980. Voyager 1 launched on 5 September 1977, arriving at Jupiter in July 1979 and at Saturn in August 1981. Journalists joined scientists and other advocates in calling for the space agency to extend the mission to Uranus and Neptune.

Public affairs operations for the Voyager mission revealed NASA's approach to disseminating information and images to the public through the mass media. The National Aeronautics and Space Act of 1958 requires the Agency to "provide for the widest practicable and appropriate dissemination of information concerning its activities and the results thereof."[1] A constant stream of press releases and briefings supplied journalists with information about the mission. NASA invited journalists, celebrities, and politicians to attend Voyager's major flyby events at the Jet Propulsion Laboratory (JPL).

---

1. National Aeronautics and Space Act of 1958, Sec. 20112 (a)(3).

Major newspapers usually published stories written by staff journalists who followed the "space beat."[2]

SCIENCE IN THE MEDIA

This chapter focuses on primarily on print news, with some attention paid to broadcast television coverage and the role of Hollywood. It draws on the work of researchers who have explored the relationship between the mass media and their audiences. Françoise Bastide analyzed the differences between accounts of the Voyager mission in popular science publications and scientific journals. Rather than finding a simple dichotomy between writing for scientists and for the general public, she saw that popular accounts might differ drastically, depending on the expectations of their writers ("enunciators") and their audiences ("enunciatees").[3] Marcel LaFollette asserted that mass media served as the primary means of culturally constructing public images of science, affecting public attitudes about science.[4] Dorothy Nelkin found that "public beliefs about science and technology tend to correspond with the messages conveyed in the media, though the direction of cause and effect is not clear."[5] Jeanne Fahnestock examined the style of science writing for a wider audience, which often emphasizes the "wonder" and the "applications" of science.[6] She found that popular science writing tended toward selective information or exaggeration, along with the omission of qualifying language to increase the certainty of claims, conveying a drastically different message than the original scientific paper. These researchers demonstrated that the mass media influenced or reflected public opinion about science.

In the late 1970s and the 1980s, Americans relied on newspapers and television (then featuring only three major networks) as their primary sources of information about current news events.[7] By the 1990s, Americans had

---

2. Newspapers allow a better comparison between earlier vs. later news coverage and remain more available to research (as opposed to television segments, which may or may not be easily available in video vs. transcript only). Therefore, this chapter focuses on the written mass media, which extends readily to online media.
3. Françoise Bastide, trans. Greg Myers, "A Night with Saturn," *Science, Technology, & Human Values* 17, no. 3 (summer 1992): 259–281.
4. Marcel LaFollette, *Making Science Our Own: Public Images of Science 1910–1955* (Chicago: University of Chicago Press, 1990).
5. Dorothy Nelkin, *Selling Science: How the Press Covers Science and Technology*, rev. ed. (New York: W.H. Freeman and Company, 1995), p. 69.
6. Jeanne Fahnestock, "Accommodating Science: The Rhetorical Life of Scientific Facts," *Written Communication* 3 (1998): 330–350.
7. Surveys have asked respondents where they received most of their information about current news events: radio, television, newspapers, magazines, books, other people, or other.

access to a greatly expanded mass media, providing around-the-clock cable TV news, as well as online news and information outlets. Using media coverage of the Voyager mission as a baseline, this chapter will also analyze and compare media coverage of the Galileo mission's return to Jupiter in 1995 and Cassini's return to Saturn in 2004. These cases reveal changes in science communication due to the evolution of mass media and hint at changing public attitudes toward science.

During the Voyager mission, media efforts to popularize the science of the mission appeared fairly obvious. In his article about Voyager 1's arrival at Jupiter published on 1 March 1979, *Los Angeles Times* science writer George Alexander begins, "Like a sailboat cresting a reef and entering the lagoon of some Pacific island, the Voyager 1 spacecraft passed through the bow shock [the shock front along which the solar wind encounters a planet's magnetic field] of Jupiter Wednesday and slipped inside the big planet's magnetic environment."[8] The simile makes an Earth-based connection to something most may have difficulty imagining and hints at the risks inherent to the mission.

During Voyager 1's planetary encounters, media coverage shifted from planned science objectives to actual scientific discoveries and images. NASA's and JPL's press releases and briefings offered more technical and scientific detail. Science journalists embellished the details by imbuing their news reports with emotional values like surprise and wonder as well as personifying the science whenever possible by adding quotes from scientists. Editors used Voyager's dramatic imagery to determine the placement of stories about the mission, which often appeared on the front page or in special sections.

The *New York Times* featured the detailed surface of Io captured by Voyager passing 173,000 miles from Jupiter at the top left of the front page and above the fold, then drew readers to the story in another section of the paper. The *Washington Post* chose to feature a spectacular mosaic of Jupiter's Great Red Spot in the middle of the front page and above the fold, along with another image of Io and starting the story below the fold.

Editorial choices in newspaper layout imply significance. Since newspapers usually fold in the middle of the page, the top half ("above the fold") offers what editors deem the most important news. The *New York Times*

Data for this question are available for 1979, 1981, 1985, and 1988. Results showed dominance in the newspaper and television categories, with an uptick in television numbers by 1988. *NSF Poll #2006-SCIENCE: Trend Dataset—Surveys of Public Understanding of Science and Technology,* conducted by Jon D. Miller and Linda Kimmel, Northwestern University (1979–1999); ORC Macro (2001); and NORC, the General Social Survey (2006), 1979–2006.

8. George Alexander, "Voyager 1 Is There: Probe Pierces Jupiter's Shield," *Los Angeles Times* (1 March 1979): A1.

provided a striking Voyager image at the top of its front page on 6 March 1979, with a story, "A Hostile Jupiter Yields Surprises," inside the paper. On the same day, the *Washington Post* showcased imagery and an accompanying article, "Voyager Records a Surprising Io" on its front page. Voyager images on these front pages led readers to stories inside. Other headlines of the day included President Jimmy Carter's mediation of a Middle East peace treaty and China's withdrawal from Vietnam. From article placement and hints within articles, the Cold War snuck into the media discourse about Voyager. A *Washington Post* columnist commented on the public's interest:

> We want to know because there may be some advantage in knowing, because we may gain an edge on the Russians, or because knowing is valuable in itself; but we also want to know because somehow the idea of exploring space connects with self-knowledge.[9]

While Cold War competition did not necessarily motivate the mission, some U.S. scientists and journalists demonstrated extra pride in Voyager's achievements.

New York Times science correspondent John Noble Wilford took a more straightforward approach in his reporting on Voyager: "The robot spacecraft sped within 174,000 miles of the multi-colored clouds of Jupiter, and with its television cameras looked deep into the eye of the huge hurricane-like feature known as the Great Red Spot."[10] He used quotations to convey emotion and humanize both the mission and its scientists. Wilford quoted Voyager project scientist Edward Stone exclaiming, "We've had a total success." Wilford also reported that when Bradford Smith of the University of Arizona "displayed the latest color photograph of the disc of Io, with its deep reds and yellow and a mingling of dark spots, he joked, 'That's better-looking than a lot of pizzas I've seen.'"[11]

In the *Washington Post,* Thomas O'Toole used the same quotations from Stone and Smith. In his reporting, O'Toole emphasized mysteries "beguiling" Voyager scientists, especially Jupiter's moon Io. He quoted the U.S. Geological Survey's Laurence Soderblom describing Io as "one of the strangest bodies in the solar system."[12] In an earlier article, O'Toole had primed

---

9. Roger Rosenblatt, "'Star Wars,' NASA and Real Life," *Washington Post* (22 August 1977): A21.
10. John Noble Wilford, "A Hostile Jupiter Yields Surprises," *New York Times* (6 March 1979): A1.
11. Ibid.
12. O'Toole covered science and technology for the *Washington Post* from 1967 to 1987. Thomas O'Toole, "Voyager Records a Surprising Io," *Washington Post* (6 February 1979): A1.

Voyager 2 image of Jupiter's Great Red Spot and South Equatorial Belt. (NASA/JPL: PIA00456)

readers by introducing the Voyagers as technological heroes, spacecraft traveling mind-boggling distances at a faster rate than previous missions, piquing curiosity over scientific questions like "Why is the Great Red Spot red?"[13]

These articles emphasized the newness of color planetary imagery (although the papers published them in black-and-white), questions raised by prior ground-based observations that now might be answered, and new questions yet to be addressed. Newspaper editorials also seemed to support the view that solar system exploration had some fundamental value. As a *Los Angeles Times* editorial eloquently stated, "Like monkeys stuck in a dark box, we use Voyager as a window into the blackness of space. We want to see what's out there. From this standpoint, the exploration of space is no high-priced public-relations gimmick or cockeyed race with the Russians. Rather, it is a fundamental expression of human nature. A few billion dollars a year seems a small price to pay."[14]

On 10 July 1977, Carl Sagan published "The Next Great Leap into Space" in the *New York Times Magazine* and "Star Wars: The Coming Conquest of Outer Space" as an opinion piece in the *Los Angeles Times*. Americans already knew Sagan as a renowned scientist, popular author, and science communicator. Both pieces mourned Voyager as NASA's last great commitment to solar system exploration and expressed concerns about the future. He outlined missions that would be within current technical capabilities and almost possible within the current NASA budget, such as a Mars rover, Titan

---

13. Thomas O'Toole, "The Compelling Giant of the Solar System: Spacecraft Voyager Will Reach Jupiter and Its Moons in March and Photograph the Entire Planet," *Washington Post* (4 February 1979): C3.
14. Michael Thacher, "Both Add Up to Curiosity: Rats Run a Maze, Humans Run a Jupiter Program," *Los Angeles Times* (9 March 1979): C7.

lander, human missions to other worlds, and more. He extolled the significance of solar system exploration:

> [F]or the first time in history, it permits us to approach with rigor, with a significant chance of finding out the true answers, such deep questions as the origins and destinies of worlds, the beginnings and endings of life, and the possibility of other beings who live in the skies—questions as basic to the human enterprise as thinking is, as natural as breathing.[15]

Sagan's *Los Angeles Times* piece had a competitive edge, pointing out U.S. and Soviet "turf" in solar system exploration.[16]

In 1977, *Star Wars* and *Close Encounters of the Third Kind* arrived in movie theatres, and Hollywood helped audiences imagine a spacefaring future.[17] Sagan's award-winning public television series, *Cosmos: A Personal Voyage*, aired from September to December 1980.[18] American culture seemed receptive to these futuristic visions, encouraged by the success of Voyager.

In November 1980, NASA Deputy Administrator Alan Lovelace wrote a letter to the Speaker of the House of Representatives in Congress: "The Voyager study of Jupiter last year provided more knowledge about the largest planet in the solar system than had been accumulated in the 369 years since Galileo began telescopic observation." He concluded, "The enclosed photographs of the sixth planet in our solar system symbolize America's preeminence in solar system exploration. I know that you share our pride in the achievements of Voyager 1 and in America's leadership in space research."[19] He clearly intended the images to provide evidence that this mission was worth funding. On 18 November 1980, Chairman Don Fuqua of the House Committee on Science and Technology also encouraged his fellow members of Congress to support a "vigorous and farsighted program of space exploration," citing the "beautiful and dramatic" Voyager 1 photos of Saturn.[20]

---

15. Carl Sagan, "The Next Great Leap into Space," *New York Times* (10 July 1977): 174.
16. Carl Sagan, "Star Wars: The Coming Conquest of Outer Space," *Los Angeles Times* (10 July 1977): D3.
17. *Star Wars* (later retitled *Star Wars Episode IV: A New Hope*), film, directed by George Lucas (20th Century Fox, 1977); *Close Encounters of the Third Kind*, film, directed by Steven Spielberg (Columbia Pictures, 1977).
18. Carl Sagan, Ann Druyan, and Steven Soter, *Cosmos: A Personal Voyage*, television documentary series, presented by Carl Sagan and directed by Adrian Malone (PBS, 1980).
19. Letter from Deputy Administrator A. M. Lovelace to Speaker of the House Thomas P. O'Neill, Jr., 26 November 1980.
20. Don Fuqua (D-FL), "Voyager Shows Space Is Our Future," *Congressional Record—House*, H 10832, 18 November 1980.

Voyager 1's encounter with Saturn in November 1980 drew the media's attention. "Voyager 1's encounter with Saturn... produced media response without parallel in the unmanned space exploration program," wrote one JPL official. "The total potential TV viewing audience was estimated at 100 million persons on four continents."[21] For more than a week during the evening news, all three television networks (ABC, CBS, and NBC) showed the latest imagery of Saturn and its moons.[22] The large audience for this encounter, roughly equivalent to the audience for recent Super Bowls, indicated tremendous public interest in the science mission and also included international viewers.

Near-natural-color image of Saturn, its rings, and four of its icy satellites (Tethys, Dione, Rhea, and Mimas) taken by Voyager 2. (NASA/JPL/USGS: PIA00400)

Hollywood movies and TV coverage nicely coincided with advocacy for continued funding for Voyager encounters with Uranus and Neptune. Administrative efforts, wide mass media coverage, and positive public opinion certainly contributed to the decision to extend the popular mission.

---

21. Interoffice memo to B. C. Murray from F. J. Colella, "Voyager Saturn Media Response," Jet Propulsion Laboratory, 17 December 1980.
22. Overall television coverage of the event lasted from 6 November to 17 November 1980. Coverage usually occurred on two of three networks, rather than all three on each day. ABC also conducted a "Special Assignment (U.S. Space Exploration)" over two days.

GALILEO TO JUPITER

News coverage of NASA's Galileo mission to Jupiter, launched in 1989, followed similar patterns in print media. Although NASA's Pioneer and Voyager missions had completed flybys of Jupiter, Galileo became the first spacecraft to remain in orbit around the planet and send a probe into its atmosphere. Before reaching its destination, Galileo flew by Venus and Earth (1990–92), visited an asteroid (1991) and discovered a moon orbiting around it (1993), and observed Comet Shoemaker-Levy 9's impact with Jupiter (1994). Galileo received extra prelaunch news coverage because of its many delays and cost overruns.

In 1987, the *New York Times* noted that the launch had been delayed five times and mission costs had ballooned when NASA announced that the spacecraft finally would launch in 1989.[23] Galileo's high-gain antenna failed to fully open on its long voyage, and multiple attempts to remedy the problem resulted in a work-around using low-gain antennas. The primary mission finally began when the spacecraft crossed into Jupiter's environment on 1 December 1995.

The *New York Times* featured the mission in its magazine section, reporting that the public had been "enchanted" by Voyager images and that Galileo's 1,000-times-more-detailed images might be even more exciting to scientists looking for "extraterrestrial water, perhaps even rudimentary life."[24] This article treated the mission with humor and humanity, musing whether "Galileo shouldn't have been called Job instead," describing the spacecraft as an "electromechanical child" growing up, and offering a sense of awe: "Within two days the probe will have vaporized, but not before putting the first human fingerprints onto one of the outer planets."

A pair of front-page articles from 8 December 1995 offered readers different takes on the mission. In the *New York Times*, Wilford reported that project scientist William O'Neil was "ecstatic" and that chief project scientist Torrence Johnson said, "This is really neat."[25] Wilford reminded readers about the antenna failure, meaning "fewer pictures and none before next summer." The article also included an illustration depicting the Galileo probe's descent into the atmosphere. Wilford conveyed a cautiously optimistic tone.

---

23. Warren E. Leary, "NASA Will Launch Unmanned Craft to Jupiter in 1989," *New York Times* (3 December 1987): A1.
24. Thomas Mallon, "Galileo, Phone Home," *New York Times* (3 December 1995): section 6 (magazine): 57.
25. John Noble Wilford, "Probe Pierces Jupiter's Clouds in First Interior Look at Planet," *New York Times* (8 December 1995): A1.

In the *Washington Post*, Kathy Sawyer poetically described the Galileo probe as the first "tiny emissary" to send messages from inside the atmosphere of an outer planet and also a "kamikaze probe dispatched from the mothership."[26] She relayed the importance of studying Jupiter, like a "Rosetta stone." In this article, William O'Neil likened the probe's descent to a "celestial ballet." Sawyer quoted Carl Sagan from a televised chat in which he said, "It's a very exciting moment to be alive and interested in these issues." Her writing showed more enthusiasm and imaginative description than Wilford's did.

Media attention turned to Galileo again when NASA issued a press release, "Galileo Probe Suggests Planetary Science Reappraisal," on 22 January 1996.[27] Project scientists had made "startling discoveries" that drastically differed from their expectations, resulting in much reevaluation of theories about planetary evolution. For example, the probe had measured higher winds, higher temperatures, and more atmospheric density than scientists had expected to find. NASA noted that these findings remained preliminary. This news did not make the front page.

On 23 January, the headline on John Wilford's story in the *New York Times* read, "Theories About Jupiter Fall as Facts Pour In."[28] Wilford summarized the findings reported in the press release as "enough to jolt scientists with surprises." He emphasized the uncertainty surrounding the findings.

In the *Washington Post*, Kathy Sawyer hooked readers by asking, "Where is the water?"[29] She explained that scientists had found a drier atmosphere than expected, as well as several other surprises that had started arguments in the science community and required reassessing theories about planetary evolution. Sawyer gave readers multiple possible explanations to puzzle over, imparting a sense of scientists' excitement over these new mysteries. Her article focused less on uncertainty about the results and more on the scientific debate, putting a positive spin on the new knowledge (rather than how old theories were wrong).

---

26. Sawyer covered space science and technology for the *Washington Post* from 1986 to 2003. Kathy Sawyer, "Galileo Starts Tour of Giant Planet; After 6-Year Trek, Spacecraft First to Transmit from Jovian Skies," *Washington Post* (8 December 1995): A1.
27. "Galileo Probe Suggests Planetary Science Reappraisal," NASA Press Release 96-10, 22 January 1996.
28. John Noble Wilford, "Theories About Jupiter Fall as Facts Pour In," *New York Times* (22 January 1996): C8.
29. Kathy Sawyer, "Jupiter Retains Atmosphere of Mystery; Surprise Galileo Data Could Force New Theories of Planetary Formation," *Washington Post* (23 January 1996): A3.

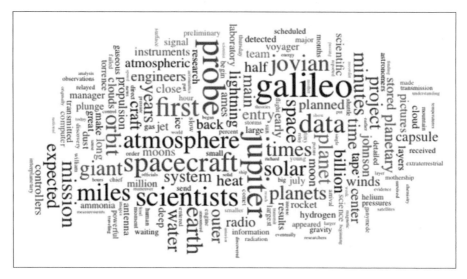

FIGURE 1. Word cloud generated from the articles in the *Washington Post* and the *New York Times* between 3 December 1995 and 24 January 1996.

Word clouds attempt to visually depict the contents of texts, making frequent words bigger. The word cloud in figure 1 depicts the contents of articles during this time period, highlighting words like "scientists," "atmosphere," and "minutes." "Billion" turned up often in references to the $1.3 billion price tag for the mission and the 2.3 billion miles the spacecraft had traveled since launch. Galileo's discoveries required more detailed scientific explanations than those of earlier missions, whose spectacular images spoke volumes by themselves. The word cloud includes some interesting terms that different writers came up with to explain complex scientific phenomena.

By the late 1990s, the media landscape had expanded to include digital forms of mass media. The 4 July 1997 Mars Pathfinder landing may have been the first NASA event to make the groundbreaking transition into digital media, redefining how people could learn about outer space. On 9 August 1997, the *New York Times* reported 566 million hits on its online Pathfinder coverage over 30 days and 47 million hits as the highest number of hits on a single day, surpassing prelanding estimates.[30] In an earlier article in its business section, the *Times* had noted that online reporting provided information faster than television and that e-mail lists allowed people to talk about

---

30. John Noble Wilford, "A Month on Mars and the Pathfinder Is Declared a Total Success," *New York Times* (9 August 1997): section 1, late edition, p. 10.

interesting news, while optimistically concluding that people gravitated toward trusted online news sources and "television did not put an end to radio."[31]

CASSINI TO SATURN

NASA, the European Space Agency (ESA), and the Italian Space Agency collaborated on the Cassini mission to Saturn as an international endeavor. The Cassini spacecraft carried ESA's Huygens probe, which would be released into the atmosphere of Titan, Saturn's largest moon. Cassini-Huygens launched on 15 October 1997 and arrived at Saturn on 30 June 2004. Cassini was the last of NASA's large-scale and expensive solar system exploration missions before the Agency's implementation of the "faster, better, cheaper" initiative.

On 1 July 2004, the headline on the front page of the *Washington Post* read, "Cassini First to Orbit Saturn; Spacecraft Slips Through Planet's Rings for Exploratory Mission." Staff writer Guy Gugliotta called the mission "unmatched in the history of space travel" and related tension in the mission control room during the spacecraft's orbital insertion.[32] In the *New York Times*, John Noble Wilford noted that the risks involved precision needed as "Spacecraft Becomes First To Enter Orbit of Saturn" (this story did not make front-page news).[33] An editorial in the *Times* stated, "Humans can marvel for only so long. A little amazement, and we're ready to get right back to the business of ordinary life.... Cassini has made its way to a place where we will all begin to marvel once more."[34]

By 2 July, Cassini's success became clear to the world through its first dazzling images. In the *Washington Post,* Guy Gugliotta focused on the reactions of scientists. Carolyn Porco, Cassini's imaging team leader, enthusiastically described the first 61 close-up images as "shocking" and "unprecedented."[35] Gugliotta reported other scientists declaring the spacecraft as "already a source of wonderment." His article did not feature any images. Gugliotta had been a national news reporter before writing about science, which perhaps explains his emphasis on people.

---

31. Amy Harmon, "Mars Landing Signals Defining Moment for Web Use," *New York Times* (14 July 1997): section D (business/financial desk), late edition, p. 1.
32. Guy Gugliotta, "Cassini First To Orbit Saturn; Spacecraft Slips Through Planet's Rings for Exploratory Mission," *Washington Post* (1 July 2004): A1.
33. John Noble Wilford, "Spacecraft Becomes First To Enter Orbit of Saturn," *New York Times* (1 July 2004): A18.
34. "Through Saturn's Rings," *New York Times* (1 July 2004), section A (editorial): 20.
35. Guy Gugliotta, "Scientists Marvel over Planet Rings; NASA's Saturn Mission Unfolding Seamlessly," *Washington Post* (2 July 2004): A3.

FIGURE 2. Word cloud generated from the articles in the *Washington Post* and the *New York Times* between 30 June 2004 and 3 July 2004.

Cassini made front-page news, below the fold, with a 2 July article in the *New York Times*. John Wilford quoted Porco describing the beauty and clarity of Cassini's black-and-white imagery as "just mind-blowing."[36] Wilford reminded readers that spectrographic analysis, not just imagery alone, would be needed to learn more about the rings. This article included a close-up image of the rings on the front page, with four more images and an illustration of the ring layers inside the paper.

Although newspapers were still providing news on space missions, digital coverage was on the rise. During Cassini's Saturn orbit insertion period, the SpaceRef website reported that the mission's website received 136.6 million hits.[37] On 15 January 2005, the day after Huygens had landed on Titan, ESA reported on its website that it had received 919,000 external visitors and 6.8 million page views.[38]

The word cloud shown in figure 2 shows words that appeared frequently in Cassini media coverage. This word cloud reveals the names of key people

---

36. John Noble Wilford, "From Ringside, Dazzling Photos Show Saturn's Swirling Wreaths," *Washington Post* (2 July 2004): section A, 1.
37. "NASA Cassini Significant Events for 07/01/04–07/07/04," 9 July 2004, *http://spaceref.com/news/viewsr.html?pid=13341* (accessed 15 August 2015).
38. "Titan Attracts Record Visitor and Media Attention to ESA," 27 January 2005, *https://www.esa.int/About_Us/Corporate_news/Titan_attracts_record_visitor_and_media_attention_to_ESA* (accessed 15 August 2015).

on the mission, such as "Porco" (imaging team leader) and "Mitchell" (program manager).

"Porco" appeared frequently due to her quotes about the content of the imagery, which added excitement to the increasingly complex science she presented. The Technology, Entertainment, and Design (TED) Conference invited Porco to give a talk on Cassini in October 2007.[39] Her TED talk led her into consulting for a new movie version of *Star Trek* (2009).[40] Her increasing visibility on the web demonstrated a new way of disseminating science through digital channels.

Cassini images have been labeled as art in some online communities and blogs. In comparison to the Hubble Space Telescope's brightly colored images, Cassini's black-and-white imagery emphasizes the starkness of space. Viewing these images online, unaffected by the limitations of print media, enables people to better appreciate their aesthetic qualities. The Cassini mission website gained a direct audience for the latest news, unfiltered by print or broadcast journalists.

CONCLUSIONS

The Voyager mission—now called "interstellar," since Voyager 1 entered interstellar space in August 2012—illustrated how mass media advanced scientific discoveries into public understanding. NASA press releases and briefings presented science that journalists expanded on to make the stories interesting, through real-world references. Journalists also added a human element to their stories through emotional cues and quotations. Although journalists often attributed surprise and wonder to the scientists involved, they also appealed to their audiences to feel wonder as well about the vast distance a small robotic spacecraft had traveled, along with the human drive for exploration. Spacecraft imagery became a source of and evidence for wonder that offered audiences awe-inspiring planetary snapshots and insights into the technological prowess needed to gaze through robotic eyes.

Galileo mission coverage followed a predictable pattern, with press releases driving news articles. Cassini broke this pattern by releasing information on the mission website. More information about new scientific discoveries

---

39. TED conferences invite speakers to discuss "ideas worth spreading," and their videos have been available online since June 2006.
40. Dennis Overbye, "An Odyssey from the Bronx to Saturn's Rings," *New York Times* (21 September 2009): D1.

The two Voyager spacecraft carry a small American flag and a Golden Record packed with pictures and sounds—mementos of our home planet. (NASA/JPL-Caltech: PIA17035)

appeared on the website than print and broadcast media were reporting.[41] Information proliferated over the web, from online news sites to amateur

---

41. Mission websites often post press releases that do not get picked up by mainstream print or broadcast media, although specialized news media may follow these developments more closely (such as *Space News* or Space.com). *Science and Engineering Indicators 2014*

space blogs and even social networking sites. Web users had the opportunity to view more images in larger sizes and at better resolution, limited only by their computer screens.

What does the transition from "old" to "new" media mean? Some digital evangelists have promoted the idea that new media have "democratized" the news, while others have expressed concerns about the shift. The internet allows users to choose what to view, and when and where to view it. Content producers might find greater audiences online than they might via "old" media. The abundance of information available on the internet, however, has become overwhelming. Users develop filters to manage the information deluge, choosing what they access based on their individual interests. Thus consumers of news take over the gate-keeping function formerly performed by producers of news.

It is difficult to gauge public enthusiasm for solar system exploration with thousands upon thousands of opinions abounding in the online environment. In the 1970s and 1980s, Carl Sagan encouraged the public to dream about the future. However, a so-called "war on science" began to take root in the 1970s and flourished by the 1990s.[42] Science skeptics have found their own place online and in the mass media alongside science enthusiasts. In addition, technology development has moved into inventing items previously imagined in science fiction.[43] Hollywood's more recent offerings appear to concentrate on space battles rather than imaginative or hopeful futures.[44] Perhaps the cultural landscape has changed, moving us away from contemplating space exploration in the ways we did during Voyager.

(National Science Board 14-01) cited that the internet had finally surpassed television as Americans' primary source for science and technology information.

42. See Chris Mooney, *The Republican War on Science* (New York: Basic Books, 2007); and Chris Mooney and Sheril Kirshenbaum, *Unscientific America: How Scientific Illiteracy Threatens Our Future* (New York: Basic Books, 2009).

43. Charles Q. Choi, "How 'Star Wars' Changed Everything," *Christian Science Monitor* (10 August 2010), *http://www.csmonitor.com/Science/2010/0810/How-Star-Wars-changed-everything* (accessed 6 June 2013).

44. The *Star Wars* franchise concentrated on mythic themes of good vs. evil and still commands numerous cult followers. Only time will tell if recent movies have similar fandoms nearly 40 years later (excepting the *Star Trek* universe as a contemporary of *Star Wars*).

PART V
Exploring the Outer Solar System

THE EUROPEAN SPACE AGENCY'S Huygens probe traveled to its target, Titan, with NASA's flagship Cassini orbiter mission to the Saturn system. In chapter 9, Arturo Russo tells the history of the Cassini-Huygens mission from a European perspective, focusing on the institutional framework and decision-making process employed by ESA to develop Huygens and the relationship developed between ESA and NASA to enable the mission to go forward.

For ESA, Huygens was more than a mere contribution to a NASA mission. As Russo notes, Huygens was ESA's first dedicated solar system exploration mission. Huygens landed on Saturn's moon Titan on 14 January 2005. Huygens is, and remains, the first and only spacecraft to land on a planetary moon other than Earth's and is the first spacecraft to land on an outer-solar-system body. Since Huygens, ESA has landed its Philae probe on the comet Churyumov-Gerasimenko (November 2014) and the Japan Aerospace Exploration Agency (JAXA) has landed its Hayabusa probe on the asteroid Itokawa (September 2005).

The Cassini-Huygens collaboration was, at times, "fraught with difficulties," as Russo explains. Nonetheless, the partners overcame them. Both Cassini (which ended its mission in 2017) and Huygens (which completed its mission on the day that it landed) are success stories that mark an important step forward in NASA-ESA collaboration.

CHAPTER 9

Europe's Rendezvous with Titan: The European Space Agency's Contribution to the Cassini-Huygens Mission to the Saturnian System

Arturo Russo

THE CASSINI-HUYGENS MISSION to Saturn and its satellite system is the most ambitious effort in solar system exploration ever mounted.[1] Launched in October 1997, the mission was realized as a joint endeavor of NASA, the European Space Agency (ESA), and the Italian Space Agency (ASI). It consists of a sophisticated spacecraft performing multiple orbital tours around Saturn, as well as a probe that was released from the main spacecraft to parachute through the atmosphere to the surface of Saturn's largest and most interesting moon, Titan. The mission's name honors two 17th-century astronomers who pioneered modern observations of Saturn and its satellites. The orbiter is named after Jean-Dominique Cassini (1625–1712), who discovered the satellites Iapetus, Rhea, Tethys, and Dione, as well as ring features such as the so-called "Cassini division." The Titan probe is named after Christiaan Huygens (1629–95), who discovered Saturn's largest satellite in 1655.

---

1. The scientific background and technical aspects of the mission are discussed in D. M. Harland, *Cassini at Saturn* (Berlin, Germany: Springer, 2007). A U.S.-focused sociological analysis is in B. Groen and C. Hampden-Turner, *The Titans of Saturn* (London: Marshall Cavendish, 2005). See also L. J. Spilker, ed., *Passage to a Ringed World: The Cassini-Huygens Mission to Saturn and Titan* (Washington, DC: NASA SP-533, October 1997); and M. Meltzer, *The Cassini-Huygens Visit to Saturn: An Historic Mission to the Ringed Planet* (New York: Springer, 2014).

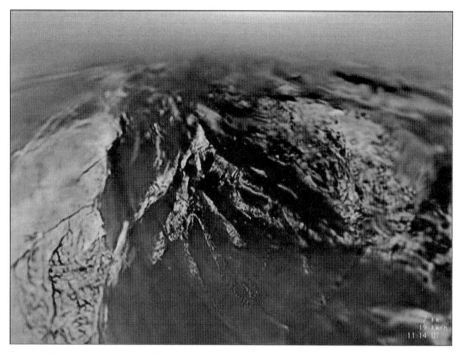

A view of Titan's surface during Huygens descent on 14 January 2005. (ESA/NASA/JPL/University of Arizona: PIA08118)

The 12 scientific instruments on the orbiter were designed for in-depth studies of the planet, its rings, its atmosphere, its magnetic environment, and a large number of its moons. The six instruments on the probe provided direct sampling of Titan's atmospheric chemistry and images of its surface. NASA provided the orbiter, ESA provided the probe, and ASI provided the high-gain antenna and other hardware systems for the orbiter. The scientific instruments and related investigations were realized by scientific teams in the United States and in ESA's member states. Both the orbiter and the probe have successfully accomplished their scientific missions. Huygens completed its mission on the very day of its descent through Titan's atmosphere, on 14 January 2005, while the nominal mission of the Cassini orbiter came to an end on 30 June 2008, four years after the spacecraft entered orbit around Saturn. NASA, however, approved two extensions of the mission, the last of which ran to 15 September 2017.

In this chapter, I will briefly discuss three aspects of the history of Cassini-Huygens as seen from a European perspective.[2] First is the institutional

---

2. A detailed analysis is in A. Russo, "Parachuting onto Another World: the European Space Agency's Huygens Mission to Titan," in *Exploring the Solar System: The History and Science*

framework that set the stage for the establishment of an important European effort in solar system exploration. For more than two decades, the European space science community felt that, for technical and financial reasons, Europe could not compete with the important programs of the United States and the Soviet Union in this field. It was only in the mid-1980s that an ambitious European planetary mission was considered as a realistic possibility, following ESA's successful Giotto mission to Comet Halley (1985–86). Huygens, in fact, was the first European mission devoted to solar system exploration.

The second aspect is the decision-making process that led to the adoption of the Huygens mission in the ESA scientific program. The founding fathers of European cooperation in space research stipulated that the European space science community at large should remain the only source of ideas and concepts of missions. These ideas and concepts are then discussed by expert groups and advisory committees in a competitive selection procedure concluding with the approval of one mission. The final decision to adopt a scientific mission in ESA's program is thus the outcome of a highly competitive process, involving the various national and disciplinary sectors of the space science community, the ESA executive staff, the European space industry, space policies in ESA's member states, relations with NASA and other potential international partners, etc.[3] The selection process of the Huygens mission is not particularly different from previous ones regarding general methodology, but this mission is the first planetary mission that entered the ESA selection process on equal conditions with other proposals, supported by a large and motivated scientific constituency.

Finally, the ESA-NASA relationship in the development of the Cassini-Huygens project is the third focus of my analysis. Originally conceived by a group of European scientists, it was soon evident that only a cooperative effort could make such an ambitious mission become a concrete reality. However, while scientific cooperation worked smoothly and resulted in the successful achievement of the mission's scientific objectives, it was not so easy to cope with the different political and institutional frameworks in which the two agencies were operating. The difference in budget procedures is particularly important. Decision-making can be very long for ESA, but once a project has been approved, its financial allocations are also approved

---

of Planetary Exploration, ed. R. D. Launius (New York: Palgrave Macmillan, 2013), pp. 275–321.

3. Other cases are discussed by the author in J. Krige, A. Russo, and L. Sebesta, *A History of the European Space Agency 1958–1987*, 2 vols. (Noordwijk, Netherlands: ESA SP-1235, April 2000).

in terms of a certain cost-to-completion. Provided no cost escalation occurs, the project becomes legally binding for member states, and there is no threat of cancellation. NASA, on the contrary, is a national agency whose overall program and budget has to be negotiated annually with the White House and Congress. Funds can always be shifted from one program to another on the basis of political considerations, lobbying, or national security priorities.

HORIZON 2000

In January 1985, the Ministerial Conference of ESA member states approved a long-term plan for space science called Horizon 2000.[4] The basic philosophy of Horizon 2000 was the establishment of two classes of projects. The first included four pre-defined "Cornerstones"—ambitious and technologically challenging missions to be realized according to a phased schedule over a 20-year period. The Cornerstone missions were devoted respectively to solar-terrestrial physics, x-ray astronomy, planetary science, and infrared astronomy. The second class included a number of standard missions, to be selected through a competitive selection procedure.

Within the framework of Horizon 2000, planetary science finally received a proper role in the European space effort. One of the Cornerstones, in fact, was devoted to an ambitious comet sample-return mission. This mission, which represented a logical step after Giotto, would eventually become the Rosetta mission, which was launched in 2004 and rendezvoused with comet Churyumov-Gerasimenko in 2014. Moreover, planetary mission proposals could be submitted for competitive selection in the standard mission program. To be precise, as astronomy and plasma physics were well represented in Horizon 2000 by previously approved missions, ESA's director of science, Roger Bonnet, felt a moral commitment to foster planetary missions in the selection process of the new standard mission. In fact, it was within this framework that the Huygens mission to Titan was eventually selected as the first new mission in Horizon 2000.

WHY TITAN?

The idea of a mission to Saturn and its satellite system can be traced back to the early 1980s, on the wave of NASA's successful Voyager missions. One of the most important discoveries of Voyager 1 was the intriguing composition

---

4. J. Krige, A. Russo, and L. Sebesta, *A History of the European Space Agency 1958–1987*, 2 vols. (Noordwijk, Netherlands: ESA SP-1235, April 2000, vol. 2, pp. 199–216; *European Space Science Horizon 2000* (Noordwijk: ESA SP-1070, December 1984). Also see R. Bonnet, "The New Mandatory Scientific Programme for ESA," *ESA Bulletin* 43 (August 1985): 8–13.

Jet Propulsion Laboratory (JPL) workers examine and repair the Huygens probe after damage was discovered during testing. (NASA: KSC-97PC-1392)

of the atmosphere of Titan, Saturn's largest moon and the second largest in the solar system after Jupiter's Ganymede. Not only was it confirmed that molecular nitrogen was the main constituent of the atmosphere, with a few percent of methane, but also the infrared spectrometer on Voyager showed that many organic molecules were present. The surface of Titan was completely obscured from the Voyager camera by a thick orange/brown smog made of a mixture of various hydrocarbon and nitrogen compounds. In fact, the dissociation of methane and nitrogen molecules, driven by solar UV radiation, cosmic rays, and electrons from Saturn's magnetosphere, produces a complex organic chemistry in Titan's atmosphere by which the fragments of the parent molecules recombine to make a large variety of carbon compounds.

To the eyes of the Voyager scientists, this planet-like satellite resembled what our Earth might have looked like some 4 billion years ago, before life started to colonize its surface and produce oxygen by photosynthesis. The fundamental difference between the early Earth and Titan is the low temperature on the latter's surface (−179°C), which makes the presence of liquid water impossible. (However, Titan is believed to have a large subsurface liquid water ocean that might be potentially habitable.) The intense organic chemistry at work in the atmosphere of primitive Earth did have a chance to lead to prebiotic chemistry and eventually to biology. Subsequent erosion, plate tectonics, and the evolution of life itself have obliterated all records of those original conditions and processes on our Blue Planet. Titan could provide Earth's human inhabitants with an opportunity to travel back in time, as it were, if they could only get there.[5]

BUILDING UP A SCIENTIFIC AND INSTITUTIONAL CONSTITUENCY

The foundations for an ESA-NASA collaboration for a mission to Saturn and Titan were established in 1982–83.[6] In July 1982, a group of 29 European scientists submitted to ESA a proposal for a Saturn/Titan mission to be realized in the framework of Horizon 2000.[7] "Project Cassini," as they named it, called for a Saturn orbiter carrying a probe to be parachuted through the atmosphere of Titan. The project was to be realized by an ESA-NASA collaboration, with Europe providing the orbiter and NASA the Titan probe. Eighteen scientific institutions from seven ESA member states were represented in the group, whose membership included representatives of four disciplines: atmospheric science, planetology, magnetosphere physics, and exobiology. The underlying idea was to study the whole of the Saturnian system, including specific objectives for the planet and its rings, the magnetosphere, the icy satellites, and Titan. This concept of "system science" would have been an important element in fostering support for the Cassini project within the European planetary science community and promoting the mission through ESA's highly competitive selection process.

The European initiative had a counterpart on the other side of the Atlantic. A Saturn orbiter–Titan probe mission was among those recommended by the Solar System Exploration Committee (SSEC) of the NASA Advisory Council. The SSEC had been established by NASA in response to the perceived survival crisis of the U.S. solar system exploration program. The so-called "core program" that the Committee discussed in its April 1983 report represented a concrete proposal for a significant effort in solar system exploration, after near-cancellation by the Reagan administration at the end

---

5. For an overview of Titan science prior to the Cassini-Huygens mission, see A. Coustenis and F. Taylor, *Titan: the Earth-like Moon*, Singapore: World Scientific, 1999); R. Lorentz and J. Mitton, *Lifting Titan's Veil: Exploring the Giant Moon of Saturn* (Cambridge, U.K.: Cambridge University Press, 2002).
6. W. Ip, D. Gautier, and T. Owen, "The Genesis of Cassini-Huygens," in *Titan: From Discovery to Encounter* (Noordwijk: ESA SP-1278, 2004): 211–227.
7. *Project Cassini: A Proposal to the European Space Agency for a Saturn Orbiter/Titan Probe Mission in Response to the Call for Mission Proposals Issued on 6th July 1982*, 12 November 1982. The author thanks Professor Wing-Huen Ip for providing him with a copy of this document.

of 1981. Besides the Saturn/Titan mission, the SSEC recommended a radar-mapping mission to Venus, a Mars orbiter devoted to geoscience and climatology, and a comet rendezvous and asteroid flyby (CRAF) mission.

These initiatives received an important institutional endorsement from the Space Science Committee of the European Science Foundation and the Space Science Board of the U.S. National Research Council. In April 1982, these two organizations established a Joint Working Group to define a framework for ESA-NASA cooperation in solar system exploration. The Joint Working Group eventually recommended that three missions should be carried out as cooperative projects by the turn of the century. Listed in order of launch, they were a Saturn orbiter and Titan probe, a multiple asteroid orbiter, and a Mars surface rover.[8]

An assessment study of the Cassini project was conducted between April 1984 and June 1985 by a team of 13 scientists, 9 from the United States and 4 from Europe.[9] Reversing the idea of the original proposal, the Titan probe was soon identified as ESA's contribution to the mission, while NASA would provide the main spacecraft, based on the Mariner Mark II spacecraft under development at the Jet Propulsion Laboratory (JPL). The latter was a key element of the SSEC core program, a family of large spacecraft dedicated to solar system exploration. The Titan probe, for its part, was considered within the technical capabilities of the European space industry, and the estimated costs were within the budget allocated to a standard mission of Horizon 2000.

The Challenger accident in January 1986 forced a dramatic redefinition of NASA's plans. The Mariner Mark II program was eventually confirmed. Spacecraft would be launched on a Titan expendable vehicle instead of the Space Shuttle, but with a two-year delay that deferred the start of the Cassini project until 1991. On this basis, ESA decided to support an industrial feasibility study of the Titan probe to be built in Europe. A number of American scientists and engineers were also involved in the study as technical consultants and as scientific advisors. The study report was published in September 1988.[10]

---

8. *United States and Western European Cooperation in Planetary Exploration*, Report of the Joint Working Group on Cooperation in Planetary Exploration (Washington, DC: National Academy Press, 1986).
9. *Cassini: Saturn Orbiter and Titan Probe*, ESA-NASA assessment study, ESA SCI(85)1, August 1985.
10. *Cassini: Saturn Orbiter and Titan Probe. Report on the Phase-A Study*, ESA SCI(88)5, October 1988.

One month later, ESA decision-making bodies were called to select the first mission in Horizon 2000.

THE ESA DECISION

On 25 October 1988, the European space science community convened in the beautiful medieval city of Bruges, Belgium, to discuss five mission proposals submitted to ESA for the selection of the next scientific mission.[11] Detailed feasibility studies had been performed for all of them, and each was supported by a significant fraction of the community. The European Titan probe in the cooperative ESA-NASA Cassini mission was one of them. Three other mission proposals addressed ultraviolet astronomy, radio astronomy, and gamma-ray astronomy, respectively. The last one, called Vesta, was a cooperative endeavor of ESA, the French space agency Centre National d'Études Spatiales (CNES), and the Soviet Space Research Institute (IKI). It aimed to visit a number of asteroids and comets using two spacecraft. Each spacecraft would carry an approach module that would be jettisoned in the vicinity of a selected asteroid and release two penetrators that would anchor themselves to the target.

As usual in the ESA selection process, after public discussion within the scientific community, the ESA scientific advisory bodies were called to issue their recommendations about which of the proposed missions should be selected by the Agency's Science Policy Committee (SPC), composed of the national delegations of ESA member states. This was a two-step procedure. First, the Astronomy Working Group (AWG) and the Solar System Working Group (SSWG) would issue a recommendation in their respective fields of interest. Second, the Space Science Advisory Committee (SSAC) would make the final recommendation to the ESA Director of Science and the SPC.

For the SSWG, the choice was between Cassini and Vesta, a very difficult choice, indeed, as both missions were dedicated to solar system exploration and considered excellent and scientifically highly interesting. The decision, of course, was a matter of politics as well as of science. From the scientific point of view, a close-up study of a number of asteroids and comets was as interesting and exciting as parachuting a probe onto a planetary body in the outer solar system. The Vesta mission promised to pursue and extend the small-body exploration program that ESA had begun with the Giotto flyby of Comet Halley, and it was presented as the forerunner of Rosetta, planned for the turn of the century. Cassini, for its part, would lead Europe

---

11. A synthesized presentation of all missions is in *ESA Bulletin* 55 (August 1988): 10–40.

to the frontiers of solar system exploration, and European industry would acquire unique know-how in the domain of atmospheric entry probes. The two missions, however, were very different as regards their political support, scientific constituency, and international framework.

Cassini had been conceived from the very beginning as an ESA-NASA collaborative project, in which ESA visibility would be secured by the fact that the Titan probe would be built in Europe and operated by the European Space Operations Centre (ESOC) in Darmstadt, Germany. A large and variegated scientific constituency had gathered in Europe behind Cassini, and it looked at this ambitious mission as a well-deserved red-carpet entry into the field of solar system exploration after the many disappointments of the past. The American planetary science community was also strongly interested in European approval of Cassini, in support of their eventual lobbying to have the mission approved by Congress.

In support of Vesta there was the powerful lobby of the French CNES. The mission, in fact, had been conceived in 1984 as a French-Soviet collaboration, with CNES responsible for building the two spacecraft and IKI for launching them.[12] The contribution of ESA had been solicited when the mission was at an advanced stage of definition. French space policy-makers insisted that Vesta would provide the European space science community with the opportunity to establish a cooperative venture with the Soviet Union, thus restoring a measure of balance in international cooperation after difficulties experienced with NASA.

Discussion within the 15-member SSWG was lively and impassioned, and only after a long debate, a consensus emerged in favor of Cassini. A formal vote was finally called, by which the SSWG recommended Cassini as the candidate project in the field of solar system science for the selection of ESA's next scientific project.[13]

It was up to the SSAC to make the final choice between Cassini and the candidate project recommended by the Astronomy Working Group, which was the gamma-ray astronomy mission. Discussion within the seven-member committee covered all aspects of the important decision to be made. On the one hand, supporters of the gamma-ray mission claimed a well-established

---

12. *Vesta: A Mission to the Small Bodies of the Solar System. Report on the Phase-A Study*, ESA SCI(88)6, October 1988.
13. A. Russo, "Parachuting onto another world: the European Space Agency's Huygens mission to Titan," pp. 275–322 in R.D. Launius, ed., *Exploring the Solar System: The History and Science of Planetary Exploration*, New York: Palgrave Macmillan, 2013, p. 296. According to D. Gautier, Cassini prevailed by 11 votes to 2 for Vesta: Ip, Gautier, and Owen, "The Genesis of Cassini-Huygens," p. 220.

The newly assembled Cassini Saturn probe undergoes vibration and thermal testing at the JPL facilities in Pasadena, California. (NASA: p48313bc)

European tradition of scientific excellence in astronomy. On the other hand, Cassini advocates stressed the importance of opening a new, fascinating territory to European space science. Moreover, by paying the ticket for the Titan probe, ESA would provide European planetary scientists with access to the NASA-built Saturn orbiter. In the event, the advocates of Cassini succeeded in convincing the majority of SSAC members to support the Saturn/Titan mission, which was thus formally recommended by the representatives of the European space science community as ESA's next scientific project.[14]

---

14. Russo, pp. 296, 298.

The ESA Science Policy Committee finally endorsed the SSAC recommendation.[15] It also decided that the Titan probe should have its own name, in order to underline that it was a separate, European-built component of the Cassini mission. Huygens thus entered the ESA scientific program as Europe's first planetary mission and the first mission in the Horizon 2000 long-term program.

UPS AND DOWNS OF INTERNATIONAL COOPERATION

While these developments occurred in Europe, Cassini's scientific constituency in the United States was working hard to have the mission approved by NASA and endorsed by Congress. In October 1989, Congress approved the Mariner Mark II program, including both Cassini and the cometary mission CRAF. NASA and ESA then issued parallel announcements of opportunity for instruments to fly on the Saturn orbiter and the Titan probe, respectively. Following peer review on both sides of the Atlantic, the two space agencies approved the recommended scientific payloads and interdisciplinary investigations. At the same time, an institutional arrangement was defined for the implementation of the scientific aspects of the mission. On 17 December 1990, a memorandum of understanding was signed by NASA and ESA, and the Cassini-Huygens mission was thus well on its way toward its scheduled launch in November 1995.[16]

The way, however, proved to be fraught with difficulties arising less from technical problems than from political uncertainty in the United States. In October 1991, Congress denied the 13 percent increase for the NASA budget requested by the White House, approving only a 3 percent increase, hardly enough to compensate for inflation. In this framework, the 1992 budget for the CRAF/Cassini program was set at $211 million, dramatically less than the requested $328 million. As a consequence, NASA decided to delay the launch of the Saturn mission until October 1997. This decision was not accepted in Europe. A two-year delay would cost ESA an additional $30 million, the ESA Director General wrote to the NASA Administrator. Such a unilateral decision "is not in the spirit of the Memorandum of Understanding," he concluded.[17]

---

15. Russo, p. 299.
16. *Science Management Plan of the Huygens Part of the Cassini Mission*, ESA/SPC(89)17, rev. 1, 15 November 1989; *ESA/NASA Memorandum of Understanding Cassini Huygens Mission*, ESA/SPC(90)20, 21 May 1990 (signed on 17 December 1990).
17. J. M. Luton, letter to NASA Administrator R. H. Truly, 7 November 1991.

No less irritation was expressed by the European space science community. SSAC Chairman David Southwood wrote to his American counterpart, NASA Space Science and Applications Advisory Committee Chairman Barrien Moore, that slipping the launch of Cassini to 1997 would create "an intolerable stress" on the ESA program. "I cannot emphasise enough the change [it] can easily induce in the climate of cooperation," Southwood concluded.[18] NASA's credibility as a reliable partner was explicitly challenged by ESA member state delegations in the SPC: "It should be impressed upon NASA that international cooperation was a valid proposition only as long as the partners honoured their commitments," pointed out the Dutch delegate.[19]

Despite all efforts, it was hardly possible for ESA and the European scientists to influence the congressional debates in the United States on the federal budget. In autumn 1989, Congress had approved the CRAF/Cassini program within a budget limit of $1.6 billion, but the cost of Cassini alone was now estimated at about $1.7 billion, and implementation of the whole program was definitely jeopardized. NASA canceled the CRAF mission and undertook a dramatic reconfiguration of the Cassini project in order to reduce its cost.

A new budgetary crisis arose in 1994, when Congress threatened to dramatically reduce the NASA budget. If approved, this reduction could lead to either Cassini or the important x-ray astronomy mission Advanced X-ray Astrophysics Facility (AXAF) (eventually called Chandra) being canceled. Prospects for Cassini were not encouraging, as the mission did not enjoy support from NASA Administrator Daniel Goldin. Cassini was the perfect antithesis of Goldin's "faster, better, cheaper" policy (see chapter 5): a mammoth mission, conceived 10 years earlier, which would not provide scientific results until more than 10 years later. Its cost was to be measured in billions of dollars, and a failure at launch or beyond would have been devastating. Moreover, its management suffered from the complexity of a large international cooperative endeavor and an 18-instrument payload coming from countless scientific institutions on two continents. Goldin did not hide his views on Cassini, and he was prepared to cancel it, or at least to submit it to a drastic revision to reduce its cost.[20]

Reporting to ESA's Bonnet on a meeting of NASA's Space Science and Applications Advisory Committee, SSAC Chairman Lodewijk Woltjer wrote

---

18. David Southwood, letter to Barrien Moore III, 28 October 1991.
19. Russo, p. 303.
20. L. Tucci, "Goldin Subjects Cassini to Cost Risk Reduction," *Space News* 5, no. 11 (14–20 March 1994): 3.

that if a choice had to be made between AXAF and Cassini, international cooperation would be a secondary consideration compared to the relative weight of various pressure groups. The overall impression was one of total uncertainty, and it would be very imprudent for ESA to depend too strongly on NASA for its long-term future projects, he concluded.[21]

In this situation, strong action was undertaken to save the mission. At the scientific level, European planetary scientists joined their American colleagues to advocate for the mission in any scientific and political forum where NASA policy was discussed. They found an influential supporter in Carl Sagan, a well-known astronomer and author of best-selling popular science books. The weekly trade paper *Space News* published an editorial claiming that the cancellation of Cassini or AXAF would be "an unacceptable option for reducing NASA's budget."[22] No less important were advocacy initiatives at the institutional level. The Italian Space Agency (ASI), which was building the antenna and the radio frequency subsystem for the Cassini spacecraft in the framework of a NASA-ASI bilateral agreement, reportedly told the Americans that Italy's important contribution to the International Space Station was at stake. An unprecedented initiative was undertaken by ESA Director General Jean-Marie Luton, who sent a formal letter to U.S. Vice President Al Gore. Underlining ESA's strong commitment to the Cassini mission, Luton concluded:

> Europe therefore views any prospect of a unilateral withdrawal from cooperation on the part of the United States as totally unacceptable. Such an action would call into question the reliability of the US as a partner in any future major scientific and technological cooperation.[23]

Finally, a strong diplomatic action was taken by ESA member state governments, whose ambassadors in Washington appealed to the State Department to avert the devastating consequences of a cancellation of Cassini.

In any event, President Bill Clinton came to NASA's aid by redirecting other spending in order to shore up the Agency's science budget. Having thus survived the attack in Congress, Cassini's advocates still faced Goldin's persistent concerns. In 1995, the NASA Administrator demanded that the

---

21. L. Woltjer, telefax to R. Bonnet, 2 April 1994, distributed to SPC delegations as annex I to ESA/SPC(94)27, 31 May 1994.
22. "Hands off AXAF, Cassini," *Space News* 5, no. 24 (20–26 June 1994): 16.
23. J. M. Luton to Al Gore, 13 June 1994. The letter is also reported in Groen and Hampden-Turner, *The Titans of Saturn*, pp. 195–197.

whole Cassini program, including the Huygens probe and the antenna under development in Italy, should undergo an independent review by a team of external experts. In Europe, this demand was viewed as an unacceptable violation of the cooperative spirit. After some tense meetings, ESA eventually accepted the review, which turned out to be a positive experience because ESA's contribution survived it and because it created confidence and strengthened cooperative spirit.

CONCLUSION

Following the 1994 political crisis and the 1995 review, the Cassini program went on smoothly. The Huygens probe was integrated and tested at Dornier's facilities in Ottobrunn near Munich, and in April 1997 it was shipped to NASA's Kennedy Space Center to be fitted to the main spacecraft. The Cassini-Huygens mission was successfully launched from Cape Canaveral on 15 October 1997. About 500 representatives of the scientific, engineering, and industrial teams in Europe that had created the Huygens probe attended the launch. After a seven-year cruise, Cassini entered orbit around Saturn on 1 July 2004. Six months later, on 25 December, Huygens was released by the mother spacecraft and started its 20-day, 4-million-kilometer cruise toward Titan. According to the mission scenario, a sequence of parachutes would deploy to slow it down, and its scientific instruments would be exposed to Titan's atmosphere during descent. If the probe survived impact with the surface, its instruments would be expected to continue to operate, providing additional information for a time ranging from a few minutes to half an hour or more. Out in space, Cassini would pick up Huygens's signals, then turn its antenna toward Earth, and relay the recorded scientific data.

On Friday, 14 January 2005, a group of nervous and excited scientists gathered in the control room of the European Space Operations Centre (ESOC) in Darmstadt, Germany, to observe this epochal event in the history of solar system exploration and enjoy the crowning achievement of their careers. For the first time since the beginning of the Space Age, a human artifact would be landed on another world in the outer solar system. The scientists and their distinguished guests, including ministers, space agency officials, and journalists, were waiting. Around noon, the news arrived that a faint radio signal from the probe had been picked up by the Green Bank radio telescope in West Virginia. Huygens had then survived the entry phase and was active! Late in the afternoon, the first scientific data, relayed by the Cassini spacecraft, arrived at ESOC. Scientists hurried to analyze the data, and soon the press got the first stunning images of Titan's surface. A long weekend of intense work—and celebrations—was about to start.

PART VI
Institutional Arrangements in Solar System Exploration

THE NEXT THREE CHAPTERS explore how institutions—institutional practices, structures, cultures, leaders—affect space projects and programs, missions, and international partnerships.

In chapter 10, James D. Burke and Harris Schurmeier report on one of NASA's earliest robotic space exploration projects—the Ranger missions to the Moon, executed by the Jet Propulsion Laboratory. Burke was JPL's first Ranger project manager, and Schurmeier succeeded him. Along with others at JPL, the two had to figure out how to establish a productive working relationship between JPL and NASA Headquarters. While Ranger had a bumpy start, with several mission failures, it ended with a string of successes and many useful lessons learned.

In chapter 11, John Sarkissian provides a deeply detailed and lively account of the building of collaborative relationships among Australia's space science establishment, NASA Headquarters, and JPL. A scientist at Australia's Parkes Radio Observatory, Sarkissian tells the story of how, beginning in the earliest days of space exploration, U.S. and Australian space scientists, engineers, and managers built durable formal and informal partnerships by means of scientific and technical exchanges and strong personal relationships.

In chapter 12, Petar Markovski examines NASA-ESA cooperation on the International Solar Polar Mission (ISPM) and the Ulysses mission to study the Sun. Like Cassini-Huygens, these NASA-ESA collaborations were fraught with difficulties due to conflicts between the goals and objectives of scientists and engineers and those of political leaders. Markovski argues that ISPM/Ulysses is an example of transnational rather than international cooperation due to the way the Ulysses spacecraft ultimately was developed. He advocates for a global, or transnational, approach to the history of space exploration, rather than the conventional international approach, which tends to frame events as competitions between nations.

While NASA's largest project in international cooperation has been a human exploration initiative, the International Space Station, the Agency maintains cooperative and collaborative agreements with more than 120 nations on science, education and outreach, and technology initiatives, including with member nations of the European Space Agency, and participates in a wide range of multilateral committees and coordination networks.[1] For the foreseeable future, international cooperation will be the way forward in space exploration.

---

1. *https://www.nasa.gov/sites/default/files/files/Global_Reach.pdf* (accessed 9 January 2020).

CHAPTER 10

Ranger: Circumstances, Events, Legacy

James D. Burke and Harris M. Schurmeier

IN THIS CHAPTER, we give our account of NASA's Ranger lunar exploration project, showing how its progress from failure to triumph laid the groundwork for the Jet Propulsion Laboratory's later lunar and planetary missions. Ranger began in 1960 in an atmosphere of management confusion and conflict, but by the time of its last flight in 1965, most of the troubles had been sorted out and NASA-JPL relations and methods had settled into the well-understood arrangement that continues to deliver success today.

Mariner 2, NASA's mission to Venus whose 50th anniversary we celebrated in 2012, derived its spacecraft design and some operations concepts from Ranger, the first U.S. attempt to deliver scientific and engineering information from the lunar surface. What follows is our review of Ranger's origin and the political background, technical experience, management relationships, and in-flight events that characterized the project and created its legacy.

In recalling our own experiences as Ranger's first (Burke) and second (Schurmeier) Project Managers, we were greatly aided by the definitive book about the project, *Lunar Impact*.[1] We have drawn other insights about Ranger from *SpaceFlight* magazine[2] and *Ambassadors from Earth*,[3] written

---

1. R. Cargill Hall, *Lunar Impact: A History of Project Ranger* (Washington, DC: NASA SP-4210, 1977), http://history.nasa.gov/SP-4210/pages/TOC.htm (accessed 29 January 2020).
2. J. D. Burke, "Personal Profile," *SpaceFlight* 26 (April 1984), pp. 178–183.
3. Jay Gallentine, *Ambassadors from Earth* (Lincoln, NE: University of Nebraska Press, 2010).

many years after the end of the project and so reflecting its longer-term historical significance. At its outset, the project's priorities were driven by the post-Sputnik urgency of competition with the USSR. "Seven Years to Luna Nine"[4] describes what the United States knew about the Soviet lunar and planetary program in the 1960s. An authoritative account of the Soviet program, including some of its management troubles, is given in *Soviet Robots in the Solar System*.[5]

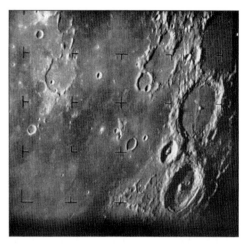

First image of the Moon taken by a U.S. spacecraft (Ranger 7). (NASA/JPL-Caltech: PIA02975)

INITIAL PLANNING FOR RANGER

During 1958 and 1959, JPL's central goals in deep space exploration were the same as they are today. Recognizing that Earth satellite programs were to become a huge business and a complex array of scientific and applications activities in a crowded field, JPL's leaders chose to concentrate the Lab's efforts mainly beyond Earth orbit. For missions to the Moon, rough landings were selected because at the time it was still thought possible that the U.S. Air Force's Atlas-Able lunar orbiters (Atlas-Able missions 4A, 4, 5A, and 5B) might succeed. (They did not.) When JPL and the Wernher von Braun team were transferred from U.S. Army auspices to those of the newly formed National Aeronautics and Space Administration, these decisions were accepted as defining JPL's role in the new civilian space agency.

All deep space mission planners knew then that an October 1960 launch window offered the first chance in human history for a mission to Mars. Briefly studied as a goal for a large spacecraft to be named Mariner A, the prospect of a 1960 mission to Mars was soon abandoned as too ambitious. A smaller craft called Mariner R, to be derived from Ranger, was chosen for a mission to Venus during a 1962 launch window. Ranger had always been considered a precursor to planetary spacecraft, so it had solar panels and a

---

4. J. D. Burke, "Seven Years to Luna Nine," *Studies in Intelligence* 10 (summer 1966). Declassified in 1994 and available through the U.S. National Archives, *https://nsarchive2.gwu.edu/NSAEBB/NSAEBB479/docs/EBB-Moon10.pdf* (accessed 29 January 2020).
5. Wesley T. Huntress, Jr., and Mikhail Ya. Marov, *Soviet Robots in the Solar System: Missions, Technologies and Discoveries* (New York: Springer, 2011).

high-gain antenna, features not necessary for lunar missions but essential for flights beyond the Moon.

In October 1960, Burke was appointed Ranger Project Manager. On 10 and 14 October, the Soviets attempted to launch robotic spacecraft to Mars. Intercepted telemetry showed that those two launch vehicles were by far the most heavily loaded rockets launched to date, and though both failed, they signaled the USSR's commitment to deep space exploration.

On 20 January 1961, President John F. Kennedy delivered an inaugural address that was almost entirely about a great contest between American values and the dark forces of communism, tyranny, and subversion emanating from the USSR. On 4 and 12 February, the Soviets launched two Venus missions. The first spacecraft failed to eject from Earth parking orbit, but the second, Venera 1, succeeded in beginning its interplanetary trip, only to fail later en route.[6] A drawing of the spacecraft showed solar panels and a high-gain antenna, so Venera was a powerful spur to Ranger.

The seeds of Ranger's most important conflicts were planted at that time. First, JPL people, accustomed to the largely hands-off management style of Army personnel and their well-established collaboration with von Braun's team at the Army Ballistic Missile Agency, were unprepared for more intrusive management by NASA. Second, management relations among the Army, Air Force, and NASA for launch services had yet to be worked out. Third, the priorities of people in the science community differed from those of engineers and managers driven by the U.S.-Soviet contest.

In the presence of these conflicts, it was nevertheless agreed by all that Ranger and the Mariner program of missions to Venus and Mars deserved high national priority, so both projects got off to a fast start. Ranger was allocated two test flights in 1961, not aimed at the Moon but intended to prove out deep space spacecraft design and operations, to be followed by three attempted rough lunar landings. The Mariner program planned for two Venus launches in 1962.

On 12 April 1961, Soviet cosmonaut Yuri Gagarin circled Earth. On 25 May, President Kennedy announced America's commitment to Apollo. On 23 August, Ranger 1 was launched.

RANGER FLIGHTS

The two Ranger test spacecraft, launched 23 August and 18 November 1961, were intended to demonstrate Sun and Earth attitude references, solar

---

6. Ibid., p. 87.

power, and high-gain communications from high-apogee orbits not aimed at the Moon. Because of Agena upper-stage failures, these two spacecraft were stranded in low-Earth orbit and unable to return any useful data. Both spacecraft did appear to be fully functional during their brief lives in orbit.

Ranger 3, launched 26 January 1962, had an Atlas guidance-system fault, but the spacecraft did get off to a reasonable start, acquiring Sun and Earth attitude references and executing a midcourse burn. But the midcourse maneuver vector, due to an undetected double-sign inversion in ground testing, was the mirror image of the planned one, so the spacecraft missed the Moon.[7]

Ranger 4, launched 23 April 1962, had its first perfect Atlas/Agena launch, and the spacecraft hit the Moon. The spacecraft's main power system was shorted out at separation from the Agena stage, however, probably by a floating conductive particle bridging two pins in the separation connector. If the spacecraft side of the connector had been female, this could not have happened.[8] Ranger 5, launched 18 October 1962, again started off well, acquiring attitude references and preparing to maneuver, but then its main power system gradually failed due to overheating of a small screw in one logic unit.

Ranger 6, launched 30 January 1964, the first Ranger mission after the project's reorganization with Schurmeier as Project Manager, had a perfect flight to the Moon but, due to a subtle and peculiar cause, returned no approach images. At staging off of the Atlas booster engines, a hot plasma cloud enveloped the launch vehicle, bridging pins in an Agena umbilical connector and burning out the spacecraft's two high-powered TV transmitters.[9] Redesigning the umbilical receptacle eliminated the possibility of this failure occurring in future missions. Rangers 7, 8, and 9 were completely successful, returning thousands of high-resolution images.

RANGER SCIENCE

Burke had what now seems a peculiar attitude toward science. He insisted that every Ranger flight must carry science instruments because there was no way to tell which flight or flights might succeed, and in-flight proof of science instruments was as important as that of any other subsystem. Though it

---

7. NASA Space Science Data Coordinated Archive, "Ranger 3, NSSDCA/COSPAR ID: 1962-001A," *http://nssdc.gsfc.nasa.gov/nmc/spacecraftDisplay.do?id=1962-001A* (accessed 29 January 2020).
8. Hall, "Which Way Ranger?" in *Lunar Impact, http://history.nasa.gov/SP-4210/pages/Ch_10.htm#Ch10_H3* (accessed 29 January 2020).
9. Hall, "Ranger 7: A Crashing Success," in *Lunar Impact, http://history.nasa.gov/SP-4210/pages/Ch_17.htm#Ch17_Top* (accessed 29 January 2020).

Ranger 3 launch from pad 12 atop an Atlas/Agena on 29 January 1962. (NASA: 62PC-3)

gave the same result, this philosophy was plainly at odds with one regarding science as the object of the project. More important, it implied that deciding on the object of the project was up to the Project Manager—an Army relic that under NASA management was soon to be dispelled.

The two Ranger test flights carried a good suite of particles-and-fields experiments to exploit their intended high-apogee orbits, plus ultraviolet telescopes to observe Earth's hydrogen corona.

The next three Ranger spacecraft addressed fundamental geophysical, geochemical, and geomorphological lunar-science objectives. Each rough-landing capsule contained a seismometer, and each spacecraft bus carried a gamma-ray spectrometer and a TV camera.

After the first five mission failures and the project's reorganization, mission goals were reduced to just high-resolution imaging before a crash, reflecting an urgent desire for some success and a modification of goals away from classic lunar science and toward support of Apollo.

During these stages in Ranger project science planning and execution, relations between scientists and the project team were mostly harmonious. The investigators were all experienced world leaders in their fields, and the project's engineers, though driven by the Soviet competitor, believed in the science goals and wanted them achieved as soon as possible.

Ranger's orderly scientific progress was marred by a nasty dispute. Early in 1962, while project engineers and managers were trying to grapple with the failures of Rangers 3 and 4, discussions at NASA Headquarters and in the science community resulted in a directive to add eight non-lunar instruments on Rangers 6 through 9. Burke strenuously objected, exacerbating already tense relations between JPL management and NASA Headquarters personnel.[10] After the failure of Ranger 5, the directive was rescinded.[11]

RANGER'S ABORTED EXTENSIONS

During much of 1963, while the effort to reduce risk and gain success with Rangers 6 through 9 was under way at JPL, discussions continued at NASA and in the scientific community about goals for more Ranger flights. Rivalry between lunar and non-lunar scientists resulted in much wasted effort. Meanwhile, all concerned were trying to respond to the findings of Ranger failure review boards.

In an effort to introduce industry management talent and reduce JPL's work overload, a contract was let to Northrop Space Laboratories for a block of flights beyond the TV missions planned in support of Apollo. Arguments over the goals for these flights led nowhere, and eventually the contract was canceled.

Five lunar orbiters managed by NASA Langley Research Center and built by Boeing and Eastman Kodak flew successfully in 1966 and 1967, covering Apollo sites so well that the last two were placed in polar orbits to map

---

10. Hall, *Lunar Impact*, pp. 128–137.
11. JPL Engineering Change Order No. 3703, initiated by S. Rubinstein, 25 October 1962 (2-1325).

the entire Moon. These missions were a much better application of available resources than more Rangers would have been.

RANGER LESSONS

One huge mistake, endorsed by all at the time, was heat sterilization of the three rough-landing spacecraft, a requirement that was abandoned for the next four flights.[12] The central lesson learned from the Ranger project, according to our own memories and documented in failure review reports, is that deep space exploration demands much more attention to risk than we were willing to allocate among the priorities of those days. Clinging to tight schedules in the face of evidence—for example, evidence that heat sterilization was damaging circuitry—was a mistake that is obvious in retrospect. Even though no Ranger failure was attributed to heat sterilizing, tests showed that it added unacceptable risk. A good legacy of these tests, however, was the successful heat sterilization of the two Viking Mars landers.

Tight schedules are good in that they enforce discipline, and fixed interplanetary schedules are mandated by celestial mechanics, but our lunar launches could have been delayed without much harm. Our Soviet competitors' record in this regard was even worse than ours. Nonetheless, undaunted by failure after failure,[13] they finally achieved history's first lunar rough landing in 1966.

Technical lessons learned from Ranger are the same as those delivered by other complicated projects in the early days of space exploration. Troubles often arise at system or subsystem interfaces that are difficult or impossible to simulate adequately in tests. The six Ranger failures included two due to the Agena upper stage. The first of these failures occurred because, during the long in-orbit coast before second burn, too much heat soaked into a switch in the engine compartment. No ground test could have revealed this problem. The second resulted from a faulty design concept in the blockhouse instrumentation that allowed the Agena to lift off with its gyros not turning. Detailed postflight testing did reveal the cause, but it is unlikely that normal preflight tests could have done so.

Though no failure can be specifically traced to it, an unnecessary weight-reduction campaign, resulting from an interface analysis error, was a distraction at a critical time in spacecraft development.

---

12. Hall, "The Question of Science and Ranger," in *Lunar Impact: The NASA History of Project Ranger, Dover Publications, 2010*, pp. 124–137.
13. Burke, "Seven Years to Luna Nine," p. 1.

Three members of the Ranger 7 television experiment team stand near a scale model and lunar globe. (NASA: P-2988b)

The four Ranger spacecraft failures all originated at interfaces. All were later duplicated in experiments designed specifically to test hypotheses, not the sort of proof testing normally done at the time. Management lessons learned from Ranger constitute its main legacy. Interagency and intercommunity conflicts bedeviled Ranger's early years. Virtually every precept of good management—clear lines of authority and responsibility, understood rules, assignment of the right people to each task, and so on—was violated. Experienced JPL people did not take kindly to invasive direction from equally competent but newly appointed engineers at NASA. Launch services confusion among the Air Force, Army, and NASA would have been even worse but for the devotion and hard work of individuals in all three agencies[14] who saw the lunar-landing goal as dominant over institutional rivalries.

---

14. Hall, *Lunar Impact*, pp. 91–95.

The attempted introduction of non-lunar science instruments, endorsed at the highest levels by NASA and its external science advisory bodies and then issued as a mandatory unilateral directive to JPL, exacerbated existing disputes and must have contributed to the project's capsize after the failure of Ranger 5.

Intolerance of failure reached an even higher level after Ranger 6, bringing into question the whole concept of a university laboratory (JPL, which is a lab of the California Institute of Technology) as the executor of large space projects. While the project's own team members struggled unsuccessfully to pin down the direct cause of the failure, the committee that investigated this failure—the Hilburn Committee—issued findings and recommendations that mostly added to a bad atmosphere around the project. Congress and the press became involved with little benefit to anyone. At last, a persistent JPL scientist, Alex Bratenahl, came up with a failure explanation fitting observations.[15] In the detonation wave launched up the vehicle at Atlas booster engine separation, ionizing plasma bridged two nearby pins in an Agena umbilical connector, turning on and burning out both spacecraft TV transmitters.

In management disputes after Ranger 6, fortunately, cool heads prevailed, and JPL was preserved as the national asset that it now remains. Strenuous technical, managerial, and political efforts focusing on the RCA camera payload may have reduced future risks, but in the end they were beside the point, as the failure did not originate in the TV system.

Seen from today's perspective, where fights do go on but upon an agreed playing field, the early Ranger battles can be counted as perhaps a necessary step in the evolution of relations among NASA Headquarters, NASA Field Centers, the Defense Department, U.S. intelligence agencies, industry, and the scientific community. The final outcome of Ranger validated the changes made toward building operational reliability and the general harmony that now prevails and delivers success.

---

15. Ibid., pp. 258–261.

CHAPTER 11
Mariner 2 and the CSIRO Parkes Radio Telescope: 50 Years of International Collaboration

John Sarkissian

IN DECEMBER 1962, the Parkes Radio Telescope tracked NASA's Mariner 2 spacecraft as it flew by Venus. Just a year earlier, Australia's Commonwealth Scientific and Industrial Research Organisation (CSIRO) had commissioned the 210-foot (64-meter) Parkes Radio Telescope as the most advanced instrument of its kind in the world. The performance parameters and innovative design features of the Parkes telescope made it a near-ideal instrument for tracking spacecraft in deep space. These factors attracted the attention of NASA and the Jet Propulsion Laboratory (JPL), which at the time were planning the next generation of large tracking antennas for the fledgling Deep Space Network (DSN). The Parkes telescope design was subsequently adapted and became the model for the large antennas of the DSN.

In order to maximize the scientific return of the Mariner 2 mission, NASA organized a coordinated international program of ground-based observations (both radio and optical) to be carried out in conjunction with the Mariner 2 encounter with Venus. Parkes was invited to participate in the program. The CSIRO considered it an excellent opportunity to demonstrate the capabilities of a 64-meter-class instrument for communication at planetary distances. The ensuing observations were a great success. The Parkes Mariner 2 tracks confirmed the suitability of the telescope's design for deep space tracking and contributed greatly to the success of future NASA-CSIRO cooperative ventures. For example, the Parkes telescope tracked Mariner 4 when it encountered Mars in July 1965 and provided the DSN with its only

64-meter capability for the mission. These historic early interplanetary missions began a long collaboration between NASA and the CSIRO in space tracking, including the Apollo lunar landing missions, the Voyager 2 encounters of Uranus and Neptune, the Galileo mission to Jupiter, the Huygens probe's landing on Titan, and, most recently, the Curiosity rover on Mars.

This chapter will describe the beginnings of this international collaboration and the special relationship that developed between the CSIRO and NASA.

THE BEGINNING

In the first decades of solar system exploration, the CSIRO's Parkes Radio Telescope had its greatest influence on the design of antennas for NASA's DSN. This influence was a result of close professional relationships established between major personalities at the CSIRO's Radiophysics Laboratory and at the California Institute of Technology's (Caltech) JPL, which operated as a NASA Field Center. To understand how Parkes came to have such an influence on the history of space tracking, it is necessary to go back to World War II, the development of radar, and the post-war foundation of radio astronomy in Australia. Major players at the CSIRO and JPL were dynamic and visionary individuals who laid some of the foundations for the modern era of space exploration.

RADAR AND THE ORIGINS OF THE CSIRO'S RADIOPHYSICS LABORATORY

In early 1939, Richard Casey, Minister of Supply and Development for the Australian Commonwealth, learned of a highly secret scientific development from Britain known as radio direction finding (RDF), or radar, as it became known. With little information to go on, but shrewdly sensing that this might be a significant development, he immediately set in motion the process of founding a secret laboratory to investigate this development. It was given the innocuous title of the Radiophysics Laboratory to hide its true purpose. For security reasons, the Radiophysics Laboratory was built as an extension of the National Standards Laboratory, part of Australia's Council for Scientific and Industrial Research (CSIR), the forerunner of the CSIRO. Soon afterwards, following the British declaration of war, Richard Casey traveled to Britain and saw firsthand the coastal chain of radar stations that would make a significant contribution to winning the Battle of Britain.[1]

---

1. Sir Frederick White, "Richard Gardiner Casey 1890–1976," *Records of the Australian Academy of Science* 3, no. 3/4 (1977), *https://www.asap.unimelb.edu.au/bsparcs/aasmemoirs/casey.htm* (accessed 8 August 2021).

Richard Casey, Ambassador of Australia to the United States, in his office in Washington, DC, 1942. (Library of Congress: fsa.8d22912)

Later that year, with the war in Europe raging, Casey resigned from the Australian Parliament and traveled to Washington, DC, to open the first Australian diplomatic mission in a foreign country. He developed a close relationship with President Franklin D. Roosevelt, with leaders of the administration and with Congress. He thus founded a firm political relationship between the United States and Australia, which proved invaluable in the dark days that followed as a Japanese invasion of Australia loomed. In 1942, Casey accepted an invitation from British Prime Minister Winston Churchill to become Australia's representative on his war cabinet.[2]

---

2. Ibid.

Meanwhile, back in Australia, the Radiophysics Laboratory carried out research and developed radar equipment suitable for use in the Pacific theater. On the Sydney cliff tops at Dover Heights, overlooking the Pacific, the Royal Australian Air Force established a coastal defense radar station. The Radiophysics Laboratory used the site as a field station for its experimental radar work. During the war, radar operators reported strong radio emissions from the Sun. However, pressing wartime needs took precedence, and investigations into the origin of these emissions had to wait until after the war.

The secret pre-war British development of radar had begun in 1935, when a Committee for the Scientific Study of Air Defence was established under the chairmanship of Henry Tizard. The "boffins," as the members of the committee became known, were led by Robert Watson-Watt. They quickly set up experimental ground radar stations and, by 1936, were able to detect aircraft at ranges of up to 100 miles. One member of this team was a brilliant, 24-year-old Welshman, Edward "Taffy" Bowen. In 1936, he was given the challenge of developing a radar unit small enough to fit in an aircraft for the principal application of night interception. By 1937, Bowen and his group had built an airborne radar system that could obtain clear echoes of ships off the English coast. Thereafter, their system became the standard for all airborne radar,[3] which later proved to be a decisive factor in defeating the German U-boat threat in the Battle of the Atlantic.

In August 1940, with the Battle of Britain at a critical phase, Henry Tizard led a seven-member mission to the United States to disclose British technical advances in radar. Among them was Taffy Bowen, who brought with him not only information on all existing projected equipment but also an early sample of the cavity magnetron, the essential and highly secret key to the development of centimeter-wave radar. Following discussions with the Tizard mission, the United States decided that its armed services would be responsible for radar development, with centimeter-wavelength development assigned to a special Microwave Committee chaired by Alfred Loomis. This committee quickly set up a Radiation Laboratory at the Massachusetts Institute of Technology (MIT), with Lee DuBridge as director. Bowen collaborated closely with this lab and established a close rapport with DuBridge. This relationship proved to be of pivotal significance in the years ahead, especially for space tracking applications. During the course of the war, the Radiation Lab grew in size and soon became the most important and productive radar laboratory in the United States. By the end of the war, lab staff numbered

---

3. Hanbury Brown, Harry Minnett, and Frederick White, "Edward George Bowen 1911–1991," *Historical Records of Australian Science* 9, no. 2 (December 1992): 151–166.

about 4,000.[4] During this period, Bowen also befriended Vannevar Bush, President Roosevelt's science advisor.

By 1943, with his work in the United States complete and the war in the Pacific swinging to the Allies' favor, Bowen was invited to join Australia's Radiophysics Laboratory in Sydney. In May 1946, he was appointed chief of the lab, a position he held for the next 25 years.[5]

THE DEVELOPMENT OF RADIO ASTRONOMY IN AUSTRALIA IN THE POST-WAR YEARS

At the end of the war, the radar labs in the United States and Britain were disbanded, and their staff returned to their peacetime professions. In 1946, Lee DuBridge was appointed president of Caltech. Australia decided to keep its Radiophysics Lab intact and redirect its research into peaceful applications. These applications included using radar to improve air navigation (important for a large country like Australia) and to study the physical processes of rain formation in clouds. Another project initiated at the time was the study of the origin of the radio emissions from the Sun that had so intrigued radar operators during the war.[6]

The radio astronomy group within the Radiophysics Lab was led by J. L. "Joe" Pawsey.[7] He pioneered the use of the "sea interferometer" (a radio analogue of a Lloyd's mirror) to investigate the solar radio emissions. At the top of a cliff at Dover Heights, just south of the entrance to Sydney Harbour, Pawsey and his colleagues used surplus Yagi antennas to observe the Sun. Radio emissions from the Sun reached the clifftop aerial along two paths, one direct and the other reflected by the sea surface. From the interference pattern so generated, it was possible to locate the source of the emission to

---

4. Ibid. Included among the battery of distinguished physicists at the MIT Rad Lab were Hans Bethe, R. H. Dicke, Robert V. Pound, E. M. Purcell, and J. H. van Vleck.
5. Ibid. In 1949, the Commonwealth Government enlarged and reconstituted the CSIR and its administrative structure. The new organization was named the CSIRO. Under Ian Clunies Ross as chairman, CSIRO pursued new research areas such as radio astronomy and industrial chemistry. The Radiophysics Laboratory was renamed the Division of Radiophysics.
6. Peter Robertson, "An Australian Icon—Planning and Construction of the Parkes Telescope," Science with Parkes @ 50 Years Young Conference, Parkes, Australia, 31 October–4 November 2011. *https://www.atnf.csiro.au/research/conferences/Parkes50th/proceedings.html* (accessed 8 August 2021).
7. Joe Pawsey's group included names that would later become well known among the international astronomical community, including Bernard Mills, Norman Christiansen, J. H. Piddington, F. J. Kerr, Ronald N. Bracewell, and J. P. Wild.

an accuracy of a few arc-minutes.[8] This measurement was accurate enough to identify sunspots as the source of much of the emissions.

Meanwhile, in 1946, British naval forces in the Pacific were demobilized, and a 24-year-old Royal Navy radar operator, John Bolton, decided to remain in Sydney rather than return home to Britain. After graduating from Trinity College at Cambridge in 1942, Bolton had joined the Royal Navy as a radar officer, but he was soon recruited into radar research at the then-secret Telecommunications Research Establishment (TRE)—Watson-Watt's old group.[9] By 1944, Bolton was serving on the aircraft carrier Unicorn in the Pacific. The day after his discharge from the Royal Navy, John Bolton met Taffy Bowen for an interview at the Radiophysics Laboratory. Bowen immediately took a liking to him and offered Bolton a position of technical research assistant. Bolton was set to work with Pawsey on the solar studies. His attention, however, soon switched to identifying other, non-solar sources of radio emission.[10]

Within the next two years, Bolton, working with colleagues Gordon Stanley and Bruce Slee, conducted observations with the sea interferometer that resulted in the identification of four new cosmic radio sources—Cygnus A, Taurus A, Centaurus A, and Virgo A. Initially, their radio positions were very poor, but by using larger, multi-element Yagi antennas, they were able to increase the sensitivity and resolution of their instruments. By the early 1950s, over 100 sources of radio emission had been discovered at Dover Heights. They included supernova remnants and other sources in our own Milky Way galaxy and in very distant galaxies. These observations established the Radiophysics Laboratory as a world-leading center of radio astronomy and opened up the study of the universe at radio wavelengths.

In 1951, Bolton, Stanley, and Slee envisaged a more powerful instrument than the 12-element Yagi array they had been using. They began a project to build a 72-foot (22-meter)-diameter "hole-in-the-ground" antenna for a survey of the region near the galactic center of the Milky Way, which at the latitude of Sydney passes almost directly overhead. With considerable ingenuity, they spent their lunchtimes, over a three-month period, excavating a dish-shaped hole in the sandy ground at Dover Heights. The surface was

---

8. J. P. Wild and V. R. Radhakrishnan, "John Gatenby Bolton 1922–1993," Australian Academy of Science, *https://www.science.org.au/fellowship/fellows/biographical-memoirs/john-gatenby-bolton-1922-1993* (accessed 8 August 2021).
9. Among other famous figures in radio astronomy who also worked at TRE were Hey, Hanbury-Brown, Bowen, Ryle, and Lovell.
10. Wild and Radhakrishnan.

consolidated with ash, and metal strips from packing cases were laid across the surface to provide reflectivity. A mast with a dipole was erected at the center of the antenna to receive the reflected radio signals. Remarkably, this instrument was the second-largest radio telescope in the world at the time. By using the rotation of Earth and altering the position of the aerial mast, it was possible to observe different regions of the sky as they passed overhead. After they had demonstrated that their design concept worked, the "hole-in-the-ground" antenna was extended to a diameter of 80 feet (24 meters) in 1953. This improved version led to detailed observations of Sagittarius A and the suggestion that it was the nucleus of our galaxy. In 1958, the International Astronomical Union ratified this view, making the position of the Sagittarius A radio source the Milky Way's zero of longitude in a new system of galactic coordinates.[11]

By 1954, the technology at Dover Heights was becoming outdated, and the work that could be done with it was exhausted. Joe Pawsey decided to shut down the station. Radio astronomy, however, continued at the other Radiophysics field stations scattered across New South Wales, most notably in the field of solar studies led by Paul Wild.

THE GIANT RADIO TELESCOPE

In the early 1950s, Taffy Bowen had been thinking about the next phase in the development of radio astronomy. By 1954, with the closure of the Dover Heights field station complete, he was convinced that the best all-round instrument to continue the CSIRO's pioneering efforts in radio astronomy would be a large, fully steerable dish antenna, or Giant Radio Telescope (GRT), in the 200- to 250-foot (61- to 76-meter) range. Bowen estimated that the cost of a GRT would be somewhere on the order of $1–2 million (USD).[12] This investment was beyond the budget of the CSIRO at the time, so Bowen sought other sources of funding. It was then that Bowen's wartime contacts came to the fore. Many of his colleagues during his radar days were in positions of authority and influence in the Australian government and in large philanthropic organizations in the United States. Bowen was

---

11. A. Blaauw, C. S. Gum, J. L. Pawsey, and G. Westerhout, "The New I. A. U. System of Galactic Coordinates (1958 revision)," *Monthly Notices of the Royal Astronomical Society*, vol. 121, p. 123, http://adsabs.harvard.edu/full/1960MNRAS.121..123B (accessed 29 January 2020).
12. Letter from Charles Dollard, president of the Carnegie Corporation, to E. G. Bowen, chief of the CSIRO Radiophysics Division, dated 14 April 1954.

determined to draw on this "old-boys network" to raise funds and make his vision a reality.[13]

FUNDING THE GRT

In August 1952, Bowen wrote to Vannevar Bush, then president of the Carnegie Institution for Science in Washington, DC, to ask if funds could be made available for his GRT.[14] The early success of radio astronomy in Australia had attracted the attention of Bush and Alfred Loomis, who had become a trustee of the Carnegie Corporation, which supported the Carnegie Institution. Both knew Bowen through wartime friendships and admired his drive and enthusiasm.[15] In due course, in May 1954, the Carnegie Corporation announced that it would provide $250,000 toward funding of the GRT in Australia.[16]

With funding from the Carnegie Corporation in hand, planning for the project could begin in earnest. In early 1955, the CSIRO set up a Radio Astronomy Trust with Richard Casey, who was by then Minister for External Affairs and Minister in Charge of the CSIRO, serving as its chairman.[17] Casey was very sympathetic and made strong representations to Prime Minister Robert Menzies to support the project. Menzies agreed, provided that at least half of total costs would be raised from private sources.[18]

In 1955, Bowen again visited the United States, seeking support from other philanthropic organizations. He received a sympathetic hearing from the Rockefeller Foundation and its president, Dean Rusk. Two factors contributed to this positive response: Richard Casey, chairman of Australia's Radio Astronomy Trust, was well known to Dean Rusk from Casey's time in wartime Washington, and Caltech president Lee DuBridge was a trustee of the Rockefeller Foundation and a great supporter of the GRT.[19] The Rockefeller Foundation agreed to contribute $250,000.[20]

---

13. Robertson, "An Australian Icon," p. 3.
14. Ibid.
15. White, "Richard Gardiner Casey."
16. Letter from Charles Dollard, president of the Carnegie Corporation, to E. G. Bowen, chief of the CSIRO Radiophysics Division, dated 21 May 1954.
17. White, "Richard Gardiner Casey."
18. Letter from Robert Menzies, the Australian Prime Minister, to Richard Casey, Minister for External Affairs and Minister in Charge of CSIRO, dated 19 April 1955.
19. White, "Richard Gardiner Casey." Also see note 10.
20. Letter from the Rockefeller Foundation to Richard Casey, Minister for External Affairs and Minister in Charge of CSIRO, dated 8 December 1955.

Further funding of $107,000 was obtained from the Rockefeller Foundation in December 1959.[21] A further grant of $100,000 from the Australian government was received in January 1960 to cover a shortfall in funds.[22] When combined with $55,000 from private Australian donations and matching funds from the Australian government, funding for the GRT eventually came to $1.42 million.[23]

DESIGNING THE GRT

With initial funding secured from the Carnegie Corporation, work began on the GRT design in 1955. That year, a publicity booklet titled "A Proposal for a Giant Radio Telescope" was released, which was intended to stimulate the interest of engineers and contractors with many unusual design concepts presented.[24] GRT designers were fortunate to learn from problems encountered in the construction of the U.K.'s Jodrell Bank 250-foot (76-meter) dish, which had commenced in 1951.

The eventual breakthrough in final design came about by accident. During a trip to the U.K. in 1955, Taffy Bowen was introduced to Barnes Wallis, the famous chief engineer of the electrical engineering company Metropolitan-Vickers. Wallis was well known as the inventor of the "bouncing bombs" of Dambusters fame during World War II. Over lunch one day, Bowen discussed plans for the GRT with Wallis, who agreed to submit a few ideas. A few months later, Wallis submitted his plans, which included several innovative design features. One was the inclusion of spiral purlins to ensure the dish surface maintained a parabolic shape as it was tilted. The second feature was a master equatorial (ME), consisting of a small optical telescope situated at the intersection of the two axes of rotation. The ME could be pointed to a particular direction in the sky with great accuracy. The dish would be "slaved" to the ME via a servo loop, thus achieving a high degree of pointing accuracy.[25] Wallis also advocated an alt-azimuth mount with the dish pivoted in the center like an inverted umbrella.

---

21. Letter from the Rockefeller Foundation to Frederick White, Chairman of CSIRO, dated 8 December 1959.
22. Robertson, "An Australian Icon." p. 7.
23. Frank Karr, "The Proposal for a Giant Radio Telescope," in *Parkes: Thirty Years of Radio Astronomy*, ed. D. E. Goddard and D. K. Milne (Clayton, Australia: CSIRO Publishing, 1994), https://www.eoas.info/bib/ASBS00850.htm.
24. Ibid. P. Robertson, "An Australian icon: planning and construction of the Parkes telescope," Science with Parkes @ 50 Years Young, 31 October–4 November 2011, p. 11.
25. Robertson, "An Australian Icon," p. 4.

The British firm Freeman Fox and Partners (FF&P) was engaged to perform a detailed design study using Wallis's ideas.[26] Radiophysics engineer Harry Minnett was appointed his lab's representative at FF&P to supervise the design and drive system. Both FF&P and Wallis favored an alt-azimuth mount because of its structural simplicity. An equatorial mount was studied but rejected because an alt-azimuth mount could support a significantly larger dish. FF&P established the feasibility of the master equatorial and servo-drive system. Given the budget, a dish diameter of 210 feet (64 meters) was planned. Since the study had also shown that a minimum operating wavelength below 21 centimeters was feasible, a figure of 10 centimeters (S-band) was selected as the optimum operating wavelength for the 64-meter dish. To minimize spillover—detection of radiation from ground sources—the telescope would have a 30-degree elevation horizon. The design study had taken three years to complete, much longer than originally planned. However, the excellence of the design was recognized, vindicating the extra time it took to get it right.[27]

CHOOSING THE SITE

The site chosen for the GRT was near the town of Parkes in New South Wales, about 217 miles (350 kilometers) west of Sydney.[28] Several requirements were taken into consideration when choosing the site. The ideal location would need to be geologically stable to provide a solid foundation. The site would need to have a mild climate free of ice and snow, with a low average wind speed year-round. It needed to be a few hours' drive from the Radiophysics Lab's headquarters in Sydney. Above all, the site had to offer a very low level of radio interference.[29] During a comprehensive four-year search, several sites were considered and shortlisted. At a meeting convened at Radiophysics headquarters in March 1958 to decide the matter, Parkes was the unanimous choice.

---

26. The firm's founder, Sir Ralph Freeman, Sr., was the designer of the Sydney Harbour Bridge, the most famous structure in Australia.
27. Harry Minnett, "The Construction of the Parkes 210-ft Radio Telescope," in *Parkes: Thirty Years of Radio Astronomy*, ed. D. E. Goddard and D. K. Milne (Clayton, Australia: CSIRO Publishing, 1994).
28. B. Y. Mills, W. N. Christiansen, and J. P. Wild, "Report on the Site Requirements for the Giant Radio Telescope," March 1958. Author's files.
29. Robertson, "An Australian Icon," p. 5.

Parkes radio telescope in Australia. (NASA/CSIRO/Shaun Amy: PIA17248)

CONSTRUCTION

In 1959, FF&P called for tenders on an international competitive basis.[30] Seven bids were received, and the winner was Maschinenfabrik Augsburg Nurnberg (MAN) of West Germany, offering the lowest bid of $1.4 million. Another factor in MAN's favor was its promise of completion in the extraordinarily short time of 21 months.[31] In July 1959, the contract was signed, and by September construction began at Parkes.[32]

From then on, things moved quickly. The Sydney firm Concrete Constructions began excavating the foundations of the telescope, and by November 1959 erection of the concrete tower began. Meanwhile, Associated Electrical Industries began work on the servo-control system in Manchester, U.K. Askania-Werke started building the master equatorial in West Berlin, and MAN starting casting some of the telescope's massive steel components.

---

30. Letter from E. G. Bowen to G. E. Mueller, Associate Director, Space Technology Laboratories, Inc., dated 9 April 1959; letter from E. G. Bowen to John Mengel, NASA, Washington DC, dated 12 May 1959.
31. Confidential bidding summary for the Australian 210-foot radio telescope, prepared by E. G. Bowen, July 1959.
32. Letter from E. G. Bowen to William Pickering, JPL, 12 May 1960.

In September 1960, the MAN construction crew arrived at Parkes. First, the steel azimuth track was positioned on the tower, followed by the turret, then the cylindrical hub. The 30 radial ribs were fabricated on the ground before being lifted, one at a time, and bolted into position to form the dish structure. The aerial cabin was hoisted into position, and then the reflective surface panels were individually placed on the dish. By late August 1961, the structural work was largely complete, having gone a little over the 21-month schedule MAN had promised. By any standard, the construction proceeded remarkably smoothly, with few problems or delays. By mid-October, the telescope was tipped for the first time.[33]

Two weeks later, on 31 October 1961, the Governor-General of Australia, Lord De L'Isle, officially opened the Parkes telescope in a ceremony attended by 500 guests.

THE CALTECH CONNECTION

As previously alluded to, there was a very interesting back story to the funding of the GRT that illustrates the very close relationship between the CSIRO and Caltech. Although radio astronomy had begun in the United States through the work of Karl Jansky and Grote Reber, by the early 1950s it was universally recognized by American astronomers that the United States was lagging behind Australia and the U.K. in the field. Lee DuBridge, who was by then president of Caltech, was eager to remedy the situation. With the 1949 opening of the 200-inch (5.1-meter) Hale Telescope at Caltech's Palomar Observatory in southern California, he had dreams of building the radio equivalent of the optical observing facilities at the Mount Wilson and Palomar observatories. He wanted to make Caltech the world's finest center of radio as well as optical astronomy.[34]

In 1951, during one of his frequent visits to the States, Bowen visited DuBridge at Caltech. During the meeting, the two men discussed the idea of a U.S. radio astronomy center, and Bowen was asked to prepare a proposal for a new observatory. DuBridge encouraged Bowen "to let your imagination run wild as several million dollars could be provided."[35] In May 1952, Bowen submitted a report to DuBridge titled "A Large Radio Telescope for Radio

---

33. Minnett, "The Construction of the Parkes 210-ft Radio Telescope"; Robertson, "An Australian Icon," p. 9.
34. Peter Robertson, *Beyond Southern Skies: Radio Astronomy and the Parkes Telescope* (Cambridge University Press, 1992), p. 117.
35. Letter from Lee DuBridge to E. G. Bowen, dated 21 February 1952.

Astronomy," proposing a single large dish in the 200- to 250-foot (61- to 76-meter) range.[36]

DuBridge wanted Bowen to be the director of the new observatory. Though Bowen was confident that the project would go ahead, he was reluctant to commit to it. For Bowen, it meant leaving the Radiophysics Lab, a group that he had guided to a position of international leadership, and starting again from scratch. For the CSIRO, the prospect of losing the man who had led the most successful of Australia's post-war research programs was not a welcome development. CSIRO Chairman Frederick White counseled patience. Bowen informed DuBridge that, while he was interested in taking up the post at Caltech, he felt duty-bound to investigate the possibility of having a large dish—a GRT—built in Australia.[37]

In July 1952, Bowen consulted with his former mentor Henry Tizard, who advised him to seek funding from the Carnegie Corporation's British Dominion and Colonies Fund, which had been suspended since the war. Interest in the fund had been accruing, and it was now flush with money. In August, Bowen wrote to Vannevar Bush, president of the Carnegie Institution, to ask whether, in addition to supporting the Caltech instrument, Carnegie would consider granting further funds for a similar dish in the Southern Hemisphere. Bowen argued that both radio astronomy centers would benefit from a collaboration that would enable cost-sharing. For Bush, Bowen's proposal could not have come at a better time, and he responded positively to it.[38]

Throughout most of 1953, GRT feasibility and cost studies were carried out by several firms in the United States and Australia. In May 1954, seed funding for the Australian GRT came through from the Carnegie Corporation, as previously described. The dream of having two large telescopes, one in Australia and the other in California, seemed to be taking form.

JOHN BOLTON ARRIVES AT CALTECH

With progress on the GRT in Australia going well, Taffy Bowen declined the offer to take up the Caltech position. In his place, he recommended John Bolton. DuBridge offered Bolton a two-year appointment as a senior research fellow in physics and astronomy, with a commitment to discuss a long-term association at the end of that term. Bowen urged Bolton to take it, adding that he could come back and run the new Australian GRT when it was finished.

---

36. Robertson, *Beyond Southern Skies*, p. 118.
37. Ibid., p. 162.
38. Ibid, p. 119.

In January 1955, Bolton arrived at Caltech to take up his new position. Two months later, Gordon Stanley, his colleague in the discrete source identifications at Dover Heights, joined him. Two years after arriving at Caltech, Bolton was promoted to professor of radio astronomy.[39]

OWENS VALLEY RADIO OBSERVATORY

Soon after arriving at Caltech, Bolton decided to build a two-element interferometer rather than a large, single-dish antenna as proposed by Bowen. Bolton and Stanley had discussed the idea years earlier, but it never went beyond the planning stage at the CSIRO. The site they selected for the U.S. radio observatory was in Owens Valley. Their goal was to be able to precisely determine the positions of radio sources. Each of the antennas for the interferometer would be 90 feet in diameter. They would be polar-mounted since, before computers became available, alt-azimuth axes were awkward to drive. Originally, the antennas were to operate at 400 megahertz (MHz), but later they shifted to a higher frequency of 960 MHz, a protected communication band. A few years later, early JPL satellite systems began to operate at that frequency, using receiver front ends designed by Gordon Stanley. This development represented the first close collaboration between JPL and the Caltech radio astronomy group.[40]

Construction of the Owens Valley Radio Observatory (OVRO) began in 1956, with Bruce Rule, Caltech's chief engineer, designing the antennas. Rule had distinguished himself in telescope design through his major role in the 200-inch Palomar telescope project.[41] Rule was considered the doyen of American optical telescope designers (John Bolton described him as Caltech's "dean" of telescope construction), and the Owens Valley 90-foot (27.4-meter) antennas were his first venture into radio astronomy.[42]

The day before the dedication of the OVRO in 1958, John Bolton made a private commitment to Taffy Bowen (who was visiting OVRO for the dedication) that he would return to Radiophysics to oversee the construction and commissioning of the GRT and direct its operations. In June 1960, to the surprise and disappointment of his colleagues at Caltech, Bolton announced that

---

39. Marshall H. Cohen, "The Owens Valley Radio Observatory: Early Years," *Engineering and Science* (spring 1994) p. 12.
40. Ibid., p. 15.
41. Ibid., p. 15.
42. J. Bolton, "Commissioning the Parkes Radio Telescope—a Retrospective View," in *Parkes: Thirty Years of Radio Astronomy*, ed. D. E. Goddard and D. K. Milne (Collingwood, Australia: CSIRO Publishing, 1994).

he would be returning to Australia as director of the new Parkes Telescope.[43] Gordon Stanley succeeded him as acting director of the OVRO.[44]

Bolton had a profound influence on Caltech. By the time he returned to Australia in 1961, the OVRO had been recognized as a world radio astronomy center, providing a much-needed boost to U.S. radio astronomy. Bolton's crew at Caltech had come from all over the world: England, Australia, New Zealand, India, Canada, and Norway. Graduate students were American and included Barry Clark, Ken Kellerman, Al Moffet, and Robert Wilson.[45] In 1978, with Arno Penzias, Wilson won the Nobel Prize in Physics for the discovery of the cosmic microwave background radiation—a project suggested to Wilson by Bolton.

THE SPACE AGE BEGINS

In October 1957, the United States was jolted by the Soviet launching of Sputnik 1. Scrambling to catch up, it quickly initiated a program of satellite launches and robotic Moon shots. Caltech's JPL recognized a coming need for a communications system that could satisfy not only the immediate requirements of the Pioneer lunar missions but also more demanding future missions to other planets.[46]

The first Pioneer lunar probe was scheduled to launch in November 1958. JPL initiated a crash program to design and build suitable tracking antennas. In February 1958, William "Bill" Merrick, head of JPL's Antenna Structures and Optics Group, was assigned to investigate an appropriate antenna design. Merrick quickly concluded that JPL could only meet requirements by minor modification of an existing design. Merrick consulted with John Bolton, whom he knew well. Bolton had recently completed a survey of precision radio astronomy instruments.[47] One of the instruments he had highlighted was an 85-foot (26-meter)-diameter antenna with a cantilevered equatorial mount, being built by the Blaw-Knox Company for the National Radio Astronomy Observatory (NRAO) at Green Bank, West Virginia. Merrick and his colleagues ultimately chose that design, and JPL immediately placed

---

43. Ibid.
44. Cohen, "The Owens Valley Radio Observatory," p. 12.
45. Wild and Radhakrishnan.
46. Craig B. Waff, "Designing the United States' Initial Deep Space Networks: Choices for the Pioneer Lunar-Probe Attempts of 1958–59," *IEEE Antennas and Propagation Magazine* 35, no. 1 (February 1993), p. 49.
47. John Bolton, "Radio Telescopes," in *Telescopes*, ed. Gerard P. Kuiper and Barbara M. Middlehurst, Stars and Stellar Systems series, vol. 1 (Chicago: University of Chicago Press, 1960), pp. 176–209.

an order for three of the antennas. The first was delivered and installed at the Goldstone Dry Lake at the U.S. Army's Fort Irwin, in the Mojave Desert about 149 miles (240 kilometers) northeast of Pasadena. The antenna was built in an astonishingly short period, from July to October 1958. From initial design to operational status, the project took only 10 months.[48] Bolton had thus played a small but significant role in the design of the initial tracking antennas of the fledgling Deep Space Network (DSN).

PARKES GETS INVOLVED IN SPACE TRACKING

In March 1959, the Pioneer 4 spacecraft flew past the Moon at a distance of 36,972 miles (59,500 kilometers). JPL tracked the spacecraft with its 85-foot (26-meter) antenna at Goldstone. When the signal was finally lost on 6 March, after it had been tracked for a then-record distance of 406,911 miles (654,860 kilometers), NASA and JPL found themselves in the frustrating position of having a fully functioning vehicle far out in space, emitting signals that they had no way of receiving.[49]

It was evident that the tracking of spacecraft at lunar and planetary distances required larger and more sensitive antennas, so JPL considered building an array of three or four large tracking antennas around the globe. The tracking characteristics of these proposed antennas were close to those of the planned Parkes radio telescope. One early plan, mooted in 1959, was to link existing large radio astronomy antennas with new antennas built specifically for tracking spacecraft. The plan was to use the 250-foot (76-meter) dish at Jodrell Bank with the soon-to-be-built 210-foot (64-meter) dish at Parkes. Two new antennas would then be built at Goldstone and another somewhere in India to complete the coverage. The two new antennas would be based on the Parkes telescope design.[50]

During the tender and construction phase of Parkes, from 1959 to 1961, regular discussions occurred between NASA/JPL and the CSIRO's Radiophysics Division about the possibility of using Parkes for tracking spacecraft. During this period, John Bolton and Bruce Rule facilitated contacts between the CSIRO and JPL. Rule helped enormously on critical aspects of the Parkes design, suggesting changes missed by FF&P that helped improve the telescope's overall performance.[51] In a letter to JPL Director

---

48. Waff, "Designing the United States' Initial Deep Space Networks," p. 52.
49. Letter from E. G. Bowen to Freeman Fox and Partners, dated 8 June 1959.
50. Ibid.
51. E. G. Bowen, "The Pre-History of the Parkes 64-m Telescope," *Proceedings of the Astronomical Society of Australia* 4, no. 2 (1981): 267–273.

William Pickering dated 12 May 1960, Bowen suggested that the CSIRO could cooperate with JPL in designing and building its proposed large tracking antennas.[52]

By 1960, NASA/JPL had settled on a plan to build a three-station ground system for communications with lunar and planetary vehicles. Initially, the stations were to be equipped with one or more 85-foot (26-meter) antennas. These stations were referred to as Deep Space Instrumentation Facilities (DSIFs). One of these stations would be located at the Commonwealth Rocket Range at Woomera, South Australia. However, the need for larger antennas was anticipated.[53]

In July 1960, Edmond C. Buckley, NASA Assistant Director of Space Flight Operations, proposed a cooperative U.S.-Australian space exploration program. Such a program was to be based on occasional use of the Parkes radio telescope for short-term data acquisition when an extremely strong and reliable signal was desirable—for example, during the terminal phase of a spacecraft impact on the surface of another planetary body.[54] The proposal was favorably received by Bowen and the CSIRO.[55] To this day, it is still the rationale for Parkes's inclusion in NASA tracking operations.

On 26 February 1960, the governments of Australia and the United States had formally agreed to cooperate in spacecraft tracking and communications through an "Exchange of Notes," generally referred to as a Space Cooperation Agreement. In this treaty, NASA and Australia jointly established a management policy that has proved successful and remains virtually unchanged to the present day. In his letter to Bowen, Buckley had suggested two approaches to cooperation: amend the treaty to allow Parkes to participate, or arrange a service contract between the CSIRO and NASA based on a similar contract with the University of Manchester, operator of the Jodrell Bank telescope. For simplicity, the latter arrangement was adopted and remains in place to the present day.[56]

---

52. Letter from E. G. Bowen to William Pickering, Director of JPL, 12 May 1960.
53. Letter from E. C. Buckley, NASA Assistant Director, Space Flight Operations, to E. G. Bowen, 29 June 1960.
54. Ibid.
55. Letter from E. G. Bowen to E. C. Buckley, NASA Assistant Director, Space Flight Operations, 4 August 1960; letter from E. G. Bowen to S. H. Bastow, Acting Chairman, CSIRO, 4 August 1960.
56. Letter from E. C. Buckley, NASA Assistant Director, Space Flight Operations, to E. G. Bowen, 29 June 1960.

PARKES AS PROTOTYPE FOR JPL LARGE-APERTURE ANTENNAS

On 15 September 1960, JPL issued a document, "Project Description, Advanced Antenna System for the Deep Space Instrumentation Facility, Engineering Planning Document No. 5," describing requirements for its new antennas.[57]

The new antennas were to provide a 6- to 12-decibel (dB) improvement over JPL's existing 85-foot (26-meter)-diameter dishes, bringing them up to the 200- to 260-foot (60- to 80-meter)-diameter class. The surface accuracy of the dishes would require optimum performance around 2,200 megahertz (MHz) (S-band). The pointing accuracy was to be 1.2 arc-minutes, slightly less demanding than the Parkes telescope's 1 arc-minute. The dishes would need to be tipped to the horizon, much lower than the Parkes telescope's 30-degree elevation limit. Slew rates would not be substantially different from those of the Parkes telescope. Finally, the new antennas would need to withstand higher wind speeds of 70 miles (110 kilometers) per hour.[58] These requirements matched those for Parkes so closely that by the inauguration of Parkes in October 1961, JPL was showing intense interest in the instrument.[59] During an inspection visit to Parkes on 29 September 1961, Edmond Buckley was shaken by the economy of the telescope, which had cost substantially less than NASA's 85-foot (26-meter) antenna at the Woomera DSIF station.[60]

JPL had set itself the target of constructing a giant dish at Goldstone by 1963 and up to two more for the DSN by 1964. This tight schedule could be met only by making virtual copies of Parkes. JPL eventually decided on a redesign, adapting some of the more innovative features of the Parkes telescope while incorporating Cassegrain optics, full tracking accuracy in winds of up to 70 miles (113 kilometers) per hour, and coverage down to the horizon. This redesign meant that JPL would not meet its original target dates but would instead take up to five years to complete the job. Eberhardt Rechtin, chief of JPL's Electronics Research Section, was the head of the project to design the JPL antennas.

In order to bridge the gap in its capabilities until JPL's large antennas were built, JPL Director William Pickering proposed in December 1961 that the Parkes telescope be formally included in NASA's fledgling DSN. The intention was to use Parkes for 6–8 hours per day, particularly for planetary probe

---

57. Letter from E. G. Bowen to Ralph Freeman, Freeman Fox and Partners, 12 October 1960.
58. Ibid.
59. Letter from E. G. Bowen to Ralph Freeman, Freeman Fox and Partners, 23 November 1961.
60. Letter from E. G. Bowen to Frederick White, Chairman of CSIRO, 5 October 1961; letter from Edmond C. Buckley to E. G. Bowen, 10 October 1961.

operations from late 1964 onward.[61] Astronomical research took precedence at Parkes, so the CSIRO could not take up the offer. However, Bowen encouraged NASA/JPL to consider building a similar large antenna in the vicinity of Parkes, arguing that the value of two large telescopes near to one another exceeded that of two telescopes taken individually.[62] This proved to be a prophetic statement because, two years later, NASA selected a site at the Tidbinbilla nature reserve near Canberra, Australia, just 186 miles (300 kilometers) south of Parkes, for a new DSN antenna. The value of this decision was not fully realized until 1986, with the Voyager 2 encounter of Uranus, when the Parkes and Tidbinbilla antennas were linked, or arrayed, to increase receiving sensitivity.

An alternative proposal offered by Pickering was to use the Parkes telescope as a passive listening device, supplementing JPL's DSN antennas. Parkes would be used to listen to the planned Mariner R probe (later renamed Mariner 2) as it neared Venus. Pickering also suggested that the CSIRO could provide technical consulting on JPL's large-aperture antenna.[63] Bowen enthusiastically supported both of these recommendations.[64]

NASA RESEARCH GRANT NSG-240-62

In February 1962, the CSIRO was awarded a NASA research grant, NsG-240-62, to report on the detailed characteristics of the newly commissioned Parkes telescope. CSIRO engineer Harry Minnett was appointed Officer-in-Charge of Advanced Antenna Design to head the study.[65] JPL's proposed large-aperture antennas had the basic form and dimensions of the Parkes telescope and incorporated the master equatorial precision-pointing system.

Under the grant, the CSIRO participated in feasibility studies and specification reviews of the JPL antennas. Detailed performance parameters of the Parkes telescope were determined in regard to structural behavior, characteristics of the drive master control systems, and radio frequency performance. In addition, vibration characteristics and dish shape in the zenith

---

61. Letter from William Pickering, Director of JPL, to E. G. Bowen, 4 December 1961.
62. Letter from E. G. Bowen to William Pickering, Director of JPL, 28 December 1961; letter from E. G. Bowen to Eberhardt Rechtin, Director of DSIF, 16 May 1962; Harry Minnett, "Progress Report No. 1 on Studies Under NASA Research Grant NsG-240-62," CSIRO Radiophysics Division RPR 141, April 1963.
63. Letter from William Pickering to E. G. Bowen, 4 December 1961.
64. Letter from E. G. Bowen to William Pickering, 28 December 1961.
65. Letter from E. G. Bowen to Eberhardt Rechtin, Director of DSIF, 2 May 1962.

and tilted positions were measured.[66] This information was deemed to be of critical importance in the design of the JPL antennas.

During the period of the grant, the CSIRO and JPL established a close working relationship, with many visits and exchanges by key personnel.[67] By the time the grant expired in December 1966, over 30 research papers had been published on the design and performance of the telescope. At that point, Parkes was not only the most advanced radio telescope in the world, but also the most extensively studied.[68]

MARINER 2

On 27 August 1962, the Mariner 2 spacecraft was launched toward an encounter with Venus. The 85-foot (26-meter) antennas of the DSN were deemed sufficient to satisfy NASA's requirements during the encounter.[69] However, NASA considered it vital that a coordinated program of ground-based radio and optical observations be carried out in conjunction with the encounter to maximize the scientific return. In June 1962, Parkes was invited to participate in this program.[70]

Taffy Bowen and Harry Minnett decided that tracking Mariner 2 would be an excellent demonstration of the Parkes telescope's capabilities for communication at great distances.[71] In addition, it would provide Parkes personnel with valuable experience.[72] Since this activity would provide valuable performance information on Parkes that would be of interest to JPL's antenna designers, tracking costs were covered by the CSIRO's NASA research grant.

This experiment was to be a simple one, involving the measurement of spacecraft position, signal level, and Doppler frequency.[73] It did not include the reception of telemetry. Mariner 2 carried an L-band (960-MHz)

---

66. Letter from E. G. Bowen to Eberhardt Rechtin, 16 May 1962; letter from E. G. Bowen to Eberhardt Rechtin, 2 May 1962.
67. The relationship developed so closely that often, when replacement parts were required for the telescope, they were shipped out to Parkes in the next diplomatic parcel and delivered within days.
68. Robertson, *Beyond Southern Skies*.
69. Letter from Paul Coleman, Jr., Mariner Program Scientist, Lunar and Planetary Programs, Office of Space Sciences, to E. G. Bowen, 2 November 1962.
70. Letter from Homer E. Newell, Director, NASA Office of Space Sciences, to E. G. Bowen, 8 June 1962.
71. Letter from E. G. Bowen to Homer E. Newell, 25 June 1962.
72. Letter from Harry Minnett to Bill Merrick, JPL Communications Elements Research Section, 14 September 1962.
73. Harry Minnett, interview by author, September 2002.

transmitter, and for these test tracks, JPL loaned Parkes a modified version of the GSDS 960-MHz transportable phase-lock receiver.[74]

Attempts to detect Mariner 2 signals began on 12 December 1962, two days before closest approach.[75] Parkes had a gain advantage of 8 dB (about 6 times) over the 85-foot (26-meter) antennas of the DSN and should have detected the signals easily. However, Parkes experienced great difficulty in finding and locking on to them. There were two reasons for this difficulty: the narrow beam width of the 210-foot (64-meter) antenna made the accurate pointing of the dish crucial, and the receiver had to be tuned very precisely since it only had a 20-Hz-wide gate.[76] The Doppler shift of the signal had to be known precisely so that the receiver could be tuned manually to the received frequency. Once the signal was detected, the receiver could lock on to it and automatically track the signal. The Parkes team of Doug Cole and Harry Minnett needed to know both the position and frequency very accurately. This proved to be extremely difficult, especially since they were calculating the position and Doppler shift by hand. They found that they could have an accurate position but incorrect frequency, or vice versa, or alternatively both the frequency and position could be wrong. They had no way of knowing which.[77] Whatever the case, they failed to detect the signal at all. After 100 frustrating hours of searching, they contacted the Woomera DSIF and asked JPL to telex the predicted positions and Doppler shifts to them. Using these data, they succeeded in finding Mariner 2 at around 7 a.m. on 20 December 1962. They were able to track the spacecraft for several hours until it set at about 1:30 p.m. later that day.[78]

The telescope's measured threshold was −150 decibel-milliwatts (dBm), and the Mariner 2 signal was about 4 dB above it (−146 dBm). This measurement was consistent with the known signal strength at the time and the measured parameters of the antenna and receiver. Also, a penalty of 3 dB was incurred because a circularly polarized feed was unavailable. (Parkes

---

74. Telex from J. H. Wilcher, JPL DSN Data Systems Development Section, to Harry Minnett, 25 October 1962; Minnett, "Progress Report No. 1."
75. "Parkes Scientists Hear Signals from Mariner 2," *Sydney Morning Herald* (26 December 1962) p. 10.
76. Minnett interview, September 2002; telex from J. H. Wilcher, JPL DSN Data Systems Development Section, to Harry Minnett, 25 October 1962.
77. Minnett interview, September 2002.
78. Harry Minnett, "Progress Report No. 1 on Studies Under NASA Research Grant NsG-240-62," CSIRO Radiophysics Division RPR 141, April 1963.

was using a linearly polarized astronomy feed.)[79] Overall, Parkes had a 5-dB advantage over the DSN 85-foot (26-meter) antennas.

Doug Cole continued to track Mariner 2 at intervals during the Christmas holiday period until the signals ceased on 3 January 1963.[80] The experiment was a success, and many lessons were learned that contributed to the success of future cooperative ventures. It also confirmed the appropriateness of the design.

MARINER 4

In 1962, NASA had a plan to launch a spacecraft to Mars in November 1963 that would deliver a 125-pound (57-kilogram) capsule to the surface of the planet in July 1964. However, NASA postponed this mission in favor of a Mars flyby mission that became Mariner 4.[81] When the flyby mission was first proposed, NASA expected the Goldstone 210-foot (64-meter) antenna would be ready in time to track the spacecraft at Mars. However, by the time Mariner 4 reached Mars in July 1965, the Goldstone dish was still about a year from completion. Consequently, NASA asked Parkes to provide backup for the DSN.

Mariner 4 carried an S-band transmitter centered on 2,300 MHz. The GSDS 960-MHz receiver, previously loaned to Parkes for the Mariner 2 tracks, was converted to operate at the higher frequencies, and a parametric amplifier from JPL was installed to increase the sensitivity of the receiver. In addition, a circularly polarized feed was constructed. The data rate from Mariner 4 was just 8 bits per second, and the receiver had an 11-Hz-wide gate. Pointing and frequency predictions as a function of time were telexed to Parkes on a daily basis. As with the Mariner 2 test tracks, Harry Minnett and Doug Cole were responsible for the Parkes operations, and costs were covered by the NASA research grant.[82]

On 21 June, Parkes began receiving Mariner transmissions. Daily tracks, centered approximately on Mariner's meridian transit, were carried out during 2-hour periods each afternoon. Horizon-to-horizon observations were obtained on 3, 14, 15, and 16 July. Regular telemetry recordings were made

---

79. Ibid.
80. Ibid.
81. Letter from W. G. Stroud, Chief, NASA Aeronomy and Meteorology Division, to E. G. Bowen, 30 November 1962.
82. Letter from Harry Minnett to Charles Koscielski, JPL RF System Development Section, 30 April 1965; letter from Charles Koscielski to Harry Minnett, 5 May 1962.

from 8 July to 27 August.[83] The telemetry was recorded on a Pemco instrumentation tape recorder using 5.5-inch reels with a playing time of about 30 minutes.[84]

Mariner 4's closest approach to Mars was scheduled to occur about 2 hours below the Parkes horizon on 15 July, and soon after that, the spacecraft would pass behind the planet.[85] Exit from occultation would occur just above the telescope's 30-degree-elevation horizon. These occultation observations were considered important since they were intended to probe the atmosphere and ionosphere of Mars.

Mariner 4 experiments with the Parkes telescope showed that the 210-foot (64-meter) dish equipped with a standard S-band parametric amplifier had a margin of about 2.5 dB over a maser-equipped 85-foot (30-meter) dish. The resulting gain in data transmission performance was demonstrated. Using identical receivers, the increase in performance with the 210-foot (64-meter) dish was close to the theoretical figure of 7.7 dB.[86]

In early September, the telemetry recordings were shipped to JPL.[87] The tapes contained the data for the 22 images of the Martian surface captured by Mariner 4. The Parkes data were later combined with data from the smaller 85-foot (30-meter) antennas. Pictures of the Martian surface produced from this combined dataset were of considerably higher quality than the pictures produced from the 85-foot data alone.

APOLLO 11

In October 1968, John Bolton visited Caltech for the dedication of the new 130-foot (39.6-meter) radio telescope at the Owens Valley Radio Observatory. One evening, he and his wife, Letty, attended a dinner party at the home of Bob Leighton. Leighton had been the Principal Investigator on the Mariner 4 mission and a colleague of Bolton's during his Caltech period. Also at the party was JPL's Eberhardt Rechtin, head of the Goldstone project. That evening, John was asked if the 210-foot (64-meter) Parkes telescope might be available to receive signals from the Apollo 11 mission, particularly during its most critical phase, when the Lunar Module (LM) would be on the lunar surface. The historic nature of the mission, combined with the fact that

---

83. D. J. Cole and P. R. Crossthwaite, "Observations of Mariner 4 with the Parkes 210-ft Radio Telescope," CSIRO Radiophysics Division Report, RPL 173, 1966.
84. "Introducing the New PEMCO Model 110 Instrumentation Tape Recorder" brochure.
85. Cole and Crossthwaite, "Observations of Mariner 4."
86. Ibid.
87. Letter from Harry Minnett to Charles Koscielski, 2 September 1965.

human lives would be at risk in space, convinced both him and Taffy Bowen to support the mission.[88]

The original Apollo 11 mission plan called for Parkes to act as a backup for NASA's 210-foot (64-meter) Goldstone dish during the moonwalk. The plan called for the astronauts to perform their extravehicular activity (EVA) shortly after landing. The Moon would not rise at Parkes until 1:02 p.m. Australian Eastern Standard Time (AEST) on landing day, by which time the EVA would be completed.

In May 1969, NASA decided to alter this mission plan to allow the astronauts a rest period in the LM before commencing the EVA. The new plan called for the EVA to start about 10 hours after landing, at 4:21 p.m. AEST, some 20 minutes after the Moon would set for the Goldstone dish. The Moon would be overhead at Parkes at that time. Parkes's role was consequently upgraded from backup to prime receiving station for the EVA. Parkes could provide the reliability and quality for telemetry and TV that the mission planners demanded.

On Monday, 21 July 1969, at 6:17 a.m. AEST, astronauts Neil Armstrong and Buzz Aldrin landed their LM, Eagle, on the Sea of Tranquility. Armstrong diverted from the plan when he exercised his option for an immediate EVA—5 hours before the Moon was to rise at Parkes. However, as the hours passed it became evident that the process of preparing to exit the LM was taking more time than planned.

The weather at Parkes on the day of the landing was miserable. While the Parkes dish was fully tipped over, waiting for the Moon to rise above its 30-degree elevation horizon, a violent squall hit the telescope. Two sharp wind gusts exceeding 70 miles per hour (110 kilometers per hour) struck the dish, subjecting the telescope to wind forces 10 times stronger than it was considered safe to withstand. The control tower shuddered from this battering, creating concern in all present. Fortunately, the winds abated, and as the Moon rose into the beam of the telescope, Aldrin activated his TV camera at 12:54 p.m. AEST.

Three tracking stations were receiving TV signals simultaneously: Parkes, Honeysuckle Creek, and Goldstone. Using its less sensitive "off-axis" detector, Parkes was able to receive TV pictures just as the TV camera was switched

---

88. This section draws on John Sarkissian, "On Eagle's Wings: The Parkes Observatory's Support of the Apollo 11 Mission," *Publications of the Astronomical Society of Australia* (PASA) 18, no. 3 (2001): 287-310. Also see John Bolton, "Parkes and the Apollo Missions," in *Parkes: Thirty Years of Radio Astronomy*, ed. D. E. Goddard and D. K. Milne (Clayton, Australia: CSIRO Publishing, 1994).

The "Apollo Antenna" built in 1967 at Goldstone. (NASA: G-67-3491)

on. Eight minutes later, the Moon had risen into the beam of the Parkes telescope's main detector, and the picture quality improved.

During the first 9 minutes of the broadcast, NASA alternated between signals from its stations at Goldstone and Honeysuckle Creek, searching for the best-quality images. Then NASA switched to transmissions from Parkes, which were of such superior quality that NASA stayed with the Parkes TV signal until the EVA was completed. This event alone repaid NASA for its investment in Parkes.

APOLLO 12

Following the success of Apollo 11, NASA contracted Parkes to support the Apollo 12 mission four months later. This landing, in the Ocean of Storms, was scheduled to occur during the Parkes coverage period.

During descent and landing, Apollo 12's LM high-bit-rate telemetry would be vital to mission control. Loss of this telemetry could lead to aborting the mission. Telemetry could be received by the 85-foot (30-meter) antennas of NASA's Manned Space Flight Network (MSFN), but only if the LM's high-gain antenna could function properly. The high-gain antenna was a single-point-failure item that needed to be pointed with extreme accuracy during descent maneuvers, so coverage by a 210-foot (64-meter) antenna would be necessary to receive data from the LM's omnidirectional antenna as an alternate route.[89] This backup plan was employed during the Apollo 11 descent, when LM telemetry was continually dropping out. The Apollo 11 signal received by the Goldstone 210-foot (64-meter) antenna was weak and variable, while the 85-foot (30-meter) dish at Goldstone received no usable data at all. Had the Goldstone 210-foot (64-meter) antenna not been available, the Apollo 11 landing would very likely have been aborted.

NASA also had a requirement for color TV coverage of the Apollo 12 EVA. The Parkes telescope's capabilities were required to provide the additional gain necessary to ensure good TV coverage.[90] Early in the EVA however, astronaut Alan Bean inadvertently pointed the camera at the Sun, rendering it inoperable, so little TV was received.[91]

In recognition of Parkes's contribution to Apollos 11 and 12, NASA granted CSIRO $90,000 to improve research facilities at Parkes.[92] In October 1970, CSIRO used the money to resurface the dish, which allowed the telescope to operate more efficiently at higher frequencies.

APOLLO 13

Parkes was not initially required for the Apollo 13 mission. The Moon's northerly declination during the mission meant that Parkes would have only 2 hours of coverage per day, at unimportant times.[93] Plans changed when, just 2 days into the mission, on 14 April 1970, an oxygen tank on the Apollo 13 Service Module exploded, severely crippling the Command Module, Odyssey.

John Bolton happened to be in his office listening to the Apollo 13 air-to-ground conversations when he heard mission commander Jim Lovell report, "Houston, we have a problem." Bolton knew that the LM could be used as a lifeboat and that return to Earth could occur during Parkes coverage time. He anticipated that Parkes would almost certainly be called in to assist.[94]

---

89. Teletype notes to E. G. Bowen, 3 September 1969; letter from NASA Administrator Thomas Paine to Senator Kenneth Anderson, Australian Minister for Supply, 29 September 1969.
90. Letter from Thomas Paine to Kenneth Anderson, 29 September 1969.
91. Bolton, "Parkes and the Apollo Missions."
92. Letter from Senator Kenneth Anderson to the Hon. J. M. Fraser, Australian Minister for Education and Science, 13 October 1969.
93. Letter from E. G. Bowen to Noel Seddon, CSIRO Radiophysics, 13 February 1970.
94. Bolton, "Parkes and the Apollo Missions."

Radiophysics Lab engineers were conducting an experiment at the telescope at that time. Bolton got them to quickly uninstall their equipment and reinstall NASA equipment instead. He had other equipment flown to Parkes from the Radiophysics head office in Sydney. The observatory staff accomplished in just 10 hours what normally took close to a week.[95]

When NASA officials finally asked for Parkes support, they were astonished to learn that Parkes's staff were aware of the problem and well on the way to being ready for the next pass of the spacecraft. Parkes senior receiver engineer David Cooke had his equipment operating in time to track Apollo 13. Parkes was able to receive weak voice signals from Odyssey that were sent via landline to Sydney and then on to Houston. The feeble signals from Odyssey were a thousand times weaker than those received from Apollo 11.[96] Microwave links established for Apollos 11 and 12 were not operational at this point. Soon engineers from Tidbinbilla, headed by Bruce Window, arrived at Parkes. Working all night, they were able to set up those links, while technicians from the Post Master General's office (the Australian telephone company) reestablished microwave links to Sydney before the next pass of the spacecraft.

Meanwhile, Mike Dinn, deputy director in charge of operations at Honeysuckle Creek, was coordinating the efforts of the Australian stations. At one point, he had up to 10 receivers tracking the spacecraft.[97] The greater sensitivity of the Parkes telescope meant that it was able to download telemetry data more quickly, saving precious time and spacecraft power. The 210-foot (64-meter) Goldstone dish was able to do the same in non-Parkes coverage periods. The two together were able to extract weak but vital telemetry and save the mission from disaster. In a gesture of friendship to the United States, CSIRO Chairman Sir Frederick White decided that NASA would not be charged for using the Parkes telescope to help Apollo 13.[98]

Parkes supported the rest of NASA's Apollo lunar landing missions. In particular, it played a major role in the Apollo 15 mission to Hadley Rille. By the time of Apollo 17 in December 1972, the 210-foot (64-meter) antenna at Tidbinbilla was finally complete and used for the first time with that mission.

---

95. Ibid.
96. Ibid.
97. Mike Dinn, "NASA, Parkes and Voyager," in *Thirty Years of Radio Astronomy*, ed. D. E. Goddard and D. K. Milne (Clayton, Australia: CSIRO Publishing, 1994).
98. Letter from Thomas Paine, NASA Administrator, to Frederick White, CSIRO Chairman, dated 8 June 1970.

With the commissioning of the Tidbinbilla dish in April 1973, Parkes was no longer required for tracking operations. Taffy Bowen retired from CSIRO in 1971, and John Bolton stepped down as director of Parkes the same year. It was the end of an era.

A NEW ERA BEGINS WITH VOYAGER 2

NASA did not employ Parkes again for tracking operations until January 1986, for Voyager 2's once-in-a-lifetime encounter with Uranus. To maximize scientific return, NASA decided to array, or link, the Parkes and Tidbinbilla 210-foot (64-meter) dishes via microwave link to double the sensitivity of the instruments. Together, they composed the world's second-largest radio telescope (after the 1,000-foot [305-meter] Arecibo dish in Puerto Rico). This linkage realized Taffy Bowen's vision of having the two dishes work together and justified his decision to locate the DSN station at Tidbinbilla. The $2 million microwave link was later used for real-time very long baseline interferometry (VLBI) observations with Parkes and Tidbinbilla. The Voyager 2 encounter with Uranus was a resounding success, followed by an encounter with Neptune in August 1989. Between encounters, in 1987, the DSN antennas were enlarged to 230 feet (70 meters) to provide greater sensitivity for the Neptune encounter.

A YEAR WITH GALILEO

The Parkes and DSN antennas linked up again for the Galileo mission to Jupiter.[99] The spacecraft's high-gain antenna had failed to deploy fully, meaning that the expected data rate of 134 kbps would not be possible. A solution was devised using the spacecraft's less powerful S-band, omnidirectional antenna. The planned data rate from this antenna was about 10 bits per second (bps). By arraying the Parkes dish with the 230-foot (70-meter) antennas at Tidbinbilla and Goldstone plus two 112-foot (34-meter) antennas at Tidbinbilla, the data rate was raised to 160 bps. By further employing new data compression algorithms for data transmission, the mission team could salvage 70 percent of the planned science. These arraying operations required Parkes for tracking duties for periods of up to 10 hours a day, every day, for 1 year—the period of Galileo's initial 11-orbit tour of Jupiter.

In order to allow radio astronomy observations at Parkes during non-track periods of the day, NASA funded a new, larger focus cabin at a cost of $3 million. This larger cabin could house up to four receivers, any one

---

99. The author has been on the staff of the CSIRO Parkes Observatory from 1996 to the present.

of which could be placed on the focus within minutes. This increased "frequency agility" made the telescope more efficient and flexible. The larger cabin also could accommodate larger and more complex receivers that could be used for innovative radio astronomy projects.

Galileo tracking commenced on 28 October 1996 and continued until 6 November 1997. The operations team achieved a 96.95 percent up time, exceeding expectations, with no tracking time lost due to operator error or equipment breakdown.

A TRAFFIC JAM AT MARS

In 2003–04, a traffic jam was looming at Mars. NASA termed this situation an "asset contention period" (ACP). Over four months, up to seven spacecraft were scheduled to be at Mars, with several more operating elsewhere in the solar system, all clustered close to the same celestial longitude as Mars. They all needed to be tracked. The DSN station at Tidbinbilla had too few antennas to cope with this pileup.

To augment tracking capabilities at Tidbinbilla, Parkes was contracted to provide extra receiving capability. This arrangement freed the Tidbinbilla antennas to track those spacecraft requiring two-way communication (the Parkes radio telescope could only receive, not transmit). Because these spacecraft would be transmitting at X-band (8.4 gigahertz), it would be essential to increase the Parkes telescope's sensitivity at these frequencies. NASA's $3 million grant to the CSIRO covered the repaneling of the Parkes dish surface in March 2003. The upgrade extended the perforated aluminum panels from 148 to 180 feet (45 to 55 meters) in diameter. The upgrade increased the sensitivity of the dish by about 30 percent (1 dB) at X-band.

On 31 October 2003 (the 44th anniversary of the telescope's commissioning), the U.S. Ambassador to Australia, J. Thomas Shieffer, visited Parkes and officially launched the Parkes Mars tracks. Over the next four months, Parkes tracked mainly Voyager 2, Mars Global Surveyor, and the Mars Exploration Rovers Spirit and Opportunity while en route to Mars.

HUYGENS HEROES

The Cassini-Huygens mission to the Saturn system was launched on 15 October 1997. It arrived on 1 July 2004 and entered into orbit about the planet.

The mission had two parts. The Cassini spacecraft was an orbiter built by NASA to study the planet and its rings and moons. The Huygens probe, built by the European Space Agency (ESA) to study the atmosphere of Titan, landed on the surface of the moon on 14 January 2005.

The Huygens probe was designed to transmit data to Cassini in two channels, at 2,040 and 2,098 MHz.[100] Since the descent of the probe would occur in view of the Pacific Ocean, Leonid Gurvits of the Joint Institute for VLBI in Europe (JIVE) organized a VLBI network around the Pacific Rim to take advantage of this alignment. The plan was to track the 2,040-MHz signal and pinpoint the position of Huygens to within 1 kilometer as it descended to the surface of Titan, enabling transverse velocity (on the plane of the sky) to be obtained as well as Doppler (radial) velocity.[101] One of the experiments during the descent was the Doppler Wind Experiment (DWE). This involved having Cassini track the 2,040-MHz signal to measure the Doppler shift of the frequency in order to determine the probe-orbiter radial velocity. When combined with the radial velocity obtained from the probe-Earth, VLBI observations enabled a measure of the winds of Titan.

JIVE arranged for up to 17 antennas to link together in this VLBI network. Five were in Australia. Others were in the United States, including the 328-foot (100-meter) telescope at Green Bank, West Virginia. The Green Bank and Parkes telescopes were essential for the observation because of their large collecting areas.[102]

The first part of the descent of the Huygens probe would be visible from Green Bank and the second part from Parkes. Twenty minutes before the probe was scheduled to land, Titan would set at Green Bank. At Parkes, the expected landing time would be 1 minute after Titan would rise.

In October 2004, Bob Preston at JPL contacted the CSIRO's Australia Telescope National Facility and his former colleague John Reynolds, the Parkes officer-in-charge, and asked if JPL could piggyback another DWE on the Parkes observations.[103] JPL planned to install radio science receivers (RSRs) at Green Bank and Parkes to detect the probe-Earth Doppler data in real time, rather than waiting weeks or months to get it from the VLBI observations. The JPL DWE measurements would enable a determination of Titan's wind speed in the probe-Earth direction as a function of altitude. By comparing observed Doppler shifts to those predicted from a smooth atmospheric descent model, any variation from predictions would indicate what

---

100. Private notes made by the author, who was present in the Parkes control room during the descent of the Huygens probe on 14 January 2005.
101. Witasse et al., "Overview of the Coordinated Ground-Based Observations of Titan During the Huygens Mission," *Journal of Geophysical Research* 111, no. E7 (July 2006): 2, doi:10.1029/2005JE002640.
102. Ibid.
103. JPL's Robert Preston, e-mail to the CSIRO Australia telescope National Facility on 27 October 2004.

the atmosphere of Titan was doing. This experiment was planned to enhance a similar experiment on the Cassini orbiter by providing two vectors for the wind speed.[104]

The Green Bank telescope detected the Huygens signal as the probe entered the atmosphere of Titan. JPL's Sami Asmar was at Green Bank monitoring the data in real time. As the probe descended, Doppler shift deviations increased and fluctuated—winds on Titan were furiously blowing the little probe about.[105]

After about an hour and a half, Titan set at Green Bank. Seventeen minutes later, it rose at Parkes, at 10:29 p.m. AEST. The Huygens signal was 2.5 times stronger than expected.[106] About 15 minutes after it had first received the signal, Parkes reported that the probe had landed on Titan—a little later than expected. It was a second moon landing for Parkes.[107]

The Huygens batteries were designed to last for about an hour after landing. But as tracking continued, the signal remained strong and showed no indication of weakening. At 1:56 a.m. AEST, when Titan set at Parkes, Huygens was still transmitting strongly.[108]

After Huygens tracking ended, it became apparent that data being relayed by Cassini was missing the 2,040-MHz telemetry. It appeared that a sequencing error by ESA controllers in Germany had resulted in the 2,040-MHz receiver on Cassini not being switched on. Although Huygens had been transmitting 2,040-MHz data, Cassini had not been receiving it. Since it was this 2,040-MHz signal that Earth-based antennas had been tracking, the Parkes and Green Bank recordings of this signal assumed greater significance in the DWE. In fact, the Parkes and Green Bank observations salvaged the entire experiment. Sami Asmar later declared, "Sometimes it pays to eavesdrop."

A LITTLE CURIOSITY GOES A LONG WAY

On 6 August 2012, at 3:31 p.m. AEST, the Mars Science Laboratory rover Curiosity landed on Mars. The CSIRO's Parkes telescope tracked the rover's ultra-high-frequency (UHF) beacon during the few minutes of the mission's

---

104. Lebreton et al., "An Overview of the Descent and Landing of the Huygens Probe on Titan," *Nature* 438 (8 December 2006): 758–764.
105. Private notes made by the author, who was present in the Parkes control room during the descent of the Huygens probe on 14 January 2005.
106. Ibid.
107. Ibid.
108. Ibid.

hair-raising entry, descent, and landing (EDL) maneuvers.[109] JPL considered EDL risks to be so great that it demanded maximum redundancy in its tracking network. Consequently, Parkes was enlisted to act as a backup for the Canberra Deep Space Communication Complex (CDSCC) at Tidbinbilla, which was the prime station for tracking during EDL.

In order for Parkes to support the mission, CSIRO staff modified an existing 70-centimeter radio astronomy receiver to operate at the UHF frequency of 401.58 MHz transmitted by the rover.[110] Two weeks before the EDL, a radio science receiver (RSR) was delivered to Parkes from Tidbinbilla and installed in the control room. Sami Asmar of JPL was present at Parkes to operate the RSR while John Reynolds set up the VLBI recording system as a backup. At 3:16 p.m. AEST, the signal was detected following cruise stage separation. It was slightly stronger than expected.[111] Parkes tracked the descent of the rover until just after parachute deployment and heat-shield separation. At 3:30 p.m. AEST, less than 2 minutes before it was scheduled to land, the rover dropped below the Martian horizon and out of direct radio contact with Earth. Fortunately, the EDL went according to plan, and the Parkes data were not needed this time.

CONCLUSION

On 31 October 2003, U.S. Ambassador to Australia J. Thomas Shieffer remarked, "The Parkes Telescope is like a trusted friend, always there when we need a hand. The relationship between the CSIRO and NASA is very much like that between the United States and Australia, as friends that share common values and dreams."[112]

The history of the Parkes telescope's support of space missions is a testament to this special relationship, which has benefited both sides equally. The CSIRO has been able to maintain the Parkes telescope's leading role in

---

109. Private notes made by the author, who was present in the Parkes control room during the entry, descent and landing (EDL) of the Mars Science Laboratory, Curiosity, on 6 August 2012 (the author was controlling the telescope); email correspondence between the author and Sami Asmar, plus various other JPL personnel, from 2011–2012, involving the detailed planning for the Parkes Observatory's support of the MSL EDL.
110. Ibid.; A. Makovsky, P. Ilott, and J. Taylor, "Mars Science Laboratory Telecommunications System Design," DESCANSO Design and Performance Summary Series, Article 14, JPL/California Institute of Technology, November 2009, p. 75.
111. Private notes made by the author, who was present in the Parkes control room during the entry, descent, and landing of the Mars Science Laboratory, Curiosity, on 6 August 2012 (the author was controlling the telescope).
112. *https://www.parkes.atnf.csiro.au/news_events/mars_ceremony/parkes_ceremony.html*.

world radio astronomy, partly through financial support from NASA. In return, NASA has had a reliable partner available to help when it was needed. Upgrades to the telescope have meant that a better and more reliable instrument would be available the next time it was needed.

Fifty years after Mariner 2, the Curiosity landing again proved the telescope's utility to NASA and the foresight of those who designed and built it.

EPILOGUE

On 27 August 1962, the first interplanetary spacecraft, Mariner 2, was launched to Venus. This also happened to be the day that I was born. In July 2015, when the New Horizons spacecraft accomplished its flyby of the dwarf planet Pluto, I could say with conviction that in the span of a single human lifetime, the entire solar system has been explored. What an amazing achievement!

CHAPTER 12

International Cooperation in Solar System Exploration: A Transnational Approach to the History of the International Solar Polar Mission and Ulysses

Petar Markovski

> COOPERATION IS EASILY ESTABLISHED as an objective but is far more difficult to implement. If it is to achieve meaning in the affairs of men, it must progress beyond lip service, slogans and token exchanges. It must go forward substantively and realistically within the existing, rather than always a future, political framework, and with due regard for modes and channels, for first and immediate steps and for ultimate objectives.[1]
>
> —Arnold W. Frutkin, NASA Assistant Administrator for International Affairs (1963–78)

In a May 1987 *ESA Bulletin*, Reimar Lüst, former director general of the European Space Agency (ESA), reflected on American and European cooperation in space, emphasizing "the importance of a free and open exchange of views between the scientific communities of the United States and of Europe." It is true, he wrote, "and we should never deny the fact, that we live in a world of conflicting, or at least, divergent, political and economic interests. But in spite of that, I do believe that many of our present problems can

---

1. Arnold Frutkin, *International Cooperation in Space* (Englewood Cliffs, NJ: Prentice Hall, 1965), p. iii.

be solved more easily when there is an international community of scientists and scholars free to follow common goals and common objectives."[2]

While I can only speculate as to whether Lüst was referring to anything specific, it would not be farfetched to think that he might be referencing a turbulent episode in NASA-ESA cooperation earlier in the decade, a result of the collapse of an agreement between the two agencies for a jointly developed International Solar Polar Mission (ISPM). Although the ISPM was not launched as originally planned—two solar probes exploring the north and south poles of the Sun—the plan was eventually reworked and launched in 1990 as the Ulysses mission. While NASA and ESA eventually carried out a joint solar polar mission, with a single spacecraft named Ulysses, the evolution of ISPM to Ulysses had a lasting impact on U.S.-European cooperation in space.[3]

This important episode in the five-decade-long history of international space cooperation also happens to be one of the most strenuous ones. The ISPM had its origins in the mid-1960s, when European space scientists worked on building a scientific constituency for a spacecraft that would explore the Sun out of the ecliptic plane (OOE), particularly at the poles and other high latitudes (hence its original designation as an out-of-ecliptic mission).[4] Through the mid-1970s, NASA and ESA established working groups and hosted a number of symposia and conferences to determine both the scientific and technical merits and capabilities of an out-of-ecliptic mission. These efforts resulted in a proposal for the ISPM, which was officially established as a joint mission with the 29 March 1979 signing of a memorandum of understanding (MOU) between NASA and ESA.[5]

To date, there have been three primary historical studies of Ulysses. Two of these analyses have focused on the origins of the mission. Historian Karl Hufbauer's account of the genesis of an out-of-the ecliptic solar mission

---

2. Reimar Lüst, "Cooperation Between Europe and the United States in Space," *ESA Bulletin* 50 (May 1987): 98.
3. Joan Johnson-Freese, "Cancelling the US Solar-Polar Spacecraft: Implications for International Spaceflight," *Space Policy* 3.1 (February 1987): 24–37.
4. See Karl Hufbauer, "European Space Scientists and the Genesis of the Ulysses Mission, 1965–1975," in *Science Beyond the Atmosphere: The History of Space Research in Europe. Proceedings of a Symposium Held in Palermo, 5–7 November 1992*, ed. Arturo Russo (Noordwijk, The Netherlands: European Space Agency, 1993), pp. 170–191; and Ludwig Biermann, "Some Aspects of the Physics of Interplanetary Space Related to Out-of-Ecliptic Studies," *Advances in Space Science and Technology*, 7 (1965): 437–447.
5. European Space Agency, "NASA Signs Agreement with ESA for 1983 Solar Polar Mission," ESA News Release, 30 March 1979; "NASA, ESA Sign Solar Polar MOU," *Aerospace Daily* (16 April 1979): 187.

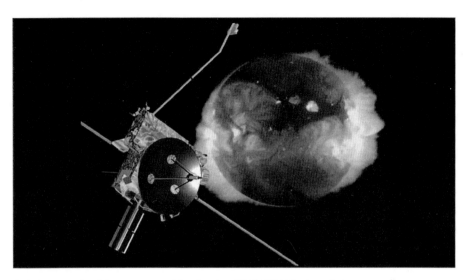

Artist's concept of Ulysses approaching the Sun. (NASA/ESA: 1418_ulysses.jpg)

focuses on the viewpoint of European space scientists whose "early visions of an out-of-ecliptic probe eventually found expression in the Ulysses mission."[6] Hufbauer's analysis builds on another, more narrative history of Ulysses, told by English space scientist Harry Elliot.[7] According to Hufbauer, his account "provides a fuller account of the steps leading up to the mission's approval" and "reveals that European space scientists, always an essential group of mission proponents, played an increasingly circumscribed role in the campaign that culminated in the ESA/NASA memorandum of understanding for the International Solar Polar Mission."[8] Joan Johnson-Freese gives a third account, in which she examines events leading to the cancellation of the U.S. spacecraft for the ISPM and its potential ramifications for international cooperation in space.[9] She concludes that the whole "poorly handled" affair, itself contingent on the political climate of the then-new Reagan administration, set a precedent and became an invaluable learning experience for Europe in international space cooperation.[10]

In this chapter, I will revisit the 25-year history of Ulysses, from its origins as a proposed OOE mission to its emergence as the dual-spacecraft ISPM

---

6. Hufbauer, "European Space Scientists," p. 170.
7. Harry Elliot, "The Genesis and Evolution of the International Solar Polar (Ulysses) Mission," *COSPAR Information Bulletin* 122 (December 1991): 82–89.
8. Hufbauer, "European Space Scientists," p. 172.
9. Joan Johnson-Freese, "Cancelling the US Solar-Polar Spacecraft," pp. 24–37.
10. Ibid., pp. 36–37.

and its eventual reemergence as Ulysses. I will pay particular attention to the multitude of actors that reshaped early conceptions of an OOE mission into Ulysses. In doing so, I will reframe the history of Ulysses from a transnational perspective, suggesting that Ulysses was a transnational project. I will focus on the flow of ideas, discussions, and events involved in defining the OOE spacecraft. Ultimately, I will argue that the transnational element is embedded within the technology itself—that is, the spacecraft, which was negotiated in various ways at various times by different individuals and groups from both Europe and the United States. This historical analysis seeks to supplant more standard nation-centered accounts of international cooperation in space. This chapter contributes to a newly emerging interest in cooperation in space, which aims to identify a new global narrative of space history.

THE HISTORY OF SPACE AND TRANSNATIONAL HISTORY

Space history as a field of inquiry has often been written as a history of Cold War competition. While this perspective has been fruitful in examining the dynamics of U.S. and Soviet space programs, the Cold War era represents only part of more than a century of space history. Historians exploring the Cold War era have focused on the political, economic, and military relationships between governments and large technoscientific programs, including national space programs. More recently, others have looked at how these types of programs have contributed to the emergence of modern national identity in both the post-colonial and post–Cold War context.[11] A few recent studies have aimed to decenter "Cold War–ness" from post-war history.[12] As these authors contend, the Cold War was a global conflict, involving not only the United States and Soviet Union, but also a range of other global actors. This emerging perspective can be conducive to the study of under-explored areas of spaceflight, such as transnational cooperation in the history of

---

11. For instance, see *Global Power Knowledge: Science and Technology in International Affairs, Osiris 21*, ed. John Krige and Kai-Henrik Barth (Chicago: University of Chicago Press, 2006); Gyan Prakash, *Another Reason: Science and the Imagination of Modern India* (Princeton, NJ: Princeton University Press, 1999); Gabrielle Hecht, *The Radiance of France: Nuclear Power and National Identity After World War II* (Cambridge, MA: MIT Press, 1998); Itty Abraham, *The Making of the Indian Atomic Bomb: Science, Secrecy, and the Postcolonial State* (London: Zed Books, 1998); Arjun Appadurai, *Modernity at Large: Cultural Dimensions of Globalization* (Minneapolis: University of Minnesota Press, 1996); and Armin Hermann, Lanfranco Belloni, and John Krige, *History of CERN* (Amsterdam: North Holland, 1987).
12. Gabrielle Hecht, ed., *Entangled Geographies: Empire and Technopolitics in the Global Cold War* (Cambridge, MA: MIT Press, 2011).

space exploration. In doing so, it might be a step forward in constructing what historian Asif Siddiqi calls a "global history of space exploration."[13] Constructing a global historical perspective on space, shying away from a nationalistic framework and concentrating on lines of cooperation between two of the biggest and most successful actors in space history, NASA and ESA, will help to reframe space history.

While the Cold War certainly had a tremendous influence upon U.S. and Soviet (and later Russian) programs, what influence did it have on programs that matured in the post–Cold War era, such as the Chinese, Japanese, and Indian programs, or programs not as connected with military development, such as ESA's? Siddiqi prescribes a new approach that looks "with new lenses as more and more 'new' narratives join the old cold-war-centered approach to space history."[14] While not advocating the overthrow of previous space histories, Siddiqi urges historians to step beyond the constricting scope of Cold War and nationalistic narratives and move toward the incorporation of "a broader matrix of approaches, including, particularly, the highlighting of global flows of actors and knowledge across borders, communities, and identities."[15] Ultimately:

> This approach might lend itself to constructing for the first time a global and transnational history of rocketry and space travel. Since a global history would theoretically be decentered and a nation's space program rendered as a more nebulous transnational process, one might expect a multitude of smaller, local, and ambiguous processes and meanings to become visible. With a new approach grounded in a global history of spaceflight, we might learn much more about how individuals, communities, and nations perceive space travel, how they imbue space exploration with meaning, and especially how those meanings are contested and repeatedly reinvented as more and more nations articulate the urge to explore space.[16]

In concentrating on these elements and bringing them to the foreground of my analysis, I will recast the so-called "standard narrative" of the history of ISPM and Ulysses. My reexamination of this history will be a step toward this larger project of providing a transnational history of cooperation in space.

---

13. Asif Siddiqi, "Competing Technologies, National(ist) Narratives, and Universal Claims," *Technology and Culture* 51.2 (2010): 425–443.
14. Ibid., p. 443.
15. Ibid.
16. Ibid., p. 443.

ULYSSES' ORIGINS AS OOE MISSION AND ISPM: 1965–79

After the launch of Sputnik in 1957, space scientists began to discuss the advantages of using spacecraft for a number of scientific investigations. Almost immediately, scientists on both sides of the Atlantic began to pursue space-based solar observatory capabilities. Between 1957 and 1975, solar science research and, by extension, the solar physics community saw drastic growth, in which scientists took advantage of three new strategies of observation: the use of high-atmospheric balloons, rockets, and spacecraft; the adoption of new telescopes and other ground-based observatories; and the use of underground solar-neutrino detectors.[17] Dramatic developments in spacecraft technology following Sputnik convinced space engineers of the prospects of interplanetary exploration with new propulsion systems, which could make an out-of-ecliptic solar science mission possible. Advances in solar physics resulting from experiments near the ecliptic plane convinced space scientists to anticipate further advances from out-of-ecliptic observations.[18]

By the early to mid-1960s (a period that Karl Hufbauer characterizes as the bountiful period for solar space science), a number of developments from both European and U.S. scientists and engineers led to the conception of a full-fledged out-of-ecliptic mission. In Europe, two champions emerged: German astrophysicist Ludwig Biermann of the Max-Planck Institute and British physicist Harry Elliot of Imperial College. Biermann's contribution included the first publication to consider the scientific value of an out-of-ecliptic mission.[19] In his paper, which came out shortly after the first international conference on the solar wind, he "considered how out-of-ecliptic studies might improve knowledge of the solar wind, the supersonic efflux from the corona responsible for anti-solar orientation of cometary plasma trails." He concluded, "the time was ripe for direct investigations of the solar wind's plasma properties and associated magnetic fields."[20] One of Britain's leading authorities in space science, Elliot, as appointed chair of the British National Committee on Space Research's Working Group 3, steered the "committee to the conclusion that an out-of-ecliptic mission to 45 degree heliographic latitude would best meet the dual desiderata of yielding novel

---

17. Karl Hufbauer, Exploring the Sun: Solar Science Since Galileo (Baltimore: Johns Hopkins University Press, 1991), p. 160.
18. Hufbauer, "European Space Scientists," p. 173.
19. Ibid.
20. Hufbauer, "European Space Scientists," p. 173; Hufbauer, Exploring the Sun, p. 240.

scientific results and stimulating the nation's aerospace industry."[21] From 1968 to 1971, Elliot had mixed success in mustering support for an out-of-ecliptic mission, but ultimately his efforts resulted in a 1972 European Space Research Organisation (ESRO) mission-definition study.[22]

By the early 1970s, U.S. space scientists were also considering the feasibility of an OOE mission. It was seen as a potential candidate for NASA's emerging solar system exploration program. By this time, U.S. scientists and engineers were already solving problems relating to an OOE mission (and, by extension, technical issues facing future interplanetary probes).[23] In July 1971, NASA Ames Research Center published a "Pioneer H Jupiter Swingby Out-of-Ecliptic Mission Study."[24] The 128-page report laid out a scientific rationale for the mission; established mission requirements, a range of mission possibilities, and a mission design; evaluated the suitability of the Pioneer spacecraft for this mission; and investigated the feasibility of a launch in 1974.[25] While the report outlined a number of different launch and hardware configurations, the proposed Pioneer OOE would use a spare Pioneer spacecraft for Pioneers F and G (which would became Pioneers 10 and 11).[26]

For the next few years, attempts by U.S. scientists to persuade NASA officials to use the backup Pioneer spacecraft for an OOE mission were unsuccessful. While a number of officials recognized the potential benefits, a few concerns arose regarding its use. Writing to NASA Associate Administrator for Space Science and Applications John Naugle, Norman Ness, chief of the Laboratory for Extraterrestrial Physics at NASA Goddard Space Flight Center, expressed concerns about the use of the backup Pioneer. According to Ness, while an OOE mission seemed "exceedingly worthwhile…scientifically," perhaps the backup Pioneer might not be the best option for fulfilling the potential of an OOE mission. Ness urged approval of an OOE mission but

---

21. Hufbauer, "European Space Scientists," p. 174.
22. Hufbauer also provides a thorough discussion of the important elements of the ESRO study, in which it concluded that ESRO should try to pursue a feasibility study as quickly as possible as the scientific merits of the mission were very appealing.
23. Three solutions: 1) for propulsion, the radioisotope thermoelectric generator (RTG) instead of solar panels; 2) a gravity assist for a swing-by of Jupiter; and 3) the development of radiation-resistant electronics for penetration of the Jovian radiation belt.
24. NASA, "Pioneer H Jupiter Swingby Out-of-Ecliptic Mission Study: Final Report," NASA Ames Research Center, 1971.
25. NASA, "Pioneer H," p. 1.
26. Letter from John Naugle to Norman E. Ness, "Pioneer H Mission," 27 August 1971, NASA Historical Reference Collection, NASA Headquarters, Washington, DC (hereafter "HRC").

asked "that the payload be entirely reconsidered."[27] In response, Naugle cited budget and time constraints posed by soliciting proposals for an entirely new spacecraft for the mission.[28] In August 1972, NASA Associate Administrator Homer Newell also questioned use of the backup Pioneer for an OOE mission. "Although Pioneer 10, presently on its way to Jupiter, is still working well," he wrote to physicist John Simpson, "we cannot assume that it will give us all the definitive information on the radiation environment of Jupiter that is required."[29] He suggested that, in the event that Pioneer 10 could not meet this goal, the backup Pioneer might be needed for a follow-up mission.

By the mid-1970s, NASA would become increasingly supportive of a joint mission, especially with larger looming budgetary concerns. By 1974, NASA had given up on the idea of using the backup Pioneer as an OOE probe. As Hufbauer has shown, two developments helped create an environment favorable for the advancement of an ESA-NASA OOE mission. First, both NASA and ESRO responded to budgetary constraints with the idea of cooperation. Second, Pioneer 10 used a gravitational assist maneuver on its way to Saturn in December 1973, demonstrating the viability of a planetary swing-by.[30]

While NASA officials seemed increasingly supportive of a joint mission with ESRO (by 1975, ESA), the views of U.S. scientists were varied. By summer 1974, some expressed concern about a perceived lack of consultation with the U.S. scientific community.[31] John Simpson, at the Enrico Fermi Institute, wrote to NASA Administrator James C. Fletcher in June 1974:

> I was shocked to learn when I was in Frascati, Italy to report on our Pioneer 10 and Mariner 10 results that NASA has invited the European space group to consider taking over this type of mission. Furthermore, a European conference on this matter was already scheduled for 2 July. I find this incredible since I can think of no other mission which could guarantee as many scientific discoveries per dollar spent on a major mission than this one. Thus this potential reduction of participation by U.S. scientists—if the Europeans choose this mission—is hard to justify within the United States. Both for strengthening U.S. science at this time and for NASA's stated objective of supporting U.S. science, this mission is outstanding, and as I understand

---

27. Letter from Norman E. Ness to John Naugle, "Proposed Pioneer H Mission," 3 August 1971, NASA HRC.
28. Letter from John Naugle to Norman E. Ness.
29. Letter from Homer E. Newell to John A. Simpson, 11 August 1972, NASA HRC.
30. Hufbauer, "European Space Scientists," pp. 176–177.
31. Letter from Nathaniel B. Cohen to John Naugle, "Out-of-the-Ecliptic Missions," 18 June 1974, NASA HRC.

it, involves a relatively small commitment in '76. I am just strongly enough oriented towards strengthening U.S. science at this time to argue that this should be an all U.S. mission if at all possible.[32]

NASA's Naugle recognized that while U.S. scientists were increasingly concerned about international cooperation, Congress was becoming more interested in the idea of cooperation in space. "Congress views such cooperation as a reduction in funding requirements," Naugle told Fletcher, "whereas the U.S. scientists regard such missions which will carry U.S. and foreign experiments as a reduction in their opportunities to do research."[33] To Naugle, and perhaps other NASA officials, cooperation looked like a good compromise, as it would produce "a net increase in the number of flights and hence a net increase in the total opportunities for U.S. scientists."[34]

By the end of 1974, in Europe, as ESRO was considering and sorting mission priorities for the 1980s, a stereoscopic mission to study coronal phenomena emerged as a compelling and worthwhile candidate for a future mission. ESRO's Launching Programs Advisory Committee (LPAC) included both OOE and stereoscopic missions as top priorities for mission-definition studies.[35] During the summer of 1974, in the United States, the idea rose of perhaps combining the OOE and stereoscopic missions. In response to Simpson's 26 June letter, Fletcher wrote, "The best chance of implementing an out-of-ecliptic mission is with a mission mode that will attract as wide a constituency as possible," and a combined stereoscopic and OOE mission would do.[36] These developments created a "ripe" atmosphere for cooperation.

At an ESRO/NASA science program review held at the European Space Technology Center in February 1974, ESRO and NASA agreed to cooperate on two joint missions, one of which was an OOE mission. ESRO suggested coupling the stereoscopic mission with the OOE mission to attract a wider and broader constituency. By the end of summer 1974, 47 European and 7 U.S. space scientists and planners had presented their finding during ESRO's "Symposium on the Sun and Solar System in Three Dimensions." By the end of the symposium, it was clear that a stereoscopic mission would not happen

---

32. Letter from John A. Simpson to James C. Fletcher, 26 June 1974, NASA HRC.
33. Letter from John Naugle to Administrator, "Out-of-Ecliptic Mission," 7 August 1974, NASA HRC.
34. Ibid.
35. Hufbauer, "European Space Scientists," p. 178.
36. Letter from James C. Fletcher to John A. Simpson, 18 August 1974, NASA HRC.

if it were not part of the OOE mission.[37] NASA favored this position, and a joint NASA-ESRO Science Working Group (SWG) was established in order to "form the optimum mission mode."[38] In the first few months of 1975, based on the SWG study, ESRO science planners recommended an OOE dual stereoscopic spacecraft, using a Jupiter gravitational assist, as the most suitable mission option.[39] This decision was one of ESRO's last for space science in Europe, because by May, ESA would become the official space agency of Europe.[40]

Following the feasibility studies of 1975, development continued on what would eventually emerge as ISPM and Ulysses. As Hufbauer has shown, ESA emphasized a number of priorities for a cooperative mission: clean interfaces, ESA involvement in choosing experiments and Principal Investigators, observations of Jupiter during the swing-by, commitment to the two-spacecraft option, and mission operations as long as possible at the 50-degree heliographic latitude.[41] Several months later, five tentative points of agreement were reached regarding the cooperative mission: "(1) a joint announcement of opportunity would be released in early 1977; (2) a joint screening committee would nominate the principal investigators; (3) a joint science team would be formed for the development phase; (4) NASA would seek new-start status for the mission in FY 1978; and (5) the two agencies would ultimately enter into a memorandum of understanding for the mission."[42] In April 1977, NASA and ESA began soliciting proposals for an OOE mission, and by March 1978, mission experiments were chosen. "A total of 16 experiments will be flown," ESA reported in a news release, "eight on each of the two spacecraft. In addition, 12 theoretical investigations will be undertaken, based on the data collected and on radio measurements. Through these experiments and investigations, more than 200 scientists belonging to 65 universities and research centres in Belgium, Canada, Denmark, France, Germany, Great Britain, Greece, Italy, Japan,

---

37. Hufbauer, "European Space Scientists," p. 181.
38. Letter from James C. Fletcher to John A. Simpson, p. 2.
39. Memo from Daniel H. Herman to Noel W. Hinners, "Telephone Conversation with Dr. George Haskell on January 20, 1975, Regarding NASA/ESRO Meeting of February 4 and 5, 1975," 23 January 1975, NASA HRC; letter from Thomas E. Burke to Gary E. Hunt, 14 March 1975, NASA HRC.
40. Hufbauer, "European Space Scientists," p. 181.
41. Ibid. See also Craig Covault, "ESRO Narrows Future Project Choices," *Aviation Week & Space Technology* (26 May 1975): 43.
42. Hufbauer, "European Space Scientists," p. 183.

the Netherlands, Norway, Switzerland and the United States will participate in this mission."[43]

While technical and scientific development of the OOE mission continued from 1977 to 1978, securing funding for the cooperative mission was increasingly a problem.[44] For instance, in May 1977, NASA anticipated a $77 million cut to its FY 1978 budget request. This cut would have a particular impact on the Agency's planetary program, especially the planned new start for a Jupiter orbiter/probe. The OOE mission was affected, as the question arose of "what effect…the delayed new start [would] have on plans to use the same basic Jupiter spacecraft design as part of the NASA/ESA proposed out-of-ecliptic mission."[45] In July, the House of Representatives appropriated $17.7 million for the Jupiter orbiter/probe mission, with the stipulation that the planned 1979 new-start for the OOE mission would use a variant of the Jupiter mission spacecraft. Without this new budget approval for the Jupiter probe mission, OOE mission plans would have been threatened.[46] Requesting more funding for the OOE mission, which by late 1977 had been renamed the Solar Polar Mission, was becoming increasingly difficult. By September 1977, NASA had secured authorization from the White House Office of Management and Budget (OMB) for an initial FY 1978 budget of $13 million for the OOE mission, arguing that it would be the only funding they could receive for FY 1978. Despite these issues, in September 1978, after intense lobbying efforts of the American space science community and Harold Glaser, Director of NASA's Solar-Terrestrial Division, President Jimmy Carter approved the Solar Polar Mission.[47] On 29 March 1979, NASA

---

43. ESA News Release, "Experiments Selected for Latest ESA/NASA Joint Mission," 13 March 1978.
44. "News Digest," *Aviation Week & Space Technology* (18 April 1977): 25. For specifics on budget debates and discussions, see "Five-Year Space Agency Plan Raises Budget to $4.7 Billion," *Aviation Week & Space Technology* (7 March 1977): 47; Craig Covault, "Potential in Space Awaits Funds," *Aviation Week & Space Technology* (21 March 1977): 59; Craig Covault, "House Unit Cut Threatens NASA Planetary Planning," *Aviation Week & Space Technology* (8 May 1977): 13; Craig Covault, "NASA Assessing Budget Slashes," *Aviation Week & Space Technology* (16 May 1977): 12; and Craig Covault, "NASA Mulls New Fiscal 1979 Efforts," *Aviation Week & Space Technology* (18 July 1977): 49.
45. Craig Covault, "NASA Assessing Budget Slashes," p. 12.
46. Craig Covault, "Jupiter Mission Approval Saves Planetary Capability, 300 Jobs," *Aviation Week & Space Technology* (25 July 1977): 21.
47. Hufbauer, "European Space Scientists," p. 186. For a more thorough discussion of both budgetary approval and lobbying efforts by both American and European scientists, see pp. 182–187.

Artist's concept of Ulysses at Jupiter. (ESA/NASA; PIA18173)

Administrator Robert A. Frosch and ESA Director General Roy Gibson signed an MOU for the International Solar Polar Mission.[48]

ISPM AT THE BRINK OF COLLAPSE AND REEMERGENCE OF ULYSSES: 1980–90

The mission that became the ISPM was already facing budget issues as early as 1978. In January 1978, NASA's budget request for FY 79 included $13 million for ISPM, one of five new-start programs. Although Congress approved the mission, it cut $5 million from the $13 million request and reallocated those funds to cover Space Shuttle cost overruns.[49] According to the March 1979 MOU, the ISPM dual-craft launch was scheduled for early 1983, aboard the "Space Transportation System on a single shuttle mission with an Inertial Upper Stage (IUS)."[50] This launch window was chosen because it provided

---

48. ESA News Release, "NASA Signs Agreement with ESA for 1983 Solar Polar Mission," 30 March 1979.
49. Craig Covault, "Inflation Absorbs NASA Funding Growth," *Aviation Week & Space Technology* (30 January 1978): 28; Washington Staff, "NASA Cuts," *Aviation Week & Space Technology* (30 January 1978): 13.
50. "Memorandum of Understanding between NASA and the ESA for the ISPM," 29 March 1979, NASA HRC.

the optimal position of Jupiter for a swing-by. Any delays would have to take into account the next possible alignment of the planet for a swing-by.

By the end of 1978, the Senate Appropriations subcommittee with jurisdiction over NASA's budget proposed that ISPM be delayed for two years, "(1) to reflect the delays in Shuttle development, and (2) because the committee was concerned that the IUS necessary to send the two spacecraft on the flight path would not be adequate and that NASA should develop a high-energy upper stage (Centaur) instead."[51] Despite $135 million already awarded for the mission by this point, ISPM was in serious danger. The Carter administration submitted an amended FY 1981 budget request to Congress calling for a two-year launch delay and roughly $43 million dollar budget cut for ISPM.[52] Protests arose from European nations. In response, U.S. Representative Edward Boland claimed, "The action threatens not only international cooperation in space, but other areas of technology as well."[53] A few months later, the House Appropriations Committee recommended in a 1980 supplemental bill that ISPM be canceled, claiming that the two-year delay would cost at least an additional $150 million. While ESA reacted to the possible cancellation with strong diplomatic protest, Representative Don Fuqua (D-FL), chairman of the House Committee on Science and Technology, successfully argued "that the cancellation of the funds would constitute legislation in an appropriations bill—a violation of House Rules."[54] This victory was short-lived, though, as NASA ultimately dropped out of the ISPM.

As Joan Johnson-Freese has shown, the fate of ISPM took a turn for the worse in the early 1980s, as "the whole budget process and attitude fundamentally changed with the November 1980 election of Ronald Reagan as President and his appointment of David Stockman as Director of the [OMB]."[55] By early 1981, it became clear that the Reagan administration's

---

51. Johnson-Freese, "Cancelling the US Solar-Polar Spacecraft," p. 25.
52. "Solar Polar Flight Delay Likely Budget Cut Result," *Aviation Week & Space Technology* (31 March 1980): 27; "House Panel NASA Cuts Follow Budget Guidelines," *Aviation Week & Space Technology* (7 April 1980): 20.
53. Quote from Alton K. Marsh, "Solar Polar Fund Threat Spurs Worldwide Protest," *Aviation Week & Space Technology* (26 May 1980): 22; "Cancellation of Solar Polar Mission To Be Recommended by Boland Panel," *Aerospace Daily* (7 May 1980): 34; "ISPM Backers Muster Effort To Save Program," *Aerospace Daily* (13 May 1980): 66; letter from Matthew Nimetz to Frank Church, 12 May 1980; NASA HRC; "Salvaging Solar Polar," *Aviation Week & Space Technology* (9 June 1980), 22.
54. Johnson-Freese, "Cancelling the US Solar-Polar Spacecraft," pp. 25–26; "ISPM Backers Muster Effort To Save Program," p. 66. Regarding the ESA response, see letter from Roy Gibson to Robert Frosch, 7 May 1980, NASA HRC.
55. Johnson-Freese, "Cancelling the US Solar-Polar Spacecraft," p. 26.

proposed budget for NASA would effectively cancel ISPM. The original FY 1982 budget request for the NASA space science program was $757.7 million, including $58 million for ISPM. After Reagan took office, OMB cut the FY 1982 space science budget by almost 23 percent, to $584.2 million.[56] This move effectively signaled the cancellation of U.S. participation in ISPM.

This decision elicited uproar among both U.S. and European delegations. U.S. politicians claimed a lack of new projects could jeopardize NASA's ability to keep its status as a leader in space. ESA declared the decision an unacceptable breach of the MOU, despite a vague reassurance by the administration that the United States would participate in the ISPM mission at a reduced capacity.[57] In March 1981, ESA Director General Erik Quistgaard told the House Science and Technology Committee, "It cannot be accepted that at such an advanced stage of the [ISPM]development, and after the commitment of more than half of the European funding, NASA presents ESA with the fait accompli of its withdrawal from an international cooperative program, and this without prior consultation."[58] He told the committee that the short-term financial advantage for NASA might come at the cost of future cooperative ventures. In the following weeks, ESA expressed willingness to work on a compromise solution, if the United States was willing to reinstate its spacecraft.[59] Despite some promising efforts in the early summer of 1981, newly instated NASA Administrator James Beggs informed Quistgaard on 9 September "that NASA would not include any request for funds for the second ISPM spacecraft in its FY 1983 budget proposal."[60] Beggs did offer

---

56. Ibid., p. 26; "Spacelab, Solar-Polar Curtailed," *Aviation Week & Space Technology* (23 February 1981): 18.
57. "IUS Cancellation Irks Europeans," *Aviation Week & Space Technology* (16 February 1981): 103; "Reagan Administration To Cancel U.S. ISPM Spacecraft," *Defense Daily* (26 February 1981): 295; "Budget Concerns," *Aviation Week & Space Technology* (23 February 1981): 17.
58. "ESA Director Hits NASA's ISPM Cut," *Aerospace Daily* (12 March 1981): 67.
59. Johnson-Freese, "Cancelling the US Solar-Polar Spacecraft," p. 29; "ESA Seeks Solar-Polar Compromise," *Aviation Week & Space Technology* (30 March 1981): 20. For reinstatement correspondence, see letter from Alan Lovelace to David Stockman, 24 April 1981, NASA HRC; telex from Erik Quistgaard to Alan Lovelace, 16 April 1981, NASA HRC; letter from David Stockman to Alan Lovelace, 22 June 1981, NASA HRC. For press coverage, see "NASA Reviews Proposal for Second European-Built ISPM Spacecraft," *Aerospace Daily* (21 April 1981): 289; "NASA Hopes To Buy Second ISPM Spacecraft From Europe," *Aerospace Daily* (24 April 1981): 314; "ESA Encouraged by Washington Response to Two-Spacecraft ISPM Program," *Aerospace Daily* (15 May 1981): 83; "Rep. Flippo Opposes European ISPM Spacecraft Offer," *Aerospace Daily* (29 June 1981): 324.
60. Johnson-Freese, "Cancelling the US Solar-Polar Spacecraft," p. 32; "NASA Drops ISPM from FY 1983 Budget," *Aerospace Daily* (16 September 1981): 81.

support and encouragement for ESA to pursue a single spacecraft mission, in which NASA would fulfill any remaining commitments, such as launch services, tracking and data support, and continued support for U.S. experiments on the European spacecraft.[61] By the end of the year, the dual-spacecraft ISPM mission was officially out of commission.

Despite the cancellation of the U.S. spacecraft, ESA decided to continue with a solar polar mission, citing substantial commitments already made.[62] With a targeted launch window of 1984, ESA had a number of considerations to deal with, primarily involving the integration of U.S. and European experiments on the craft. In early 1982, ESA sought continued assurance of support from NASA and Congress.[63] ESA also stressed continuing discussions regarding the establishment of a framework for future cooperation—the start of what Johnson-Freese characterizes as a strategy that ultimately made ESA a stronger, autonomous, and more independent space agency.[64] In July 1984, ESA announced the renaming of the ISPM to Ulysses. ESA suggested that the new name was chosen as a reference to the hero in Homer's *Odyssey* and to Dante's *Inferno*. Perhaps the new name also reflected the long, arduous journey of mission development.[65] Ulysses was scheduled to be launched aboard the Space Shuttle on 15 May 1986, but the Challenger accident of 28 January 1986 intervened. A new launch date would be determined after NASA restored the Shuttle Program.[66] Ulysses was finally launched on Shuttle mission STS-41 on 6 October 1990.

---

61. Johnson-Freese, "Cancelling the US Solar-Polar Spacecraft," p. 32; "ESA Likely To Proceed with One-Spacecraft ISPM Program," *Aerospace Daily* (25 September 1981): 139; "ESA Considers Options for Solar-Polar Mission," *Aviation Week & Space Technology* (28 September 1981): 26; Jeffrey M. Lenorovitz, "Solar Polar Plans Advance Despite Pullout by NASA," *Aviation Week & Space Technology* (28 December 1981):12; letter from James Beggs to Harrison Schmitt, 2 October 1981, NASA HRC.
62. Jeffrey M. Lenorovitz, "Solar Polar Plans Advance Despite Pullout by NASA," *Aviation Week & Space Technology* (28 December 1981): 12.
63. "Europe Seeks Assurance on Solar Project," *Aviation Week & Space Technology* (15 February 1982): 135.
64. Johnson-Freese, "Cancelling the US Solar-Polar Spacecraft," p. 37; Jeffrey M. Lenorovitz, "Europe's Cooperative Space Efforts Expand as Costs, Complexity Grow," *Aviation Week & Space Technology* (3 June 1985): 137.
65. ESA News Release, "Ulysses—A New Name for the International Solar Polar Mission," 31 July 1984.
66. NASA, "NASA Postpones Galileo, Ulysses, Astro-1 Launches," *NASA News* (10 February 1986); ESA News Release, "Consequences of the Challenger Accident on the Joint ESA/NASA Ulysses Mission," 17 February 1986.

The Ulysses spacecraft undergoes testing. (NASA: s90-45985)

OOE, ISPM, AND ULYSSES AS A TRANSNATIONAL HISTORY

The history of the OOE mission's evolution into ISPM and eventually Ulysses makes for a compelling narrative. Its long history, spanning 25 years from conception to reality, is fraught with challenges that both NASA and ESA (as well as its predecessor organization ESRO) faced regarding international cooperation. From a transnational standpoint, the (long) history of Ulysses tells a more rich and globalized history that is part of the history of international cooperation more generally. In particular, I highlight how the lines and flows of transnational cooperation contribute to the development of technology.

What makes the history of Ulysses transnational? Its main technological component, the spacecraft itself, is an example of a transnational object. The mission and spacecraft were negotiated along transnational lines, in which a host of actors and institutions played a role. Initially, an OOE mission was proposed and championed by European space scientists, some of whom were involved in the shaping of space programs in Europe. As the feasibility of an OOE mission began to be discussed in the global community of space scientists (that is, among Americans and Europeans), Europeans had a key role in building a scientific constituency. The OOE mission emerged as a potential candidate for the Pioneer program as Pioneer H—conceived as a joint mission by NASA (at least initially), in part due to budget concerns.

The American space science community reacted with concern about losing research opportunities in a cooperative mission. NASA was concerned about using the Pioneer probe backup for a new mission. By the mid-1970s, both ESRO and NASA advisory committees had determined the feasibility of stereoscopic observations for an OOE mission. Both institutions seemed to agree that this option would appeal to a broader scientific constituency to justify program approval. NASA and ESA pursued a number of more concrete cooperative agreements, culminating in the signing of an MOU for the ISPM. Budgetary concerns during the Reagan administration affected the shape of the mission, leading to the cancellation of one of two planned probes. By the 1980s, ISPM, renamed Ulysses in 1984, had become a single-probe mission. Despite the "failure" of cooperation on ISPM, an American-European hybrid OOE mission designed to study the polar regions of the Sun was launched on the Space Shuttle.

The transnational approach that I have taken to the history of Ulysses highlights the changing meanings and imaginings of cooperation and collaboration between various actors and organizations, such as space agencies, politicians, space scientists and engineers, and other advocates. At different times, different individuals saw different values (or perhaps no value at all) in cooperation on an OOE mission. Ulysses is an interesting case study for a transnational analysis as it began as a failed project, the dual-spacecraft ISPM. Yet the project lived on, in the sense that a material transnational object, the Ulysses probe, was actually built and launched under a different form of cooperation.

So what exactly failed? I suggest that negotiations and lines of cooperation leading to the breakdown of ISPM were a normative representation of cooperation between the two agencies. Eventually a critical mass of issues and concerns led to the cancellation of the U.S. spacecraft. In this chapter, I have demonstrated why and how adopting a transnational perspective might enrich our understanding of international cooperation in space exploration more generally. Adopting a transnational perspective might improve understanding of the multiple imagined and varied meanings of collaboration constructed by both NASA and ESA.

EPILOGUE

Linda Billings

THE PAST HALF CENTURY of robotic solar system exploration has been a remarkable ride, from early flyby reconnaissance missions to landing and roving on Mars.

The accomplishments of NASA's four Mars lander-rover missions—Mars Pathfinder, the twin Mars Exploration Rovers (MERs), the Mars Science Laboratory (MSL), and Mars 2020—have been especially remarkable. MSL's Curiosity rover is still operating on the surface of the planet, NASA's Mars Insight lander mission launched in May 2018, the Mars 2020 rover Perseverance landed on the planet on 18 February 2021, and the MER Opportunity rover ended long operations in June 2018.

Following its 2015 flyby of the dwarf planet Pluto, NASA's New Horizons spacecraft is now on its way into the far-flung Kuiper belt at the edge of the solar system. NASA's Juno spacecraft, which entered the atmosphere of Jupiter on 4 July 2016, is expected to operate until July 2021. NASA's Europa Clipper mission is being developed to launch sometime in the 2020s. And NASA's Dawn mission to the asteroids Vesta and Ceres has completed its science operations.

The European Space Agency's ExoMars 2020 mission, now scheduled for launch in 2022, plans to deliver a European rover and a Russian surface platform to the planet's surface. Continuing its successful Venera Venus-exploration program, which has landed 10 probes on the surface of the planet, Russia plans a Venera-D orbiter-lander mission to Venus. China, India, and Japan all have ambitious plans for exploring the solar system. In 2021, the China National Space Administration placed its Tianwen-1 spacecraft in orbit around Mars, and the United Arab Emirates placed its Hope spacecraft in orbit around Mars. However, while ambitions run high, budgets for solar system exploration remain tight, in the United States and elsewhere. International cooperation is no longer an option but a must for high-priced missions such as Mars sample return.

As the cost of both robotic and human exploration missions continues to rise, NASA will continue to struggle with balancing funding for these two enterprises. In recent years, NASA has attempted to foster greater

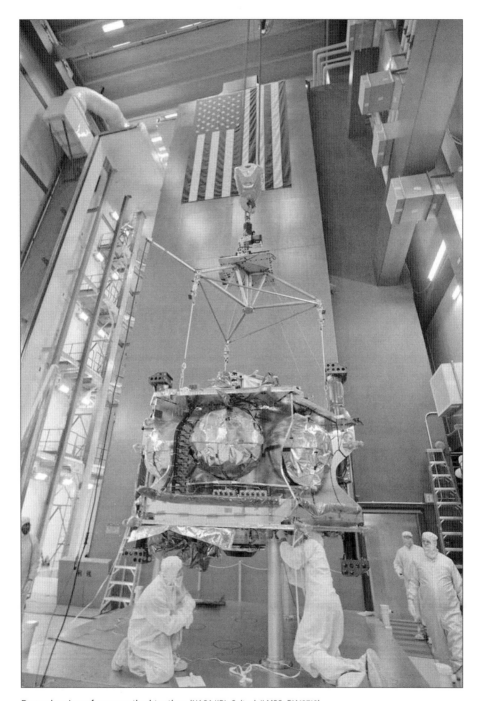

Preparing Juno for acoustical testing. (NASA/JPL-Caltech/LMSS; PIA13718)

collaboration and cooperation between its scientific and human-exploration camps. Tensions persist, however. Human exploration has been—and likely always will be—considerably more expensive than robotic exploration. The ideological underpinnings of scientific and human exploration differ as well.

Scientific exploration by robotic missions tends to be justified on scientific grounds. Solar system exploration has improved understanding of the origin and evolution of the solar system, and thus of Earth, and its climate, and its life. Many members of the space community talk of space exploration—especially human exploration—as our "destiny." Though we use the term freely in everyday discourse, the concept of destiny is fundamentally a religious idea, an odd choice for justifying a technoscientific enterprise and perhaps not suited to serve as a long-term rationale for space exploration.

As the historian Stephen Pyne has said, exploration is a cultural invention:

> There is frequently a tendency to generalize "exploration" into a universal expression of the human gene, to equate "discovery" with "curiosity" or with "human spirit." That it is, but not uniquely…. Exploration…appears to be a cultural invention…. Its vitality as an institution depends on the vitality of the whole civilization with which it interacts. To survey the motives for exploration is to survey all the motives that animate a thriving civilization….
>
> The point is that exploration must share and participate in a moral universe with its civilization. This is not a question of purpose so much as legitimacy. In this sense exploration is a shared act of faith. It reinforces and reinterprets in updated garb myths, beliefs, and archetypes basic to its originating civilization.[1]

Advocates of colonizing other planets argue that humanity is destined to extend its presence into the solar system and beyond, that settling other planets and mining extraterrestrial resources will benefit all of humankind. Critics claim that colonizing other planets will likely extend our Earthly problems—resource depletion, unequal distribution of wealth, conflict, and violence—to other worlds, that extraterrestrial settlement and resource exploitation will benefit only a small elite, leaving the poor and disenfranchised on a ruined Earth.

What value does humanity glean from space exploration? What is the real value of space exploration in the 21st century? Does it enrich human

---

1. Stephen J. Pyne, "The Third Great Age of Discovery," in *The Scientific and Historical Rationales for Solar System Exploration*, ed. Carl Sagan and Stephen J. Pyne (Washington, DC: Space Policy Institute, 1988), pp. 14, 18.

existence? Fulfill a cultural imperative? Offer critical additions to knowledge? Enhance economic strength and technological competitiveness? Improve international relations? Advance education? Improve the quality of life? Feed spiritual needs? How can space exploration best benefit humanity in this century and beyond? These are questions worth pondering as we continue to explore space.

For the foreseeable future, robotic solar system exploration will be delving deeper into the histories of solar system bodies—the Moon, Mars, Venus, dwarf planets, asteroids, the giant planets Jupiter and Saturn and their moons.... Robotic missions will intensify their investigations of potentially habitable environments beyond Earth—top candidates now include Mars, Europa, Titan, and Enceladus. And the search for evidence of past or present life on Mars will continue, building on advances in the identification of biosignatures and the development of life-detection technologies. There is no doubt that the next 50 years of solar system exploration will be as fascinating as the last.

APPENDIX

Program for "Solar System Exploration@50," 25–26 October 2012

SOLAR SYSTEM EXPLORATION @50
at the Lockheed Martin Global Vision Center,
2121 Crystal Drive, Arlington, VA

THURSDAY, 25 OCTOBER 2012

8:30 a.m.

OPENING REMARKS: **James H. Crocker**, Vice President and General Manager, Civil Space, Lockheed Martin Space Systems Company

9:00 a.m.

KEYNOTE SPEECH: **Peter Westwick** (University of Southern California): *Exploring the Solar System: Who Has Done It, How, and Why?*

9:45 a.m.

PANEL 1: POLITICS AND POLICY IN THE CONDUCT OF SOLAR SYSTEM EXPLORATION

PANEL CHAIR: **Marcia Smith** (Space and Technology Policy Group)

Dwayne Day (National Research Council): *The National Research Council's Role in the American Planetary Exploration Program*

Roger Handberg (University of Central Florida): *The Politics of Pure Space Science, the Essential Tension, Human Spaceflight's Impact on Scientific Exploration*

Jason W. Callahan (The Tauri Group): *Funding Planetary Science: History and Political Economy*

John M. Logsdon (George Washington University) and **Andre Bormanis** (Independent Writer/Producer): *The Survival Crisis of the Planetary Program*

11:45 a.m.

LUNCH KEYNOTE SPEAKER: **James L. Green** (NASA): *NASA's Solar System Exploration Paradigm: The First Fifty Years and a Look at the Next Fifty*

1:00 p.m.

PANEL 2: THE LURE OF THE RED PLANET

PANEL CHAIR: **Janet Vertesi** (Princeton University)

Richard W. Zurek (JPL): *Mars After 50 Years of Space Exploration: Then, Now, and Beyond*

David Grinspoon (Denver Museum of Nature & Science): *Evolving Concepts of Planetary Habitability in the Age of Planetary Exploration*

Erik M. Conway (JPL): *Dreaming of Mars Sample Return, from Viking to the Mars Science Laboratory*

W. Henry Lambright (Syracuse University): *NASA, Big Science, and Mars Exploration: Critical Decisions from Goldin to Bolden*

3:15 p.m.

PANEL 3: PUBLIC PERCEPTIONS, PRIORITIES, AND SOLAR SYSTEM EXPLORATION

PANEL CHAIR: **Heidi Hammel** (Space Science Institute)

Linda Billings (George Washington University): *Survivor(?): The Story of* S. Mitis *on the Moon*

William R. Macauley (Freie Universität Berlin): *"Instant Science": Space Probes, Planetary Exploration, and Televisual Media*

Laura Delgado López (Institute for Global Environmental Strategies): *Killer Asteroids: Popular Depictions and Public Policy Influence*

Giny Cheong (George Mason University): *Voyager: Exploring Through the Public Eye*

5:30 p.m.

Solar System Exploration @50 Reception (Hosted by Lockheed Martin)

FRIDAY, 26 OCTOBER 2012

8:30 a.m.

KEYNOTE SPEECH: **Wesley T. Huntress, Jr.** (NASA Advisory Committee), and **Mikhail Marov** (Keldysh Institute): *First on the Moon, Venus, and Mars: The Soviet Planetary Exploration Enterprise*

9:30 a.m.

PANEL 4: EXPLORING THE OUTER SOLAR SYSTEM

PANEL CHAIR: **Ralph McNutt** (Applied Physics Laboratory)

Torrence V. Johnson (JPL): *Outer Solar System Exploration: An Archetype of the Scientific Method*

Arturo Russo (University of Palermo): *Europe's Rendezvous with Titan: The European Space Agency's Contribution in the Cassini-Huygens Mission to the Saturnian System*

Robert Pappalardo (JPL): *Revealing Europa's Ocean*

11:30 a.m.

Lunch and conversation

1:00 p.m.

PANEL 5: INSTITUTIONAL ARRANGEMENTS IN SOLAR SYSTEM EXPLORATION

PANEL CHAIR: **Joan Johnson-Freese** (U.S. Naval War College)

J.D. Burke (JPL): *Foundations of Solar System Exploration at JPL: How the First Mariners and Rangers Built Them*

John Sarkissian (CSIRO): *Mariner 2 and the CSIRO Parkes Radio Telescope: Fifty Years of International Collaboration*

Michael Neufeld (National Air and Space Museum): *Transforming Solar System Exploration: The Applied Physics Laboratory and the Origins of the Discovery Program, 1989–1993*

Petar Markovski (University of Oklahoma): *International Cooperation in Solar System Exploration: The Cases of Ulysses and Giotto*

3:15 p.m.

PANEL 6: ROUNDTABLE—FROM THE PAST TO THE FUTURE

MODERATOR: **Andrew Chaikin** (Independent Space Historian)

Glenn E. Bugos (Ames Research Center): *Precursor Missions: The Science of What Comes Next*

Amy Paige Kaminski (NASA): *Faster, Better, Cheaper: A Sociotechnical Perspective on Programmatic Choice, Success, and Failure in NASA's System Exploration Program*

G. Scott Hubbard (Stanford University): *Exploring Mars: Following the Water*

Chas Beichman (Caltech): *The Search for and Study of Extra-Solar Planets: Extending Planetary Science into the Realm of Classical Astronomy*

ACKNOWLEDGMENTS

THANKS ARE DUE TO MANY PEOPLE who made this symposium possible, starting with members of the organizing committee: then–NASA Chief Historian Bill Barry; Roger Launius; Nadine Andreassen, Kristen Erickson, Steve Garber, and Steve Williams of NASA Headquarters; and Gregg Vane of the Jet Propulsion Laboratory. Lockheed Martin Space Systems Company generously agreed to host the symposium at its Arlington, Virginia, conference center. Thanks are also due to our very able panel chairs for the conference: Marcia Smith, Janet Vertesi, Heidi Hammel, Ralph NcNutt, Joan Johnson-Freese, and Andrew Chaikin.

In the NASA History Division, thanks to the late NASA Chief Archivist Jane H. Odom, her successor Robyn Rodgers, and archivists Colin Fries and Elizabeth Suckow for their help finding key documents. Interns Claire Smrt and Gwendolyn Rak went above and beyond the call of duty by carefully formatting the manuscript while Andrew Parco and David Skogerboe greatly helped by selecting photos; Catherine Baldwin graciously oversaw all their work. Special thanks to Yvette Smith, who edited an early version of this manuscript. In the Headquarters Photo Library, Gwen Pitman and Connie Moore provided a number of key images in their usual friendly, helpful, and professional ways. Thanks to NASA Acting Chief Historian Brian Odom for shepherding these proceedings to publication.

On the production side, the Communications Support Services Center (CSSC) at NASA Headquarters did its customary exemplary, professional job to bring this work from a manuscript to a published book. In particular, Jennifer Way, Shawna Byrd, Lisa Jirousek, and Andrew Cooke expertly copyedited the manuscript; designer Michele Ostovar skillfully laid out the book and created the index; and Tun Hla carefully oversaw the printing.

My apologies to anyone I've forgotten.

ABOUT THE AUTHORS

LINDA BILLINGS is a consultant to NASA's Astrobiology Program and Planetary Defense Coordination Office in the Planetary Science Program Office of the Science Mission Directorate at NASA Headquarters in Washington, DC. She also is Director of Communication with the Center for Integrative STEM Education at the National Institute of Aerospace in Hampton, Virginia. She earned her Ph.D. in mass communication from Indiana University. Her research interests include science and risk communication, social studies of science, and the rhetoric of science and space. Her papers have been published by the NASA History Division; *Space Policy*; *Acta Astronautica*; *Scientific American*; the *Bulletin of Science, Technology, and Society*; *Space News*; and *Advances in Space Research*. She was elected a fellow of the American Association for the Advancement of Science in 2009.

JAMES D. BURKE is an alumnus of Caltech and a former U.S. naval aviator, employed at the Jet Propulsion Laboratory from 1949 to his retirement in 2001. In retirement, he is active in the Planetary Society, the Space Generation Advisory Council, and the International Space University (ISU), where he has been a faculty member in each ISU Space Studies Program since 1989. Burke's main professional interest is in the exploration and settlement of the Moon. He is a fellow of the British Interplanetary Society and a member of the American Geophysical Union, the Division for Planetary Sciences of the American Astronomical Society, the American Institute of Aeronautics and Astronautics, and the European Geosciences Union. Married since 1950 to his wife, Caroline, with five children and three grandchildren, he is a pilot, lifelong yachtsman, and determined advocate of educating young people toward enjoying learning and achievement.

JASON CALLAHAN has worked as a science, technology, and policy analyst in Washington, DC, for over a decade. He received a master's degree in international science and technology policy from the George Washington University and a master's degree in history and sociology of technology and science from the Georgia Institute of Technology.

GINY CHEONG is a senior analyst at the U.S. Government Accountability Office. She has a master's degree in history from George Mason University and a master's in digital sociology from Virginia Commonwealth University. She did further graduate research on NASA and public communication of space science through mass media and popular culture from the 1980s through the 2000s. She also worked for 10 years at NASA Headquarters, supporting the NASA History Program Office and the NASA Academy for Program, Project and Engineering Leadership (APPEL).

ERIK CONWAY is the historian at the Jet Propulsion Laboratory. His duties include research and writing, conducting oral histories, and contributing to the Lab's historical collections. Before JPL, he worked as a contract historian at Langley Research Center. Conway enjoys studying the historical interaction between national politics, scientific research, and technological change. For his current research in robotic Mars exploration, he analyzes the effects of changing policies on project management and planetary science. His book *History of Atmospheric Science at NASA* was published by Johns Hopkins University Press in 2008. He is also a coauthor on two articles on the history of climate science: "From Chicken Little to Dr. Pangloss: William Nierenberg, Global Warming, and the Social Deconstruction of Scientific Knowledge" (with Naomi Oreskes and Matthew Shindell) in *Historical Studies in the Natural Sciences* (2008) and "Challenging Knowledge: How Climate Science Became a Victim of the Cold War," (with Naomi Oreskes) in *Agnotology: The Making and Unmaking of Ignorance* (2008).

LAURA DELGADO LÓPEZ is an analyst in the NASA Science Mission Directorate's Policy Branch, which provides policy support to the Directorate's 90-plus science missions. Prior to joining NASA, she was an advocacy lead at Harris Corporation's Space and Intelligence Systems segment, a project manager for the Secure World Foundation, and the Earth Observations Associate at the Institute for Global Environmental Strategies. She is a former editor-in-chief of the peer-reviewed journal *Space Policy* and serves on the Advisory Committee of the Secure World Foundation. Her research has focused on issues related to Earth observations, space politics and policy, international cooperation, space security and sustainability, and public opinion. Her work has been featured in *Space Policy*, *Astropolitics*, and *Space News* and has led to media appearances in major Spanish-speaking media outlets, including CNN en Español.

KRISTEN J. ERICKSON, selected as NASA's Director for Science Engagement and Partnerships, oversees the restructuring of science education and communications for NASA's Science Mission Directorate. From 2009 to 2014, she led science engagement efforts for NASA's Planetary Science. Division. Successes included the 2012 Mars Curiosity Landing awareness campaign, the 2012 Transit of Venus engagement, and other solar system mission activities. From 2006 to 2009, she led NASA's Strategic Communications effort, including leading NASA's 50th anniversary and Apollo 40th anniversary celebrations. Since starting her career at NASA Johnson Space Center, she also has held leadership positions in the Space Shuttle Program, Office of Biological and Physical Research, and various staff offices. She holds degrees from Texas A&M University and Harvard University.

JAMES L. GREEN has been NASA's Chief Scientist since 2018. He received his Ph.D. in space physics from the University of Iowa in 1979 and began working at NASA's Marshall Space Flight Center. In 1985, he moved to Goddard Space Flight Center, where he worked until 2006, when he became the Director of the Planetary Science Division at NASA Headquarters. Under his leadership, more than a dozen planetary missions have been successfully executed, including the New Horizons spacecraft flyby of Pluto, the MESSENGER spacecraft to Mercury, the Juno spacecraft to Jupiter, the dual Gravity Recovery and Interior Laboratory (GRAIL) spacecraft to the Moon, the Dawn spacecraft to Vesta and Ceres, and the landing of the Curiosity rover and the InSight lander on Mars.

ROGER HANDBERG is a professor in the Political Science Department of the University of Central Florida, specializing in space policy, national security policy, and judicial politics. He also teaches courses dealing with government policies in science and technology, economic and business policy, and American security policy—particularly military space policy and ballistic missile defense. He has published 9 books and more than 161 articles and book chapters and has presented over 130 papers. His most recent books include *Chinese Space Policy: A Study in Domestic and International Politics* (2006), *International Space Commerce: Building from Scratch* (2012), and *Reinventing NASA and the Quest for Outer Space* (2003).

W. HENRY (HARRY) LAMBRIGHT is professor of political science and public administration and director of the Science and Technology Policy Program of the Center for Environmental Policy and Administration in the Maxwell School of Citizenship and Public Affairs at Syracuse University in Syracuse,

New York. His research interests include federal decision-making on space technology, environmental policy, transboundary issues, national security, the integration of science with policy, ecosystem management, biotechnology, technology transfer, and leadership issues. Lambright has written scores of articles and has written or edited nine books, including *Powering Apollo: James E. Webb of NASA* (1995). His most recent book, which he edited, is *Why Mars: NASA and the Politics of Space Exploration* (2014). He earned his Ph.D. from Columbia University in 1966.

PETAR MARKOVSKI received his bachelor of science in astrophysics from the Lyman Briggs School of Michigan State University and his master of arts in the history of science at the University of Oklahoma. His master's thesis was titled "A Comparative History of Hipparcos and FAME: Space Astrometry in the 20th Century." He is working on his doctoral dissertation, titled "The Globalization of Space Science and Technology: The History of International and Transnational Cooperation at NASA and ESA." His research interests include the history of technology, the history of modern astronomy, and the history of the Space Age and modern Europe. His past research projects have included a historical examination of attempts by NASA and the European Space Agency (ESA) to develop and launch astrometric observing satellites. An avid gamer, he enjoys games of the digital, board, and card varieties.

ARTURO RUSSO is a former professor of the history of physics at the University of Palermo, Italy. His research interest is the history of 20th-century physics. He has published books and essays on the history of quantum physics, the science-industry relationship in Italy and the United States between the two World Wars, the history of cosmic-ray physics, the history of particle physics at the European Organization for Nuclear Research (CERN), and the history of space research and of space telecommunications in Europe. He was involved in the European Space Agency History Project.

JOHN SARKISSIAN is an operations scientist at the Commonwealth Scientific and Industrial Research Organization's (CSIRO's) Parkes Radio Observatory in Australia. His main responsibilities are operations and systems development at the radio telescope. He is a member of the Parkes Pulsar Timing Array (PPTA) team, which is endeavoring to use precision pulsar timing to make the first direct detection of gravitational waves. He is also a member of the small, informal team searching for the missing Apollo 11 slow-scan TV tapes. He came to Parkes in 1996 to support the Galileo mission to Jupiter. He managed Galileo tracking operations at the observatory and performed one-third of the daily tracking duties. He has received NASA Group Achievement Awards for his work on the Parkes Radio Telescope X-band Upgrade Task Team in 2004 and the Huygens Probe Earth Detection Team in 2005. He also received official NASA commendations for his Galileo support in 1997 and for the search for the missing Apollo 11 tapes in 2010.

PETER WESTWICK is an adjunct professor of history at the University of Southern California (USC) and director of the Aerospace History Project at the Huntington-USC Institute on California and the West. He received his bachelor of arts in physics and Ph.D. in history from the University of California at Berkeley. He is the author of *Into the Black: JPL and the American Space Program, 1976–2004* (2006), which won the American Institute of Aeronautics and Astronautics Gardner-Lasser Aerospace History Literature Award and the American Astronautical Society's Eugene Emme Astronautical Literature Award; and *The National Labs: Science in an American System, 1947–1974* (2003), which won the Book Prize of the Forum for the History of Science in America. He is also editor of *Blue Sky Metropolis: The Aerospace Century in Southern California* (2012), which the LA Public Library named to its Best Non-Fiction of 2012. Most recently he coauthored, with Peter Neushul, *The World in the Curl: An Unconventional History of Surfing* (2013), a *Los Angeles Times* bestseller. He is currently working on a history of the National Academy of Sciences and a history of the Strategic Defense Initiative.

ACRONYMS

AAM	Apollo Astronomy Mount
AAS	American Astronomical Society
ACP	asset contention period
AEST	Australian Eastern Standard Time
AIAA	American Institute of Aeronautics and Astronautics
AMS-02	Alpha Magnetic Spectrometer-02
AMSAT	Radio Amateur Satellite Corporation
APL	Applied Physics Laboratory
APPEL	Academy for Program, Project and Engineering Leadership
ASI	Italian Space Agency
AU	Astronomical Units
AWG	Astronomy Working Group
AXAF	Advanced X-ray Astrophysics Facility
bps	bits per second
Caltech	California Institute of Technology
CDSCC	Canberra Deep Space Communication Complex
CERN	European Organization for Nuclear Research
CGI	computer-generated imagery
CNES	Centre National d'Études Spatiales, or National Centre for Space Studies
COMPLEX	Committee on Planetary and Lunar Exploration
CONTOUR	COmet Nucleus TOUR
CRAF	comet rendezvous and asteroid flyby
CSIR	Council for Scientific and Industrial Research
CSIRO	Commonwealth Scientific and Industrial Research Organisation
DAMIEN	Detecting and Mitigating the Impact of Earth-Bound Near-Earth Objects
DART	Double Asteroid Redirection Test
dBm	decibel-milliwatt
DOD	Department of Defense
DOE	Department of Energy
DSIF	Deep Space Instrumentation Facility

DSN	Deep Space Network
DWE	Doppler Wind Experiment
ED	Department of Education
EDL	entry, descent, and landing
ELV	expendable launch vehicle
ERTS	Earth Resources Technology Satellite
ESA	European Space Agency
ESOC	European Space Operations Centre
ESRO	European Space Research Organisation
EVA	extravehicular activity
FBC	faster, better, cheaper
FF&P	Freeman Fox and Partners
FY	fiscal year
GDP	Gross Domestic Product
GPRA	Government Performance and Results Act
GRAIL	Gravity Recovery and Interior Laboratory
GRT	Giant Radio Telescope
HMEC	Historical Mars Exploration Collection
HRC	Historical Reference Collection
HRMS	High Resolution Microwave Survey
IAWN	International Asteroid Warning Network
ICRP	Independent Comprehensive Review Panel
ICSU	International Council for Science/International Council of Scientific Unions
IGY	International Geophysical Year
IKI	Space Research Institute of the Russian Academy of Sciences
InSight	Interior Exploration using Seismic Investigations, Geodesy, and Heat Transport
ISEE-3/ICE	International Sun-Earth Explorer-3/International Cometary Explorer
ISPM	International Solar Polar Mission
ISRO	Indian Space Research Organization
ISS	International Space Station
ISU	International Space University
IUS	Inertial Upper Stage
JAXA	Japan Aerospace Exploration Agency
JIVE	Joint Institute for VLBI in Europe
JPL	Jet Propulsion Laboratory
JSC	Johnson Space Center
JUICE	JUpiter ICy moons Explorer
JWST	James Webb Space Telescope

KSC	Kennedy Space Center
LA	Los Angeles
LADEE	Lunar Atmosphere and Dust Environment Explorer
LAPD	Los Angeles Police Department
LCROSS	Lunar CRater Observation and Sensing Satellite
LDEF	Long-Duration Exposure Facility
LEO	low-Earth orbit
LM	Lunar Module
LMSS	Lockheed Martin Space Systems
LPAC	Launching Programs Advisory Committee
LRL	Lunar Receiving Laboratory
LRO	Lunar Reconnaissance Orbiter
MAN	Maschinenfabrik Augsburg Nurnberg
MAVEN	Mars Atmosphere and Volatile EvolutioN
MAX-C	Mars Astrobiology Explorer-Cacher
MCO	Mars Climate Orbiter
ME	master equatorial
MEMS	microelectromechanical systems
MER	Mars Exploration Rover
MESSENGER	MErcury Surface, Space ENvironment, GEochemistry and Ranging
MIT	Massachusetts Institute of Technology
MOM	Ministry of General Machine Building
MOU	memorandum of understanding
MPIAT	Mars Program Independent Assessment Team
MPL	Mars Polar Lander
MRO	Mars Reconnaissance Orbiter
MSC	Manned Spacecraft Center
MSFN	Manned Space Flight Network
MSL	Mars Science Laboratory; Mars Smart Lander
MSR	Mars sample return
NAC	NASA Advisory Council
NASA	National Aeronautics and Space Administration
NEO	near-Earth object
NEOO	Near-Earth Object Observations
NEOWISE	Near-Earth Object Wide-field Infrared Survey Explorer
NIH	National Institutes of Health
NRAO	National Radio Astronomy Observatory
NRC	National Research Council
NRL	Naval Research Laboratory
NSF	National Science Foundation

NSTC	National Science and Technology Council
OMB	Office of Management and Budget
OOE	out of ecliptic plane
OSIRIS-REx	Origins, Spectral Interpretation, Resource Identification, Security-Regolith Explorer
OSS	Office of Space Science
OSSA	Office of Space Science and Applications
OVRO	Owens Valley Radio Observatory
PASA	*Publications of the Astronomical Society of Australia*
PDCO	Planetary Defense Coordination Office
PHS	Public Health Service
PPTA	Parkes Pulsar Timing Array
PQ	Planetary Quarantine
PSIG	Project Science Integration Group
R&D	research and development
RDF	radio direction finding
RSR	radio science receiver
RSRP	Rocket and Satellite Research Panel
RTG	radioisotope thermoelectric generator
SEI	Space Exploration Initiative
SELENE	Selenological and Engineering Explorer
SESAC	Space and Earth Science Advisory Committee
SETI	Search for Extraterrestrial Intelligence
SLS	Space Launch System
SMART-1	Small Missions for Advanced Research in Technology
SMEX	Small Explorer
SMPAG	Space Mission Planning Advisory Group
SPC	Science Policy Committee
SSAC	Space Science Advisory Committee
SSB	Space Science Board
SSEC	Solar System Exploration Committee
SSWG	Solar System Working Group
SWG	Science Working Group
TED	Technology, Entertainment, and Design
TRE	Telecommunications Research Establishment
UARRP	Upper Atmosphere Rocket Research Panel
UHF	ultra-high-frequency
USC	University of Southern California
VLBI	very long baseline interferometry
VSE	Vision for Space Exploration
WIA	Women in Aerospace

THE NASA HISTORY SERIES

REFERENCE WORKS, NASA SP-4000

Grimwood, James M. *Project Mercury: A Chronology.* NASA SP-4001, 1963.

Grimwood, James M., and Barton C. Hacker, with Peter J. Vorzimmer. *Project Gemini Technology and Operations: A Chronology.* NASA SP-4002, 1969.

Link, Mae Mills. *Space Medicine in Project Mercury.* NASA SP-4003, 1965.

Astronautics and Aeronautics, 1963: Chronology of Science, Technology, and Policy. NASA SP-4004, 1964.

Astronautics and Aeronautics, 1964: Chronology of Science, Technology, and Policy. NASA SP-4005, 1965.

Astronautics and Aeronautics, 1965: Chronology of Science, Technology, and Policy. NASA SP-4006, 1966.

Astronautics and Aeronautics, 1966: Chronology of Science, Technology, and Policy. NASA SP-4007, 1967.

Astronautics and Aeronautics, 1967: Chronology of Science, Technology, and Policy. NASA SP-4008, 1968.

Ertel, Ivan D., and Mary Louise Morse. *The Apollo Spacecraft: A Chronology, Volume I, Through November 7, 1962.* NASA SP-4009, 1969.

Morse, Mary Louise, and Jean Kernahan Bays. *The Apollo Spacecraft: A Chronology, Volume II, November 8, 1962–September 30, 1964.* NASA SP-4009, 1973.

Brooks, Courtney G., and Ivan D. Ertel. *The Apollo Spacecraft: A Chronology, Volume III, October 1, 1964–January 20, 1966.* NASA SP-4009, 1973.

Ertel, Ivan D., and Roland W. Newkirk, with Courtney G. Brooks. *The Apollo Spacecraft: A Chronology, Volume IV, January 21, 1966–July 13, 1974.* NASA SP-4009, 1978.

Astronautics and Aeronautics, 1968: Chronology of Science, Technology, and Policy. NASA SP-4010, 1969.

Newkirk, Roland W., and Ivan D. Ertel, with Courtney G. Brooks. *Skylab: A Chronology.* NASA SP-4011, 1977.

Van Nimmen, Jane, and Leonard C. Bruno, with Robert L. Rosholt. *NASA Historical Data Book, Volume I: NASA Resources, 1958–1968.* NASA SP-4012, 1976; rep. ed. 1988.

Ezell, Linda Neuman. *NASA Historical Data Book, Volume II: Programs and Projects, 1958–1968.* NASA SP-4012, 1988.

Ezell, Linda Neuman. *NASA Historical Data Book, Volume III: Programs and Projects, 1969–1978.* NASA SP-4012, 1988.

Gawdiak, Ihor, with Helen Fedor. *NASA Historical Data Book, Volume IV: NASA Resources, 1969–1978.* NASA SP-4012, 1994.

Rumerman, Judy A. *NASA Historical Data Book, Volume V: NASA Launch Systems, Space Transportation, Human Spaceflight, and Space Science, 1979–1988.* NASA SP-4012, 1999.

Rumerman, Judy A. *NASA Historical Data Book, Volume VI: NASA Space Applications, Aeronautics and Space Research and Technology, Tracking and Data Acquisition/Support Operations, Commercial Programs, and Resources, 1979–1988.* NASA SP-4012, 1999.

Rumerman, Judy A. *NASA Historical Data Book, Volume VII: NASA Launch Systems, Space Transportation, Human Spaceflight, and Space Science, 1989–1998.* NASA SP-2009-4012, 2009.

Rumerman, Judy A. *NASA Historical Data Book, Volume VIII: NASA Earth Science and Space Applications, Aeronautics, Technology, and Exploration, Tracking and Data Acquisition/Space Operations, Facilities and Resources, 1989–1998.* NASA SP-2012-4012, 2012.

No SP-4013.

Astronautics and Aeronautics, 1969: Chronology of Science, Technology, and Policy. NASA SP-4014, 1970.

Astronautics and Aeronautics, 1970: Chronology of Science, Technology, and Policy. NASA SP-4015, 1972.

Astronautics and Aeronautics, 1971: Chronology of Science, Technology, and Policy. NASA SP-4016, 1972.

Astronautics and Aeronautics, 1972: Chronology of Science, Technology, and Policy. NASA SP-4017, 1974.

Astronautics and Aeronautics, 1973: Chronology of Science, Technology, and Policy. NASA SP-4018, 1975.

Astronautics and Aeronautics, 1974: Chronology of Science, Technology, and Policy. NASA SP-4019, 1977.

Astronautics and Aeronautics, 1975: Chronology of Science, Technology, and Policy. NASA SP-4020, 1979.

Astronautics and Aeronautics, 1976: Chronology of Science, Technology, and Policy. NASA SP-4021, 1984.

Astronautics and Aeronautics, 1977: Chronology of Science, Technology, and Policy. NASA SP-4022, 1986.

Astronautics and Aeronautics, 1978: Chronology of Science, Technology, and Policy. NASA SP-4023, 1986.

Astronautics and Aeronautics, 1979–1984: Chronology of Science, Technology, and Policy. NASA SP-4024, 1988.

Astronautics and Aeronautics, 1985: Chronology of Science, Technology, and Policy. NASA SP-4025, 1990.

Noordung, Hermann. *The Problem of Space Travel: The Rocket Motor.* Edited by Ernst Stuhlinger and J. D. Hunley, with Jennifer Garland. NASA SP-4026, 1995.

Gawdiak, Ihor Y., Ramon J. Miro, and Sam Stueland. *Astronautics and Aeronautics, 1986–1990: A Chronology.* NASA SP-4027, 1997.

Gawdiak, Ihor Y., and Charles Shetland. *Astronautics and Aeronautics, 1991–1995: A Chronology.* NASA SP-2000-4028, 2000.

Orloff, Richard W. *Apollo by the Numbers: A Statistical Reference.* NASA SP-2000-4029, 2000.

Lewis, Marieke, and Ryan Swanson. *Astronautics and Aeronautics: A Chronology, 1996–2000.* NASA SP-2009-4030, 2009.

Ivey, William Noel, and Marieke Lewis. *Astronautics and Aeronautics: A Chronology, 2001–2005.* NASA SP-2010-4031, 2010.

Buchalter, Alice R., and William Noel Ivey. *Astronautics and Aeronautics: A Chronology, 2006.* NASA SP-2011-4032, 2010.

Lewis, Marieke. *Astronautics and Aeronautics: A Chronology, 2007.* NASA SP-2011-4033, 2011.

Lewis, Marieke. *Astronautics and Aeronautics: A Chronology, 2008.* NASA SP-2012-4034, 2012.

Lewis, Marieke. *Astronautics and Aeronautics: A Chronology, 2009.* NASA SP-2012-4035, 2012.

Flattery, Meaghan. *Astronautics and Aeronautics: A Chronology, 2010.* NASA SP-2013-4037, 2014.

Siddiqi, Asif A. *Beyond Earth: A Chronicle of Deep Space Exploration, 1958–2016.* NASA SP-2018-4041, 2018.

MANAGEMENT HISTORIES, NASA SP-4100

Rosholt, Robert L. *An Administrative History of NASA, 1958–1963.* NASA SP-4101, 1966.

Levine, Arnold S. *Managing NASA in the Apollo Era.* NASA SP-4102, 1982.

Roland, Alex. *Model Research: The National Advisory Committee for Aeronautics, 1915–1958.* NASA SP-4103, 1985.

Fries, Sylvia D. *NASA Engineers and the Age of Apollo.* NASA SP-4104, 1992.

Glennan, T. Keith. *The Birth of NASA: The Diary of T. Keith Glennan.* Edited by J. D. Hunley. NASA SP-4105, 1993.

Seamans, Robert C. *Aiming at Targets: The Autobiography of Robert C. Seamans.* NASA SP-4106, 1996.

Garber, Stephen J., ed. *Looking Backward, Looking Forward: Forty Years of Human Spaceflight Symposium.* NASA SP-2002-4107, 2002.

Mallick, Donald L., with Peter W. Merlin. *The Smell of Kerosene: A Test Pilot's Odyssey.* NASA SP-4108, 2003.

Iliff, Kenneth W., and Curtis L. Peebles. *From Runway to Orbit: Reflections of a NASA Engineer.* NASA SP-2004-4109, 2004.

Chertok, Boris. *Rockets and People, Volume I.* NASA SP-2005-4110, 2005.

Chertok, Boris. *Rockets and People: Creating a Rocket Industry, Volume II.* NASA SP-2006-4110, 2006.

Chertok, Boris. *Rockets and People: Hot Days of the Cold War, Volume III.* NASA SP-2009-4110, 2009.

Chertok, Boris. *Rockets and People: The Moon Race, Volume IV.* NASA SP-2011-4110, 2011.

Laufer, Alexander, Todd Post, and Edward Hoffman. *Shared Voyage: Learning and Unlearning from Remarkable Projects.* NASA SP-2005-4111, 2005.

Dawson, Virginia P., and Mark D. Bowles. *Realizing the Dream of Flight: Biographical Essays in Honor of the Centennial of Flight, 1903–2003.* NASA SP-2005-4112, 2005.

Mudgway, Douglas J. *William H. Pickering: America's Deep Space Pioneer.* NASA SP-2008-4113, 2008.

Wright, Rebecca, Sandra Johnson, and Steven J. Dick. *NASA at 50: Interviews with NASA's Senior Leadership.* NASA SP-2012-4114, 2012.

PROJECT HISTORIES, NASA SP-4200

Swenson, Loyd S., Jr., James M. Grimwood, and Charles C. Alexander. *This New Ocean: A History of Project Mercury.* NASA SP-4201, 1966; rep. ed. 1999.

Green, Constance McLaughlin, and Milton Lomask. *Vanguard: A History.* NASA SP-4202, 1970; rep. ed. Smithsonian Institution Press, 1971.

Hacker, Barton C., and James M. Grimwood. *On the Shoulders of Titans: A History of Project Gemini.* NASA SP-4203, 1977; rep. ed. 2002.

Benson, Charles D., and William Barnaby Faherty. *Moonport: A History of Apollo Launch Facilities and Operations.* NASA SP-4204, 1978.

Brooks, Courtney G., James M. Grimwood, and Loyd S. Swenson, Jr. *Chariots for Apollo: A History of Manned Lunar Spacecraft.* NASA SP-4205, 1979.

Bilstein, Roger E. *Stages to Saturn: A Technological History of the Apollo/Saturn Launch Vehicles.* NASA SP-4206, 1980 and 1996.

No SP-4207.

Compton, W. David, and Charles D. Benson. *Living and Working in Space: A History of Skylab*. NASA SP-4208, 1983.

Ezell, Edward Clinton, and Linda Neuman Ezell. *The Partnership: A History of the Apollo-Soyuz Test Project*. NASA SP-4209, 1978.

Hall, R. Cargill. *Lunar Impact: A History of Project Ranger*. NASA SP-4210, 1977.

Newell, Homer E. *Beyond the Atmosphere: Early Years of Space Science*. NASA SP-4211, 1980.

Ezell, Edward Clinton, and Linda Neuman Ezell. *On Mars: Exploration of the Red Planet, 1958–1978*. NASA SP-4212, 1984.

Pitts, John A. *The Human Factor: Biomedicine in the Manned Space Program to 1980*. NASA SP-4213, 1985.

Compton, W. David. *Where No Man Has Gone Before: A History of Apollo Lunar Exploration Missions*. NASA SP-4214, 1989.

Naugle, John E. *First Among Equals: The Selection of NASA Space Science Experiments*. NASA SP-4215, 1991.

Wallace, Lane E. *Airborne Trailblazer: Two Decades with NASA Langley's 737 Flying Laboratory*. NASA SP-4216, 1994.

Butrica, Andrew J., ed. *Beyond the Ionosphere: Fifty Years of Satellite Communications*. NASA SP-4217, 1997.

Butrica, Andrew J. *To See the Unseen: A History of Planetary Radar Astronomy*. NASA SP-4218, 1996.

Mack, Pamela E., ed. *From Engineering Science to Big Science: The NACA and NASA Collier Trophy Research Project Winners*. NASA SP-4219, 1998.

Reed, R. Dale. *Wingless Flight: The Lifting Body Story*. NASA SP-4220, 1998.

Heppenheimer, T. A. *The Space Shuttle Decision: NASA's Search for a Reusable Space Vehicle*. NASA SP-4221, 1999.

Hunley, J. D., ed. *Toward Mach 2: The Douglas D-558 Program*. NASA SP-4222, 1999.

Swanson, Glen E., ed. *"Before This Decade Is Out..." Personal Reflections on the Apollo Program*. NASA SP-4223, 1999.

Tomayko, James E. *Computers Take Flight: A History of NASA's Pioneering Digital Fly-By-Wire Project*. NASA SP-4224, 2000.

Morgan, Clay. *Shuttle-Mir: The United States and Russia Share History's Highest Stage*. NASA SP-2001-4225, 2001.

Leary, William M. *"We Freeze to Please": A History of NASA's Icing Research Tunnel and the Quest for Safety*. NASA SP-2002-4226, 2002.

Mudgway, Douglas J. *Uplink-Downlink: A History of the Deep Space Network, 1957–1997*. NASA SP-2001-4227, 2001.

No SP-4228 or SP-4229.

Dawson, Virginia P., and Mark D. Bowles. *Taming Liquid Hydrogen: The Centaur Upper Stage Rocket, 1958–2002.* NASA SP-2004-4230, 2004.

Meltzer, Michael. *Mission to Jupiter: A History of the Galileo Project.* NASA SP-2007-4231, 2007.

Heppenheimer, T. A. *Facing the Heat Barrier: A History of Hypersonics.* NASA SP-2007-4232, 2007.

Tsiao, Sunny. *"Read You Loud and Clear!" The Story of NASA's Spaceflight Tracking and Data Network.* NASA SP-2007-4233, 2007.

Meltzer, Michael. *When Biospheres Collide: A History of NASA's Planetary Protection Programs.* NASA SP-2011-4234, 2011.

Gainor, Christopher. *Not Yet Imagined: A Study of Hubble Space Telescope Operations.* NASA SP-2020-4237, 2020.

CENTER HISTORIES, NASA SP-4300

Rosenthal, Alfred. *Venture into Space: Early Years of Goddard Space Flight Center.* NASA SP-4301, 1985.

Hartman, Edwin P. *Adventures in Research: A History of Ames Research Center, 1940–1965.* NASA SP-4302, 1970.

Hallion, Richard P. *On the Frontier: Flight Research at Dryden, 1946–1981.* NASA SP-4303, 1984.

Muenger, Elizabeth A. *Searching the Horizon: A History of Ames Research Center, 1940–1976.* NASA SP-4304, 1985.

Hansen, James R. *Engineer in Charge: A History of the Langley Aeronautical Laboratory, 1917–1958.* NASA SP-4305, 1987.

Dawson, Virginia P. *Engines and Innovation: Lewis Laboratory and American Propulsion Technology.* NASA SP-4306, 1991.

Dethloff, Henry C. *"Suddenly Tomorrow Came…": A History of the Johnson Space Center, 1957–1990.* NASA SP-4307, 1993.

Hansen, James R. *Spaceflight Revolution: NASA Langley Research Center from Sputnik to Apollo.* NASA SP-4308, 1995.

Wallace, Lane E. *Flights of Discovery: An Illustrated History of the Dryden Flight Research Center.* NASA SP-4309, 1996.

Herring, Mack R. *Way Station to Space: A History of the John C. Stennis Space Center.* NASA SP-4310, 1997.

Wallace, Harold D., Jr. *Wallops Station and the Creation of an American Space Program.* NASA SP-4311, 1997.

Wallace, Lane E. *Dreams, Hopes, Realities. NASA's Goddard Space Flight Center: The First Forty Years.* NASA SP-4312, 1999.

Dunar, Andrew J., and Stephen P. Waring. *Power to Explore: A History of Marshall Space Flight Center, 1960–1990.* NASA SP-4313, 1999.

Bugos, Glenn E. *Atmosphere of Freedom: Sixty Years at the NASA Ames Research Center.* NASA SP-2000-4314, 2000.

Bugos, Glenn E. *Atmosphere of Freedom: Seventy Years at the NASA Ames Research Center.* NASA SP-2010-4314, 2010. Revised version of NASA SP-2000-4314.

Bugos, Glenn E. *Atmosphere of Freedom: Seventy Five Years at the NASA Ames Research Center.* NASA SP-2014-4314, 2014. Revised version of NASA SP-2000-4314.

No SP-4315.

Schultz, James. *Crafting Flight: Aircraft Pioneers and the Contributions of the Men and Women of NASA Langley Research Center.* NASA SP-2003-4316, 2003.

Bowles, Mark D. *Science in Flux: NASA's Nuclear Program at Plum Brook Station, 1955–2005.* NASA SP-2006-4317, 2006.

Wallace, Lane E. *Flights of Discovery: An Illustrated History of the Dryden Flight Research Center.* NASA SP-2007-4318, 2007. Revised version of NASA SP-4309.

Arrighi, Robert S. *Revolutionary Atmosphere: The Story of the Altitude Wind Tunnel and the Space Power Chambers.* NASA SP-2010-4319, 2010.

GENERAL HISTORIES, NASA SP-4400

Corliss, William R. *NASA Sounding Rockets, 1958–1968: A Historical Summary.* NASA SP-4401, 1971.

Wells, Helen T., Susan H. Whiteley, and Carrie Karegeannes. *Origins of NASA Names.* NASA SP-4402, 1976.

Anderson, Frank W., Jr. *Orders of Magnitude: A History of NACA and NASA, 1915–1980.* NASA SP-4403, 1981.

Sloop, John L. *Liquid Hydrogen as a Propulsion Fuel, 1945–1959.* NASA SP-4404, 1978.

Roland, Alex. *A Spacefaring People: Perspectives on Early Spaceflight.* NASA SP-4405, 1985.

Bilstein, Roger E. *Orders of Magnitude: A History of the NACA and NASA, 1915–1990.* NASA SP-4406, 1989.

Logsdon, John M., ed., with Linda J. Lear, Jannelle Warren Findley, Ray A. Williamson, and Dwayne A. Day. *Exploring the Unknown: Selected Documents in the History of the U.S. Civil Space Program, Volume I: Organizing for Exploration.* NASA SP-4407, 1995.

Logsdon, John M., ed., with Dwayne A. Day and Roger D. Launius. *Exploring the Unknown: Selected Documents in the History of the U.S. Civil Space Program, Volume II: External Relationships.* NASA SP-4407, 1996.

Logsdon, John M., ed., with Roger D. Launius, David H. Onkst, and Stephen J. Garber. *Exploring the Unknown: Selected Documents in the History of the U.S. Civil Space Program, Volume III: Using Space.* NASA SP-4407, 1998.

Logsdon, John M., ed., with Ray A. Williamson, Roger D. Launius, Russell J. Acker, Stephen J. Garber, and Jonathan L. Friedman. *Exploring the Unknown: Selected Documents in the History of the U.S. Civil Space Program, Volume IV: Accessing Space.* NASA SP-4407, 1999.

Logsdon, John M., ed., with Amy Paige Snyder, Roger D. Launius, Stephen J. Garber, and Regan Anne Newport. *Exploring the Unknown: Selected Documents in the History of the U.S. Civil Space Program, Volume V: Exploring the Cosmos.* NASA SP-2001-4407, 2001.

Logsdon, John M., ed., with Stephen J. Garber, Roger D. Launius, and Ray A. Williamson. *Exploring the Unknown: Selected Documents in the History of the U.S. Civil Space Program, Volume VI: Space and Earth Science.* NASA SP-2004-4407, 2004.

Logsdon, John M., ed., with Roger D. Launius. *Exploring the Unknown: Selected Documents in the History of the U.S. Civil Space Program, Volume VII: Human Spaceflight: Projects Mercury, Gemini, and Apollo.* NASA SP-2008-4407, 2008.

Siddiqi, Asif A., *Challenge to Apollo: The Soviet Union and the Space Race, 1945–1974.* NASA SP-2000-4408, 2000.

Hansen, James R., ed. *The Wind and Beyond: Journey into the History of Aerodynamics in America, Volume 1: The Ascent of the Airplane.* NASA SP-2003-4409, 2003.

Hansen, James R., ed. *The Wind and Beyond: Journey into the History of Aerodynamics in America, Volume 2: Reinventing the Airplane.* NASA SP-2007-4409, 2007.

Hogan, Thor. *Mars Wars: The Rise and Fall of the Space Exploration Initiative.* NASA SP-2007-4410, 2007.

Vakoch, Douglas A., ed. *Psychology of Space Exploration: Contemporary Research in Historical Perspective.* NASA SP-2011-4411, 2011.

Ferguson, Robert G. *NASA's First A: Aeronautics from 1958 to 2008.* NASA SP-2012-4412, 2013.

Vakoch, Douglas A., ed. *Archaeology, Anthropology, and Interstellar Communication.* NASA SP-2013-4413, 2014.

Asner, Glen R., and Stephen J. Garber. *Origins of 21st-Century Space Travel: A History of NASA's Decadal Planning Team and the Vision for Space Exploration, 1999–2004.* NASA SP-2019-4415, 2019.

MONOGRAPHS IN AEROSPACE HISTORY, NASA SP-4500

Launius, Roger D., and Aaron K. Gillette, comps. *Toward a History of the Space Shuttle: An Annotated Bibliography.* Monographs in Aerospace History, No. 1, 1992.

Launius, Roger D., and J. D. Hunley, comps. *An Annotated Bibliography of the Apollo Program.* Monographs in Aerospace History, No. 2, 1994.

Launius, Roger D. *Apollo: A Retrospective Analysis.* Monographs in Aerospace History, No. 3, 1994.

Hansen, James R. *Enchanted Rendezvous: John C. Houbolt and the Genesis of the Lunar-Orbit Rendezvous Concept.* Monographs in Aerospace History, No. 4, 1995.

Gorn, Michael H. *Hugh L. Dryden's Career in Aviation and Space.* Monographs in Aerospace History, No. 5, 1996.

Powers, Sheryll Goecke. *Women in Flight Research at NASA Dryden Flight Research Center from 1946 to 1995.* Monographs in Aerospace History, No. 6, 1997.

Portree, David S. F., and Robert C. Trevino. *Walking to Olympus: An EVA Chronology.* Monographs in Aerospace History, No. 7, 1997.

Logsdon, John M., moderator. *Legislative Origins of the National Aeronautics and Space Act of 1958: Proceedings of an Oral History Workshop.* Monographs in Aerospace History, No. 8, 1998.

Rumerman, Judy A., comp. *U.S. Human Spaceflight: A Record of Achievement, 1961–1998.* Monographs in Aerospace History, No. 9, 1998.

Portree, David S. F. *NASA's Origins and the Dawn of the Space Age.* Monographs in Aerospace History, No. 10, 1998.

Logsdon, John M. *Together in Orbit: The Origins of International Cooperation in the Space Station.* Monographs in Aerospace History, No. 11, 1998.

Phillips, W. Hewitt. *Journey in Aeronautical Research: A Career at NASA Langley Research Center.* Monographs in Aerospace History, No. 12, 1998.

Braslow, Albert L. *A History of Suction-Type Laminar-Flow Control with Emphasis on Flight Research.* Monographs in Aerospace History, No. 13, 1999.

Logsdon, John M., moderator. *Managing the Moon Program: Lessons Learned from Apollo.* Monographs in Aerospace History, No. 14, 1999.

Perminov, V. G. *The Difficult Road to Mars: A Brief History of Mars Exploration in the Soviet Union.* Monographs in Aerospace History, No. 15, 1999.

Tucker, Tom. *Touchdown: The Development of Propulsion Controlled Aircraft at NASA Dryden.* Monographs in Aerospace History, No. 16, 1999.

Maisel, Martin, Demo J. Giulanetti, and Daniel C. Dugan. *The History of the XV-15 Tilt Rotor Research Aircraft: From Concept to Flight.* Monographs in Aerospace History, No. 17, 2000. NASA SP-2000-4517.

Jenkins, Dennis R. *Hypersonics Before the Shuttle: A Concise History of the X-15 Research Airplane.* Monographs in Aerospace History, No. 18, 2000. NASA SP-2000-4518.

Chambers, Joseph R. *Partners in Freedom: Contributions of the Langley Research Center to U.S. Military Aircraft of the 1990s.* Monographs in Aerospace History, No. 19, 2000. NASA SP-2000-4519.

Waltman, Gene L. *Black Magic and Gremlins: Analog Flight Simulations at NASA's Flight Research Center.* Monographs in Aerospace History, No. 20, 2000. NASA SP-2000-4520.

Portree, David S. F. *Humans to Mars: Fifty Years of Mission Planning, 1950–2000.* Monographs in Aerospace History, No. 21, 2001. NASA SP-2001-4521.

Thompson, Milton O., with J. D. Hunley. *Flight Research: Problems Encountered and What They Should Teach Us.* Monographs in Aerospace History, No. 22, 2001. NASA SP-2001-4522.

Tucker, Tom. *The Eclipse Project.* Monographs in Aerospace History, No. 23, 2001. NASA SP-2001-4523.

Siddiqi, Asif A. *Deep Space Chronicle: A Chronology of Deep Space and Planetary Probes, 1958–2000.* Monographs in Aerospace History, No. 24, 2002. NASA SP-2002-4524.

Merlin, Peter W. *Mach 3+: NASA/USAF YF-12 Flight Research, 1969–1979.* Monographs in Aerospace History, No. 25, 2001. NASA SP-2001-4525.

Anderson, Seth B. *Memoirs of an Aeronautical Engineer: Flight Tests at Ames Research Center: 1940–1970.* Monographs in Aerospace History, No. 26, 2002. NASA SP-2002-4526.

Renstrom, Arthur G. *Wilbur and Orville Wright: A Bibliography Commemorating the One-Hundredth Anniversary of the First Powered Flight on December 17, 1903.* Monographs in Aerospace History, No. 27, 2002. NASA SP-2002-4527.

No monograph 28.

Chambers, Joseph R. *Concept to Reality: Contributions of the NASA Langley Research Center to U.S. Civil Aircraft of the 1990s.* Monographs in Aerospace History, No. 29, 2003. NASA SP-2003-4529.

Peebles, Curtis, ed. *The Spoken Word: Recollections of Dryden History, The Early Years.* Monographs in Aerospace History, No. 30, 2003. NASA SP-2003-4530.

Jenkins, Dennis R., Tony Landis, and Jay Miller. *American X-Vehicles: An Inventory—X-1 to X-50.* Monographs in Aerospace History, No. 31, 2003. NASA SP-2003-4531.

Renstrom, Arthur G. *Wilbur and Orville Wright: A Chronology Commemorating the One-Hundredth Anniversary of the First Powered Flight on December 17, 1903.* Monographs in Aerospace History, No. 32, 2003. NASA SP-2003-4532.

Bowles, Mark D., and Robert S. Arrighi. *NASA's Nuclear Frontier: The Plum Brook Research Reactor.* Monographs in Aerospace History, No. 33, 2004. NASA SP-2004-4533.

Wallace, Lane, and Christian Gelzer. *Nose Up: High Angle-of-Attack and Thrust Vectoring Research at NASA Dryden, 1979–2001*. Monographs in Aerospace History, No. 34, 2009. NASA SP-2009-4534.

Matranga, Gene J., C. Wayne Ottinger, Calvin R. Jarvis, and D. Christian Gelzer. *Unconventional, Contrary, and Ugly: The Lunar Landing Research Vehicle*. Monographs in Aerospace History, No. 35, 2006. NASA SP-2004-4535.

McCurdy, Howard E. *Low-Cost Innovation in Spaceflight: The History of the Near Earth Asteroid Rendezvous (NEAR) Mission*. Monographs in Aerospace History, No. 36, 2005. NASA SP-2005-4536.

Seamans, Robert C., Jr. *Project Apollo: The Tough Decisions*. Monographs in Aerospace History, No. 37, 2005. NASA SP-2005-4537.

Lambright, W. Henry. *NASA and the Environment: The Case of Ozone Depletion*. Monographs in Aerospace History, No. 38, 2005. NASA SP-2005-4538.

Chambers, Joseph R. *Innovation in Flight: Research of the NASA Langley Research Center on Revolutionary Advanced Concepts for Aeronautics*. Monographs in Aerospace History, No. 39, 2005. NASA SP-2005-4539.

Phillips, W. Hewitt. *Journey into Space Research: Continuation of a Career at NASA Langley Research Center*. Monographs in Aerospace History, No. 40, 2005. NASA SP-2005-4540.

Rumerman, Judy A., Chris Gamble, and Gabriel Okolski, comps. *U.S. Human Spaceflight: A Record of Achievement, 1961–2006*. Monographs in Aerospace History, No. 41, 2007. NASA SP-2007-4541.

Peebles, Curtis. *The Spoken Word: Recollections of Dryden History Beyond the Sky*. Monographs in Aerospace History, No. 42, 2011. NASA SP-2011-4542.

Dick, Steven J., Stephen J. Garber, and Jane H. Odom. *Research in NASA History*. Monographs in Aerospace History, No. 43, 2009. NASA SP-2009-4543.

Merlin, Peter W. *Ikhana: Unmanned Aircraft System Western States Fire Missions*. Monographs in Aerospace History, No. 44, 2009. NASA SP-2009-4544.

Fisher, Steven C., and Shamim A. Rahman. *Remembering the Giants: Apollo Rocket Propulsion Development*. Monographs in Aerospace History, No. 45, 2009. NASA SP-2009-4545.

Gelzer, Christian. *Fairing Well: From Shoebox to Bat Truck and Beyond, Aerodynamic Truck Research at NASA's Dryden Flight Research Center*. Monographs in Aerospace History, No. 46, 2011. NASA SP-2011-4546.

Arrighi, Robert. *Pursuit of Power: NASA's Propulsion Systems Laboratory No. 1 and 2*. Monographs in Aerospace History, No. 48, 2012. NASA SP-2012-4548.

Renee M. Rottner. *Making the Invisible Visible: A History of the Spitzer Infrared Telescope Facility (1971–2003)*. Monographs in Aerospace History, No. 47, 2017. NASA SP-2017-4547.

Goodrich, Malinda K., Alice R. Buchalter, and Patrick M. Miller, comps. *Toward a History of the Space Shuttle: An Annotated Bibliography, Part 2 (1992–2011)*. Monographs in Aerospace History, No. 49, 2012. NASA SP-2012-4549.

Ta, Julie B., and Robert C. Treviño. *Walking to Olympus: An EVA Chronology, 1997–2011*, Vol. 2. Monographs in Aerospace History, No. 50, 2016. NASA SP-2016-4550.

Gelzer, Christian. *The Spoken Word III: Recollections of Dryden History; The Shuttle Years*. Monographs in Aerospace History, No. 52, 2013. NASA SP-2013-4552.

Ross, James C. *NASA Photo One*. Monographs in Aerospace History, No. 53, 2013. NASA SP-2013-4553.

Launius, Roger D. *Historical Analogs for the Stimulation of Space Commerce*. Monographs in Aerospace History, No. 54, 2014. NASA SP-2014-4554.

Buchalter, Alice R., and Patrick M. Miller, comps. *The National Advisory Committee for Aeronautics: An Annotated Bibliography*. Monographs in Aerospace History, No. 55, 2014. NASA SP-2014-4555.

Chambers, Joseph R., and Mark A. Chambers. *Emblems of Exploration: Logos of the NACA and NASA*. Monographs in Aerospace History, No. 56, 2015. NASA SP-2015-4556.

Alexander, Joseph K. *Science Advice to NASA: Conflict, Consensus, Partnership, Leadership*. Monographs in Aerospace History, No. 57, 2017. NASA SP-2017-4557.

ELECTRONIC MEDIA, NASA SP-4600

Remembering Apollo 11: The 30th Anniversary Data Archive CD-ROM. NASA SP-4601, 1999.

Remembering Apollo 11: The 35th Anniversary Data Archive CD-ROM. NASA SP-2004-4601, 2004. This is an update of the 1999 edition.

The Mission Transcript Collection: U.S. Human Spaceflight Missions from Mercury Redstone 3 to Apollo 17. NASA SP-2000-4602, 2001.

Shuttle-Mir: The United States and Russia Share History's Highest Stage. NASA SP-2001-4603, 2002.

U.S. Centennial of Flight Commission Presents Born of Dreams — Inspired by Freedom. NASA SP-2004-4604, 2004.

Of Ashes and Atoms: A Documentary on the NASA Plum Brook Reactor Facility. NASA SP-2005-4605, 2005.

Taming Liquid Hydrogen: The Centaur Upper Stage Rocket Interactive CD-ROM. NASA SP-2004-4606, 2004.

Fueling Space Exploration: The History of NASA's Rocket Engine Test Facility DVD. NASA SP-2005-4607, 2005.

Altitude Wind Tunnel at NASA Glenn Research Center: An Interactive History CD-ROM. NASA SP-2008-4608, 2008.

A Tunnel Through Time: The History of NASA's Altitude Wind Tunnel. NASA SP-2010-4609, 2010.

CONFERENCE PROCEEDINGS, NASA SP-4700

Dick, Steven J., and Keith Cowing, eds. *Risk and Exploration: Earth, Sea and the Stars*. NASA SP-2005-4701, 2005.

Dick, Steven J., and Roger D. Launius. *Critical Issues in the History of Spaceflight*. NASA SP-2006-4702, 2006.

Dick, Steven J., ed. *Remembering the Space Age: Proceedings of the 50th Anniversary Conference*. NASA SP-2008-4703, 2008.

Dick, Steven J., ed. *NASA's First 50 Years: Historical Perspectives*. NASA SP-2010-4704, 2010.

Billings, Linda, ed. *50 Years of Solar System Exploration: Historical Perspectives*. NASA SP-2021-4705, 2021.

SOCIETAL IMPACT, NASA SP-4800

Dick, Steven J., and Roger D. Launius. *Societal Impact of Spaceflight*. NASA SP-2007-4801, 2007.

Dick, Steven J., and Mark L. Lupisella. *Cosmos and Culture: Cultural Evolution in a Cosmic Context*. NASA SP-2009-4802, 2009.

Dick, Steven J. *Historical Studies in the Societal Impact of Spaceflight*. NASA SP-2015-4803, 2015.

INDEX

4pi airbag lander, 126–128, 131, 133
67P/Churyumov–Gerasimenko comet, 11, 223, 228
81P/Wild comet, 12
2003 SD220 asteroid, **197**
2011 AG5 asteroid, 189
2012 DA14 asteroid, 186, 190
25143 Itokawa asteroid, 12, 181, 223
132524 APL asteroid, 9

A

Able missions, **49**
Advanced X-ray Astrophysics Facility (AXAF) (Chandra), 102, 236, 237
Air Force. *See* U.S. Air Force
Alabama, 140
Aldrin, Buzz, 274
Alexander, George, 209
ALH84001 meteorite, 66, **112**
Allen, Carlton, 176, 181
Allton, Judith, 176, 178, 181, 183
Alpha Magnetic Spectrometer-02 (AMS-02), 93, 104
alternative-space (alt-space) movement, 19, 27. *See also* New Space movement; *see also* Space 2.0
Alvarez, Luis and Walter, 157, 188, 196
American Physical Society, 100
American Rocket Society, 47
Apocalypse, The (TV film), 195
"Apollo Antenna," **275**

Apollo Applications program, 96. *See also* Apollo-Soyuz Test Project (ASTP)
Apollo Astronomy Mount (AAM), 102
Apollo program, **4**, 11, 13, 26, 37, 38, 51, 52, 54, 56, 93, 96, 97, 102, 104–106, 160–163, 167, 170–179, 190, 243, 246, 252, 273–278
Apollo 11, **4**, 273–275
Apollo 12, **4**, **161**, **162**, 275–276
Apollo 13, **4**, 276–278
lunar rover, 115
Apollo-Soyuz Test Project (ASTP), 52, 97, 327
Applied Physics Laboratory (APL), 45, 46
Ares I expendable launch vehicle, 103, 104
Ares V launch vehicle, 103, 113, 138
Ariane launch vehicles, 98
Armageddon (film), 185, 187, 193, 194, 199, 204
Armstrong, Neil, 274
Army. *See* U.S. Army
Arvidson, Raymond, 131
ASI. *See* Italian Space Agency
Asmar, Sami, 281, 282
Asteroid Initiative, 109
asteroids, 7, 9, 12, 15, 74, 104, 109, 152, 157, 158, 181, 185–206, **192**, 214, 223, 231, 232
2003 SD220, **197**

337

2011 AG5, 189
2012 DA14, 186, 190
25143 Itokawa, 12, 181, 223
132524 APL, 9
Apophis, 189
asteroid belt, 74
Chelyabinsk "superbolide" event, 158, 186, 190, 199, 201
impact risks, 158, 185, 185–206
mining, 15
Vesta, 12, 74, 232, 233, 303
Asteroids! (animated short), 190, 206
Asteroid v. Earth (TV movie), 190, 206
astrobiology, 3, 66, 109, 137, 145, 169, 183
Astrobotic Technology Corp., 20
Astromaterials Acquisition and Curation Office, 176
Astronomy Planning Board, 59
astrophysics, 41–45, **43, 44, 45**, 64, 71, 77, 79–82, 92
Athena rover design, 122
Atlas-Agena launch vehicle, 51, 244, **245**, 247, 249
Atlas Centaur launch vehicle, 73
Augustine, Norman, 104
Augustine Committee, 104
Australia, 251–283

B
Baldwin, Ralph, 196
Barringer Crater, **198**
Bastide, Françoise, 208
Bean, Alan, 162, 173, 276
Beggs, James, 99, 298
Berkner, Lloyd, 46, 49
Berlin Wall, 120
Biermann, Ludwig, 290
Big Science, 107, 141–143, 155, 156

Billings, Linda, vii, viii, 157, 159, 313
biological isolation garments, 163
Boeing Corporation, 100, 246
Bohr, Niels, 30
Boland, Edward, 297
Bolden, Charles "Charlie," 108–110, 141, 143, 150–156, **151**
Bolton, John, 256, 263–266, 273, 276–278
Bonestell, Chesley, 89
Bonnet, Roger, 228, 236
Bowen, Edward "Taffy," 254–259, 262–264, 267, 269, 270, 274, 278
Boxer, Barbara, 105
Bratenahl, Alex, 249
Briggs, Geoffrey, 116, 121
Brookhaven National Laboratory, 46
"bubble team" study, 125, 127, 134
Buckley, Edmond C., 267, 268
Burke, James D., 22, 239, 241, 243, 244, 246, 313
Bush, George H. W., 64, 65, 100, 101, 103, 113, 118, 119, 143, 148
Bush, George W., 103, 109, 113, 135, 146, **147**, 148
Bush, Vannevar, 255, 258, 263

C
California, 23, 95, 143, 146, 262, 263
California Institute of Technology (Caltech), 12, 45, 111, 115, 249, 252, 255, 258, 262–265, 273
Callahan, Jason, 33, 35, 313
Cape Canaveral, FL, 9, 238
Carnegie Institution, 258, 263
Carr, Michael, 117
Carter, Jimmy, 98, 210, 295
Casani, John, 127
Casey, Richard, 252, **253**, 258
Cassini, Jean-Dominique, 225

Cassini-Huygens mission, **4, 6, 7**, 10, 29, **65**, 69, 70, 158, 209, 217–219, 223, 225–281, **234**
Centaur upper stage booster, 61, 73, 117, 297
Centers for Disease Control and Prevention (CDC), 163
Centre National d'Études Spatiales (CNES), 121, 122, 232, 233
Ceres, 74, 303
Challenger Space Shuttle accident, 61, 62, 64, 66, 94, 99, 106, 231, 299
Chandra X-ray Observatory. *See* Advanced X-ray Astrophysics Facility (AXAF) (Chandra)
Chandrayaan-1 mission, **5**
Chang'e missions, **4, 5**, 31
Chapman, Sydney, 46
Chelyabinsk meteor impact, 158, 186, 190, 199, 201
Cheney, Dick, 109, 146, 147
Cheong, Giny, 158, 207, 314
China, 20, 28, 31, 303
China National Space Administration, 31, 303
Cinemark USA theater chain, 192
Clarke, Arthur C., 196
Cleave, Mary, 148
Clementine spacecraft, **4**
climate change, 31, 103, 152
Clinton, Bill, 113, 144, 237
Close Encounters of the Third Kind (film), 212
Cold War, 27, 28, 31, 43, 45, 50, 70, 102, 113, 120, 190, 210, 288, 289
Cole, Doug, 271, 272
colonialism, 20
colonizing other planets, 305
Colorado, 192, 196

Columbia Space Shuttle accident, 94, 103, 146
Columbia Accident Investigation Board, 103
Columbus, Christopher, 30
Comet/Asteroid Impacts and Human Society (book), 200
COmet Nucleus TOUR (CONTOUR) mission, **71**, 74
comet rendezvous and asteroid flyby (CRAF) mission, 231, 235, 236
comets, 7, 24, 74, 169, 187–190, 196, 199, 200, 202, 228, 232
  67P/Churyumov–Gerasimenko, 11, 223, 228
  81P/Wild, 12
  Halley, 188, 227, 232
  Shoemaker-Levy 9, **187, 189**, 187–189, 196, 214
  Tempel 1, **75**
commercial cargo program, 105, 137, 138
Commercial Crew Development program, 138
commercial spaceflight, 27, 63, 105, 137, 152, 186
Committee on Planetary and Lunar Exploration (COMPLEX), 59, 60, 64, 66, 67, 111, 114, 115, 122, 134, 140
Commonwealth Scientific and Industrial Research Organisation (CSIRO), 251–283
Compton Gamma Ray Observatory, 102
computer-generated imagery (CGI), 193
Congress, 26, 36, 37, 44, 47, 48, 51, 52, 54, 55, 57, 60, 74–78, 80, 91, 93–95, 100, 101, 105, 116, 120, 138, 139, 144, 148, 152–154, 156, 189, 196,

212, 228, 233, 235–237, 249, 253, 293, 296–299
Conley, Catharine, 179
Conrad, Charles "Pete," **161**, 162, 173, 174
Constellation program, 73, 103, 104, 137, 138, 148, 150, 152
Conway, Erik M., 107, 108, 111, 314
Cook, Captain James, 30
Cooke, David, 277
Copernican revolution, 30
Cornerstone missions, 228. *See also* Horizon 2000 plan
"Cosmic Ancestry," 159, 179
Cosmos (TV series), 26, 212
Cunningham, Glenn, 119
Curiosity rover, **5**, 11, 12, 17, 18, 25, 26, 28, 90, 91, 107, 109, 112, 121, **133**, 140, 154–156, 183, 252, 281, 283, 303

D

Darwinian revolution, 30
data management, 23
David, Leonard, 178
Dawn spacecraft, **7**, **71**, 74, 303
decadal surveys, 3, 52, 63, 64, 71, 72, 77, 78, 92, 106, 111, 116
Deep Impact (film), 185, 193, 195, 204
Deep Impact spacecraft, **7**, **71**, 74, **75**
Deep Space 1 mission, **7**, **65**
Deep Space Instrumentation Facilities (DSIFs), 267, 268, 271
Deep Space Network (DSN), 3, 20, 23, 43, 130, 251, 252, 266, 268–272, 278, 279
de Grasse Tyson, Neil, 26
Delgado López, Laura, 157, 185, 314
Department of Defense (DOD), 37–41, **39**, 55, 76, 86–88, 195

Department of Energy (DOE), 38, **39**, **40**, **41**, 84–86
Department of State, 46, 70
Detecting and Mitigating the Impact of Earth-Bound Near-Earth Objects (DAMIEN), 158
Digital Equipment Corporation, 115
digital media, 216–222
Dinn, Mike, 277
direct landing concept, **129**
Discovery program, 65, 66, 68, 73, 74, 101, 102, 154
discretionary spending, 37–39, **38**, **39**, 58, 62
doomsday scenarios, 193, 194
Doppler radar, 128
Doppler shift, 271, 280–281
Doppler Wind Experiment (DWE), 280, 281
Dordain, Jean Jacques, 151, 153
Dornier, 238
Double Asteroid Redirection Test (DART), 201
Dover Heights radio telescopes, 254–257, 264
Dryden, Hugh, 49, 50
DuBridge, Lee, 254, 255, 258, 262, 263
dwarf planets, 1, 7, 9, 73, 74, 283, 303. *See also* Ceres; *see also* Pluto
Dyson, Freeman, 22

E

Earth observation, 102, 103
Earth Resources Technology Satellite (ERTS), 102. *See* Landsat satellite program
Earth science, 41, 42, 44, **45**, 61, 71, 77, 79–82, 92, 102, 103, 152
Eisenhower, Dwight D., 47, 76

Elliot, Harry, 287, 290, 291
Ellis, R. H., 163, 164, 166, 167, 172–174, 178, 179
Enlai, Zhou, 32
EPOXI mission, 74
Erickson, Kristen J., 1, 315
Europa Clipper mission, 303
Europe, 28, 70, 139, 225–238, 285, 287, 288, 290, 293, 294, 300
European Science Foundation, 231
European Space Agency (ESA), 10, 11, 69, 70, 108, 110, 137, 139, 151–152, 156, 217–218, 223, 225–238, 279, 281, 285–287, 289, 292, 294–301, 303
    Astronomy Working Group (AWG), 232
    Science Policy Committee (SPC), 232, 235, 322
    Solar System Working Group (SSWG), 232, 233
    Space Science Advisory Committee (SSAC), 232
European Space Operations Centre (ESOC), 233, 238
European Space Research Organisation (ESRO), 291–294, 300, 301
ExoMars mission, 137, 139, 151–153
    ExoMars 2020 rover, **5**, 110, 303
    ExoMars Trace Gas Orbiter, **5**, 110, 139
expendable launch vehicle (ELV) program, 63, 98
Explorer program, 56, 79
extinction events, 157, 188, 189, 196
extrasolar planets, **92**
extraterrestrial life, search for, 28, 91, 109, 145, 169, 180, 183, 214, 229, 306
extremophiles, 169

F

Fahnestock, Jeanne, 208
failures, mission, 1, 8, 17, 61, 68, 72, 74, 95, 107, 123, 124, 144, 145, 155, 243, 244, 246–249
Farmer, Jack, 132
"faster, better, cheaper" (FBC) paradigm, viii, 66–68, 72, 94, 101, 107, 109, 121, 123, 140, 144, 145, 155, 217, 236
Favero, M. S., 165, 166, 167, 172
federal budget, 25, 33, 35–88, **38**, 93, 105, 112, 114, 120, 236
federal debt, 36, **37**, 82–84
Figueroa, Orlando, 154
Fisk, Lennard, 63
Flatow, Ira, 179
Fletcher, James C., 56, 292, 293
Florida, 9, 140
flyby missions, 3–10, **4–7**
"follow-the-water" strategy, 109, 155
Ford, Gerald, 57
Freeman Fox and Partners (FF&P), 260, 261, 266
French Guiana, 20
Frosch, Robert A., 59, 296
Frutkin, Arnold, W., 285
funding, 25, 28, 33, 35–88, 91, 93, 100, 105, 109, 113, 118, 120, 121, 130, 131, 135, 138, 140, 147, 148, 152–153, 197, 212, 213, 227, 235–237, 295–298, 303
Fuqua, Don, 212, 297

G

Gagarin, Yuri, 50, 243
Galileo orbiter, **4**, **6**, **7**, 10, 23, 29, **57**, 58–59, 98, 99, 116, 158, 175, 179, 189, 209, 214–216, 219, 252, 278, 279

Galileo probe, 6
Galloway, Eilene, 48
Garver, Lori, 150
Garvin, James, 130, 131, 135
George E. Brown, Jr., Near-Earth Object Survey Act, 197, 341
Germany, 53, 120, 233, 238, 261, 281
Giant Radio Telescope (GRT), 257–260, 262–264. *See also* Parkes Radio Telescope
Gibson, Roy, 296
Giotto spacecraft, **7**, 227, 228, 232
Glaser, Harold, 295
Glenn Research Center Propulsion Systems Laboratory Control Room, **19**
global climate change, 31
Glover, Ken, 174
Goldin, Daniel, 65, 66, 68, 70, 72, 101, 108–109, 135, 141–148, **145**, 150, 155, 236, 237
Goldstein, Barry, 127
Goldstone Deep Space Communications Complex, **23**, **197**, 266, 268, 272–278, **275**
Google Lunar XPRIZE, 20, 27
Gorbachev, Mikhail, 120
Gordon, Richard, Jr., 162
Gore, Al, 70, 144, 237
Graf, James, 127, 129, 130
"Grand Tour," 53–55
gravitational assist, 8, 9, 291, 292, 294
Gravity Recovery and Interior Laboratory (GRAIL) spacecraft, 5
"Great Bombardment" theory, 29
Great Observatories spacecraft program, 43, 102
Green, James L., 1, 15, 315
Green, Richard H., 165–167, 172

Green Bank radio telescope, **197**, 238, 265, 280–281
Greenberg, Daniel, 90
Griffin, Michael, 109, 143, 148–151, **149**, 155, 156
Gross Domestic Product (GDP), 36, **37**, 82–84
Grunsfeld, John, 153, 154
Gugliotta, Guy, 217
Gurvits, Leonid, 280

H
Halley's Comet, 188, 227, 232
Handberg, Roger, 33, 34, 89, 315
Harper's Magazine, 188
Hartwell, William, 189
Hayabusa probe, **7**, 181, 223
heat sterilization of spacecraft, 247
Hein, Marv, 174
heliophysics, 41–43, **44**, **45**, 71, 77, 79–82, 92
Helios missions, **53**
heliosphere, 9
Herodotus, 21
High Resolution Microwave Survey (HRMS), 91
high-tech industry, 28
History Classics: Mega Disasters, 193
Hiten spacecraft, **4**
Honeysuckle Creek tracking station, 274, 275, 277
Hope spacecraft, 303
Horizon 2000 plan, 228, 230–232, 235
House Committee on Science and Technology, 212, 297
Houston, 150, 163, 194, 276, 277
Hubbard, Scott, 72, 73, 130
Hubble Space Telescope, 57, 58, 66, 91, 93, 99, 102, 120, 150, 219
Hufbauer, Karl, 286, 287, 290, 292, 294

Human Microbiome Project, 181
human spaceflight, vii, 13, 15, 20,30, 33, 34, 41, 42, 47, 50–52, 56, 64, 73, 89–106, 113, 140, 142, 143, 147–148, 150, 151, 153–155 180, 303, 305
Huntress, Wesley, 144
Huygens, Christiaan, 225
Huygens probe, **7**, 69, 70, 217, 218, 223, 225–228, **229**, 235, 238, 252, 279–281. *See also* Cassini-Huygens mission

I

Impact (miniseries), 193, 194, 199
India, 20, 28, 303
Indian Space Research Organization (ISRO), 11
infrared astronomy, 2, 102, 228, 229
Ingenuity (Mars helicopter), **5**, 12
Interior Exploration using Seismic Investigations, Geodesy, and Heat Transport (InSight) lander, 5, 110, 154, 303
International Asteroid Warning Network (IAWN), 158, 202
international cooperation, 25, 69–70, 227, 230–231, 233–238, 240, 267, 285–303
International Council for Science/International Council of Scientific Unions (ICSU), 46, 200
International Geophysical Year (IGY), 46, 47, 49, 76
International Mars Analysis of Returned Samples Working Group, 108
International Polar Year, 46
International Solar Polar Mission (ISPM), 69, 70, 285–302
International Space Station (ISS), 20, 70, 93, 100, 101, 103–106, 113, 137, 138, 144, 146, 152, 237, 240

Space Station Freedom (previously called Space Station Alpha), 70, 100, 119
interstellar space, 8, 98, 219
interstellar winds, 9
Intrepid Lunar Module, **161**, 162
Isakowitz, Steve, 131
ISEE-3/ICE mission, **7**
Italian Space Agency (ASI), 128, 217, 225, 226, 237
Itokawa. *See* asteroids

J

Jaffe, Leonard, 171, 172
James Webb Space Telescope (JWST), 92, 138, 152, 153
Japan, 20, 28, 303
Japan Aerospace Exploration Agency (JAXA), 12, 223
Jet Propulsion Laboratory (JPL), vii, 17–19, 22, 26, 28, 45, 58, 67, 68, 90, 95, 96, 105, 110, 115, 116, 118, 119, 123–135, 139–141, 148, 149, 154, 158, 165, 171, 207, 209, 213, **229**, 231, **234**, 239, 241–243, 246, 248–252, 264–273, 280, 282
Jodrell Bank telescope, 259, 266, 267
Johns Hopkins University Applied Physics Laboratory, 45, 148
Johnson, Lyndon, 48, 106
Johnson, Torrence, 214
Johnson-Freese, Joan, 287, 297, 299
Joint Institute for VLBI in Europe (JIVE), 280
Jolly, Steve, 127
Joyce, J. Wallace, 46
Jucunda, Sister Mary, 25
Juno orbiter, **6**, 10, 73, 303, **304**
Jupiter, **6–7**, 8–10, 53–55, 57, 58, 73, 98, 116, 186–189, **187, 189**, 196, 199,

207, 209–212, 214, 215, 252, 278, 291, 292, 294–297, **296**, 303, 306
Great Red Spot, 209–211, **211**
moons of, 6, 8, 29, 30, 169, 175, 179, 209, 210, 229, 306
JUpiter ICy moons Explorer (JUICE) spacecraft, **6**
Jupiter Orbiter probe, 57, 58. *See also* Galileo orbiter

K

Kazakhstan, 20, 120
Kennedy, John F., 50, 96, 243
Kenyon College, 170
Kepler-186f. *See* Extrasolar planets
Keyworth, Jay, 58
Kissinger, Henry, 32
Knittel, M. D., 165–167, 172
Korolev, Sergei, 15
Kuiper Belt, 9, 303

L

La Fin du Monde (novel and film), 187, 203
LaFollette, Marcel, 208
Lambright, W. Henry, 108, 109, 141, 315
lander missions, **4–7**, 11
Landsat satellite program, 102
Lanzerotti, Louis, 63
Last Days on Earth (TV movie), 193, 205
Layman, Bill, 125
Leighton, Bob, 273
Library of Congress, 48
life, extraterrestrial, 13, 28, 109, 141, 143, 145, 169–171, 180, 183, 214, 229
evidence of, 66, **112**, 141, 144
Life (magazine), 26
Lindsay, John F., 176
Lockheed Martin Corporation, 100, 122, 123, 125–129, 140

Long-Duration Exposure Facility (LDEF), 181, 182
Loomis, Alfred, 254, 258
Los Angeles, 26
Los Angeles Times, 209, 211, 212
Lovelace, Alan, 212
low-Earth orbit (LEO), 3, 13, 55, 99, 104–106, 194, 195, 244
Lowell, Percival, 89
Lucifer's Hammer (novel), 194, 203, 204
Lunakhod missions, **4**
Luna missions, **4**, 8, 242
Lunar and Planetary Institute, 175, 176, 179
Lunar and Planetary Missions Board, 52, 59, 60, 76
Lunar Atmosphere and Dust Environment Explorer (LADEE) spacecraft, **5**
Lunar CRater Observation and Sensing Satellite (LCROSS) spacecraft, **4**, 73
Lunar Geophysical Network, **4**
Lunar Geoscience Orbiter, 62
Lunar Orbiter missions, **4, 49**
Lunar Precursor Robotic program, 73
Lunar Prospector spacecraft, **4**, 65
Lunar Receiving Laboratory (LRL), 161, 163, 164, 168, 170, 172, 177
Lunar Reconnaissance Orbiter (LRO), **5**, 10, 11, **71**, 73
Lunar Science Conference, 163, 167, 171
Lüst, Reimar, 285, 286
Luton, Jean-Marie, 237

M

Magellan spacecraft, **4**, 10, **57**, 99
Manned Space Flight Network (MSFN), 275
Manning, Rob, 127
Mariner Mark II program, 231, 235

Mariner missions, vii, 1, **2**, **4**, **5**, 8, 17, 18, 22–24, 29, **49**, 51, **53**, 55, 73, 196, 241–243, 251, 269–273, 283, 292
  Mariner 2, vii, 1, **2**, **4**, 17, 23, 241, 251, 269–272, 283
  Mariner 4, **4,** 251, 272, 273
  Mariner 10, **4,** 8, 73, 292
Markovski, Petar, 239, 240, 285, 316
Mars, **5**, 10–13, **12**, 17, 22, 30, 51, 52, 55, 56, 64, 66, 67, 73, 90, 96, **97**, 101–104, 107–156, 169, 179, 180, 182, 183, 231, 243, 252, 273, 279, 303
  Jezero Crater, 12
  moons of, **5**
  Thaumasia region, **97**
Mars 2, 4, and 5 spacecraft, **5**
Mars 2020 Perseverance rover, **5**, 12, 91, 107, 110, 139, 303
Mars Astrobiology Explorer-Cacher (MAX-C), 111, 137
Mars Atmosphere and Volatile EvolutioN Mission (MAVEN), **5**, 11, 110, 137, **151**
Mars Climate Orbiter (MCO), 24, **65**, 67, 68, 72, 107, 121
Mars Exploration Office, 125
Mars Exploration Program, 132, 141–156
Mars Exploration Rovers (MER), **5**, 26, 28, **71**, 73, 107, 122, 128, 130, 131, 140, 146, 279, 303
Mars Express orbiter, **5**, 11, 110
Mars Global Network mission, 119
Mars Global Surveyor, **5**, **65**, 73, 121, 130, 131, 279
Mars Helicopter Ingenuity, **5**, 12
"Mars Next Decade" program, 154
Mars Observer spacecraft (previously named Mars Geoscience/Climatology Observer), **60**, 61, 62, **65**, 101, 107, 119, 121, 144, 155
Mars Observer Mission Failure Investigation Board, 61
Mars Odyssey orbiter, **5**, 11, **71**, 72, 73, 110, 121
Mars Orbiter Mission, **5**, 11
Mars Pathfinder, **5**, **21**, 26, **65**, 125–128, **145**, 216, 303
  Sojourner rover, **5, 21, 145**
Mars Polar Lander (MPL), 24, **65**, 67, 72, 107, 121–125, **123, 124**, 128
Mars Polar Lander Special Review Board, 67, **124**
Mars Reconnaissance Orbiter (MRO), **5**, 10, 11, **71**, 73, 110, 130, 131, 136, 137
Mars Rover Sample Return Science Working Group, 116–119, 121
Mars sample return (MSR), 107, **108**, 111–141, **123**, 145, 146, 148, 149, 151, 152, 155, 180
Mars Science Laboratory (MSL) Curiosity rover, **5**, **12**, 73, 107, 109, 111, 112, 121, **133**, 134–137, 140, 149–151, 154, 156, 281–282, 303. *See also* Curiosity rover
Mars Science Working Group, 121
Mars Scout mission, 73, 129, 136
Mars Smart Lander (MSL), 128, 131, 132, **134**, 135
Mars Surveyor Orbiter, 128, 129
Mars Surveyor program, 67, 73, 121–123, 144, 145, 155
Mars Telecommunications Orbiter, 128, 136
Maryland, 95, 148, 177
mass media, 158, 186, 189, 207–209, 213, 216, 219, 221
McCleese, Dan, 132, 141

McCurdy, Howard E., 190, 193, 194
McDougall, Walter, 31
Menzies, Robert, 258
Mercury, 1, **4**, 8, 26, 29, 73
Mercury 7, 26, 94
MErcury Surface, Space ENvironment, GEochemistry, and Ranging (MESSENGER), **4**, 8, **71**, 73
Merrick, William "Bill," 265
Meteor Crater, **198**
meteor impacts, 185–206
microbiology, space, 160, 167
microspacecraft, 22, 23
Mikulski, Barbara, 105
miniaturization of spacecraft, 22
Ministry of General Machine Building (MOM), 20
Minnett, Harry, 260, 269–272
Mission to Planet Earth (MTPE), 103
Mitchell, F. J., 163, 164, 166, 167, 172–174, 178, 179
Mobile Geobiology Explorer, 132
Mojave Desert, **23**, 266
Moon, 1, **4**, 8, 10–13, 21, 29, 31, 40, 50–52, 54, 64, 96, 103, 104, 107, 109, 110, 113, 135, 147, 148, 152, 155, 157, 159–184, **161**, 194, 241–244, **242**, 246, 247, **248**, 265, 274–276
  Ocean of Storms, 162, 275
Moore, Barrien, 236
Morrison, Don, 176–178, 183
Mount Wilson Observatory, 262
movies, 29, 185–206, 213, 221
MSL Science Definition Team, 134
Muirhead, Brian, 125, 127
Muldrow, Edna, 185, 188
Multidisciplinary Platform, 132
Murray, Bruce, 58

N

National Aeronautics and Space Administration (NASA), 26, 33–36, 38, **39**, **40**, **41**, 47, 74, 89–106, **95**, 111–140, 141–156, 160–179, 182, 189, 195–197, 201, 207, 209, 214–217, 223, 225–238, 241–249, 251, 252, 266–279, 281–283, 286, 289, 291–301, 303
  Aerospace Safety Advisory Panel, 59
  Astronomy Missions Planning Board, 52
  budget, 35–88, **38**, **42**, 93, 96, 98, 100, 101, 103, 105, 112, **114**, 116, 120, 130, 131, 135–139, 147, 152–154, 156, 197, 211, 228, 235–237, 295–298
  Human Spaceflight Directorate, **95**
  Lunar and Planetary Missions Board, 52, 60, 76
  Office of Manned Space Flight, 50, 56
  Office of Space Science (and Applications) (OSSA), 50, 51, 55, 56, 59, 60, 63, 72
  Planetary Defense Coordination Office, 158, 201
  Planetary Exploration Division, 65
  Planetary Science Division, 72
  Science Mission Directorate, vii, 51, 59, 79, **95**, 138, 142, 147, 149
  Space Exploration Initiative office, 148
NASA Administrator, role of, 141–156
NASA Advisory Council (NAC), 33, 59, 60, 62, 69, 72, 76–78, 230
  Research and Technology Advisory Council, 59
  Solar System Exploration Committee (SSEC), 60–63, 69, 230–231

Space and Earth Science Advisory Committee (SESAC), 62, 63
Space Program Advisory Council, 52, 59
Space Science Steering Committee, 51, 52
NASA Centers
  Ames Research Center (ARC), 22, **149**, 172, 291
  Glenn Research Center (GRC), **19**, 143
  Goddard Space Flight Center (GSFC), 105, 149, 173, 291
  Headquarters, 50, 51, 95, 116, 121, 128, **147**, 179, 183, 239, 246, 249
  Jet Propulsion Laboratory (JPL). *See* Jet Propulsion Laboratory (JPL)
  Johnson Space Center (JSC) (formerly Manned Spacecraft Center [MSC]), 105, 116, 119, 125, 160, 161, 163, 167, 171, 176, 181
  Kennedy Space Center (KSC), 105
  Langley Research Center (LaRC), 246
  Marshall Space Flight Center (MSFC), 18, 105, 115, 173
National Academy of Sciences, 3, 49, 50, 76, 105, 106, 111, 171. *See also* National Research Council (NRC)
National Advisory Committee for Aeronautics (NACA), 59
National Aeronautics and Space Act of 1958, 48, 76, 90, 207
National Air and Space Museum, vii, **168**
National Institutes of Health (NIH), 38, **39**, **40**, **41**, 84–86, 181
National Reconnaissance Office (NRO), 102
National Research Council (NRC), 3, 33, 50, 76, 92, 95, 152, 182, 183, 188, 199, 231. *See also* Space Science Board/Space Studies Board (SSB). *See also* Committee on Planetary and Lunar Exploration (COMPLEX)
  decadal surveys, 3, 52, 63, 64, 71, 72, 77, 78, 92, 106, 111, 116
National Science and Technology Council (NSTC), 158
National Science Foundation (NSF), 38, **39**, **40**, **41**, 75, 76, 84–86, 95, 106, 197
National Space Council, 64, 65, 119, 120
Naugle, John, 60, 62, 291–293
Naval Research Laboratory (NRL), 45
Navy. *See* U.S. Navy
Near Earth Asteroid Rendezvous (NEAR) Shoemaker spacecraft, 7, **65**
near-Earth objects (NEOs), 189, **192**, 195–202
Near-Earth Object Wide-field Infrared Survey Explorer (NEOWISE), **192**
Near-Earth Observations program, 109
Nelkin, Dorothy, 208
Nelson, Bill, 150
Neptune, 7, 8, 53–55, 207, 213, 252, 278
Ness, Norman, 291
Newell, Homer, 47, 49–51, 292
New Frontiers program, 9, 72, 73
New Horizons spacecraft, 1, **6**, **7**, **9**, 10, 30, **71**, 73, 283, 303
New Millennium program, 101
New Space movement, 19
New York City, 143, 185, 191
New York Times, 209–211, 214–218
Nixon, Richard, 18, 54, 55, 97, 99, 116

O

Obama, Barack, 73, 104, 105, 109, 137, 150, 152–155
Odishaw, Hugh, 49
Odyssey Command Module (Apollo 13), 276–277
Office of Management and Budget (OMB), 55, 58, 82, 84, 86, 94, 109, 112, 120, 130, 144, 148, 152, 153, 156, 295, 297, 298
Office of Science and Technology Policy (OSTP), 58
O'Keefe, Sean, 109, 135, 143, 146–148, **147**, 155
Omega: The Last Days of the World (film), 188, 205
O'Neil, William, 214, 215
Öpik, Ernst, 196
orbiter missions, **4–7**, 10–11
Origins program, 101
Origins, Spectral Interpretation, Resource Identification, Security-Regolith Explorer (OSIRIS-REx) spacecraft, **7**
Orion crew vehicle, 103, 104
O'Toole, Thomas, 210
out-of-ecliptic (OOE), 286–288, 290–295, 300–301
Owens Valley Radio Observatory (OVRO), 264, 265, 273

P

pallet lander, **126**, 126–128, 131–134, **134**, 140
Palomar Observatory, 262, 264
panspermia hypothesis, 159, 175, 178, 179
Parkes Radio Telescope, 251–283, **261**
Pawsey, J. L., 255–257
Peekskill, NY, meteorite event, 201

Pentagon. *See* Department of Defense (DOD)
Perseverance. *See* Mars 2020 Perseverance rover
Peterson, K., 191
Pew Research Center, 190, 202
Philae probe, 7, 11, 223
Phoenix lander, **5**, **71**, 73
Pickering, William, 17, 47, 267–269
Pioneer missions, **4**, **6**, 8, **9**, 49, 51–53, **53**, 56, 214, 265, 266, 291, 292, 300, 301
Pioneer Venus Orbiter and Multiprobe, **4**, 52, **53**, 56
planetary defense, 195, 197, 202
Planetary Defense Coordination Office (PDCO), 158, 201
Planetary Explorer program, 56
Planetary Observer program, 61, 62
Planetary Protection Program, 122, 163, 169, 171, 176, 180–183
planetary science, vii, 3, 21, 35–88, **42**, **43**, **44**, **45**, **49**, **53**, **57**, **65**, 92, 111, 116, 138, 139, 153, 228, 230, 233
Planetary Society, 99
Pluto, 1, **9**, **10**, **30**, 54, 72, 73, 283, 303
popular culture, 157, 185–206
Porco, Carolyn, 217–219
press releases, 207, 209, 219, 220
Preston, Bob, 280
private industry in space exploration, 19, 20
Project Science Integration Group (PSIG), 132, 134
Prometheus, 103
public opinion polls, 190, 202
public outreach, 26, 207–222
public perceptions, 25–27, 157–158, 186, 201, 202, 208, 213, 221
Pyne, Stephen, 30, 305

Q

quarantine, 162, 164, 170, 171
Quayle, Dan, 65, 66, 119
Quistgaard, Erik, 298

R

radar, development of, 252–255
Radiation Laboratory (MIT), 254
Radio Amateur Satellite Corporation (AMSAT), 20
radio astronomy, 232, 252, 255–258, 262–266, 278–279, 282–283
Radio Astronomy Trust, 258
radioisotope thermoelectric generator (RTG), 13, 133, 134, 291
Radiophysics Laboratory, 252, 254–256, 260, 263, 277
Raleigh, Sir Walter, 32
Ranger missions, **4**, 19, 24, 29, **49**, 96, 241–249, **242**, **245**, **248**
Rea, Donald, 116
Reagan, Ronald, 58, 98, 99, 113, 297, 298
Rechtin, Eberhardt, 268, 273
Rendezvous with Rama (novel), 194, 196, 203
Reynolds, John, 280, 282
Rivellini, Tomasso, 125, 128, 131
Rockefeller Foundation, 258, 259
Rocket and Satellite Research Panel (RSRP), 47–49
Roosevelt, Franklin D., 253, 255
Roscosmos, 139
Rose Parade, 17
Rosetta mission, 7, 11, 228, 232. *See also* Philae probe
rover missions, **4–7**, 11
Rule, Bruce, 264, 266
Rummel, John D., 163, 168, 171, 172, 176–181, 183
Rusk, Dean, 258
Russia/Soviet Union, 8, 20, 22, 28, 45, 47, 50, 70, 100, 104, 113, 116, 118, 120, 153, 183, 212, 227, 232, 233, 242, 243, 246, 247, 265, 288, 289, 303
  Ministry of General Machine Building (MOM), 20
  Space Research Institute of the Russian Academy of Sciences (IKI), 20, 232, 233, 349
Russo, Arturo, 223, 316

S

Sabahi, Dara, 125, 127
"Safe on Mars" sample return, 136
Sagan, Carl, 26, 211, 212, 215, 221, 237
Sakigake spacecraft, **7**
Salvation (TV series), 157
sample return, **4–7**, 11–12, 104, 107, 108, 110–116, 118, 121, 123, 125–128, 130–132, 135–141, 145, 146, 148–149, 151, 152, 155, 180, 181, 303
Sandford, Scott, 181, 182
Sarkissian, John, 239, 251, 316
Saturn, **6**, 8, 10, 53–55, 69, 96, 98, 169, 207, 209, 212, **213**, 217, 218, 223, 225–238, 279, 292, 306
  moons of, **6**, 30, 69, 169, **213**, 217, 218, 223, **226**, 225–238, 252, 279–281, 306, 309
Saturn rockets, 13, 51
Sawyer, Kathy, 112, 215
Schmitt, Harrison, 96
Schurmeier, Harris M., 239, 241, 244
Science Advisory Committee (Eisenhower Administration), 76
Science Citation Index, 168
Search for Extraterrestrial Intelligence (SETI), 91
Selenological and Engineering Explorer (SELENE)/Kaguya spacecraft, **4**

Senate, 121, 142, 146, 150, 297
Shirley, Donna, 116, 117
Shoemaker-Levy 9 comet, 186–189, **187**, **189**, 196, 214
Siddiqi, Asif, 289
Simpson, John, 292, 293
Singer, Fred, 46
skycrane landing, **133**, **134**, 136, 139, 140
Skylab missions, 52, 96, 102
Slee, Bruce, 256
Slovic, Paul, 186, 191
Small Missions for Advanced Research in Technology-1 (SMART-1) spacecraft, 4
Smith, Bradford, 210
social media, 26, 91, 158, 201
Soderblom, Laurence, 210
solar space science, 290
solar studies, 256–257
solar system exploration paradigm, 1–13
solar system explorers, 18–20, 23
    gender of, 18, 20
    race/ethnicity of, 18, 20
    socioeconomic class of, 18, 20
solar wind, 2, 11, 49, 110, 209, 290
South Africa, 20
South Pole Aitken Basin Sample Return, **4**
Southwood, David, 236
Soviet Union. *See* Russia/Soviet Union
Space 2.0, 20
space-based solar observatory, 290
Space.com, 175, 178, 220
spacecraft design, 22, 23, 61, 241, 243, 295
Space Exploration Initiative (SEI), 64, 109, 120, 143, 144, 148, 155
Spaceguard Survey, 196
Space Launch System (SLS), 13, 105, 106

Space Mission Planning Advisory Group (SMPAG), 158, 202
Space Research Institute of the Russian Academy of Sciences (IKI), 20, 232, 233
space science, vii, 3, 33, 34, 36, 41, 42, 44, 47, 50–52, 57–60, 62–64, 69, 70, 72, 75–79, 89–107, 155, 156, 180, 215, 227–228, 232–234, 236, 239, 290, 294, 298, 301
Space Science Advisory Committee (SSAC), 232–236
Space Science Board/Space Studies Board (SSB), 33, 49, 50, 52, 54–56, 59, 63, 64, 66, 71–72, 74, 76–78, 95, 114, 116, 231
Space Science Steering Committee, 51, 52
Space Shuttle Program, 34, 55–57, 61, 62, 66, 69, 93, 97–106, 112, 116, 120, 135, 296, 299
    Challenger (STS-51L) accident, 61, 62, 64, 66, 94, 99, 106, 231, 299
    Columbia (STS-107) accident, 94, 103, 146
Space Task Group, 97
Space Transportation System (Shuttle), "Spacewatch Workshop," 196
SpaceX Corporation, 20
spinoffs, 28, 29
Spitzer Space Telescope (Spitzer Infrared Telescope Facility [SIRTF]), 102
Sputnik, 47, 48, 265, 290
Squyres, Steven, 111
Stanley, Gordon, 256, 264, 265
Stardust mission, **7**, **65**, 181
Star Trek (TV program and films), 219, 221
Star Wars (film), 212, 221
Stern, Alan, 148, 149

Stockman, David, 58, 98, 297
Stone, Edward, 210
Strategic Defense Initiative Organization "Star Wars," 65, 66, 148
Streptococcus mitis, 159–184
Stuhlinger, Ernst, 25, 28
Suisei spacecraft, 7
Sun, 69, 110, 255, 286, **287**, 301
Superconducting Super Collider (SSC), 100
Super Soaker squirt gun, 29
Surveyor missions (lunar), **4**, 29, **49**, 157, 160–168, **161**, **165**, **168**, 171–179, 182

T

Taylor, Gerald R., 167, 168, 171
Technology, Entertainment, and Design (TED) Conference, 219
television coverage of NASA missions, 208, 209, 212, 213
Tempel 1. *See* comets
Tennessee Valley Authority (TVA), 106
Tianwen-1 spacecraft, 303
Tidbinbilla antenna, 269, 277–279, 282
Titan (moon of Saturn), **7**, 30, 61, 69, 169, 217, 218, 223, **226**, 225–238, 252, 279–281, 306, 309
Titan launch vehicles, **60**, 101, 117
Tizard, Henry, 254, 263
tracking of spacecraft, 3, 20, 53, 251, 252, 254, 265–270, 277–282
Truly, Richard, 64, 65, 119, 143
Trump administration, 109, 110
TRW Space and Technology Group, 66
Tunguska event, 188, 199

U

Ulysses mission, **6**, **65**, 69, 285–290, **287**, 294, **296**, 299–301, **300**

United Arab Emirates, 303
United Nations (UN), 103, 202
United Nations Conference on Environment and Development (UNCED), 103
United Space Alliance, 100
Upper Atmosphere Rocket Research Panel (UARRP), 46, 47, 76
Uranus, 7, 8, 53, 55, 207, 213, 252, 269, 278
U.S. Air Force, 98, 242, 243, 248
U.S. Army, 19, 242, 243, 245, 248
U.S. Navy, **162**
U.S. Public Health Service Center for Disease Control and Prevention, 163

V

Van Allen, James, 46, 47
van der Woude, Jurrie, 24
Vanguard program, 47
Vega missions, **4**, **7**
Venera missions, **4**, 8, 243, 303
Venus, vii, 1, 2, **4**, 8, 10, 17, 29, 52, 54, 56, 96–99, 214, 231, 241–243, 251, 269, 270, 283, 303, 306
Venus Climate mission, **4**
Venus Express spacecraft, 10
Venus In-situ mission, **4**
very long baseline interferometry (VLBI), 278, 280, 282
Vesta (asteroid), 12, 74, 232, 233, 303
Vestine, Ernest H., 46
Vietnam War, 54, 210
Viking missions, **5**, 19, 24, 26, 43, 52, **53**, 55–57, 73, 96, **97**, 107, 111, 115, 141, 247
Vision for Space Exploration (VSE), 103, 109, 135, **147**, 148
von Braun, Wernher, 15, 89, 242, 243

model of space exploration, 89, 106
Voyager missions, **6–7**, 8, **9**, 23, 26, 27, 29, 51–53, **53**, 55–57, 96, 98, 158, 196, 207–214, **211**, **213**, 219, **220**, 221, 228, 229, 252, 269, 278, 279
 Golden Record, **220**

W

Wallis, Barnes, 259, 260
"war on science," 221
Washington Post, 209, 210, 215–217
Wasserberg, Gerry, 111
Watson-Watt, Robert, 254, 256
Webb, James, 50, 52
Weiler, Ed, 71, 144, 146, 148–153, 155
Weissman, Paul, 200, 201
West Virginia, 197, 238, 265, 280
Westwick, Peter J., 15–17, 317
White, Frederick, 263, 277
White House, 54, 55, 57, 58, 60, 64, 69, 70, 74–76, 79, 82, 84, 86, 93, 109, 112, 120, 121, 137, 144, 146–148, 150, 152–154, 156, 201, 228, 235, 295
Wikipedia, 159, 160, 168

Wild, Paul, 257
Wilford, John Noble, 210, 214–218
Will, George, 27
Williams, David, 173, 178
Wilson, Robert, 265
Window, Bruce, 277
Woltjer, Lodewijk, 236
Woomera station, 267, 268, 271
word clouds, **216**, **218**
World War II, 252–255

X

X-33 and X-34 next-generation launch vehicle programs, 103
X Factor, The (TV series), 193

Y

Yagi array, 255, 256
Yutu rover, **4**

Z

Zolensky, Michael, 181–183
Zond missions, **4**, 8
Zurek, Rich, 129